Praise for Michael Dregni's
Django: The Life and Music of a Gypsy Legend

"Dregni's musical analysis will send fans running to the stereo, digging out
the old recordings and listening with fresh ears. Guitarists will have a feast
reading about Django's technique and his famous Selmer Maccaferri guitar.
Although Django will always be a larger-than-life figure, Dregni has given us
a much clearer picture of the man behind the myth. 'Django' is, for now, the
definitive biography, and we are in Dregni's debt for considerably advancing
our understanding of the remarkable Django Reinhardt, his music and the
world he lived in."

—David French, *Los Angeles Times Book Review*

"Django Reinhardt as he has never been seen . . . . Dregni clarifies a lot of
history while weaving an illuminated web of contexts around his subject. He
vividly describes Gypsy life and mores, and anti-Gypsy bigotry; unearths new
aspects of Reinhardt's life and work; discusses Parisian musette, American
'hot' jazz and bebop, and classical music."

—Gene Santoro, *The New York Times Book Review*

"Extremely informative . . . . An important appreciation of an oft-forgotten
musician . . . . Dregni carefully dissects Reinhardt's virtuoso playing style
without resorting to technical jargon, and he spends plenty of time tending to
Reinhardt's passionate soul—artistic, gypsy and otherwise."

—Mitch Myers, *DownBeat*

"A compelling portrait of this colorful musician, one that gives equal time to
Reinhardt's fascinating story as well as ample musical analysis."

—*JazzTimes*

"An encyclopedic account of the Gypsy jazzman's life and times that provides
an abundance of new information, finds new connections between what was
already known, and clears up many misconceptions along the way."

—*Guitar Player*

"The great strength of his book is his tireless research into the world of Django's gypsy roots. He has tracked down and interviewed as many of Reinhardt's relatives as he can find, as well as older gypsies who knew and worked with him. The result is a more complete portrait of Reinhardt's inner life, including his relationships with his parents, his wife and many other women, and two sons. There is even a detailed account of the tragic fire that cost him two fingers . . . . *Django* is a remarkable book, and its outsider's perspective is part of the reason."

—*New York Sun*

"A rags-to-riches story of a unique talent whose works continue to touch aspiring guitarists of all genres."

—*Library Journal* (starred review)

"In this carefully researched biography, rich with details from interviews with family members, friends and musicians, Dregni brings legendary Gypsy jazz guitarist Django Reinhardt into the spotlight . . . . Dregni casts Django as a mercurial, charismatic Romany innocent, alternately transfixed by dajo life and dismissive of it. Colorful descriptions of the nightclubs of jazz-age Paris and sensitive appraisals of Django's musicianship add to the book's appeal."

—*Publishers Weekly*

"The book is alive from beginning to end, and after awhile you feel like you were there as Django's career unfolds. Dregni insures that the story behind the music will not fade. Musicians, guitarists, students of the history of WWII, and those who love a good biography will love this book."

—Frank Forte, *Just Jazz Guitar*

"Uncovers the influences that helped fuse Reinhardt's unique talent and background with a developing music scene that would eventually become a lasting art form."

—*Vintage Guitar Magazine*

Django

The Life and Music of a Gypsy Legend

Michael Dregni

OXFORD
UNIVERSITY PRESS

OXFORD
UNIVERSITY PRESS

Oxford University Press, Inc., publishes works that
further Oxford University's objective of excellence
in research, scholarship, and education.

Oxford   New York
Auckland   Cape Town   Dar es Salaam   Hong Kong   Karachi
Kuala Lumpur   Madrid   Melbourne   Mexico City   Nairobi
New Delhi   Shanghai   Taipei   Toronto

With offices in
Argentina   Austria   Brazil   Chile   Czech Republic   France   Greece
Guatemala   Hungary   Italy   Japan   Poland   Portugal   Singapore
South Korea   Switzerland   Thailand   Turkey   Ukraine   Vietnam

Copyright © 2004 by Michael Dregni

First published by Oxford University Press, Inc., 2004
198 Madison Avenue, New York, New York 10016
www.oup.com

First issued as an Oxford University Press paperback, 2006
ISBN-13: 978-0-19-530448-0

Oxford is a registered trademark of Oxford University Press

The Library of Congress has cataloged the cloth edition as follows:

Dregni, Michael, 1961–
Django : the life and music of a Gypsy legend / Michael Dregni.
p.   cm.
Includes bibliographical references and index.
ISBN-13: 978-0-19-516752-8
1. Reinhardt, Django, 1910–1953.
2. Guitarists—France—Biography.
3. Jazz musicians—France—Biography.
I. Title.
ML419.R44D74   2004
787.87'165'092—dc
2004006214

Every effort has been made to locate the holders of rights to the photos that appear in this book;
we regret if any have been inadvertently overlooked.

1 3 5 7 9 8 6 4 2

Printed in the United States of America
on acid-free paper

To Boing-Boing and Bam-Bam

Contents

Django

Django

Like us
you have no king
no set of rules
but you have a mistress:
Music

—Manouche poet Sandra Jayat,
"Django," 1961

Django, il était la musique fait l'homme.

—Emmanuel Soudieux

1

Awakening
1910–1922

HE WAS KNOWN AS DJANGO, a Gypsy name meaning "I awake." His legal name—the name the gendarmes and border officials entered into their journals as his family crisscrossed Europe in their horsedrawn caravan—was Jean Reinhardt. But when the family brought their travels to a halt alongside a hidden stream or within a safe wood to light their cookfire, they called him only by his Romany name. Even among his fellow Gypsies, "Django" was a strange name, a strong, telegraphic sentence due to its first-person verb construction. It was a name of which Django was exceedingly proud. It bore an immediacy, a sense of life, and a vision of destiny.

He was born in a caravan at a crossroads in the dead of winter. Following the dirt paths and cobblestone roads north from the Midi of France in the fall of 1909, his father, Jean-Eugène Weiss, steered the family's single horse to pull their caravan creaking and swaying onto the wide open plains of Belgium. Here, the land was so flat it gave the impression one could see to the ends of the earth. The wet wind whipped down from the Atlantic unimpeded in its cold fury. Riding on the wind came dark rains that seemed never-ending, turning day into night for months on end until one prayed for even the weakest rays of sun. Reining in his horse, Jean-Eugène brought the family's perennial travels to a halt at the crossroads of Les Quatre Bras. As they had done for countless years past, the family would weather the winter in a rendezvous outside the Belgian village of Liberchies in the southwestern Hainaut region. They camped amid a small troupe of fellow Romanies to huddle through the coldest months alongside the Flache ôs Coûrbôs—the Pond of the Ravens— named for a coven of the black birds that haunted the surrounding trees. With fresh water from a stream and fodder for their horse from the fallow fields, the family settled in as much as they ever settled anywhere.

Jean-Eugène's caravan—called a *vurdon* in Romany and *roulotte* in French—
was a typical Gypsy home of the era. The family lived in a wooden box mea-
suring roughly seven feet wide by fourteen feet long and six feet high. This
box was mounted atop two axles bearing wooden-spoked wheels. Traces and
tack held their single horse while a simple bench supported the driver. At the
rear, steps led to the entry door. The typical Romany caravan of the time had
small windows on either side letting in daylight; these windows were covered
by handcrafted lace curtains—the kind of domestic touch that made a caravan
a home. Inside, a cast-iron stove was bolted to the floor; fed on wood and
coal, it glowed transparent red in the winter and warmed the whole of the
caravan. Across the front end, a bedchamber dominated, surmounting chests
of drawers storing belongings, quilts, and blankets. A corner of the caravan
was set aside as a shrine with a framed lithograph turned into an object of
worship. The image depicting the French Gypsies' patron saint, Sara-la-Kâli,
was draped with strands of vari-colored beads and lit by votive candles. Underneath the caravan hung wooden crates containing tarps, tools, water buckets, feed for the horse, and cages for ducks and chickens that might be spirited
away from farmsteads along the road. Running the roofline and around the
doorway was carved scrollwork painted in the most brilliant golds, scarlets,
and indigos possible and shining like a gilt crown on a religious effigy. Within
this small home-on-wheels lived the family: Jean-Eugène, his wife Laurence
Reinhardt, Jean-Eugène's ten-year-old daughter, and another, younger son,
both of whose names have been lost.

Beyond the half-moon rooftop and spindly stovepipe of the family's caravan,
the staunch red-brick houses of Liberchies led up to the grand gothic church of
Saint-Pierre-de-Liberchies, its heavenward spire towering high over the level
countryside. The Belgians said of themselves that they were born with a rock in
their stomach to start building their houses, so infatuated were they with their
homes and the security of a firm foundation. Now, in wintertime, the solid
houses of the 700 inhabitants of Liberchies were warmed by charcoal braziers.
Electric radios bringing news of the world and diversion in the dark evenings
were winning pride of place on mantels. And around town, the automobile was
coming to rule the roads, terrifying Romany horses as the horseless carriages
rattled by. The modern world of 1909 had left the Gypsies in its dust.

Still, the arrival of Jean-Eugène's family and their *kumpania*, or traveling
clan, of Gypsies was celebrated each autumn by the people of Liberchies with
a bazaar organized in their honor, the Kermesse du Fichaux. Swirling with
color into the gray of a Belgian fall, the Gypsies sold the jewelry, baskets, and
lacework they fashioned as well as wares from their far travels. They told
fortunes, unwinding the paths of a life from the tangle of lines on a palm,
auguring greatness and love, selling charms to ward off evil. Some specialized
in mending wicker chair seats. Others patched copper cooking pots the Belgian village women brought; with a concerto of pounding, a pot could be

made as good as new with metalwork changed little since the armoring of knights. Still other Gypsies traded horses with the farmers, wheeling and dealing, examining teeth for age and hooves for lameness. The Gypsies were known as *maquignons*—literally, horse fakers—who magically dressed up horses for sale, and the farmers looked for their timeless trademark tricks—shoe polish hiding grizzled hair, a diet of water to fill out ribcage staves, a spike of ginger in the anus for spirit. It was all an ages-old exchange between the Gypsies and townspeople of Europe.

Jean-Eugène was *un vannier*—a basketmaker. Yet he also wore other hats, a necessity for survival on the road. Now 27, he was born in 1882, although no one remembered where. In the sole surviving photograph of him, taken in Algeria in 1915, Jean-Eugène looks more like the prosperous mayor of a French city than a traveling Gypsy. His dark hair is combed back from his broad forehead above virile eyebrows and the penetrating eyes that dominate his face. His cheekbones are pronounced, his mouth hidden behind the usual mustache, a symbol of masculinity affected by most Gypsy men as soon as they can cultivate one. Dapper in a dark suit, he appears distinguished and, above all, wise from a lifetime of having seen many things in many lands with those piercing eyes. As the Romany proverb went, He who travels, learns.

Basketmaking was labor Jean-Eugène only did when times were tough. He boasted a special talent: Jean-Eugène was an entertainer, another timeless métier of the Gypsies. He could juggle with the best circus sideshowmen and tease audiences with the mysteries of legerdemain. But Jean-Eugène's pride was in playing music—violin, cymbalom, piano, guitar—and directing a dance orchestra of Romanies. It is this pride that shines in his eyes in the photograph: He is seated at his piano with his band arrayed around him. And while the hands of the musician next to him look like those of a peasant who could be holding a plow as indifferently as they grip his viola, Jean-Eugène's hands are crossed before him in regal manner. Even in this ancient photograph, they look like the fine hands of an artist.

To earn a few francs on the side, Jean-Eugène tuned pianos. He also repaired other musical instruments. He might find a damaged violin at a flea market, barter for it on the cheap, rebuild it, and sell it again down the road. But it was as a musician that he supported his family. He modified the rear of his family's caravan to create a diminutive, canvas-covered traveling theater stage on which he and his wife performed for townsfolk their magical and musical menageries.

Laurence Reinhardt was introduced on the family's stage as *La Belle* Laurence. Among the Romanies and in honor of her dark beauty, Laurence was known as Négros—Spanish for "black." She made jewelry to sell, but she came alive as a dancer. At 24, she was renowned for her ravishing flow of movement, and even in her old age, Négros was moved to dance as soon as the music began. She traded on her exotic tea-toned complexion, raven-black hair, and tall stature. In a photograph of the time, she is handsome with a masculine strength to her face—a jutting jaw that seems determined even in repose and eyes that look like they feared nothing.

It was on the eve of one of the family's performances in Liberchies that Django was born. The night of Sunday, January 23, 1910, was bitter with cold. The townsfolk gathered for the annual show of Jean-Eugène and his Romany troupe at the inn of Adrien Borsin known familiarly as Chez Borsin. Happy for entertainment as an anodyne against the emptiness of winter, the townsfolk were looking forward to Jean-Eugène's music, the burlesque comedy of his friend Louis Ortica, and the dance of *La Belle* Laurence. But this year, events conspired against the evening.

Négros was in her caravan alongside the Pond of the Ravens, lost in the pains of childbirth.

She had set off on foot to walk into town to perform at Chez Borsin when the contractions began. Jean-Eugène continued on to perform while the Gypsy women ushered Négros back to the camp, lit candles against the darkness, and gathered clean cloths to deliver her first child.

As the distant sound of applause came to them from town, Django was born.

THREE DAYS LATER on January 26, Jean-Eugène and Négros wrapped Django against the cold and set out with their fellow Romanies for the church of Saint-Pierre-de-Liberchies. They filed into the baptistery dressed in their finest suits and most brilliant dresses, fedoras held humbly in hand. Joining the Gypsies were several townspeople, also in their Sunday best. Adrien Borsin stood front and center. He was a stout, rotund man who appeared to enjoy his restaurant's fare to the fullest. At Borsin's side was his sister, Isabelle, a staunch matron with primly trimmed hair. Symbolizing the rare friendship between the Romanies and the townsfolk, the Borsins were serving as Django's sponsors and godparents.

Following the name-giving ceremony and baptism, Jean-Eugène and Négros hosted a celebration for their newborn son. Chez Borsin was alive again with a feast and music. The family's clan of Manouche Gypsies did not celebrate marriages, but a baptism—especially a couple's firstborn—was a grand affair.

Jean-Eugène applied for a birth certificate for his son with the town secretary, Henri Lemens, on January 24. In the exquisite penmanship of a turn-of-the-century bureaucrat, Lemens entered Django's legal name as "Jean Reinhardt." For his part, Jean-Eugène gave his own name as "Jean-Baptiste Reinhard"—an alias to mask him from the French gendarmes who sought him for military conscription—and he signed with the practiced yet unsure hand of an illiterate at the bottom of the birth certificate, "J. B. Reinhard." Lemens ignored the orthography and added a final "t" to the newborn's name, corresponding to the French pronunciation of the Alsatian name.

Such a revision of a Romany's identity was common throughout Europe, a simple yet subtle act of cruelty, a reworking of a person's legal being by an all-powerful border official or bureaucrat. The hegira of Gypsy names began with requirements that Romanies bear Christian given names and family surnames for identification. These random names were chosen by chance during a Gypsy's travels and bore little meaning for their owners; among themselves, they went solely by their Romany names. They adopted surnames of the country in which they lived in a charade of assimilation to mask their Gypsy identity. When they crossed a border or signed a document, officials often transliterated and twisted their legal names in spelling and eventually even in pronunciation. At the same time, Gypsies surreptitiously altered their own surnames as needed, changing their legal identities like they changed their shirts. Jean-Eugène's surname was often written phonetically in France as Vées, and he and his brothers sometimes also hid behind the alias Schmitt when the gendarmes were on their trail. Négros's Alsatian surname of Reinhardt—literally someone from the heart of the Rhineland—was likely chosen for expedience by her ancestors who long lived around Strasbourg in Alsace. By these various forces, Django was registered as Jean Reinhardt.

Django was given the legal name Jean in honor of his father, but it was his Gypsy name that bore his true identity. Gypsies chose a Romany name for their child evoking a physical attribute, such as Baro (Big, or often, First Born), or natural phenomena, including Chata (Shadow) or Zuna (Sun). Animal names served as totems—such as Bero (Bear)—while girls were given flowery names like Fayola (Violet) and Draka (Grape). Names might mirror a child's personality or the parent's hopes, including Grofo (Noble) and Schnuckenack (Glorious Music). Tchavolo or Tchocolo (Boy or Son) and Tchaj (Girl or Daughter) were simple references to the child's sex whereas other names like Bimbam and Boulou were onomatopoeia echoing a baby's babbling.

In naming their firstborn son Django, Négros and Jean-Eugène chose a Romany verb and not a noun or adjective for his name. They saw something special in this child.

As a youth, Django became a proficient robber of chickens. Among his people, the Romanies believed it a noble skill to trick or steal from the non-Gypsy world around them. It was also a skill that brought curses from non-Gypsies, fostering distrust and ultimately hatred toward Django's people. Yet to the Romanies such thievery was part of survival on the road.

Silence was the key to abducting a chicken. The fowl could not be allowed to alert its owners of its plight. Like most good tricks, it was simple, and was handed down among Gypsies from father to son. As part of a *paguba*, or raiding party, the robber stole up on an unsuspecting hen with coat or cloth held ready. Before the chicken had a chance to rouse its owners with a storm of clucking, the cloth was dropped over its head. The robber then stuffed the chicken under his arm, twisted its neck with a practiced jerk of the wrist, and disappeared from the farmyard as silently as he arrived.

Django also became an adept trout tickler. Wherever his family traveled, he was drawn to the closest water to fish, casting into the surf along the Midi coast or in country streams. When he lacked a cane pole or tackle, Django poached fish in a technique decried by the gendarmes as *pêcher à la chatouille*, fish tickling. Lying on his stomach in the grasses along a riverbank, he moved his hands in a systematic search along the water bottom until he came upon a fish, his fingers gently tickling the fish's belly to lull and lure it in until he could grasp the silver body and catapult it out of the creek.

Yet the true delicacy of the French Gypsies was the hedgehog, an animal the French would never consider eating. The creature was known affectionately as a *niglo* in Romany, and the Gypsies felt a kinship for this strange little rodent with its prickly hide. The hedgehog lived hidden beneath hedgerows—nether regions no other animal wanted as its home.

Hunting a *niglo* required wiles and a good nose. Romanies trained dogs to track hedgehogs much as pigs were used to root out truffles. Once a dog found its quarry, the hedgehog was chased into a cloth sack and clubbed on the head.

Most Romanies had treasured *niglo* recipes, and Négros no doubt had her own. Hedgehogs have a rich meat, gamy yet delicate, best when caught in autumn when they have put on fat for their winter hibernation. They were cured overnight on a caravan rooftop as it was believed moonglow enhanced flavor. To clean off the quills, Gypsies poked a hole in the hedgehog's hide, then blew into the carcass, inflating it until the skin was taut so the prickles could be easily shaved away. *Niglos* were often cooked on a spit over open flames or stewed in a ragoût. The classic recipe, however, called on Gypsy enterprise and ingredients found along the road to roast the *niglo* in a clay sarcophagus. With its prickles still in place, the hedgehog was sliced open across the belly and gutted, the liver saved as the supreme delicacy. After stuffing the *niglo* with fresh rosemary, thyme, and wild garlic, the Romany cook would stitch up the incision. The hedgehog, prickles and all, was rolled in wet river clay; the resulting soccer ball-sized lump was roasted in a fire's coals for an hour or so. When the clay rang to the rap of a knuckle, the shell was broken open, the hardened clay prying away the prickles. With a prayer of *latcho rhaben*—Romany for *bon appétit*—the hedgehog was feasted on.

For Django, tickling trout and hunting hedgehogs were early lessons in living: The rules of the road required resourcefulness. And the everyday act of stealing a chicken likely opened Django's eyes—in life he could have whatever he wanted as nothing barred him from taking it by any means necessary, whether it was in his Gypsy world or from the larger, foreign world surrounding him.

DJANGO WAS BORN in Belgium by chance, just as he could have been born in France, Italy, or anywhere else on his family's travels. He was sometimes referred to as a Belgian Gypsy, due to his birthplace; as a French Gypsy, as he lived most of his life in France; or even as a German Gypsy as his family came from the Alsace. But nationality was not important. His cultural heritage as a Romany was his sole allegiance.

Django was a Manouche Gypsy. Based on kinship between Romany and Sanskrit, the Gypsies are believed to have originated in India. When Islamic leader Mahmud of Ghazni invaded India in 1001, a defending army was conscripted from lower-caste Indians to battle the Muslims through northern India and into Persia for three decades. From Persia, some of the warriors returned to India, others hired on as mercenaries to new nations or migrated westward. They traveled what became known as the Romany Trail leading into Byzantium and on to Europe, where their arrival was first noted in Serbia in the 1300s. Others moved through North Africa, eventually crossing into Europe via Spain in the 1400s.

Europeans, believing these dark-skinned wanderers came from Egypt, corrupted "Egyptian" into "Gypsy." Through time, they were also christened with a variety of other names. They were called Tziganes for their work as animal traders, known as "athingani" in Byzantium; as Sinti as they were believed to have originated from along the Indian Sind River; or as Manouche from the Romany *manus* and the Sanskrit *manusa*, or "true man." In Spain, they became known as Gitanos, or Gitans in French. Now, many prefer to be known collectively as Roma or Romany, a name derived from their word for "human." The Roma's military heritage has been passed down in their most common term for a non-Gypsy, *gadjo*, or the plural *gadjé*, from a Sanskrit word meaning "civilian" or "non-military person."

The Romany's history was one of persecution. Forced from their homes, they were conscripted by the ruling Aryan caste. Arriving in the Balkans, they were enslaved. In Europe, popular folklore long held that Gypsies wrought the nails to crucify Jesus on the cross, and laws were passed in most European countries to rid them of the perceived Gypsy scourge. Gypsies were first chronicled in France in 1418 with the first expulsion orders following on their heels in 1427. In a 1560 decree, Gypsies were committed to a lifetime of pulling oars in French galleys. Louis XIV directed French bailiffs in 1682 to round up Gypsy men as slaves; the women were to be flogged, then banished. France deported Gypsies to Africa's Mahgreb, Gambia, and Senegal as well as to Louisiana in the New World. While Europeans prided themselves on not having India's social castes, they did have a place for Gypsies—outcasts. Chased away from civilization, the Gypsies became nomadic of necessity rather than desire, a people of the diaspora, without a homeland or a promised land.

The earliest traces of the Reinhardt clan date to the 1700s. Police records note them traveling the Rhine River valley, through the forests of the duchy of Swabia, and into Switzerland. Three generations of Reinhardts led a dreaded bandit gang terrorizing their namesake Rhineland. Antoine-Alexandre Reinhardt—known as Antoine de la Grave—marauded the region before being captured and executed in Giessen in 1726. His grandson Jacob, better known as Hannikel, bested Antoine's reputation, ruthlessly raiding towns and then retreating into the shadows of the Black Forest. Yet Hannikel too ended his days hanged by the neck with his brother Wenzel at Sulz in 1787. Family lore recalled that Django's grandparents moved from Bavaria to Strasbourg when the Franco-Prussian war of 1870 forced them to flee westward. Wherever they traveled, Django's ancestors carried what mattered with them: The essence of their culture—their language, customs, trades, and music—was portable, always ready for the road. Their history was unwritten, their footsteps blown over with dust almost as soon as they passed by.

On Django's birth certificate, Jean-Eugène listed the family's place of residence as Paris, but their true home was the caravan. It was here that a second son was born to Négros and Jean-Eugène at a campsite on the outskirts of Paris on March 1, 1912. Named Joseph Reinhardt, he was known to all as Nin-Nin, a common Romany diminutive and term of endearment. A daughter soon followed, named Sara for the patron saint, yet called Tsanga—literally, the Pincher, describing her role in tussles with her elder brothers. With Jean-Eugène's two children from a previous marriage and his and Négros's three young ones, the family continued their travels, their single horse pulling the caravan at a slow trudge to the horizon.

IN 1915 when Django was five years old, Jean-Eugène quit his family. A French Gypsy proverb advised, Love your horse more than your wife; she may leave you without warning, but a good horse never will. Now, Négros was the one left behind with the family's horse.

Divorce and abandonment were rare among the Manouche. Yet Jean-Eugène had an earlier wife, the mother of his elder daughter and son, although no one remembers what became of her. Now, when Jean-Eugène deserted Négros, she was stranded with Django, Nin-Nin, and Sara to raise without a father.

Jean-Eugène's abandonment left a hole in Django's life. The family crossed paths with Jean-Eugène at various times over the coming years in Algiers and Paris, but he never returned to live with his wife and children. Négros was forced to support them by weaving baskets, caning chair seats, and crafting jewelry. Her specialty was bracelets made from spent artillery shellcasings collected on the battlefield of the Marne following World War I. She taught Django to dig the shells out of the trenchworks, washing away the earth to uncover the brass that was cut into bangles, engraved with designs, and sold to keep the family fed.

With Jean-Eugène gone, Négros took the horse's reins and steered the caravan in a regular route following the seasons and the opportunities they brought to survive. When the narcissuses bloomed and the swallows returned to swirl above the rooftops of Paris, she led her family to the French Midi or further south into Italy. Here, she sold her bracelets to flush summer visitors on the Mediterranean. As the fields of lavender blossoms faded in the Midi, signaling the arrival of autumn and the end of the lucrative tourist season, the family made its way north to Paris. In winter, Négros and her brood returned to the hospitality of Liberchies to wait out the cold.

For the festival days of May 24 and 25, Négros shepherded her children on a pilgrimage to Les Saintes-Maries-de-la-Mer on the far tip of the Rhône delta along the Camargue coast. This was the barren land of wild white horses and *gardian* cowboys, salt marshes and stone towns struggling to hold on in a harsh realm. The family parked among the fields of caravans of Manouche and Gitans from across Europe. Négros and her children paid homage to the Gypsies's adopted Saint Sara during a week of devotion and music. During their travels, the Romanies assimilated Catholicism into their lives, sometimes blending it with their Hindu beliefs, sometimes supplanting them. Whereas the Catholic *gadjé* celebrated the town's two namesake saints—Sainte-Marie-Jacobé and Sainte-Marie-Salomé, the aunts of Jesus—the Gypsies honored their bastard Saint Sara. According to orthodox legend, Sara was the servant of the two Saintes-Marie, accompanying them after the Crucifixion when they were cast out of Palestine by the Romans in a boat with no oars only to wash up on the shores of France. Gypsy mythology, however, held that Sara was a Provençal Gitane who saved the Saintes-Marie when their boat capsized in a storm off the Camargue. The effigies of the two Maries stood in honor in the consecrated chapel of the fortified medieval church Notre-Dame-de-la-Mer. But Négros guided her children past them to descend stone stairs into a crypt where a wooden statue of Sara waited; she was relegated to this chamber as she was not a true saint recognized by the Vatican and beatified only by the Romanies. Django entered this grotto blackened by the candles of generations of devotees to bow down before the dark-skinned statue of Sara, known in Romany as Sara-la-Kâli, or Black Sara. Négros then presented her children for Sara's mute benediction or proffered a child's photograph among the numerous other alms and ex-voto medallions attesting to miracles rendered, left behind by countless Romanies through time in tribute to Sara's powers. If the Reinhardt family wished to give special thanks, they stitched an ornate robe to drape over the statue, which was blanketed by dozens of such robes by the pilgrimage's end. Following their homage, the Gypsies carried the statue of Sara on their shoulders to be purified in the saltwater of the sea.

With the coming of winter, Négros turned her horse again toward Belgium. In Liberchies, she and her children were welcomed back, but without

the money from Jean-Eugène's music, their caravan stood out for its dilapidated state. Django and Nin-Nin made friends among the Belgian boys, and
Nin-Nin attended the town's school for three years for a few months at a
time. But despite Négros's attempts, Django bore no interest in school. He
seemed impatient with the confines of youth, yearning to break free. Over
the years, Django attended school at haphazard intervals, preferring to escape
to explore the countryside, drink coffee with the Gypsy men in bars, and
shoot billiards. His was a life lived purely for the moment.

When World War I broke out, Négros and her children abandoned their
caravan outside Paris to flee on foot among the refugees evacuating eastern
France. They walked for weeks along the roadside, Négros leading her sons
and daughter, carrying the belongings they could shoulder, accepting rides in
wagons when offered, marching along at a child's pace when there was no
other choice. They eventually reached the Midi, then continued along the
coast to the Italian port of Livorno. They found berths on a boat for Corsica,
then boarded another ship bound for Algeria.

Perched above the Barbary Coast, Algiers was known as the White City
for its whitewashed buildings that blinded the eye in the African sun. By contrast, Algiers's casbah was a world of brilliant color with market stalls wandering in a labyrinth around the fort and the Grand Mosque Jamaa-el-Kebir's
minaret. This was the Arab quarter, but it was also home to Muslim Xorax
Gypsies as well as Afrikaya Gypsies—Manouche who had emigrated or been
cast out of France long before. Négros found rooms neighboring the casbah
to sell her baskets and jewelry. And it was here, among other Gypsies from
their troupe, that they again encountered Jean-Eugène, leading his orchestra
for dances and spare change.

IN 1920 when the war had ended and Django was ten years old, Négros brought
her family back to Paris and the caravan they had abandoned among the Romany encampments encircling the capital. Beyond shifting between campsites around Paris, the family was settled for the first time in Django's life.

Paris was a changed world. The city had been a diamond aglow in the
glitter of *la Belle Époque*. Now, following the war to end all wars, France was
in a state of shock. To forget the horrors, Paris threw itself full fury into *les
années folles*—the crazy years—of high living and fresh fads, casting out the
old and dashing like a bayonet charge into the future. It was part self-induced
amnesia, part anesthesia. Paris resurrected itself as a city of a new era in art,
music, and literature. It was the modern world's capital, the city of the new
century, boasting a métro and sewers and clean drinking water for all. And
with the arrival of municipal electrification and Georges Claude's artificial
rainbow of neon, the glories of Paris could now be witnessed day and night,
earning the city a new nickname—the City of Light.

Paris was still protected by its ring of medieval ramparts, and it was here on the doorsteps of the city that Django's family lived. Outside the fortifications, the city's glory came to a dead end. Surrounding Paris was a vast nether region known as *la Zone*. Here, outside the City of Light, was a city of blight: It was in *la Zone* that Paris's cesspool cleaners dumped their waste each night and here as well that the human refuse of the city found refuge. This was not the Paris of broad boulevards, monuments, and cathedrals. Instead, whole cities of shantytowns crowded the fortification ports like beggars holding out their hands for the smallest offering. The ramshackle hovels crafted from cast-off boards and stone rubble were homes to the dispossessed. The inhabitants of *la Zone* were known derisively by Parisians as *les zonards*—and many feared the Gypsies as the worst vermin among them.

The Manouche and Gitans parked their caravans in *la Zone* where they could find streamwater along the lost river of Paris, *la Bièvre*, and it was here that Négros brought Django and her other children and settled in among their clan. These Gypsy camps of *la Zone* were described by French poet Serge:

> Down there in the Gypsy camp a guitar juggles with a popular melody. One can hear distant dance music, dizzying waltzes, the sweetness of an accordion. Campfires are everywhere, each with its own cooking pot. Chickens are stewing and guitars going wild. Heavy, gray clouds roll over *la Porte de Clignancourt*, leaving behind a drizzling rain. One flounders in the rutted roadways of molasses-like mud, in the small lakes and quagmires, on this slope where stands the camp of the Manouche, an immense assembly of caravans, *vurdons*, and *roulottes*, making *la Zone* a colorful puzzle of an itinerant city of more than five hundred vehicles parked side by side in crazy disorder. At night, the five hundred *roulottes* sparkle like oriental palaces. And through it all comes a song—brutal, sordid, flowing onward, with a plaintive cry for *la Zone*, where enchantment itself may perhaps be hidden, somewhere in the rottenness.

Négros and the other Gypsies favored campsites in *la Zone* near their livelihoods in the flea markets. They moved between encampments outside the Porte de Choisy or Porte d'Italie on the southeastern side of Paris near the Kremlin-Bicêtre flea market and their beloved horsetrading market at the Vaugirard galleries; Porte de Montreuil and its endless thieves' market to the east; and Porte de Clignancourt to the north with its vast *marché aux puces de Saint-Ouen*. Each weekend, Négros led her children to these markets blossoming out of the mud of *la Zone* and named in honor of the fleas that inhabited the upholstery of the old furniture and rags for sale. She hawked her wares amid the glorious anarchy of the markets.

La Zone became Django's world. He led a gang of Gypsy boys that proudly called themselves *les Foulards rouges*, or Red Scarves, a symbol of the Parisian working class. Django's gang fearlessly stole pears from the walled orchard of the Saint-Hippolyte priory, sweet juice dripping down their faces as they ate the forbidden fruit. Ambushing an enemy gang's leader, known to all as Le Grand Loucheur, or Big Cross-Eyes, Django stood tall before him and demanded in his best outlaw growl, "Your money or your life!" Le Grand Loucheur chose to leave Django flat on his back with a black eye. Other days, they tried to derail trams on the avenue d'Italie, jamming the rails with iron bolts stolen from the nearby Panhard factory, praying with religious fervor for a spectacular crash. When the horsedrawn wagons slowed to a crawl to climb the hill on avenue des Gobelins, Django and his gang spirited away coal to resell. Often the brothers gathered scrap metal in wheelbarrows to barter to foundries. One day, they found a boxing ring erected at a café on the avenue d'Italie. Invited to take their turn, Django and Nin-Nin pummeled each other while the locals threw coins to spur them on. The brothers, battered and unsteady on their feet, walked away with their arms about each other's shoulders and their pockets full.

Négros tried once more to send Django to school. A traveling classroom for Gypsy children was organized by a former teacher known as *père* Guillon. Forced to retire early due to his fondness for red wine, Guillon started his own school in *la Zone* in a converted bus. But Django and the other Gypsy children, used to their freedom in *la Zone*, had little regard for the authority of this *gadjo* dipsomaniac. Django preferred school in the streets and cinema.

Even as a youth, Django was a fool for games and gambling. He would wager on anything, anywhere—cards, dice, and especially, billiards. With his winnings, Django sometimes treated himself and Nin-Nin to a movie. Or better yet, they found a way around buying tickets. Django was drawn to the cinema like an innocent to the inferno. At the grand Luxor movie palace in Barbès, Django and Nin-Nin were regular gate-crashers. The afternoon matinee featured two films, separated by an intermission when the audience mingled in the lobby to buy treats. Django and Nin-Nin slid in among the crowd to watch the second feature, and their ploy worked well for weeks until one day when Le Luxor held a showing for a nearby school. Among the freshly scrubbed and uniformed schoolchildren, the two grubby Gypsy boys were easy marks and the cinema manager collared them. But he struck a deal with Django and Nin-Nin: If they set up the movie posters in front and performed odd jobs around the cinema, he would grant them gratis admission. With their modest labor complete, Django and Nin-Nin found seats and roared with laughter at the antics of Charlie Chaplin. They thrilled to cliffhanger serials and for 90 minutes lived the life of pirates sailing before the wind, dreaming of crossing rapiers with D'Artagnan against Richelieu's guards and hiding their faces in horror as Fântomas hatched his nefarious plots. From the cinema, Django learned how to walk with a gangster's swagger. He learned of honor among thieves and the codes of chivalry. And he learned how to tilt his fedora over one eye just so.

The earliest known photograph of Django, taken in 1920 when he was ten, captured him with a group of other Gypsies, including the fierce Négros.

Django wears a bedraggled suit with a carelessly crooked tie and that jauntily tilted fedora, many sizes larger than his head. While the others in the photo look down to the ground or off into the distance with feigned interest, only Django looks back out of the image straight into the eye of the camera, self-assurance radiating from his impossibly dark eyes, defiance in their depths.

On his lips is an infinitely mischievous smile.

THEN THERE WAS THE MUSIC. Melodies played on cymbaloms, banjos and guitars, harps and pianos, and above all, violins. Throughout his childhood, Django was surrounded by music. His father and mother fashioned a livelihood from music and dancing. At Les Saintes-Maries-de-la-Mer, music went hand in hand with religious homage, Manouche violinists playing their songs influenced by Eastern European Tzigane traditions while the Spanish Gitans strummed out guitar-fueled flamenco. In the Parisian flea markets, Gypsies offered melodies on violins and banjos in exchange for spare coins. And around the Romany campfires wherever they were lit, music accompanied family events, from baptisms to funerals. For the Manouches and Gitans, music was as intrinsic to life as air.

Jean-Eugène continued to lead his dance orchestra. He had seven brothers, all musicians, including pianist Nellone and multi-instrumentalist Guiligou, proficient on violin, banjo, and guitar. In the 1915 photograph of Jean-Eugène, his band—wearing fezzes for the occasion—comprised two violinists, a bassist, and two guitarists, one holding a twin-necked harp guitar, in addition to Jean-Eugène's piano. This was an ambitious orchestra for the day. It was rare to have a piano in a traveling Gypsy band, but Jean-Eugène heroically hauled the upright along in his caravan during his journeys. Django's sister Sara remembered their father's band playing smart hotels in Paris and along the Côte d'Azur as well as in the open-air dancing pavilions known as *guinguettes* along the River Marne outside the capital at La Varenne-Saint-Hilaire. Sara sometimes accompanied her father's violin on piano, their repertoire including popular songs, light opera airs, early one-steps, classic Chopin waltzes, and Gypsy melodies as well as the *Czardas* of Vittorio Monti and the *Sérènade* of Frantisek Drdla.

Django's first instrument was the violin. The classic instrument of Romany musicians due to its portability, it was ideal for the anguished sounds of popular Gypsy violinists Jean Goulesco and Georges Boulanger. Django learned the instrument from his father, his uncle Guiligou, or other relatives in the call-and-response teaching style common among Romanies: An elder taught a child the melody and chords to a song, painstakingly displaying the fingerings and patiently playing the song over until the child knew it by heart. According to family lore, Django learned much of his musical skill under his

uncle Guiligou's tutelage, and Sara remembered Django playing violin with
his father's ensemble when he was between the ages of 7 and 12.

When he was ten years old, Django came upon his cousin Gabriel playing
a battered banjo. Django was enthralled by the instrument and the melodies
Gabriel picked out. He may have learned the rudiments of banjo from Gabriel,
copying his cousin's fingerings and following his melodies on the instrument.
With these songs in his head, Django begged his mother for a banjo of his
own. Négros laughed off this request as a child's whim—and moreover, she
did not have the 50 francs for an instrument. It was not until Django was 12
that he received a banjo, given to him by a Manouche acquaintance named
Raclot, who understood the boy's fascination for music. Raclot's gift to Django
was a diminutive banjo-guitar, a common instrument of the day featuring a
banjo resonator coupled to a six-string guitar neck. This banjo-guitar became
Django's focus. He strained to teach his awkward fingers to follow the melody
lines that he had a near-magical skill for remembering after hearing them
only once or twice. Forcing his right hand into the arcane shapes of chords
stretched across the fretboard, he played until his fingertips glowed red—and
then beyond, building thick calluses of skin that could suddenly split open on
the unforgiving steel strings and coat the frets with his blood. Django was
inventive in finding items to use as picks—the tip of a spoon, a sewing thimble
of his mother's, a two-sous piece, and a bit of whalebone that once served as a
shirt-collar stiffener all found new use in his hands. Django played the melodies he learned from his father and tidbits like the old French children's song
"Au Clair de la Lune" as well as the soldiers' favored dirty song, "La Madelon,"
an ode to a barmaid of fairy-tale beauty far from the horror of the trenches.
Django carried his banjo-guitar with him everywhere through the day and cradled
it in his arms as he slept. Négros remembered him plucking at his instrument
until his fingers ached: "Once, when I returned to our caravan, I found him
with the tips of his fingers all red and swollen. I thought that he had five whitlows
at one time." On another day, teacher *père* Guillon came to the caravan in search
of his errant pupil only to find Django plucking at his banjo. "Is that what
prevents you from learning to read?" the teacher asked. In answer, Django only
bowed his head and played his banjo harder than ever.

Witnessing Django's growing skill, Négros bought a real guitar for her
son after selling a necklace of faux pearls in the Clignancourt market. Cousin
Gabriel taught Django how to chord it, and they set up to perform on street
corners. Django soon found another accompanist in a banjo-playing hunch-
back named Lagardère, and together they ventured into Paris to play their
duets. Their music sounded so good to their ears that they continued to roam
the city with their instruments for three days. Finally realizing how much
time had passed and what his mother's response was going to be, Django
chose to stay safely by Lagardère's side instead of returning to his caravan.
Négros, meanwhile, was in a panic. She scoured the city for her son, even

taking the bold step for a Gypsy of notifying the police of her missing child. She finally found him at 3 A.M. playing his banjo in a café in the place d'Italie. The beating Django received terrified his accompanist: "That's your mother?" Lagardère asked. "I would say instead that she's a panther." The repentant Django could not reply—he was begging Négros for mercy.

On weekends, Django often made the journey to the Porte de Clignancourt and a dance hall called Chez Clodoche. Amid the bustle of white-aproned waiters and the clatter of diners, Django stood silent in a remote corner to listen as his father and uncles played their music. When other Romany waifs were chased out like flies by the exasperated waiters, Django darted beneath a table, keeping attuned both to the arrival of the waiters' footsteps and the sounds of the band. He was particularly impressed by his uncle Guiligou's guitarwork. Concentrating on remembering how he fretted his instrument and the melodies played, Django repeated the fingerings on his own guitar back home. Then, one day, his uncle found Django hiding and at the same time watching him with rapt attention. Guiligou asked Django if he could play guitar, to which he proudly nodded. Guiligou proffered his own guitar and asked for a song. Django took up the guitar, playing not just a few chords but picking out the intricacies of a melody. Guiligou was astonished. He grabbed his brothers and directed Django to play his song again for the full audience. Soon, Django was serving his apprenticeship on the banjo, playing alongside his father and Guiligou at Chez Clodoche each Saturday.

There was another Romany guitarist in *la Zone* whom Django also sought to emulate. He was a Gitan named Auguste "Gusti" Malha. Short and round, Malha was the sort of unremarkable man one passed on a Parisian street without noticing as he picked your pocket. Yet Malha put his nimble fingers to better—if less-profitable—use. Malha was a virtuoso who picked the strings as if he had six fingers on each hand. He first won renown at 14 in Brussels alternating with equal aplomb between guitar and banduria, a Spanish mandolin with flat back and six strings doubled in their tunings. In Paris, Malha played alongside the dance hall accordionists, his many gem-encrusted rings flashing in the spotlight, a symbol of success to Django.

Django also learned from the Gitan virtuoso Poulette Castro. Poulette was a rarity among the Parisian Gypsies for he could read music and played in the pit orchestra at Paris's Théâtre du Châtelet accompanying the opera divas. Having traveled throughout Europe and even England, he boasted a great repertoire of waltzes, traditional songs, and Gypsy melodies. For generations after, "*le grand* Gitan" was summoned forth in stories told by Romany musicians, his music surviving to haunt the melodies composed by his followers.

Poulette performed alongside his brother Laro Castro, a wizard of the banduria. The Castro brothers also played in the ensemble Le Quatuor à Plectre—the Plectrum Quartet—joined by two other Gitan musicians, Coco and Serrani Garcia. Le Quatuor à Plectre was recorded accompanying singer

Rosita Barrios on a variety of gay Spanish songs then the rage of Paris. The
all-string ensemble featured instruments of various timbres, doubling up on
the melody lines to create an enchanting multilayered sound highlighted by
trills and tremolos.

Django likely learned the genesis of his right-hand technique from Poulette
while watching the Gitan in Clignancourt cafés. Poulette taught Django to
play in a style similar to Spanish *flamencos* without resting his right hand on
the guitar's soundboard. Again like a *flamenco*, Poulette and others instructed
Django to bend his wrist almost perpendicular to the strings, keeping his
wrist loose and supple for quick strumming. Therefore, to reach different
strings, Django moved not with his wrist but from his elbow. Yet instead of
strumming the strings with his fingernails as a *flamenco*, Poulette taught Django
to use a plectrum for increased volume.

It was this technique that the 12-year-old Django used in playing his banjo
with his whalebone plectrum. Nin-Nin, imitating his elder brother, also learned
banjo, and starting a tradition that would last for decades, served as Django's
accompanist. Together, they wandered Paris from the medieval passageways
of *la Mouffe* to working-class Ménilmontant, past the windmills of Montmartre
to the belly of Paris in the food markets of Les Halles. They busked for coins
at the *marché aux puces* at the Porte de Montreuil, or set up to play for laborers
drinking their after-work beers in the cafés encircling the place d'Italie. Everywhere they went, they played their banjos, passing their battered borsalinos
around to collect the proffered sous when the song was done.

One day, Django was picking his banjo at a café near the Porte d'Italie
called À la Route de Dijon. Another Gypsy in the bar—a tall, thin Italian
Zingaro with a head of rich dark curls like a black sheep's fleece—listened as
Django played Johann Strauss's "Blue Danube." This Italian Gypsy heard
something special in the boy's picking, and he introduced himself. His name
was Vétese Guérino; Django may have heard of him for he played accordion
in the dance halls of all Paris. If Django was willing, Guérino offered to hire
him as an accompanist for the princely sum of ten francs a night.

2

Panam
1922–1928

BEFORE HE COULD MAKE HIS DEBUT with Vétese Guérino, Django had to ask permission of his mother. He was only 12, but he was in a hurry to grow up. Despite Négros's ruling hand, Django roamed *la Zone* at will, venturing far and wide throughout Paris, armed with just his banjo. All the while, Négros spent her days peddling her basketry and jewelry in the flea markets. In the past, Django's drive to play his instrument led him to wander away for days on end. Playing in Guérino's band, Négros would know his whereabouts during the night hours. The allure of a second income in the family may also have been enticing—especially the riches Guérino promised. So, with Négros's approval, Django set off with his banjo-guitar to accompany the accordionist in the dance halls of Paris.

He was a slender, small Gypsy youth overshadowed by the size of this diminutive banjo. Yet entering the dance hall, Django crossed the threshold to adulthood. His skill with a banjo was recognized by established, professional musicians and he was accepted among them.

Django was being paid for playing his banjo, rewarded for his skills and talent. With the same banjo his mother bought for him, he earned money for her, paying her back many times over as a provider for the family. He never believed himself ordinary; he had faith in his own talents, and now others too saw something special in him. Django's joy at this recognition was overflowing.

Django had also entered into the *gadjo*'s world. This was a large realm beyond the comforts of his family's small caravan, one strange and unforgiving, with new rules, a different language. Django grew up on the tattered edges of this world, tricking and conniving against it. He had been the outsider, the pariah. But now no longer was he that Gypsy waif with his infernal banjo shooed away by waiters from the cafés. He was accepted into the *gadjo* world—or at least a small corner of it. For a Gypsy boy, this must have been another awakening.

In the few surviving photographs of Django from this time, he has traveled far from the rapscallion of youth. In an age-stained studio portrait from 1923 or 1924, Django looks composed and confident. He is now dressed with care, perhaps because this photograph was taken in a studio, or maybe because it reflected a new sense of self. Guérino bought him a stylish suit and a new banjo-guitar, replacing his ragged coat and battered banjo of the past. This neat, dark suit actually appears to fit Django, and his hair is combed back from his brow with an exquisite, practiced hand. The collar of his shirt is carefully turned down, a collar pin holding his well-knotted tie high for all the world to see in the dandy's style of the day. He stares back into the camera without averting his eyes as if it's a dare for a duel. On his face is a look of such defiant pride that he seems almost disdainful, even haughty.

Yet this portrait is as much of his new banjo-guitar as it is of Django. He holds the instrument front and center and it fills the middle of the frame. The banjo seems too large for the boy, and although it looks like a quaint child's toy, a plaything precious and cute, that is obviously not how Django thinks of the instrument. His whole being is intent on the banjo: his legs crossed to support it, his back bent forward to play, his arms enveloping it. Django grips this banjo like a weapon—a weapon with which to wage war for his ambitions.

MUSETTE WAS AN UNIQUE EXPRESSION of a place, a people, and a period. Jazz was born in New Orleans, the blues in the Mississippi Delta, the tango in Buenos Aires, flamenco in Sevilla, fado in Lisbon. Paris gave birth to musette.

Musette originally referred to a type of bagpipe, but it soon became the name for a music. The hailed king of the pipes was Antoine "Bousca" Bouscatel. Born in 1867 in the Cantal region of the French Auvergne, he received his first pipes when he was eight years old. Bouscatel spent his days alone in the Auvergnat alps tending his family's cows and goats and teaching himself to play. It was this music of a goatherd that Bouscatel brought to Paris.

He arrived in the capital in 1890 when he was 23. Like many Auvergnat farmhands, he came to Paris seeking a better life, part of a wave of immigration from the Auvergne. Bouscatel settled in what were then the fringes of the city in *la Roquette*, the Faubourg Saint-Antoine near where the old Bastille once stood, far from the grand boulevards and Opéra. The neighborhood was known in Auvergnat argot as *la Bastoche*, and it became a veritable village of the Auvergne transplanted into the heart of Paris.

The Auvergnats arrived on the city streets like poor country cousins. They vended coal for heating during winter and transported water year round for drinking and bathing, carrying the buckets as beasts of burden at the ends of wooden beams straddling their shoulders like oxen yokes. They stood out amid the Parisians, dressed in their regional clothes of flowing blue blouses known as *biaudes*, broad-brimmed black felt hats, and brilliant red scarves knotted at the neck, their arrival heralded by the clack of their wooden clogs on the cobblestones. Yet the Auvergnats soon won the grudging respect of Paris for their drive and desire to get ahead; Honoré de Balzac created a caricature of the thrifty, industrious Auvergnat immigrant in his wheeler-dealer Rémonencq in *Le Cousin Pons* of 1848, who "thirsted for gold like the devils in hell thirst for the dew of paradise." Many Auvergnats graduated to establish cafés that sold wine instead of water, yet still offered good black Auvergnat coal to heat people's homes.

The cafés became a center of Auvergnat life in Paris. They were simple inns, without the brasswork and Art Nouveau finery of an Alsatian brasserie or the fanfare that doubled as ambiance in a bistro. They typically had no tables or chairs and boasted just a bar—a wooden counter if times were tough or a true zinc bar when they were good. Many of the proprietors also played the musette, and when the wine so moved them, they could be induced to pump up their bagpipes and play a song of the old days. Others hired musicians such as Bouscatel and invited friends on Sundays to dance the Auvergnat 3/4-time *bourrée*. These balls were private family affairs, a respite from the work week, a small taste of the dew of paradise in the limbo of the big city.

The musette's song could soon be heard five nights a week as full-time dance halls were established known as *bals musette*. By 1880, there were some 150 dance halls in Paris's working-class neighborhoods. In November 1890, *Le Figaro* reported in an amused if somewhat panicked tone that there seemed to be a *bal musette* in every Auvergnat shop in Paris.

Bouscatel was working during the day as a boilermaker and coppersmith, common work among Auvergnats. But when night descended, he packed up his musette and set out to play. He honed his crude country style and no longer sounded like a goatherd: Recordings of Bouscatel display a musician able to coax enchanting sounds from his crude instrument and play rousing *bourrées* that kept the good times alive. By 1903, Bouscatel was the star of a small bistro named Au Chalet, crowded in between scrap-metal dealers' shops and groceries on the street known to all as the Auvergnat heaven on Earth, rue de Lappe.

Rue de Lappe was a plain, ugly street, a mongrel of a Parisian boulevard, but whatever charm it lacked during daytime was made up for by its bewitching allure at night when the street came alive. While upper-class Paris promenaded along the Champs-Élysées, the Auvergnat boilermakers let off steam here. The short street shot straight from rue de la Roquette to rue de Charonne and was wide enough for just one cart to pass—usually the gendarmes' Black Maria. The factory workers and neighborhood toughs arrived in droves with the darkness, jostling each other to gain entrance, twirling around the dance floor with the shop girls, and settling their grievances with switchblades. As dawn finally arrived, rue de Lappe woke each day in a bed of litter and broken glass, gray-faced with a hangover and grieving the morning after—but with no regrets and ready to do it all again as soon as the grace of darkness descended.

It was on rue de Lappe that Bouscatel was crowned the king of the musette. He gave up his day job to perform through the nights, and by 1910, Au Chalet was in Bouscatel's hands and renamed Chez Bouscatel. Over the years, Bouscatel expanded his *bal* into a grand dance hall. He appeared each evening still wearing his *biaude* blouse, felt hat, and red scarf, symbols of Auvergnat tradition applauded by his crowds, even though they had traded their old farm wear for work clothes suited to the factories. Bouscatel also still cultivated a grand moustache in the best Auvergnat style. Like many pipers, he wore on his ankles bracelets of bells with which he kept time and provided his own simple accompaniment. Often, he played solo. Other times, he led a trio of a violin and hurdy-gurdy. With a shout of "*Hé les enfants!*" Bouscatel pumped up the red-velvet-covered airbag with his right arm, blew into the mouthpiece, and the night began.

THE MELODY of the bagpipe's song was soon to be interrupted. By the late 1800s, another wave of immigrants began arriving in Paris—Italians—bringing their own musical instrument, the accordion. This robotic kin of the bagpipes was a complete band in a box, and the Italians played their own traditional songs and light opera airs with a sound that waltzed from sad to sweet and back again.

An accordionist first climbed up on the dais of a Parisian *bal* to play for the dancers in 1879. The instrument was new to the dance halls and people flocked to hear the novel sounds. The accordion was dramatically more flexible than the pipes, capable of stretching to numerous octaves, painting a wider palette of tones, and playing numerous styles of music and emotions. To win jobs in the *bals* and displace the pipers, the Italian accordionists belted bells to their ankles and adopted the Auvergnat repertoire as if it were their own.

The pipers rose up against this threat to their livelihood and patrimony. In an outraged panic, a piper dashed off a call to arms to an Auvergnat newspaper: "Death to these foreign squeezeboxes that are good only to make bears dance, but absolutely unworthy to start the legs of our charming women of Cantal in to dancing." Heeding the cry, pipers organized in 1895 a fraternal union with Bouscatel at its head. The war was on.

Prominent among the Italian accordionists was Charles Péguri. He was the eldest son of Félix Péguri, who left his native Piedmont for Marseille in 1872 before venturing to Paris in 1890 to open an atelier fabricating and repairing accordions. Félix had three sons, all of whom became accordionists—Charles, Michel, and Louis. Like his father, Charles was both an accordion maker and player, yet he held grander ambitions. In 1905, in the midst of the war between the pipers and accordionists, Charles packed up his accordion to introduce himself to the piper's king, Bouscatel.

Chez Bouscatel was alive that night with Auvergnats dancing to Bouscatel's music. Péguri stood in the shadows, his accordion hidden at his feet, awaiting a break in the songs. When Bouscatel exchanged his pipes for something cool to drink, Péguri hoisted his own instrument and approached the dais. His greeting in Italian-inflected French won a cold eye from Bouscatel, but Péguri introduced himself. Bouscatel responded with a curt dismissal: He needed no accompanist as the bells on his ankles provided all the band he required. But Péguri continued, stating proudly that he was an accordionist. Bouscatel's ire rose at this impertinence. Onlookers remembered his condemnation: "It's strange, that machine. You make music with it?" Bouscatel sneered. But he had likely already admitted to himself that the accordion boasted qualities his simple pipes lacked. He asked Péguri to play for him, and from the first notes, onlookers remember Bouscatel's eyes became eloquent, at once sad and yet impressed. Finally, he set down his drink, climbed onto the stage next to Péguri, and pumped up his pipes to join in. They began their song, playing side by side, bagpipes and accordion in harmony. The duet won over the dancers, who gathered up partners and swung across the floor. When the music came to an end, they demanded more from a pleased Bouscatel and relieved Péguri. With the people's response to their song, Bouscatel hired Péguri to accompany him at Chez Bouscatel. It was a truce in the war between pipers and accordionists. It was also the beginning of a new music.

Although the union between bagpipes and accordion may only have been a marriage of convenience, it was followed by a marriage of love. On May 27, 1913, Charles Péguri wed Bouscatel's daughter. Like a strategic medieval marriage between heads of state, the king of the bagpipes was now forever linked with the new king of the accordion.

Yet even though he accepted the accordion into his hallowed dance hall, Bouscatel was uneasy about this upstart. Sharing a drink late one night after the *bal* was quiet, Bouscatel and his hurdy-gurdy player, Baptiste, bemoaned the arrival of the accordion. Bouscatel pronounced a funeral elegy for his musette: "The days of my bagpipes are numbered, and those of your hurdy-gurdy too! This character with his accordion carries with him our ruin! . . . The accordion is a miracle that falls from the sky. It is a revolution on the way. Did you hear? It is complete, it is hot, it is alive. And it is a whole orchestra, this instrument of the devil! It takes the breath out of you, this accordion of Satan. Listen well to what is conspiring against Bouscatel. It is fate. And when I am dead, people will still be dancing on rue de Lappe."

By the time Bouscatel died in 1945, his premonition had come true. The musette was playing its swan song in the *bals* by the mid 1910s; the accordion had joined in, played supporting harmony, and then quickly took center stage to play the melody in the halo of the spotlight. In the wake of Bouscatel and the other pipers, the music the accordionists now played—whether it was *bourrées*, Italian airs, or a unique and growing repertoire of *bals* favorites—became known simply as musette. The Auvergnat bagpipes had given their name to the music that replaced them.

MUSETTE EVOLVED into a sophisticated form of music in the 1910s and 1920s primarily at the hands of one man, accordionist Émile "Mimile" Vacher. There were other accomplished accordionists following Charles Péguri during this era—players such as Louis and Michel Péguri, Émile Prud'homme, Joseph Colombo, Adolphe DePrince, Medard Ferrero, Marceau Verschueren, Jean Vaissade, and Fredo Gardoni. But it was Vacher who synthesized the traditions of Bouscatel and Péguri to pioneer almost single handedly the music of musette.

Vacher grew up to the sound of an accordion. Born May 7, 1883, in Tours, he was brought to Paris by his mother when he was an infant. In the capital, his mother moved in with an accordionist named Louis-Paul Vacher. Émile fell under the music's spell, begging for lessons, and soon accompanying his adoptive father in a duo. In 1898, when Émile was just 15 years old, the two began playing dance halls, and in 1910, the Vacher family purchased the Bal de la Montagne Sainte-Geneviève in *la Mouffe*. Here, in the medieval passages of the Rive Gauche, where the ancient rue Mouffetard joined rue de la Montagne Sainte-Geneviève in the shadow of the Panthéon, the Vacher's *bal* became the humble cathedral of musette.

Émile Vacher grew into a paternal-looking man, befitting his role as the father of musette. He was a husky person with an ample supply of chins. With hands the size of hams and fingers like plump sausages, he made even his monstrous accordion seem diminutive as he gripped the box and rocked the bellows. Vacher drew such an enchanting sound from his accordion one onlooker reported that his music sent women into ecstasy.

Vacher commanded a wide repertoire of music. Along with the *bourrées*, he unreeled popular quadrilles, polkas, mazurkas, Spanish paso dobles, and maxixes from Rio de Janeiro; the tango, foxtrot, cakewalk, biguine, rumba, and *le shimmy* were fashionably late arrivals on the scene. He also composed accordion waltzes that became known as *valses musette*. These waltzes were breezy tunes that swept the dancers into their gay sound. Their mechanics were largely standardized: a major-key A section theme followed by a B section that led back to the melody line.

In addition, Vacher played the java, a dance that became the pride of musette. Legend held that the java got its name at Le Rat Mort, a grand *bal* reigning over place Pigalle in Paris's red-light district. Here, the women were infatuated with the 3/4-time Italian mazurka "Rosina" that they danced in quick, minced steps with their hands planted on their partners' derrières. Throughout the nights, the dancers demanded the band play "Rosina," calling out for encores, "*Ca va?*" which in the Auvergnat accent came across as "*Cha va?*" Paris woke one morning and a new dance had been born. Yet the debut of a new dance was contentious. Some staunchly Auvergnat *bals* bore signs proclaiming "The java is forbidden." Others cursed the java: Louis Péguri said the java was "a dance derived from the waltz but with a step that was debauched and vulgar." Others decried it succinctly as a *mazurka massacrée*, whereas Parisian novelist Francis Carco summed up all bal dancing, stating, "Here, dance is not an art." Art or not, the dancers begged for encores, and Vacher hurried to compose fast-paced javas for his fans.

At his dance hall, Vacher's band was also changing with the times. One evening, his band included an awkward little drum kit played by Vacher's adopted father. This addition to the traditional musette sound was inspired by the hot new jazz music arriving in France with the American Army bands of World War I. Almost overnight, drums replaced the piper's bracelet of bells, giving the music a percussive drive and modern rhythmic movement. The musette drum kit was quaint, consisting of just three components—kick bass, snare drum, cymbal—and was fittingly known in musette argot as *un jazz*.

Another strange instrument soon also appeared at Vacher's side. The banjo arrived, like the drum kit, via America in the hands of jazz-band and minstrel-show musicians. Three different types came into vogue—the elfin banjo-mandolin, four-string tenor, and six-string banjo-guitar. Vacher adopted it as the ideal accompaniment to the accordion with its percussive sound like a drum, harmonic chords like a harp, or bass lines of a string bass. And it was blessed with a sharp volume and trebly tone that cut through the accordion's powerful voice.

THE FIRST NOTES from a banjo in a dance hall may have been shocking, but Vacher's next move created more waves—both in the immediate and long term. Appearing at his side was a Gypsy, a banjo player known as Mattéo Garcia. The music of the Auvergnat pipers had been usurped by Italian accordionists, then charged by the earliest American hot jazz. Now, a new influence to musette arrived in the person of Garcia, who opened the door for other Gypsy musicians and their musical sensibilities.

Little is known of Mattéo Garcia. He was likely related to Coco and Serrani Garcia, the bandmates of Poulette Castro. He played his music in the 1910s and 1920s; by 1921, he was accompanying Vacher at the most notorious of all *bals musette*, Au Petit Jardin. Yet no photos remain, no recordings survive. Garcia remains a shadowy figure, his story lost to the wastelands of *la Zone*.

Garcia was the composer of "Minch valse," his sole surviving composition, yet it was a singular masterwork that built his fame as the godfather of a distinguished style of *valse musette* known as the *valse manouche* for its Gypsy composers. The melody of Garcia's "Minch valse" was borne on rippling arpeggios running in ascending melodic lines. The title of this rhapsody, however, had a jocular, base background that was straight off the dirty floors of the dance halls. *Minch* was vulgar Romany slang for "cunt."

Garcia was soon joined by Gusti Malha. Inheriting Garcia's chair as Vacher's accompanist, Malha was prized as an accompanist due to his lightning-fast fingers and trustworthy rhythm chording. But there was something more to his music. Even though he was musically illiterate like most Romanies of the day, Malha added what the accordionists called *passion rabouine*—Gypsy passion—to their sound. Thus, his services were vied for among the bandleaders—including Michel and Louis Péguri, Gardoni, and Albert Carrara—who jealously stole him away from each other like the spoils of a never-ending musical war.

Whereas Garcia's legacy rests on just the one waltz that became by forfeit his masterpiece, Malha was prolific. But beyond numerous simple melodies, Malha was the uncredited composer of the quintessential "Reine de musette," and herein lay a tale indicative of the place of the Gypsies in both the *bals* and the *gadjo* world at large.

"Reine de musette" is a romance in musical miniature. The melody is sweetly nostalgic like the remembrance of an old love. Then the B section arrives on a note of trepidation like a lover's spat, before the song resolves itself in the crescendo of a warm embrace. After composing the waltz, Malha sold it for 40 francs to pianist Jean Peyronnin, who played alongside him in Vacher's band. Peyronnin required a sixth composition bearing his name to become a member of the vaunted Société des Auteurs, Compositeurs et Éditeurs de Musique (SACEM). This organization was a sort of union and musical old boys club that copyrighted songs; being a member was both an honor and a necessity to work your way up in the music world. The tale of "Reine de musette" tells of the outsider nature of the Romany musician: Here was Malha, one of the best known and most prolific of Gypsies, and even though he himself boasted enough compositions to join SACEM, he steered clear of the musical establishment. Malha aided a Frenchman in gaining SACEM membership and paid no heed to possibly ephemeral royalties from publication and other musicians' recordings of the song. For himself, he took his payment up front in money he could count.

Among his compositions, Malha remains most famous for his classic "La valse des niglos," a jewel of a minor-key waltz building on the legacy of Garcia's "Minch valse." These pioneering waltzes of Garcia and Malha display a distinctive style showing the hand of a banjo player as composer rather than an accordionist, with melody lines that fall readily under the fingers on a banjo-guitar neck. Lacking the accordion player's ability to sustain notes, the guitarists instead filled the air with furious flurries of sound, ornamenting the melodic lines with triplets and tremolos, virtuosity impressive to the Gypsies. Garcia and Malha incorporated elements of the accordionists' playing into their waltzes, especially in the roller coaster melodies of ascending and descending arpeggios and chromatic runs. This character of musette melody came from the right-hand button "keyboard" favored by accordionists of the day as the sensible layout made rapid two- or three-octave arpeggios a simple dash for the fingers across the buttons. Vacher and others used these arpeggios liberally in composition and ornamentation, and Garcia and Malha wholeheartedly adopted this style to their banjos.

Garcia and Malha's signature was the introduction of minor instead of major-key melodies. These Romany themes were often spiced by harmonic minor-seventh chords, sixth and ninth notes, and even diminished chords, all adding flavor. In addition, their waltzes were three-part compositions. The A section theme was followed by the B with a quick-moving melody line of near-non-stop triplets. The waltz reached its crescendo here, dancers spinning to the music in a move known as *la toupie*, named for a child's spinning top. The waltz returned to the theme before moving into the C section, which typically jumped to a major key and featured a relaxed melody, giving dancers a chance to catch their breath before launching back into the theme.

Garcia and Malha's music was due not to sophisticated training, but rather to playing what pleased and provoked their untutored ears. The Gypsies had learned how to translate their talents of making music around the campfire into a way to make a living. Along the path, musette was forever enriched. Nowhere did this come alive as in Malha's "La valse des niglos," a sophisticated waltz of melancholy and sentimentality. Malha christened his melody in homage to the hedgehog—and in turn, to Romany culture.

IN THE *BALS MUSETTE*, the banjo—that misshapen, shrill-voiced freak of a musical instrument—was known affectionately and descriptively as *un jambon*, a ham. Arriving each evening at the dance hall as the sun set behind the rooftops, Django carried his banjo under his arm. Just as a butcher wrapped a ham in paper, Django carefully protected his *jambon* in cast-off newspaper. He lacked money for a proper case.

To reach the stage, Django followed the lead of Guérino in scaling a ladder to a balcony known as a *surplomb*. Once they were in place with their instruments, the owner stowed the ladder away. The balcony saved valuable floor space for paying customers in the tight dance halls. It also served a simple sonic purpose: The typical dance hall was no Opéra, and by placing the musicians above the dancers' heads, their unamplified instruments could be heard over the hubbub of the hall. Django and Guérino were left on the mezzanine to play their music through the night above the clouds of cigarette smoke and amid the stars cast by the reflecting ball.

Enthroned on the balcony, Guérino was the ruler of all. Accordionists were treated with regal reverence, a respect accorded in lesser degree to their court of musicians. Guérino and the others bore their names emblazoned in multicolored rhinestones and faux jewels on their accordions, and when the spotlight shone just right, the reflection blinded the eyes. If that was not enough, each accordionist commanded a self-proclaimed title more outlandish, more boastful than the other: Their advertising posters and record labels saluted them as *Le Virtuose, Le Célèbre, Le Beau, Le Magicien de l'accordéon* . . .

The dancers adored the song of the accordion. The squeezebox defined musette, and the regulars identified themselves with its sound. In homage,

they christened the accordion with pet names in argot. Some of the slang
terms were simply descriptive, such as *piano à bretelles* (piano with suspenders), or were affectionately belittling, like *le poumon d'acier* (the iron lung) and
boutonneux (pimple-face, for the button keyboard). Others called it *le piano du
pauvre* (the piano of the poor), which might be used alternately to disparage
or with pride. Yet the most colorful names were honorary titles—*la boîte à
sanglots* (the box of sobs) and *la boîte à frissons* (the box of thrills). To many, it
was simply *la boîte magique*.

Befitting the magical world of escape the accordion and dance halls promised, Django, Guérino, and other musicians often dressed in fantastical garb
provided by the dance halls. Some nights, they were Argentine gauchos. Other
evenings, they portrayed sailors dressed in the signature white-and-blue-striped
jerseys of the French maritime. Or, ironically, they wore the blue blouses and
red scarves of the Auvergne. At another *bal*, they might button themselves up
in black evening dress—which, in the world of the dance hall, may have been
the most incongruous costume of all.

As dusk fell across the darker side of Paris—known in slang then as *Panam*—
gas lamps were lit and neon lights charged. The dance halls glowed like a
promised land. At the entrances, men impatiently lined up outside to be pat-
ted down and searched for weapons—brass knuckles, stilettos, pistols. Anything they carried that could be used in a fight was confiscated. But out of
age-old chivalry, the women were not searched, and it was tucked into their
garters that a knife might make its clandestine entrance.

Most dance halls did not charge a fee at the door. Instead, the men had to
pay by the dance, purchasing tokens minted by each *bal*. A token cost 25 centimes or five sous, the price of a dance. They were stamped out of cheap
aluminum or brass in shapes from squares to hexagons to diamonds, yet all
bore the legend *Bon pour une danse*. These false coins were a fitting currency
for the make-believe world of the *bals*.

From his seat at Guérino's side, Django could gaze out over the dance
halls and the unvarying decor: Set at the perimeters of the rooms, the tables
were nailed to the floor so the furniture couldn't furnish ammunition for fights.
They were surrounded by garish red banquettes—chairs too were taboo. Large
mirrors covered the walls, making the simple dance hall appear like a palace.
Colored streamers festooned the ceiling, stretching from the four corners to
the center of the room. Here, they ended at the prismed reflecting ball that
cast a confetti of light over the dancing couples, carrying them off into a
dreamworld far away from the present.

Just as the dance hall had its décor, it also had its fashion and code of
behavior among *les mulots*, the "mice," slang for dance hall regulars. The women
wore dark skirts held up by suspenders over bright-colored short-sleeved
blouses—made of satin if they had a good job or a good-paying bad job. Hair
fashions changed with the times, but there was one rage that survived—spit

curls. With a dab of saliva, the women fashioned elaborate coils of hair flattened onto their forehead or temples, and the spit curl remained the hallmark of *bal musette* beauty. The men's dress was based on work clothes. They typically wore black trousers and blue workshirts set off by their beloved red scarves tied around their necks. Snap-brim caps topped their heads, worn either menacingly low over their eyes or cocked back from their foreheads. And the men removed these hats in deference to nothing and no one.

As Django and Guérino struck up a waltz, the men beckoned women to dance from long distance across the hall. In the *bals*, no man ever bowed to a woman. Instead, men stared down women from across the room and called to them with a loud, almost sinister *psst!* As photographer Brassaï, a habitué of the *bals*, remembered, "The sounds—*Psst! Psst!*—shot from table to table in all directions before every dance, like an orchestra of crickets!" After the dancers took to the floor and spun their way through a few choruses, Django and Guérino halted their song and the owner called out, "*Passez la monnaie!*" The men then anted up their tokens, and Django and Guérino again started their songs.

To cool down the dancers after a turn, the bars served bizarre concoctions all their own. Ghastly colored drinks called *diabolos* were the fad. Green, red, violet, or orange, they were made with blends of crème de menthe, grenadine, and a healthy dose of alcohol to be sipped through straws. Drinks were never provided in bottles, as those bottles could double as weapons to split open someone's skull.

Fights could be provoked in countless ways. By accepting an invitation for a drink with *un mulot*, a woman might be agreeing to raise her skirt for him and her refusal could spark a row. Other accounts were settled outside the *bals* between rival gangs, regulars vowing allegiance to different dance halls, or natives of various neighborhoods—the Auvergnats of *la Bastoche* might that night hunt down the *Mémilmouche*, the roughnecks of Ménilmontant. And then there were the Belleville gangsters known as *les apaches*, emulating the Wild West Indians they read about in pulp magazines or watched in the early moving pictures.

Django and Guérino's music served as accompaniment to the theater of the *bals*. The dance halls were alive with the poetry of the night, but also with pitfalls. Behind the mask of a handsome man might have lurked a sharp-dressed pimp seducing girls and recruiting the labor force for the streets and brothels. Or that charming girl responding to a call to dance might have been a prostitute, shepherded by her sharp-dressed pimp to the wolfpack of men. Other *bals* hired B-girls who enticed men into the dance halls like sirens. Within this nightworld of the working class, Django was on his own. While Guérino may have promised Négros he would watch over her son, the accordionist was not immune to the charms of the *bals*. In this milieu, Django grew up quickly.

When the music ended for the night and the crowd turned out into the early morning, the vigilant Négros was waiting at the dance hall for Django.

She wanted to be sure her son sidestepped the seductions of *Panam*. Django's banjo protected again in its newspaper case, they would make their way together through the fortifications and home to their caravan in *la Zone*.

ARMED WITH HIS BANJO, Django arrived in the *bals* as though he was storming the Bastille. He seated himself next to the accordionists, inheriting the sideman's chair that once belonged to Poulette Castro, Mattéo Garcia, and Gusti Malha. Yet while Django's banjo work followed this lineage, it was suffused with his own personality. Even at 12 and while still learning the banjo, he played with a virtuosity and power that was stunning, startling—even a bit frightening. He did not enter the *bals* with a plan to attack the barricades of musette, but in the surviving recordings he played not so much as a sideman but as if he were leading a one-man coup d'état.

One of the first indications of Django's ambitions came early in the 1920s during a banquet for Les Amis de l'Accordéon at a restaurant in La Villette. Gathered about the tables were all of Paris's accordionists—the good, the bad, and those who played, as the saying went, with a fork in the right hand, a boxing glove on the left. To entertain the entertainers, Django was one of several invited to the stage. Taking up his banjo-guitar, he struck the first notes of the most celebrated and difficult of all polkas in the *bal* repertoire, "Perle de cristal," originally composed for the arabesques of a flute. The melody is a blaze of triplets that can twist an accordionist's fingers into a knot, and to prove their proficiency, the best bands accelerated the tempo up to a blistering finale. But after negotiating his way through the melody, Django did not bring the song to its usual crescendo. Instead, he started in again, unreeling variations on the well-worn melody, pulling notes out of thin air, bending the song to his wishes. Django saw no reason to conform to the strict dictates of the melody; it was simply a starting point to playing *music*. As they said under their breaths in the *bals*, Django was playing "with a drawn knife" and looking for a fight in freely interpreting the sacred and inviolable musette. Jazz influenced musette in its instrumentation, but the line was set at swinging the music, and when Django finally hit his last note, one can only imagine the looks on the accordionists' faces and perhaps a hesitation before they applauded this daring young man with his banjo.

One of Django's fellow banjoists, Frenchman Roger Chaput, remembered the effect Django had on himself and the purist musette world. Born in 1909 in Montluçon Allier but raised in Ménilmontant, Chaput learned guitar and mandolin in a bistro from an ancient Italian known as Papa Jean. Hanging around the *bals* of Porte de Bagnolet, Chaput was soon accompanying accordionists Michel Péguri and Albert Carrara as well as leading several elegant banjo musette recordings. "Django arrived one day in about 1925 with a banjo missing his bass E string," Chaput recalled. "He started in to play. He created these incredible variations—but he was just a *môme*, just a little punk kid, when I first heard him play. I said to myself, that's astounding! The following day, I was searching the Gypsy encampments to find him again."

Django was fortunate to begin his career at Guérino's side. The accordionist was not only regaled throughout Paris as a dance hall star, but also as an innovator. As such, Guérino was open to Django's zeal. If Django had begun in the band of one of the musette traditionalists, his fervor might have been silenced from the start.

Like many accordionists, Guérino was Italian—from Napoli. Yet Guérino was the sole Gypsy among them. And like many Gypsies, his story was clouded. Guérino traveled Europe in his caravan, steering his horse to France in 1903, surviving by playing dances and giving lessons. By 1915, Guérino was established at Paris's *bal* Le Petit Gravilliers. Then, sometime in the 1930s, he disappeared from the scene, dying soon after from cancer. As befitting his vague story, only a handful of photographs of Guérino remain. His was a wide face with deep eyes and a strong brow capped by woolly hair that won him the nickname "Tête de mouton"—Sheephead. From the photos, there is an obvious strength in his broad shoulders, ideal for pumping the bellows of his accordion through long nights.

During his career, Guérino searched out Romany accompanists, such as his brother, vocalist and guitarist Meneghi Guérino, and Malha. His fellow Gypsies may have been more sympathetic to his nontraditional ideas of music as he was not locked into playing just musette but augmented his repertoire with Italian waltzes and popular tunes.

Guérino's song list was not all that set him apart. His accordion was also modern. Guérino played a button-keyboard chromatic, which was typically built with three steel reeds per note. Yet Guérino eschewed the classic "wet" musette sound with one reed tuned precisely to a note and supplemented by the other two reeds tuned sharp and flat around it. This provided players such as Vacher the trademark plaintive sound with "vibration" surrounding every note in a sentimental quavering like a street singer's crooning. Guérino instead had his accordion reeds tuned "dry," with the reeds closely in tune. This gave him a sound that was forceful, even jazzy and American.

Django began playing his banjo-guitar with Guérino at a *bal musette* on rue Monge in *la Mouffe*. After this stand, they moved to Vacher's Bal de la Montagne Sainte-Geneviève, then to Chez Marteau near the place d'Italie.

Accompanying Guérino through the nights, Django likely built up a repertoire of hundreds of songs. Being alphabetically and musically illiterate, he carried this trove of melodies and harmonizing chord progressions in his head. For Django—as well as most other Gypsies—music was an oral tradition; as one of his later musical partners stated, "I wonder if, in his younger days, he even knew that printed music existed." While songs were published and copyrighted, it mattered little beyond the legal domain as many in the musette world couldn't read music, or didn't bother to, learning the songs by example. Django became a human jukebox with a vast repertoire of waltzes, tangos, javas, and chanson filed in his memory.

After playing alongside Guérino, Django was hired away by Maurice Alexander. Born in 1900, Alexander was a rarity among accordionists. He was a Parisian, and not just from any quarter but from the high-class Passy neighborhood. He began playing accordion at seven, later racing a bicycle in the Tour de France, and then by 1918, leading a band at the Bal des Vertus. With Django at his side, Alexander performed at the *bal* Chez Berlot, then moved on to Chez Bouscatel and the landmark Bal Ça Gaze. But Django didn't stay in one place for long. Alexander was a conventional accordionist, and Django soon left him, probably in search of better pay or greater musical challenges.

By 1926, he was accompanying accordionist Fredo Gardoni. Italian by descent, Gardoni was born in Switzerland, in 1898. Although he was not Romany, Gardoni lived in a caravan parked among the Gypsies. Over the years, he became one of France's most beloved musicians; as he sang in boast, "My heart is an accordion." At his peak, he was imposing and magnificently regal in bearing. He weighed more than 300 pounds, boasted a smile aglitter in golden teeth, and lived with the jovial and carefree mentality of a baby. He was also an infamous womanizer: A compatriot termed him not simply a bigamist but a *tri*gamist. When Django first joined Gardoni, the accordionist too was at the beginning of his career: "Django made his debut with me at La Rose Blanche, a dance hall near the Porte de Clignancourt by the the old customs barrier, two steps from the Gypsy caravans in *la Zone*. It was a true dance hall where you could eat mussels and fries, drink a glass of white wine, and dance. I found Django the Gypsy sitting on the steps of a caravan. It was right near mine. He was making miniature Gypsy caravans in wood, like toys, with Lilliputian horses. They were beautifully done. Little caravans and he had not forgotten anything: chimney, curtains, stairs, just like the real ones. Already Django, at nine years old [*sic*: he was more likely 12], was playing the guitar like a phenomenon."

Again, Django wandered on and was soon playing alongside Jean Vaissade. An Auvergnat born in 1911, Vaissade was also a child prodigy, starting on violin at age seven before taking up accordion. Vaissade performed at all the famous dance halls, but in his travels, he never heard anything like Django, and he remembered their first meeting: "It must have been around 1925 or 1926. At that time Fredo Gardoni was playing at La Chaumière, a dance hall near the Porte de Clignancourt that isn't there any more. Django, who lived just outside in *la Zone*, often came to sit in, eagerly replacing the band's regular banjoist for several numbers. Already everyone admired him, for if he didn't yet have the mastery he was eventually to display, he was already carving out a style that was different from anyone else's. I remember thinking how fantastic he was when I heard him play."

The problem for many of the bandleaders impressed by Django was that even by hiring him, you didn't always get him. If Django happened upon a better opportunity—a hot dice game, a worthy billiards challenger, or if he simply was not in the mood—he enlisted someone else to take his place. This occurred all too often for some accordionists, as Nin-Nin or their cousin Eugène "Ninine" Vées arrived with their banjos in Django's stead. As Vaissade said with a twinkle, "All of Django's family passed through my band!" For Django's part, he may have grown bored of the routine, playing the identical songs over and over—especially if an accordionist demanded he play them the same each time. Or perhaps Django was simply young, unreliable, and irresponsible. Or again, it may have been another case of his flaunting the bandleaders's authority as he chafed under their rein and sought to assert his freedom. And still, the accordionists took Django back; his skill with the banjo was worth the headache. While there was disagreement among bandleaders about who had discovered Django, they all agreed on his talent. As Vaissade said, "He stuck his fingers to his nose and played incredible, complicated things the other banjo players that worked with us could not have even imagined. Although he was our accompanist, it was we who were unable to follow him! He played almost too strongly and, deep down, we were always afraid that he would overshadow our accordions!"

Nowhere did this come across more strongly than in Django's musette recordings. Only some dozen sides have been found that are known to include him, however. It's likely Django recorded at further sessions and played on other lost sides, but his musette legacy lives in just this handful of recordings.

Django's earliest known sessions occurred in spring and summer 1928 when he was just 18. At Vaissade's side, he entered the Compagnie Gramophone du Française studio in Pigalle's Cité Chaptal on June 20, 1928. Vaissade's choice of instrumentation was common to the *bals*: His accordion was backed by Django's banjo and another musician playing *jazzflûte*, a sort of slide whistle. This whistle was the dance hall version of a jazz band trumpet, a bizarre but typical accompaniment to musette bands due to its sustained, soothing sound that smoothed out the harsh treble of the accordion and banjo; it was like a string or horn section on a budget. Django and Vaissade recorded four songs characteristic of dance hall repertoires. A mix of chanson, waltzes, and light opera airs, they were jolly tunes tailored to dancing, including the street-organ favorite "Griserie" and "La Caravane," an air from Raoul Moretti's 1927 operette *Le Comte Obligado*, then the rage in Paris.

On these sides, Django played with power and assurance belying his age. When he hit on-the-beat rhythmic chords to bolster the accordion's melody, he strummed his banjo with a piston's punch driving the beat. But he was obviously not content with this role for long; such playing appeared to bore his youthful impetuosity and dreams of dance hall grandeur. Django seemed to be throwing down the gauntlet, challenging the accordionist to a duel over the song. Soon, he was adding a strummed half-note accent after the beat, and then, in a shake of his wrist, triple-time chords, bringing the song to full gallop, creating an undercurrent of swinging energy within the trio's sound. In the next chorus, he pattern-picked harmony behind the accordion, dropping effortlessly into tremolos on the secondary chords that built tension to deliver the song to its dénouement.

The recording engineer must have been impressed by this banjoist too: He arranged the musicians in the studio around the single microphone giving Django's banjo prominence and bringing out its sound in the front on the mix. Usually, the accordionist was seated closest to the mic in deference to his prestige. This novel mix did not suit Gramophone director Piero Coppola. Shocked by the brash banjoist's accompaniment, he allowed four sides to be released, but six other songs cut at the same time were cast out. Proud as Django may have been of the session, Vaissade remembered the problem with the overloud, overzealous banjo: "It was several years before I dared set foot in the place again."

Yet Django did not fall out of favor with Vaissade. Following the Gramophone session, he returned at Vaissade's side to record for the small Idéal label. Obviously, Vaissade did not sign any sort of exclusive contract; he was happy to pocket whatever session fees labels paid without regard to hurting sales of his other recordings as he likely received no royalties. Django too was pleased to take part in the session as he was paid a 500-franc fee, riches beyond his youthful dreams. This session took place in May or June 1928 in the venerable Pathé Palace recording studio neighboring the Opéra. Along with Francesco Cariolato on xylophone, Django and Vaissade recorded six sides. While the engineer tamed the volume of Django's banjo, his playing was still as forceful. Yet in the interplay between accordion and xylophone, these songs have a cartoonlike character that is cute instead of impressive.

On the Idéal labels, Django was listed as "Jiango Renard." Since Django could not spell his own name, a label clerk wrote it out phonetically on the discs. It was the first of many derivations of his name to appear over the years.

Django's name was transcribed on his next session as "Jeangot." Sometime in about August 1928, he joined accordionist Marceau in recording for the F. Henry label. Marceau Verschueren was one of the few musette musicians to study music, taking courses in theory at the Lille Conservatoire. On this date, with Django on banjo and Erardy on *jazzflûte*, Marceau cut the *fox-trot oriental* "Au Pays de l'Hindoustan," which was nothing but a veiled version of "The Sheik of Araby," and Marceau's original "Miss Columbia," a so-called *marche américaine*. The Marceau sides display a band in tight form. The recording levels—always a black art in those days of acoustic instead of electric recordings—are balanced between instruments, adding to the cohesive feel. Behind Marceau, Django's playing is so purely musical that his accompaniment is intrinsically part of the song.

Django also recorded at least once with Alexander, but the story behind these sides remains obscure. During summer 1928, Alexander cut two sessions for the Henry label resulting in 12 sides. His band members were not spelled out on the labels, yet the banjoman on some sides plays with a verve and virtuosity that echoed Django's early recordings and may well be him. Django also remembered backing the obscure singer Chaumel, who released "Sur la Place de l'Opéra" and "E Viva la Carmencita" on the Henry label in about 1928 with Alexander and an unidentified rhythm banjoist. Only a handful of these Alexander and Chaumel sides have been found, and there isn't conclusive evidence the banjo player was Django.

The banjo—Django's *jambon*—was a musical paradox. It was an instrument built for sheer volume, the embarrassing quality of its tone a secondary concern. In honor of its sound as well as its odd shape, dance hall musicians also had another nickname for the banjo—*la poêle*, the frying pan. It was only a short step away from the derogatory name with which they cursed a poor-sounding instrument—*une casserole*. Yet in Django's hands, his banjo—this musical instrument likened to various culinary objects—came alive to sing a lyrical song.

DJANGO'S AMBITIONS did not end as an accompanist. During his years playing in the dance halls from 1922 through 1928 when he was between the ages of 12 and 18, Django composed at least four waltzes of his own. These songs followed the tradition of Gypsy banjomen Mattéo Garcia and Gusti Malha. And like these predecessors, Django sadly did not record his compositions at the time.

Years later, after he had left the dance halls behind, Django cut one of his waltzes. The circumstances are a mystery, but during 1935 Django recorded a test pressing of a sole waltz listed on the label simply as "Valse manouche." Django performed on his guitar accompanied by his sister Sara Tsanga on piano. This "Valse manouche" featured a charming melody, almost like a sentimental lullaby. The B section was unique, however, a flamenco interlude with long tremolos rising up to arpeggiated and strummed chords. Recorded in the key of A major with the B section moving to E, the waltz was harmonized with ambitious chord colorings—minors, sixths, and diminished sevenths—that breathed life into the melody.

Another one of Django's waltzes survived due to a recording made in Paris in 1939 by Le Trio Ferret, a group of Gitan dance hall guitarists. Pierre "Baro" Ferret led the trio, accompanied by his brother Jean "Matelo" Ferret and cousin René "Challain" Ferret and backed by bassist Maurice Speilleux. At the time, this session was unremarkable. The sides were timepieces—quaint, all-string recordings of *valses manouche*, a remembrance of things past. Yet decades later, the session proved priceless in saving three historic songs that may have been lost forever—Garcia's "Minch valse," Malha's "La valse des niglos," and Django's piece.

Django's waltz was first released under the name "Gin Gin," but would be known as "Chez Jacquet: À la Petite Chaumière" when it was next recorded in 1959 by Matelo. Like "La valse des niglos," it was a quintessential *valse manouche*. Django composed it in a major key, but the harmony was again flavored by exotic chords, enhancing the melody's beauty. And Le Trio Ferret's version was enchanting. Baro's delicate lines of arpeggios mirrored the playing of a musette accordionist whereas his strong vibrato called forth ages of Gypsy violinists. Matelo and Challain's accompaniment was singular in its ambiance, creating an ageless mood with a sound like a balalaïka chorus. Behind Baro, they added counter-harmonies and filigrees to accent the melody, seamlessly tying the song together into a small masterpiece.

Two other waltzes composed by Django also endured due to Matelo, who recorded them in 1959. Matelo cut "Chez Jacquet" as well as a rubato version of the "Valse manouche" theme Django recorded in 1935, here titled "Choti." In addition, he played another waltz by Django, "Gagoug," which he also interpreted in free time.

The fourth waltz composed by Django and salvaged by Matelo was the sentimental and bittersweet "Montagne Sainte-Geneviève." Its melody was a cascade of arpeggiated minor chords accentuated by an interlude in major with breathless tirades of triplets. But above all, this waltz was likely designed to impress: The song was a bravura showpiece mirroring Django's youthful fervor and echoing his ambitions. He probably performed the song in the dance halls of rue de la Montagne Sainte-Geneviève, his fingers dashing from one end of the banjo fretboard to the other, crisscrossing the neck in a display of virtuosity that dazzled dance hall crowds and sent them spinning like tops across the floor—while accordionists such as Vaissade, a false smile glued to their lips and droplets of sweat itching at their brow, struggled to keep up.

IT WAS IN ABOUT 1925, when he was some 15 years old and flush with his dance hall success, that Django met a Manouche girl of 14 named Sophie Irma Ziegler. Hers was a dark beauty—deep brown hair, supernaturally dark eyes, and the full, round face that was the coveted look of the day. Yet, perhaps surprisingly, it was her cheeks that first caught your glance. They were bright and rosy and warm, and against her olive skin, they set her face aglow. For her complexion, she was known around the campfires as Naguine or La Guigne after the wild cherries that grew in the French mountains. Django was bewitched. And for Naguine, he was a first—and only—love. "It hit me like a bolt of lightning," she remembered of her meeting Django. "Love at first sight."

Naguine's family ventured to Paris from Tuscany, parking their caravan in *la Zone* outside the Porte d'Italie alongside the fires of various cousins. Concerning her family's more distant lineage, she was unsure: "They were from Hungary . . . I think." For now, her life and her future were focused on Django.

Django must have been proud of the dashing adult figure he cut. He was just 15, but he earned money from the *gadjé*, more money than most Manouche could hope to reap in a year of selling baskets or jewelry. And with his banjo, he wooed women with a song. Naguine was swept into his world. "He played very well," she remembered, adding with a smile, "but he didn't know how to dance."

Django and Naguine stayed together for two years, Django still living in the caravan of his mother Négros, Naguine with her family. "He took me along with him to all of the dance halls," she remembered. "At Ça Gaze in Belleville, a dance hall full of underworld toughs wearing their typical caps and red scarves, I was afraid and Django scolded me: 'Why be afraid? It's stupid, because you are the most beautiful girl here.' And so, I smiled and I tried not to be afraid.

"At La Java, Django earned a lot of money, because Monsieur Alexander was very generous with him. But Django instantly burned all of this money at poker. And then we were stuck without a sou, but we were not unhappy because we were in love and love helped us live."

But all that changed one day in 1927. Django dropped Naguine like a spent cigarette.

Another woman had caught his fancy, a Manouche girl named Florine Mayer who was older at 17 and, in Naguine's resentful eyes, more beautiful. Mayer came from a family of gorgeous women. A sole surviving photograph from a family album shows the women of the clan surrounding Django, who appears like a prince—slim, handsome, and debonair with his newly culti-vated moustache. From their mother, Josephine Renaud, to Florine herself, all had lustrous black hair framing their faces, warm olive skin, and smiling eyes above smiles on their lips that would stop the breath of any man. In honor of her beauty, Florine was known simply and truthfully as "Bella," Ital-ian for "beautiful."

For Naguine it was like the thunderclap following that bolt of lightning: "I set out again for Tuscany. I cried all along the road, I was desperate and hopeless, I wanted to die. But I knew that my hour would come again, that I would have a second chance with Django, that the good Lord would give me this second chance . . . And so, I had patience, living under the sun of Italy."

Django was once again in love. He and Bella were both 17 when they stole away from their families for several days. Upon their return, their union was received as a marriage. This "runaway marriage" was the common and hon-orable form of marriage among the Manouche. The Gitans married after elabo-rate bartering between the groom and bride's families, followed by a wedding ceremony and party. Gitans considered elopements scandalous, provoking disputes and even wars between family clans. But runaway marriages were the sole manner among the Manouche. A Manouche boy and girl eloped together,

passed several days—or even several hours—away from their families, and
when they returned their marriage was consummated in the eyes of all. The
Manouche had no marriage ceremony or celebration; the festivities were saved
for the baptism of the couple's firstborn child. As Négros explained, "It is
love, and nothing else, that seals the union between a man and a woman."

Following their marriage, Django and Bella were received by her mother
and father, Henri "Pan" Mayer, a compact yet fierce-looking man behind a
glorious handlebar mustachio. In the Manouche tradition, Bella's parents made
the present of a caravan to the newlyweds, a helping hand on the road to their
married life—as the Manouche saying went, To give a push to the wheel of
the new caravan. Django and Bella parked their new home near the caravans
of their families outside the Porte de Clignancourt.

Within a short time, Bella was pregnant. Django was to be a father.

3

La Musique Diabolique
1926–1928

AT THE SAME TIME Django was making a name for himself in the dance halls, he was also making a discovery on the other side of Paris. Next to Le Rat Mort on place Pigalle stood the grand restaurant l'Abbaye de Thélème. Here sometime in 1926, Django came upon a novel sound. Through the nightclub's windows he could hear the music: It was hot, exotic, strange. It was music so amazing, so different that the world seemed to have changed the direction it spun. Clarinets howled. Saxophones honked. Trombones wailed. Trumpets screamed. And it was all propelled by wild drumming. The sound was unlike anything Django had ever heard, beyond anything he could imagine. Each afternoon, he made a pilgrimage from his family's caravan to the restaurant; sometimes banjo player Roger Chaput or other dance hall musicians ventured along. Django became a regular at the window, straining to hear. He sat on the cobblestones of place Pigalle with a breadcrust to eat, listening through the night until the restaurant shut its doors. They called this music "jazz"—a strange, foreign word that soon translated into any language around the globe.

That this was the devil's music was beyond doubt to most Parisians. From the dance hall regulars to the literati, jazz was a four-letter word, a shocking cacophony of discord, an anarchy of music and tribal drumming fit only for the black savages who created it. The *bals* barred their doors against its entry into their sacred dance halls, and at La Java, accordionist Maurice Alexander led Django aside to offer him some fatherly advice: Beware this music.

But jazz was a siren song to Django. He was hearing Billy Arnold's Novelty Jazz Band, direct from the United States. All of the musicians in the group were African Americans—Arnold himself led the band from his piano bench, directing his combo of horns pumped by the heartbeat of drums. Arnold's band was far from the best of jazz, but no matter. It was the best music Django had ever heard.

JAZZ INVADED FRANCE with the American doughboys of World War I. On New Year's Day 1918, the New York National Guard's 15th Heavy Foot Infantry Regiment (Colored)—soon to earn its sobriquet of the Harlem Hellfighters—landed on French soil at Brest. Organized in 1916 under the command of white Colonel William Hayward, the 15th was formed primarily of recruits from Harlem. When conscription lagged, Hayward created a regimental orchestra to attract enlistees. Already within his ranks happened to be one of the most famous black bandleaders in New York City, Private James Reese Europe, who heeded the call to arms with patriotic zeal and was assigned to a machine-gun company. Europe led Harlem's famed Clef Club orchestra, cut dance music for Victor records, and served as a black booking agent for white high society. He was the ideal man for the job, and Hayward commanded: "Organize for me the best damn band in the United States Army." Europe built a band boasting 65 recruits, including the crème of the Harlem jazz world: cornetist and drum major Noble Sissle, drummer Buddy Gilmore, trumpeter Arthur Briggs, Chicago cornetist Jaçon Frank De Braithe, and dancer Bill "Bojangles" Robinson. And Europe's band was not just about music. It was a full-fledged Broadway show on the march, including musicians playing a refined blend of ragtime, cakewalk, brass band music, and popular dance tunes as well as entertainers who sang, danced, and performed comedy. When the Harlem Hellfighters landed at Brest, they marched off the SS *Pocahontas* led by their band blowing their horns.

The music won French hearts. Just as the Hellfighters infantry soon became the most decorated American unit in World War I, the regiment's band was lauded wherever it went. General John "Black Jack" Pershing, commander of the American Expeditionary Force, requisitioned them for a six-week goodwill tour playing across France to boost the morale of Allied soldiers and French civilians. Drum major Noble Sissle was awestruck by the effects of his own music and farsighted in divining the powers of jazz. He described a French concert:

> Lieutenant Europe, before raising his baton, twitched his shoulders, apparently to be sure that his tight-fitting military coat would stand the strain, a musician shifted his feet, the players of brass horns blew the saliva from their instruments, the drummers tightened their drum-heads, everyone settled back in their seats, half closed their eyes, and when the baton came crashing down with a swoop that brought forth a soul-rousing crash, both director and musicians seemed to forget their surroundings; they were lost in scenes and memories. Cornet and clarinet players began to manipulate notes in that typical rhythm (that rhythm which no artist has ever been able to put down on paper), as the drummers struck their stride, their shoulders started shaking in time to their syncopated raps.
>
> Then it seemed the whole audience began to sway, dignified French officers began to pat their feet, along with the American general, who temporarily lost

his style and grace. Lt. Europe was no longer the Lt. Europe of a moment ago, but Jim Europe, who a few months ago rocked New York with his syncopated baton. . . .

The audience could stand it no longer, the jazz "germ" hit them and it seemed to find the vital spot, loosening all muscles and causing what is known in America as an "eagle rocking it." . . .

All through France, the same thing happened. Troop trains carrying Allied soldiers from everywhere passed us en route, and every head came out of the window when we struck up a good old Dixie tune. Even German prisoners forgot they were prisoners, dropped their work to listen and pat their feet to the stirring American tunes.

But the thing that capped the climax happened up in northern France. We were playing our colonel's favorite ragtime, "The Army's Blues," in a little village where we were the first American troops there, and among the crowd listening to the band was an old woman about sixty years of age. To everyone's surprise, all of a sudden she started doing a dance that resembled "Walking the Dog." Then I was cured and satisfied that American music would one day be the world's music.

With the armistice, the Hellfighters returned home to play in the victory parade down New York City's Fifth Avenue. The band was then demobilized. Musicians began searching for work again, but in the postwar recession, jobs were tight. Faced with Jim Crow laws and the undercurrent of racism, many Hellfighters looked back fondly on their stay in France, where they had been treated well no matter their skin color. Trumpeter Bill Coleman stated simply, in Paris "a jazz musician was considered as a human being." The Hellfighters' heralded trumpeter Arthur Briggs and drummer Buddy Gilmore were some of the first to pack their bags and return to Paris. As the title to Sam M. Lewis and "Mighty" Joe Young's hit song of the day warned, "How 'Ya Gonna Keep 'Em Down on the Farm (After They've Seen Paree)?"

World War I had left France with a wounded soul. After staring into the eyes of Armageddon, the established order of life and beliefs were shaken: almost two million French soldiers were dead, four million wounded, and vast portions of the country devastated. Facing the future now meant forgetting the past. As French actress Arletty remembered, "People wanted to forget the war, they spent without counting, went out night after night, living from one day to the next with the sole notion of catching up for the wasted four years that had gone by." The United States's role in helping win the war swept in a wave of hope in things American. All that was new was seen as better than anything that was old—in politics, literature, art, and music, the ancient order was challenged by novel ways of thinking, seeing, and hearing. And at the avant-garde was jazz. With the sounds of the Hellfighters' music still echoing in their ears, club owners and dancers yearned for that beguiling American jazz.

Les années folles of the Jazz Age erupted in Paris in the 1920s. Nightclubs in Pigalle hired Briggs, Gilmore, Coleman, and other African American musicians as soon as they arrived. And arrive they did. A headline in *The New York Age* newspaper on February 8, 1919, proclaimed "French Now Want Colored Musicians from the United States." A small migration began, following in the Hellfighters' old marchsteps.

Django was listening to the fruits of this migration. Billy Arnold's Novelty Jazz Band first came to Paris in December 1921 after a stand in London. Arnold's band was well named: It was indeed a "novelty" band, playing slapdash "jazz" full of gimmicks. In Arnold's few recordings of the time—such as "Stop It" from 1922 and "Louisville Lou" from 1925—the band lacked even a modicum of swing. The rhythm section of the drum and piano stumbled over each other at every beat while the caterwaul of horns was out of tune and downright corny, even for the times—which was saying a lot. Still, it was hot and it was new, and Arnold's band inspired Django and other French musicians— dance hall musicians, proto-jazzmen, and even classical musicians like pianist Jean Wiener and composer Darius Milhaud. Wiener organized a concert in 1921 including Arnold's band playing jazz tunes in between works by Stravinsky, Milhaud, and Bach; whereas composer Albert Roussel stalked out of the concert, slamming the door behind him, Maurice Ravel complimented Wiener for his audacity.

If Django found Billy Arnold, he probably also stumbled on other jazz bands in Pigalle, Montparnasse, and even in the upscale venues along the Champs-Élysées. Throughout the 1920s, Paris bloomed with nightclubs featuring African American jazz bands. A novel black vaudeville show entitled *Revue Nègre* made its debut at the Théâtre des Champs-Élysées in 1925, featuring dancers, singers, and musicians including clarinetist Sidney Bechet, who had been shanghaied by an earlier band onto a boat bound for Europe in 1919. The star of the show was African American dancer Josephine Baker, who almost overnight became the rage of Paris. From the dawn of the 1920s, Parisian artists and high society went crazy for black exoticism, mirrored in the Primitivist art of Modigliani, Picasso, Robert Delaunay, and others since discovering African sculpture. Jazz fit the fad, and black musicians became the toast of the town, their music joyfully labeled *le tumulte noir*—the black noise.

It was a friend of the Hellfighters' Jim Europe, drummer Louis Mitchell, who had the strongest musical influence on the Jazz Age in Paris. Mitchell played in London as early as 1914. Now, Mitchell's Jazz Kings with cornetist Cricket Smith headlined at the Casino de Paris' Le Perroquet cabaret for five years starting in 1918, accompanying French stars such as Mistinguett with her world-famous legs and that ace French lover, Maurice Chevalier. Dancing to jazz liberated the French after the discipline of European ballroom steps. For the booming numbers of American tourists of the Hemingway crowd, it was no coincidence that the best of times of the Jazz Age in Paris corresponded with the worst of times of Prohibition in the United States. Many headed straight for Pigalle and Montparnasse nightclubs to dance, drink, and make up for lost time. And from his bandstand, Louis Mitchell directed the music that became the overture for *les années folles*.

THIS MUSIC SOUNDED so natural, so pure—and therein lay its deceptive beauty. In earlier years, Django listened to the Gypsy violinists and banjo players and resurrected their melodies on his banjo. Now, he tried to do the same with the songs he heard Billy Arnold play. It marked the beginning of a new epoch for Django: From listening to Arnold and hearing recordings of early jazz, Django was absorbing and assimilating American jazz, striving to master the harmonies they played, their scales and arpeggios, their phrasing, the bent notes and smears, and most of all, that sense of rhythmic movement inspired from black dance that infused the music, the swaggering gait known as swing. Django no longer wanted to sound like a Gypsy or play Gypsy music and would rarely ever record Gypsy tunes. From the far side of the Atlantic, through the fleeting sound of jazz bands on a Pigalle stage and the more enduring magic of records played in his caravan, he sought an acculturation—to play his guitar like a African American jazzman.

Yet jazz was not as simple as it sounded.

As Django heard, jazz was a fomenting musical revolution. It struck at the basis of European classical music, then undisputed in it supremacy as the Western world's standard. The vanguard of this new jazz was the symphonic slapstick of Nick La Rocca's Original Dixieland Jazz Band of New Orleans, whose 1917 recordings are widely regarded as the first jazz records. The white band's songs were played at furious tempos fired by the drums' heat and instrumental histrionics, from barnyard mews to howling gimcrackery. With its use of brass and woodwind instruments, the ensemble alternately amazed and scandalized the European musical establishment, and La Rocca blustered for promotional value that he was a "musical anarchist." Outraged critics agreed, screaming that the Original Dixieland Jazz Band was hell-bent on murdering music.

Drumming drove this jazz with rhythms founded in black dance that were syncopated and dynamic. To many in the early days, jazz *was* drumming and grandstanding drummers like Louis Mitchell drew crowds with their spectacle and novelty—as well as shock value.

The time structure of jazz also heralded a rebellion against European classical and popular music, as Django no doubt realized. Most of the French popular music that Django played in the dance halls was to a marching 2/4 or a waltz's 3/4 time, both signatures that stressed a bar's first beat. Jazz was typically played in 4/4, providing a freedom within its greater number of beats to the bar. To make it swing, the second and fourth downbeats were stressed, but that swing was a nearly insurmountable task for Europeans musicians. As French trombonist Léo Vauchant remembered, "when the French would play, there was no sense of beat. They were playing things with rubato—there was no dance beat. It didn't swing. It didn't move."

Once these fundamentals were understood, there was above all the art of improvisation, a concept that went against conservatory training. European musicians—as well as many white *and* black American musicians struggling to play jazz—were so used to reading the notes they were to play that improvising was like learning the language of music anew. Jazz was not musical nihilism, as Nick La Rocca preached, but musical liberation. Still, after years of rigorous conservatory training, it was an impossible transition for some. As pianist Jean Wiener said, "People understood almost too well that jazz was improvisation—but they didn't understand how to do it. So you got jazz bands whose only purpose was to make as much noise as possible—bells, klaxons, drums, revolvers, etc." Vauchant had to write out detailed arrangements notating all of the syncopation before his fellow French musicians could play it. American bandleader Paul Whiteman faced a similar dilemma with early bandmembers who needed him to score their "improvised" solos.

For Django, music *was* improvisation. He learned music by listening and then improvising—and then improvising on his improvisations. The Romany musical tradition was built on improvisation, whether it was adding flowery notes to a violin song in a brasserie, flourishes to a flamenco buleria, or composing "original" pieces based on existing melodies, as with many Eastern European Tziganes songs. Django had none of the dogma of conservatory training or even the dictates of reading music to slow him down. Some musically illiterate jazzmen such as Sidney Bechet even held fierce superstitions against learning to read music; Bechet feared the science of reading music would destroy his magical powers of improvisation. Whether Django held similar beliefs, it's not recorded. Yet even when hanging out after hours in the musicians' favored bars such as L'Alsace à Montmartre or Tabac Pigall, he never bothered to join discussions about musical theory or jazz aesthetics. Django preferred to wrap himself around his banjo and explore music with his hands.

From the time Django first heard Billy Arnold, jazz filled his imagination. The music was not only exotic and new but also represented freedom to Django. It left behind the strict traditions of musette for new rhythms and opportunities to play the sounds he heard in his head. Django built up a small repertoire of American jazz numbers, playing the melodies by memory. And as he recreated the themes, it was a simple step for Django to then play variations. He had performed improvisations on "Perle de cristal" for Les Amis de l'Accordéon; now, he improvised on American jazz numbers in the dance halls when a bandleader let him showcase his specialty. The dancers were not fond of this new jazz, but they liked to watch their Django and his antics of virtuosity, playing *un hot*—a solo—improvising choruses, reworking the melody lines, adding to them, accentuating them. And when he struck the last note of his versions of the current American jazz hits such as "Dinah" and "The Sheik of Araby," the dancers applauded Django with equal abandon.

DJANGO WAS ACCOMPANYING accordionist Maurice Alexander at La Java one night in late October 1928 when a man in impeccable black evening dress and smoking a large cigar entered the *bal musette*. His face was jovial and warm—yet a long, deep scar that sliced across his left cheek made one hesitate before trusting his smile. He stood just five feet, four inches tall, but bore a beautiful woman on each arm, one dressed in a sumptuous mink coat, the other in a jacket of Tuscan lamb, their Chanel *le numero cinq* overpowering the sweaty scent of the dancers. He made his way through the crowd, which parted like the fabled sea of old. La Java was one of the roughest dance halls in one of the toughest quarters of all Paris, Belleville. Situated in a grand old Belle Epoque galerie, the dance hall was a dank underground cave, a truly infernal underworld. The appearance of this suave entourage raised the hackles of the regulars, and they greeted them with whistles and lingering appraisals of their diamond necklaces, estimating what they'd bring if hocked in the flea market. Yet as the song came to an end with a crescendo of accordion and banjo, this man who had won such stares kept his eyes fixed on Django on the balcony above.

The interloper was Englishman Jack Hylton, a name that even many of the dance hall regulars would have recognized. He was the impresario of the most famous symphonic jazz orchestra in Europe. Named John Hilton at birth, he later modified his name to Jack Hylton to add some showmanship dash. A pianist and singer, he began in 1921 transcribing recordings of Paul Whiteman and established Jack Hylton and His Orchestra, modeled after the polished sounds of the American's band. From opposite sides of the Atlantic, Whiteman and Hylton's symphonic jazz sanitized the uncouth elements of hot jazz that made it dynamic and revolutionary, bringing it back into the fold of classical music. Hylton's orchestra was the Rolls-Royce of jazz bands—not merely a dance orchestra but a full traveling show, replete with singers, dancers, and comedians. In 1929, Hylton's orchestra would give 700 performances while traveling 63,000 miles and selling 3,180,000 records—one record every seven seconds. Gone was the barnyard braying of the Original Dixieland Jazz Band, but lacking as well were the raucous improvised solos and the daring drumming that first excited dancers. His brand of music replaced rhythmic syncopation with complex harmonies, hot improvised solos with elaborate string arrangements, slapdash jams with grandiose full-orchestra finales. Whiteman and Hylton's showmanship groomed jazz to make it presentable to a proper audience. In the process, they turned jazz into bourgeois music.

Now, Hylton had come in search of Django. The bandleader must have heard of Django's skill at improvising over American jazz numbers. Hylton had just finished a tour of the English provinces and was on his way to Germany to perform on October 28 before starting a month-long stand on November 1 at Berlin's Scala-Theater. En route, he had come for Django.

Hylton cut through the crowd at La Java and approached the musicians. He introduced himself to Django, who for all of his 18 years of age must have been speechless in response.

Hylton said he was in Paris specifically to hear Django play. Banjo players and guitarists who could improvise jazz were a rare commodity. In response, Django may have strummed his banjo and picked out one of Billy Arnold's melodies. And then Hylton spoke the words he had traveled all that way for, an offer to join his orchestra.

Django probably looked over Hylton and liked what he saw: Rewards of the jazz life beyond just playing the music—tuxedos, cigars, and a woman on each arm who outshone the *bal*'s reflecting ball. That he would accept was probably a foregone conclusion.

And with that, they set a rendezvous to sign contracts the next day at eight o'clock at the bar Chez Fred Payne on Pigalle's rue Blanche.

AFTER HYLTON LEFT LA JAVA and the dance hall closed for the night, accordionist Alexander walked Django to a taxi stand along the rue de Lyon. The City of Light was finally as dark as the rest of the night, the prostitutes and musicians the last to head homeward for a well-earned rest. As they parted, Alexander halted Django to offer some more paternal advice. He told him he didn't want to prevent Django from walking his own path, yet this jazz was a new thing—and by no means a sure thing. Musette had proven itself; it would last. If things did not work out in the Englishman's jazz band, Alexander offered to always keep a chair open for Django.

With that, they parted and Django took a taxi home. As legend has it, Django was so overcome by the events of the evening that he forgot his banjo in the back seat of the taxi and it was lost forever.

4

Wanderings
1928–1934

ALL WAS SILENT as Django returned to his caravan outside the Porte de Clignancourt in the early morning hours of October 26, 1928, after playing La Java. Night settled over *la Zone* like mercy, cloaking the squalor in its shadow, returning the world to darkness. Caravans were parked in haphazard order throughout the no-man's land, quiet reigning. Django was likely thinking still of the offer from Jack Hylton as he climbed the short ladder, knocked thrice at the door as was his fashion, passed through the small doorway, and entered to find his caravan in bloom. Bella had fashioned bouquets of celluloid flowers for the burial later that day of a Manouche boy. The father of this child, a Gypsy named Zeze, requested the flowers for the boy's resting place in the pauper's graveyard at Thiais. Dozens of plastic flowers now blossomed within the caravan—immense chrysanthemums, gigantic dahlias, and outrageous roses, all larger than life and more colorful than nature could have made.

Bella, several months pregnant, was already asleep. Hearing Django enter, she awoke and reached for a match and candle stub. She lit the candle, but in her sleepy state, fumbled, and the candle fell to the floor and rolled away into a bouquet of celluloid petals. The flowers turned to flames. In a heartbeat, the caravan was an inferno.

Django ran to Bella and pulled her from the bed. With fire consuming the caravan, she dashed through the doorway, her hair aflame. Django tried to fight back against the blaze but the heat and smoke in the small space were overwhelming. He grabbed a blanket to shield himself. Gasping for breath within the smoke yet still holding the blanket over him with his left hand, he collapsed amidst the flames. Outside, Bella, singed to the scalp, was shouting to wake the surrounding caravans: "Django is inside!" The other Manouche rushed out to see the caravan burning like a pyre. Inside, Django, half gone but driven by some deep survival instinct, was struggling to get to his feet and drag himself to the doorway.

He was afire as he crashed from the caravan and out into the night. The other Gypsies rolled him to the ground, smothering the flames. Bella's father, Pan Mayer, led them in gathering Django up and rushing him and Bella to the Hôpital Lariboisière, the far away public "hospital of the poor," near the Gare du Nord in the northeastern Tenth Arrondissement.

Lariboisière was a somber palace of a hospital, its architectural majesty shrouding another reality inside. Built to care for the city's poor, the hospital was known as the Versailles of Misery and was the last hope for the poverty-stricken sick and injured. At the registration, Django was signed onto the docket as patient number 18763, his admittance to the Ward Nélaton under-lined in red as *une affaire judiciare*, requiring gendarmes to check into the fire's suspicious circumstances. For now, the doctors injected Django with morphine to ease his agony. Then they began the horrifying task of scraping off the remains of his burned clothes to ascertain what lay beneath. They discovered his left hand, which had held up the blanket to shield the flames, was grotesquely charred. In addition, his body's right side was scorched from knee to chest. Fearful gangrene would set in, a doctor prescribed that his right leg be amputated immediately to save his life. But Django refused to have his leg cut off. Not trusting the doctors and their unnatural ways, Négros commanded the other Gypsies about her and they spirited Django away from the hospital.

They carried Django back to their encampment, and the old women de-scended upon him. Packing his burns with secret, age-old concoctions of *drab*—homemade poultices of wild herbs—they prayed that medicinally or magically, he be restored to life.

Yet in the coming weeks, Négros realized Django was not recovering. Fur-ther medical treatment was necessary, as distasteful as it might be to return and ask again for the doctors' aid. With the help of her fellow Manouche, Négros transported Django this time to the Hôpital Saint-Louis, near the place de la République. With careful attention, Django's suppurating burns finally began to heal. His leg was saved.

His left hand was another matter; it was semi-paralyzed by the flames that had eaten away the skin and consumed the muscles, tendons, and nerves, and doctors held little hope that Django would recover its use. Yet his doctor at the public Hôpital Saint-Louis also ran a private clinic in the Fourteenth Arrondissement; here, he told Négros, he could better treat Django. But treat-ment at the private clinic was expensive, he warned. Pan Mayer and Négros hawked everything they could, selling off their belongings, collecting all the money they had to pay the clinic to operate on Django's hand. On January 23, 1929—the day of Django's nineteenth birthday—he was taken to the clinic where he was knocked out with chloroform. His wounds were washed clean of pus, then burned for a second time with silver nitrate to shut them, providing a new chance to heal.

After the operation, Django was transferred back to Saint-Louis and confined to bed. Négros was waiting outside each morning at nine when the hospital opened and never left her son's bedside until the nurses chased her away at closing time each evening. She cared for Django the whole time he was in the hospital, changing dressings and cleaning the slow-healing burns that contorted his left hand. She also kept a close eye on the doctors and nurses whom she never truly trusted, fearful perhaps of their earlier prescription to cut off his leg and conversely blaming them for not fixing his wounds with all of their modern-day medical wisdom.

During Django's convalesence, the doctor wisely counseled Négros to bring Django his guitar to comfort him. Nin-Nin dutifully arrived, carrying a brand new guitar that he laid in the bed beside his brother.

In January 1930 as he turned 20, Django was summoned for French military service. When the call was ignored, a government agent came to track Django down. Arriving at the Manouche encampment, the agent was told Django was not there. Interrogating the Gypsies further, he finally learned Django was in the hospital. Doubting the veracity of any illness, the agent went to Saint-Louis to judge Django's health for himself. He found Django bedridden, his hand bound in bandages. The agent exempted him from service, crossing his name from the list: The military had no use for a cripple.

On festival days, Django was carted to family gatherings in a wheelchair, his hand hidden beside him in wraps. After food was served and feasted upon, someone invariably produced a violin and began to play; soon other instruments were brought out to join in. At the first lines of the first song, the music may have warmed Django, but as the song went on and he watched the others play, the music could become too painful and he likely turned away, back to the sterile world of the hospital.

In his bed still lay the guitar Nin-Nin brought him. Within the ward's confines, Django picked it up and strummed with his right hand. He was probably relieved to feel his picking hand function properly, although it may have been unsure after all this time. Still, his left hand was practically a clawed hook, the back shrunken into a knot of scars. His two small fingers were largely paralyzed, the tendons and nerves damaged, the digits a near-useless contortion of flesh. His index and middle fingers were likely stiff and difficult to control, but he could move them. And his thumb, which he rarely used in fretting but was all important in providing grip to the guitar neck, was unscathed. Django had no choice but to put his faith in just his index and middle fingers, and during the long months of convalescence, he forced them into motion, limbering the muscles, retraining the tendons to his command. He cautiously walked his fingers up and down the guitar's fretboard, his right hand patiently picking out melodies to the slow pace of his left hand's movement. Limited in the number of fingers he could employ, he also forced himself to rethink his approach to the fretboard. Instead of playing scales and arpeggios horizontally across the fretboard as was the norm, he searched out fingerings that ran vertically up and down the frets as they were easier to play with just two fingers. He created new chord forms utilizing a minimum of notes—often just triads with his two good fingers on the bass strings. He pushed his paralyzed fingers to grip the guitar as well, his smallest digit on the high E string, his ring finger on the B, and sometimes barring his index finger to fashion chords of four to five notes. He then slid his hand up and down the fretboard, employing these chord forms to craft a fluent vocabulary. As he played in his hospital bed, his fingers came to life again and old melodies were reborn—a waltz bringing back memories of nights at La Java, a jazz theme reviving remembrances of Billy Arnold's band. Django was slowly winning back willingness in those two fingers to make music.

After some six months of solitary practice in the hospital, Django joined the other Gypsy musicians at a family festival one spring day in 1930. With time and the aid of crutches, he could walk as before, and when the other musicians began a song, he left the circle of music again, this time to return with his guitar. Looks of pity must have passed between the musicians. But then Django joined into the song, fretting his guitar in his bizarre new fashion, keeping pace with the tempo, moving his left hand up and down the fretboard to find chords that others could play in a minimum of movement within a contained horizontal "box" of notes. Then, when the song came back to the top of a chorus he must have picked his moment to launch into a solo with all the audacity of his former self, just his index and middle fingers dancing vertically along the fretboard, two fingers on six strings, forced to move at least twice the speed of anyone else's four fingers and then faster yet as he threw in flourishes and single-finger chromatic dashes all the way up the fretboard on one string and then continuing across the strings, flaunting and then flouting his handicap. The other musicians' looks of pity must have turned in an instant to disbelief. Among the Manouche women and children and old men there were screams and tears and impassioned embraces.

They would swear to their dying day that a true miracle had taken place right before their very eyes.

DJANGO WAS HAUNTED by nightmares of flames. Following the fire, the horror of the conflagration and the burns left on his body instilled him with a fear that could not be extinguished. In the deep of night, he woke up terrorized by his memory and soaked in sweat.

Three weeks after the fire and while he was still confined to bed, Django and Bella's child was born. Following the fire, Bella stayed in Lariboisière until November 16 recovering from her own burns. Discharged, she now gave birth to a boy named Henri in honor of her father. This little Henri they called *l'Ourson*, or "bear cub." Over time, the nickname transformed into Lousson.

But during the months after the fire, something changed in Django's relationship with Bella. Perhaps it was due to the trauma of the fire and the shock of his wounds; maybe it was just differences between two people. It's even possible that Bella turned away from Django, believing him a cripple who could now only make a living as a beggar—one of those who displayed his handicap to make passersby pay for their pity. Despite their newborn son and the goodwill of Bella's father, who paid for much of Django's hospitalization, Django and Bella went their own ways. She soon remarried another Gypsy named "Niglo" Baumgartner, and Lousson was given his stepfather's family name and now known officially as Henri Baumgartner.

On the spring day in 1930 when Django finally left the Hôpital Saint-Louis for good on the arm of Négros, he was greeted by a new surprise. Waiting for him on the sidewalk in front of the hospital was Naguine. Recently returned from Tuscany, she had searched everywhere for Django. When she heard word of his tragedy, she set out immediately for the hospital and here she stood, waiting with patience for his release.

She now handed him a bouquet of tulips, saying simply, "Here! These flowers are real. They won't start on fire."

DJANGO AND NIN-NIN began once again to wander the streets with their guitars, playing in cafés and tipping their fedoras for centimes. Django chose not to return to the *bals musette* where a job with any accordionist was his for the asking. Yet he did not know where to go next. In the past 18 months, Jack Hylton had likely forgotten about him and the fans at the few jazz clubs in Paris were clamoring for African American jazzmen. No one was asking for a Gypsy guitarist to play jazz.

Still, Django was not too proud to accept a handout from his former fellows. Accordionist Jean Vaissade and banjoist Julien La Torre visited Django in his caravan. Startled by his abject poverty, Vaissade told him, "Listen, Little One: You're not too well off right now, are you? We'll take up a collection among the musicians, and you can come along to Ça Gaze some night and pick it up." Moved by empathy for their banjoist friend, Vaissade rounded up a fair sum among the dance hall regulars. Django arrived one evening at Ça Gaze, walking across Paris to Belleville as he lacked money for a ride. When Vaissade presented him with the gift and Django proffered his thanks, Django then asked directions to another site in the city. Vaissade explained he could take this bus or that train. But Django finally exclaimed, "Oh, well, I'll just take a taxi instead!" After handing over his collection, Vaissade was left breathless.

Despite the goodwill of his fellow musicians, Django turned his back on the confines of playing *musette*. Smitten by jazz, he and Nin-Nin frequented the Can-Can, a grand brasserie and meeting place for professional musicians next to Pigalle's famed Bal Tabarin. Here, Django met pianist Stéphane Mougin, a fledgling French jazzman. Mougin had been a promising student at the Conservatoire National until it was discovered that he also fooled with jazz, at which point he was denied first prize and had to settle for second; the professors refused to acknowledge a jazzman with their honors. After that, Mougin turned his back on the conservatory, studied jazz, and as early as 1929 wrote frequent articles on jazz theory and esthetics in the new Parisian journal *La Revue de Jazz*, the world's first magazine devoted to the music. Mougin was impressed by Django's playing and offered him a job as his accompanist for one hundred francs a night. Together, they played their jazz at Maurice Chevalier's Les Acacias, a swank new club near the place de l'Étoile.

In spring 1931, Django packed up to travel to the sunshine of the Côte d'Azur, following the wanderings of his parents before him. Django heeded this pattern to the seasons over the next several years—and often throughout his life: He spent spring and summer in the Midi, where the tourists and vacationers were ready for a good time. Come autumn, he returned to Paris's nightclubs. This spring, he set out walking from Paris to the Riviera with Naguine at his side: "Django made up his mind to leave with me for the Midi," she remembered. "We made our way there, town by town. We didn't have a sou and we were as sad as the stones. I tried to make a bit of money by selling a few pieces of lace, at least enough to keep body and soul together."

Django and Naguine walked to Nice where Django looked for work. The city was in the prime of the summer season with the Riviera sun warming the wealthy along the water's edge. The rich came to the Riviera to flaunt their money and have the best time they could buy at casinos, cabarets, and night-clubs along the world-renowned Corniche. Yet Django lacked even a guitar of his own to play, so he could find no work.

Giving up on Nice, Django and Naguine moved along to Cannes, the crown jewel of the Côte d'Azur. Overlooking the sea stood the Carlton Hôtel, its wedding-cake façade capped by twin domes modeled after the breasts of the famous courtesan La Belle Otero, who in the 1910s seduced men with her singing and dancing—not to mention her brassiere made of gems. Next door to the Carlton was the nightclub Banco. Here, Django got a job playing jazz. Headlining on the bill was African American violinist Eddie South.

Django had immense respect for the violin from listening to his Gypsy elders play, yet hearing South must have been a revelation: Here was the Romanies' favored instrument turned to jazz. Ironically, South himself was greatly influenced by Gypsy violinists. Born in the small city of Louisiana, Missouri, on November 27, 1904, South's parents followed the migration to Chicago when he was a child. A prodigy, he entered Chicago's College of Music and was on his way to becoming a classical violinist when he was stopped by the color of his skin: There were no chairs for blacks no matter how well they played. South switched to jazz, performing with violinists Charles Elgar and Darnell Howard before joining Erskine Tate's orchestra and directing Jimmy Wade's Moulin Rouge Syncopators. In 1927, South formed his Alabamians, a tight jazz combo with guitar, piano, drums, and clarinet. Yet South's fascination for classical music never left him. While in Europe from 1928 through 1931, he enrolled in the Paris conservatory to study with Firmin Touche, but also frequented the Russian cabarets where Romany violinists like Jean Goulesco were the stars. In autumn 1929, South left for Hungary and the Budapest Academy of Music, one of the world's leading violin schools. Here, he studied with Jenö Hubay, a friend of Franz Liszt who put the establishment's seal of approval on Gypsy violin playing by appropriating this music into his *Hungarian Rhapsody*. Hubay too was influenced by Hungarian Tziganes, composing czardas evoking Gypsy melodies. The violin playing of the Romanies opened a new world to South, and throughout his career he utilized Gypsy melodies as a jumping off point for jazz improvisations.

Alternating sets with South at Cannes's Banco nightclub, Django must have been enthralled by the violinist's music. In his version of the Romany song "Two Guitars," which he cut in Paris in 1929, South moved effortlessly in the slow-paced intro from smooth classical phrasing to deep blues to melancholy Tzigane lines before the melody erupted into its quick-tempoed chorus that he improvised with jazz-inflected licks. It was a bravura performance combining all his disparate influences into a unified, brilliant whole. And it was through this convoluted path—a southern African American fiddler raised on jazz, schooled at the best conservatories, and influenced by Eastern European Gypsy music—that Django likely first heard a violin play jazz. Django would never forget that sound.

WHEN DJANGO'S CANNES STAND ended, he and Naguine wandered on to Toulon. The city was a far cry from the elegance of Nice or Cannes, but it too was always ready for a good time as the ships of the French navy were based from the harbor and the sailors haunted the quarter known as Chicago. In the Toulon port, a spider web of palm trees, sunshine, and fast, easy living lured sailors and vacationers to the nightclubs. Arriving in the city, Django and Naguine made for the part of the city frequented by Gypsies, the down-and-out section La Rôde. Here, they met up with Nin-Nin, and together, Django and his brother went in search of work, finally finding a regular spot at the bistrot Chez Thomas in the old city. Naguine set out to tell people's fortunes, reading the lines in their palms to cross her own hands with a few coins.

The summer nights on the Côte d'Azur were mellifluous in their warmth, and Django and Nin-Nin sometimes made their way down to the beach to play. One night in 1931, they were playing for a growing crowd between the fishing boats at the water's edge when a man approached them from out of the darkness. He introduced himself as Louis Vola. He owned a bakery but was also a musician, just on his way home after performing with his band at the club Le Lido. Impressed by the guitarwork, Vola invited Django and Nin-Nin to come sit in.

Vola was indeed a musician, but he would always prove a better bandleader than instrumentalist. He was born in La Seyne-sur-Mer across the bay from Toulon on July 6, 1902, to Italian parents working in France. Growing up in Genova, he studied solfeggio and violin. He then moved to Paris where he ran a lathe building André Citroën's automobiles, but on weekends, he returned to his true love, playing drums in the *bals musette*. In 1925, he left for Yugoslavia to play accordion in cafés. Upon his return to Paris in 1928, he led a band performing at bars with a repertoire of everything from musette to American dance tunes. Yet Vola's playing was always energetic rather than refined, functional rather than graceful. Still, Vola had a survivor's instinct—a key to lasting as a musician, especially when better musicians than himself gave up and quit. And this instinct served him well as a bandleader: He was often in the right place at the right time to find the best jobs with the best musicians. Now, he enticed Django and Nin-Nin to join his dance band at Le Lido.

Soon after Django began playing guitar with Vola, engineers from the Gramophone label arrived in Toulon as part of a southern tour to record local talent. The engineers liked what they heard from Vola's band, and on May 28, 1931, Gramophone recorded eight sides by Vola, three of them featuring Django. For the dancing crowd at Le Lido, the ensemble played a broad range of music, and the songs recorded reflected the repertoire, including the tame French tango "Canaria" and the sugary chanson "C'est une valse qui chante." A pared-down ensemble recorded the tango "Carinosa" in a dynamic arrangement highlighted by Django's long arpeggiated runs in harmonic counterpoint to the melody. The music was forgettable, but it was his first venture back into a recording studio since the caravan fire of 1928, and his playing was stronger and fleeter and more harmonically bold than ever.

ONE EVENING in July 1931, after they had been in Toulon for a month, Django and Nin-Nin were playing their guitars in the Café des Lions near the harbor along quai Stalingrad. After the duo left the bar to find fresh audiences, a painter who was renting an apartment above the café came rushing down the stairs in just his slippers and dressing gown, looking for whoever had been making the music. The dilettante painter was Émile Savitry. With carefully cropped short hair, fine grooming, and banker's spectacles, Savitry looked the part of an up-and-coming French businessman. Yet Savitry had been saved from such a fate by his fascination for everything else in the world—art and music and anything in between. Savitry was a bohemian's bohemian who virtually lived at the cafés of Montparnasse among other painters, poets, and

philosophers passionately enthusing over exotic art and revolutionary theo-
ries in discussions that lasted for years. Born in Saigon in 1903, Savitry had
recently returned from Tahiti to settle for the season in Toulon.

Hearing the guitars playing jazz in the café below, Savitry at first thought
it was a record, since the quality of music was so superior. When the café
crowd applauded the end of a song, however, Savitry hurried down to see the
musicians, but like apparitions they were gone. He asked a waiter about the
guitarists, but although the waiter remembered seeing them stop by to play
for coins from time to time, he did not know them—beyond remembering
that one of the guitarists had a crippled hand yet still played better than anyone he had ever heard. Savitry asked the waiter to call him if the musicians
ever returned.

Several days later, the waiter knocked at Savitry's apartment door to say
the character was downstairs again. When Savitry asked if he was playing
guitar, the waiter responded, "No, billiards." Thinking it was all a joke, Savitry
replied angrily, "It's not a billiards player I'm looking for, but a guitarist!"
Reassured, Savitry ventured downstairs to find two ragged Romanies. Nin-
Nin was stretched out on a bench asleep; Django was shooting pool, dressed
like some exotic, deposed aristocrat from a far-off land. When Savitry asked
them to play a song, Django waved him away: He didn't have his guitar, he
said with a nonchalant shrug. But now that he had finally caught up with these
two, Savitry was not about to let them slip away again. He found two guitars
and cajoled Django into playing a tune. Nin-Nin was awakened and sleepily
took up the proferred instrument, playing accompaniment as Django launched
into the melody, reworking the theme, exploring its nuances, toying with it.
Savitry was astonished. His first impressions reinforced, he excitedly invited
them upstairs to his room. He had something he wanted to share with them.

Inside his apartment, Savitry set about playing a record with all the reverence of a religious ritual. He went straight to the gramophone, selected a 78,
speared it on the spindle, started it spinning, and then carefully lowered the
needle arm. Django had heard jazz before, from the live music of Billy Arnold
to recordings of Jack Hylton and others. But jazz had moved ahead at a dramatic pace. Leaving behind the days of Louis Mitchell and the Original
Dixieland Jazz Band, the music was entering a new era of more sophisticated
harmonization and accomplished musicianship. It was this new jazz that Savitry
now placed on his gramophone, playing side after side of smooth arrangements by Duke Ellington and His Cotton Club Orchestra and swinging string
jazz by Joe Venuti's Blue Four with Venuti's violin backed by Eddie Lang's
guitar. Then Savitry played Louis Armstrong's "Indian Cradle Song."

Recorded with his nine-man orchestra in far-off New York City on May 4,
1930, Armstrong's song was jouncy and free. Between his gravelly voice singing the lullaby and his trumpet calling out like archangel Gabriel's divine

horn, Armstrong summed up the history of jazz to that point and then wiped it away in a new sound dramatically more sophisticated and stylish.

Django was overwhelmed. "He was like a large animal, mute and dazed in the blaze of the sun," Savitry recalled. "But soon he came alive again. The intense eyes, listening ears, hands folded on his stomach, like a prior in prayer in front of a holy image, he remained there, upright, motionless; but this statue suddenly found its incredible power of perception—nothing escaped him. Right away, he understood Armstrong. Right away, he preferred Armstrong's formidable playing over the erudite technique of the orchestra of Duke Ellington. Guided by an instinct of astounding precision, he was able to judge these musicians, almost instantly. I put 'Savoy Blues' on the record player and, suddenly, Django leaped up to the ceiling: the guitarist who accompanied Armstrong was out of tune. 'It's just not possible!' Django was truly revolted, revolted as only very pure souls can be, and he began to sweat, almost as in fright."

Django had heard Tzigane music since his childhood, czardas and waltzes played with Romany verve, raucous javas in the *bals musette*, jazz in Pigalle. Now, hearing Louis Armstrong, all of that was in the past. A new fire burned. Listening to Armstrong's trumpet, Django put his head in his hands, unashamedly starting to cry. "*Ach moune! Ach moune!*" he repeated over and over again—a Romany expression of stupefaction and admiration, meaning, ironically, "My brother! My brother!"

THE TRIO CONTINUED to spin records until eventually Savitry sent Nin-Nin out to buy sandwiches. As he watched Nin-Nin and Django devour the food, Savitry realized the two were near-starving. He queried them about their circumstances and they finally told him they had been playing in Toulon's cafés and brothels along the port and eating only when they could find food.

The following day, Savitry invited Django and Nin-Nin back for lunch. As they ate, Savitry informed them that he was leaving town to visit his family; he offered them the key to his apartment and invited them to make themselves at home. Django and Nin-Nin were astounded by the generosity, disarmed by Savitry's trust in them. Returning two days later, Savitry found the two brothers as well as Naguine sound asleep, encamped in his rooms. Embarrassed by their actions, Django introduced his wife to their absent host. Savitry, counter to their expectations, was pleasantly surprised they had taken him up on his offer, happy to find he had not lost his Gypsy musicians again.

Django, Nin-Nin, and Naguine now settled in with Savitry. They spent their days lounging in comfort, listening to records and playing guitars, emulating the sounds of the American jazzmen, copying the melodies of Armstrong, copping his licks.

One morning, Savitry opened his door to insistent pounding. He found a short yet sturdy Gypsy woman with her hands on her hips and her eyes aflame.

Without preamble, she demanded, "Monsieur Bandit, what have you done with my children? Where are they? Where can I see them?" It was Négros, who had arrived in Toulon in search of her wayfaring sons. Pleased to find them, she then asked Savitry for ten francs and disappeared again. She returned minutes later laden with food and cooking utensils that must have been worth hundreds of francs, and set about feeding them all.

Satisfied with her children's whereabouts, Négros returned to Paris a week later. Django, Nin-Nin, and Naguine decided to follow her, yet they didn't have money for train tickets. With Savitry's introduction, they were hired to play at the Coq Hardy, a grand restaurant overlooking the port. Savitry then sought out dinner jackets for Django and Nin-Nin, and dressed in style, they performed at Coq Hardy for the week. Django and Nin-Nin alternated sets with the main band, the Russian Federoff Orchestra, whose members crowded around the guitarists to listen in amazement to Django interpreting Tzigane music, improvising over melodies such as Monti's *Czardas*. Paid their wages, Django and Nin-Nin were feeling flush, and with this change in their circumstances, the brothers decided not to return to Paris after all. Instead, Django invited Savitry to dinner, ordering a Rabelaisian feast that cost him everything he had earned. When Savitry reproached him for his profligate ways, Django laughed. "But why not?" he responded. "Next week we can start all over again." The bohemian Savitry had been upstaged by a true bohemian.

AS SUMMER 1931 wore on, Louis Vola heard of a new nightclub opening at Cannes's Palm Beach Hotel, the most prestigious address on the Côte d'Azur. Built out on the Pointe de la Croisette and secluded from the merely wealthy for the richest of the rich, the Palm Beach had been christened by the Comtesse de Caraman-Chimay in 1929, opening the doors to a fashionable crowd—the wayward scions of European royalty, graying playboys and nubile princesses, well-heeled and loud-voiced American tourists, and Hollywood stars and starlets. At the dawn of the 1930s, while the Great Depression was raging elsewhere, the Palm Beach played a leading role in creating the glamor for which the Riviera would soon be famous.

The Palm Beach's new cabaret was named La Boîte à Matelots—the Sailors' Hangout—and, festooned with nets, buoys, and a fishing boat as a stage, offered swank slumming. La Boîte à Matelots' manager Léon Volterra had already hired English bandleader and violinist Jack Harris and his group, but there was still an opening for a second band to alternate sets. Vola went to find Django and Nin-Nin to bring his ensemble to Cannes.

Finding Django was simpler said than done. Vola set off for La Rôde, where he had been told Django was playing boules with fellow Romanies. By the time he arrived, Django had left, and the Gypsies were mum concerning his whereabouts, thinking Vola was a *clisté*—Gypsy slang for a gendarme. They were old hands at this and wanted to give Django time to make good his getaway. In fact, after finishing his morning boules game, Django, Nin-Nin, and Naguine had set off for Paris on foot. Vola and his band opened in Cannes without their guitarists.

Django, Nin-Nin, and Naguine had meanwhile walked much of the way to Cannes. Under the palms on La Croisette, Naguine pointed to some fishing boats on the shore and suggested they sleep amid the boats. Django hatched his own plan: "Listen! If we play it right, we can book into the most expensive hotel in Cannes. Tomorrow you'll get some cash together somehow or other." Out to take the air the next day, they ran into Vola at the Palm Beach. When Vola asked them where they were staying, Django replied that they had a room at the Hôtel Georges V, the domain of the smart set. Vola could not believe his ears. The personnel at the Georges V believed Django to be some sort of Hindu prince and had extended their best service to him and his princess wife. Naguine meanwhile was off reading palms to pay their bill. Taking matters into his own hands, Vola helped them rent the villa next to his in a less-expensive neighborhood.

That same evening, Django joined Vola at La Boîte à Matelots, appearing in the band's sailor garb of blue-and-white striped mariner jerseys, navy pantaloons, and espadrilles. Vola and Django played through the finale of the 1931 summer season at the Palm Beach, joined by Nin-Nin and another Gypsy guitarist and circus acrobat named Tapolo.

Torn in his allegiances between his Romany community and his commitments in the *gadjo* world, Django did not always show up for the nightly sets. This sent Vola into a frenzy to search Cannes for his wayward guitar player. "I always had to go find him," Vola remembered. "As soon as I paid him, I could be assured that I wouldn't see him again for two or three days, and I'd have to run after him, tracking him down." One day, Naguine's uncle happened by in his caravan, inspiring Django with visions of the open road, and he left to travel for 15 days while Vola sought him in vain. Sometimes he found Django in a beguiling game of billiards at the railroad station, other times in the midst of a Romany party either at their bungalow or in a nearby encampment. Looking for the errant Django before their show one day, Vola peeked into a caravan only to discover it stocked with the finest of silver cutlery, all marked with the proud imprint of the Palm Beach.

THE FRENCH GYPSIES had a saying, "A Gypsy without a horse is not a Gypsy." During summer 1931, Django gave up his horse and caravan, at least for the time being. When he, Nin-Nin, and Naguine moved into Savitry's Toulon apartment, it was likely the first time in Django's life that he had lived indoors. Beyond convalescing in the hospital, the rest of his life had been spent in a caravan.

Moving indoors was not as simple as turning a door handle. As Naguine swore, "For us, houses are like prisons. I would rather have an automobile than the most beautiful château." It was not easy to trade forests and mountains for a horizon of rooftops and chimneys. Some illiterate Gypsies struggled to read the numerals designating apartments and wandered the halls searching out telltale signs of their doorway. Others found the silence disturbing; staying indoors for the first time, they could not sleep unless they left the faucet running as they were was used to the lullaby of a nearby stream. Some could not brave sleeping beneath sheets that reminded them of a corpse's shroud. Django and Naguine couldn't bear the harshness of electric lights, preferring kerosene lanterns that lit their rooms with a hospitable glow recreating the ambiance of the caravan they left behind.

And there was a further concern. In the apartment or hotel room Django and Naguine inhabited there was always a fear of *moulôs*—spirits—of those who had come and gone before. As a later acquaintance remembered, "He had fear of the most unbelievable things. One day, we told him that around here there was a bicycle that rolled along all by itself, without a person riding it. He became frozen in panic and would not go outdoors all afternoon nor even that evening." Another stated, "He was always an extremely superstitious man. There was nothing in the world that could make him walk by a cemetery at night because he was afraid of the dead, which he believed rose in the darkness from their tombs." Django believed wholeheartedly in luck and fate and all the mysteries that his imagination could create concerning this world—and the world beyond.

Django's stay with Savitry lasted only a short time, but he, Nin-Nin, and Naguine moved from there into the Cannes villa. This small house became their home for the summer, but at age 21 Django simply did not know how to keep house. Django's Romany cousins were suspicious of the whole thing and came to his rescue; they examined his villa to assure themselves he was there of his own volition and had not been kidnapped or locked up. Vola described the scene: "In the garden there was a table that stayed set for months on end with great loaves of *quatre livres* bread, bottles of wine, camemberts, pâtés, and other victuals. Whatever time of day or night it was, any one of them might sit down and dig in to a snack. Some slept in the garden, on the grass, or in hammocks strung up between pine trees. 'Monkeys' in the trees would often grab at the hair of terrified visitors—but these 'monkeys,' one need hardly add, were Django's cousins, Manouches who happened to be passing through and climbed over the walls of the nearby villas on the lookout for a good haul. As more and more of them arrived, there were soon Gypsies everywhere. They were camping on the beach and leaving litter everywhere. It was a true disaster. At last one day the mayor of Cannes told me, 'You'll have to get rid of them, these friends of yours. This is no longer possible!'" Happily for the mayor and Vola, the summer season soon ended.

Returning to Paris in autumn 1931, Django moved in again with Savitry, who had a large courtyard atelier on rue Vitu in the Fifteenth Arrondissement. Savitry remembered the arrival of the Reinhardt clan—including Django, Nin-Nin, Naguine, and Négros—who quickly made the studio their own: "In the space of a few days, the atelier resembled the villa at Cannes. It was strangely, improbably charming. Négros rapidly assumed command. She was the first one up in the mornings. As soon as we'd given her five francs she'd be off on the scrounge. She began by making her first call at the tobacco shop in the rue Saint-Charles to drink a coffee and buy a packet of Gauloises. She'd be back around twelve, her shopping baskets brimming over—even including a bottle of apéritif! I will never understand how she did it! . . . Django had the right to do whatever he wished and his mother was always fussing about after him. In the morning Négros ran a hot iron over his trousers so that they wouldn't make his legs cold when he got dressed. Django was the pasha. Little by little, more of his so-called cousins began to arrive. First of all they were suspicious and wondered however Django could bear to live with 'peasants' in a real house. They inspected all the rooms, trying to make out how it all worked. Then they settled down to have a bite with us, picking their teeth with their knives. Django played music truly as he wished and just for himself, accompanied by his brother and several other Manouche who happened by. I saw the most fantastic characters spend night after night there listening to Django, including whole families and their brats. We led a free and easy life. Everybody brought something along with him and the table was always set with something to eat. Then, when we were all tired, we'd lie down, each of us finding a nook that suited him—except in the attic, that is, which I'd decorated with souvenirs I'd brought back from the South Seas. The Gypsies were terrified by them—most of all by the shark skeletons, which were hung on wires from the ceiling and, being phosphorescent, glowed in the dark. These shark skeletons were the terror of Django and he pulled sheets over his head to hide from them. I must say I've never understood why with the uproar we made day and night in the atelier that the neighbors never complained. Most of the tenants in the building were White Russians, many of whom were taxi drivers. One can only think they enjoyed it. Often you'd see them leaning out their windows listening to Django's music."

During winter 1931, Django and Naguine moved into a room in the Montmartre Hôtel Poirier on place Emile-Goudeau neighboring Le Bateau-Lavoir, the dilapidated piano factory-turned-artist warren once inhabited by Picasso and others. Here again, Django and Naguine viewed their room as a camping spot. It was a typical, dingy Montmartre hotel room: torn flowered wallpaper, an enormous cupboard holding their clothes, an elderly eiderdown bearing cigarette burns covering the bed, and net curtains hanging drearily down the windows, letting in more dust than light. A shadowy screen masked off the washbasin, where Naguine rigged up a kitchen of sorts, cooking on an alcohol-fueled camp stove. In this single room lived not only Django and Naguine but her pet monkey as well, found somewhere on their travels. When not being cuddled and cooed over by Naguine, the monkey dug through the dirty dishes in the bidet, searching out remains of meals past. One moment it ate the soap, the next it was chewing on the linoleum floor. The monkey was as undomesticated as its owners, and the hotel owner soon demanded of Django, "When are you going to get rid of your menagerie?" But Django only replied with a shrug. And when he and Naguine had the opportunity, they snuck out of the hotel, avenging their dignity by leaving their devastated room and an unpaid bill in reprisal. Django often cursed the owner, calling him "peasant," a common Manouche imprecation for *gadjé* enslaved to their land and belongings.

Although Django had given up his caravan for the time being, he soon found a new horse—an automobile. Seeing the rich of the Riviera cruising La Croisette, Django immediately lusted for an automobile of his own. He would suffer a weakness for cars all his life, and naturally they had to be the fastest and flashiest. A Hispano-Suiza carried the proper prestige, but it was not speedy enough. A Bugatti was quick, but there was no place to sleep in it. A Rolls-Royce would have been just right, but he couldn't afford it.

The wheel of fortune finally rolled his number in summer 1932. Django and Naguine were in Cannes again, Django playing with Vola at the Palm Beach. One day, Django cornered Vola and pleaded with him, "I need 5,000 francs. I must buy a tiara for my mother. She deserves one. And I want to decorate our horses. For us, the horse is a queen. Give me an advance . . . if not . . . if not, I will die." Faced with this onslaught, Vola caved in to Django's begging and handed him an advance on his salary. An hour later, Django returned at the wheel of a 1926 American Dodge convertible, grinning from ear to ear.

A handful of photographs were taken of Django and his new steed in front of the Palm Beach. The car was a monster with an ostentatious chromed radiator standing tall in front like a Greek temple. While the car showed its age alongside the new, streamlined machines of the 1930s, it was still big and brassy and bold as befitting Django's tastes. And Django was obviously pleased as could be with his purchase. In one of the photos, he leans against the engine cowling with the studied air of a playboy. His hand jauntily on his hip and a brilliant white snap-brim golfing cap cocked over one eye, he looks like the sheik of Araby in person.

Savitry remembered the Dodge—and Django's driving: "When I visited Django, he had just bought the enormous white American convertible—at least, it had been white once, but it still went like a bomb, though the chrome was all rusty and corroded. Only the framework of the canopy was left. He drove about majestically, as proud as a peacock of his automobile. He was off like a flash whenever he had a moment to spare. He'd go have an aperitif at Nice or Juan-les-Pins and then visit the Gypsy camps around and about, or else go for a quiet fish in the streams. His car was everywhere to be seen, weaving in and out of the Rolls-Royces along La Croisette or tearing around the hairpin bends in the mountains. And each night he took good care to see that it was parked in the place of honor in front of the Palm Beach—to the extreme annoyance of the casino playboys."

Django lacked a driver's license, but that didn't stop him from driving. He ignored the automobile's mechanical deficiencies and never checked the oil; he could only be bothered to refill the gas tank, a necessity to making the car go. One day while out motoring with Vola, the Dodge's engine caught fire. In a panic, Django aimed the car onto the beach, beseeching Vola to douse the flames with handfuls of sand. Suddenly exasperated with the old Dodge, Django told Vola, "This jalopy is worthless. Let's just push it into the sea. The waves will take it. That's all it deserves!" And so he left the Dodge, abandoned to its fate.

The next day, Django appeared at the Palm Beach with another automobile, this time a 45-horsepower Renault speedster. This pure racer was tuned to circle a track at 130 kilometers per hour and boasted open exhaust pipes without mufflers. The Renault was basically a scull on wheels and there were no creature comforts for passengers. Vola shook his head over the car, reporting that the owner had been only too happy to find a sucker to buy it.

To initiate the Renault, Django invited Naguine, Nin-Nin, and several musician friends for a ride. Driving out of Cannes at high speed, they came upon a truck and bus blocking the road. Django hit the brakes—only to discover that there were none. The brakes were so worn that they failed to even slow the hurtling race car. To avoid an accident, Django acted fast. He swerved off the road, but in the process sideswiped the wall of a château, carving an immense gash into Naguine's arm.

Naguine's injury and another lost automobile did not satisfy Django's appetite, however. He soon bought an elderly car-camper that belonged to some vacationing Belgian grocers who needed cash fast after being ruined at baccarat. Django parked his new camper on the beach, and swarms of his Gypsy cousins joined him and Naguine for a party. The fesitivities were broken up by gendarmes dispatched by the tireless mayor of Cannes. Chased from the beach, Django and his cousins left behind a wake of whiting backbones, sardine tins, and peelings. Again that night, Django proudly parked his decrepit car-camper in what he probably now considered his reserved place in front of the Palm Beach. Manager Volterra was forced diplomatically to request he move it.

IT WAS WHILE LIVING in a Montmartre hotel during winter 1931 that Django made the acquaintance of three Romanies who would become some of his most important musical partners. One day, Naguine stepped out of their room to find a diminutive Gypsy waif with his ear to their door. Stammering his apologies, the boy said he had been passing by when he heard music and stopped to listen. Naguine invited him in and introduced Django, who was lying sprawled out on his bed—one of his favorite spots—smoking another cigarette, and picking his guitar, improvising jazz melodies. The boy was Jean "Matelo" Ferret. He and his brothers were also living in the hotel; they were all guitarists too. Yet after listening to Django's playing, Matelo solemnly pledged to throw his own guitar away. Instead, Django invited Matelo to retrieve his instrument and the two began playing together, Django teaching the boy the theme "Sugar." It was the first jazz melody Matelo ever learned.

Matelo and his two brothers had ventured that fall from Rouen to Paris to play their guitars in the capital's dance halls and Russian cabarets. Matelo's eldest brother was Pierre Joseph Ferret. Born in 1908, his nickname "Baro"—meaning "Big One" in Romany—attested to his status. He would later also earn the sobriquet "Camembert" for his fondness of the cheese, a nickname no one would ever dream of calling him to his face. Baro was a handsome man—dangerously handsome. He had a hawk-like face with sharp eyes, a prominent nose, and a dashing profile that would have made even Hollywood idol John Barrymore green with envy. He also had a broad, generous smile, yet it was a smile that could have two sides to it.

Baro was 23 when he came to the capital accompanied by his middle brother, Étienne "Sarane" Ferret, who was just 19. The nickname "Sarane" honored an ancestor who was a famed musician. Shorter and more compact than his elder brother, Sarane nevertheless shared Baro's good looks, wearing his coarse, wiry hair slicked back from his brow in the elegant style of the times.

The Ferret family was Gitan. Though their roots were in Andalucía, the Ferrets had lived in Rouen for several generations. Having settled in the city, the Ferret brothers never lived in a caravan; they had grown up in an apartment. Theirs was a modern Gypsy family, sedentary rather than voyageurs.

The Ferrets were a clan of musicians. Their mother, Douderou, was a great lover of light opera while their father, Hippolyte "Gousti" Ferret, was a horse trader. Their sisters Nina and Nine were both singers. Baro and Sarane had been taught to play first banjos and then guitars by their uncles Baro the Elder, Pebbo, and Fillou Ferret. These uncles were well traveled and could play many forms of Gypsy music, from the flamenco of Spain to the Tzigane sounds of Eastern Europe. The uncles played in the dance halls of Rouen, where Baro and Sarane served their apprenticeships before quitting the city for Paris.

Leaving their family, Baro and Sarane had said good-bye to their younger brother, Matelo. Born on December 1, 1918, Matelo's name meant "sailor" and honored his godfather—a common naming tradition—who served in the French navy. Matelo was small, almost elfin, but boasted a huge, infectious smile that appeared to encompass all those around him. He often accompanied his elder brothers busking for coins on the Rouen streets. His first instrument was violin, taught him by one of his uncles. He learned banjo from his uncle Fillou, and made his public debut in a Rouen dance hall at 12. Matelo was goaded into abandoning the banjo by his guitar-playing uncle Pebbo, who detested the percussive instrument's noise. He then took up banduria and eventually guitar. But when Baro and Sarane set out for Paris, Matelo was devastated. Left behind, he made his own clandestine plans. Shortly after his elder brothers settled in Paris, 13-year-old Matelo ran away to join them. And it was here that he met Django.

Through Matelo's encounter with Django, the other Ferret brothers were soon introduced. As musicians and eldest siblings—a position of grave respect among Gypsies—Django and Baro became best friends. They would also become great rivals.

DURING FALL 1931, Django and the Ferrets found steady work in a new venue, Paris's Russian cabarets, which invaded the capital following the Russian revolution. The majority of jobs for Romany musicians in Paris were not in the *bals* and certainly not in jazz bands nor theater or classical orchestras. Most of the many Gypsy musicians played in large orchestras in the Russian cabarets.

Since the revolution, Paris had been flooded by fleeing White Russians— deposed princes and princesses, the newly landless gentry, and those whose political beliefs didn't run the same color as the Red revolutionaries. Within a short time after the civil wars, some 60,000 White Russians crowded into Paris—the city where Marx drafted his revolutionary communist writings. It wasn't long before a nightclub of their own opened: On October 22, 1922, the Château Caucasien in Pigalle celebrated its premiere with two orchestras and three floors of entertainment, an event that drew Paris high society and inspired the rapid opening of numerous other Russian cabarets—the Troïka, Kazbek, Minoutka, Esturgeon, and more. Waiting on the wealthy were the former famous of Russia: The Tsar's chef made borscht at L'Ermitage Muscovite, where the maître d'hôtel was a one-time admiral in the Imperial fleet. Each cabaret featured a band, usually composed of Gypsies—either those who had recently fled Russia and Eastern Europe, or those already settled in France; as long as they could play, their origin didn't matter.

Django and the Ferrets played their guitars in the Tzigane orchestras at the Casanova and Shéhérazade. The Casanova opened in 1926 at 10 avenue Rachel in Montmartre with a thoroughly modern theme based on movies. The Shéhérazade opened at 3 rue de Liège on December 3, 1927, inspired by the Russian ballet. The interior was a sheik's palace of arched grottos and flowing fabric draped from the ceilings like a harem tent all lit by the crystalline light of Arabian lamps. Waiters dressed in Cossack uniforms, and tables were set with the best silver and china. Shortly after it opened, the Shéhérazade hosted the Kings of Spain, Sweden, Norway, Denmark, and Romania as well as the king of playboys, the Prince of Wales. Sumptuous in their decor, luxurious in service, and stunning in entertainment, the Casanova and Shéhérazade were the cabarets of kings and the kings of cabarets.

The music of the Russian cabarets was an amalgam of classical music, Russian folk traditions, and Eastern European melodies as sifted through the musical sensibilities of the Gypsy performers. Django and the Ferrets joined in the Tzigane orchestras behind leaders such as cymbalom virtuoso Nitza Codolban and Bulgarian Gypsy Jean Goulesco, who played a velvet-toned violin rich in gothic sentimentality. He was a virtuoso of violin trickery, honed before the Tsar's court: He performed dazzling pizzicato melodies and bow-slides that evoked the call of cuckoos and nightingales, romantic music that had even charmed the Tsar's éminence grise, Rasputin. Romanian Tzigane violinist Georges Boulanger played each song like an epic narrative, such as the infamous "Sombre dimanche," a song so sad it inspired suicide and was thus forbidden in Budapest.

In addition, there was Karp Ter Abramoff's balalaïka orchestra with its repertoire of Russian folk music. Django and the Ferrets likely learned to mimic the balalaïka on their guitars in the Tzigane orchestras, a possible source of the tremolo chordal accompaniment that became prominent in the Gypsies' harmonizing.

While Django only played the Russian cabarets sporadically in these early years, Matelo Ferret became enamored with the music. At just 13, he was hired into Romanian Tzigane violinist Ionel Bageac's orchestra at the Casanova and was soon also accompanying Codolban and Tzigane violinist Yoska Nemeth. Over the years, Matelo became one of Goulesco's favored sidemen and in the process, he developed his own unique style of Tzigane music played on guitar.

IN WINTER 1933, Django returned at last to the recording studio. He accompanied singer Eliane de Creus, but these were forgettable recordings of forgettable songs. After several years of wandering and playing various styles of music, Django finally found himself back with Vétese Guérino in one of the most dynamic and musically accomplished musette bands ever. This ensemble cut a series of records that became an apogee of musette—and led the way to the development of a new style of jazz-influenced musette. Yet ironically, Django played the sideman on these cuts—and not only to the accordionist but also to his best friend, Baro Ferret.

Throughout 1932 and 1933, Django's path had led him back to Guérino. In spring 1932, Django and Naguine again packed up for Cannes, where Django rejoined Vola at the Boîte à Matelots. Baro and Sarane also played the Palm Beach, taking over Django's old chair alongside Guérino. Near the season's end, Django and Vola were fooling around in the Palm Beach bar after their set was finished, copping the style of Jack Harris's band. Their jazzy take on the music caught the ear of the managers and they were hired to return for the 1933 summer season in place of Harris. Vola's band also won a spot at a second Boîte à Matelots that Léon Volterra was opening in Paris.

While waiting for their stint to start at the Paris Boîte à Matelots in autumn 1932, Django and Vola's band played in the capital at Cyro's and the Ambassy. Joining the band was violinist Sylvio Schmidt, whom Vola hired instead of another violin player named Stéphane Grappelli; Vola had been warned away from Grappelli, who was rumored to be unreliable. Django and Naguine lived that winter in the Ouest-Hôtel in Montparnasse. To get around Paris, Django eschewed the métro as he couldn't read the names of the stations. Anyway, the métro was below him: He preferred taking a taxi—and often used the same cab, the driver enlisted as his own private chauffeur.

Paris's La Boîte à Matelots opened to fanfare on December 22, 1932. Volterra had bought the El Garron nightclub in Pigalle, and the interior decoration by avant-garde artist Pol Rab mimicked the Cannes cabaret with its stage fashioned from a boat. Opposite the stage above the entrance was a balcony for a second band: At the inauguration in Paris, Guérino and his ensemble played from this perch. Vola's orchestra featured the bandleader on accordion, Django, Nin-Nin, and Roger Chaput on guitars, pianist Marco, tenor saxophonist Jean-Jean, bass saxman Rumolino, violinist Léon Ferreri, and drummer Bart Curtiss. When Vola left for another band, Guérino took over the main stage. Django returned to Guérino's side, along with Baro and Sarane as well as Gusti Malha and Nin-Nin, who traded off accompanying Guérino like a game of musical chairs.

On March 19, 1933, Guérino led his group to record a series of sides that were released on the Odéon label as Guérino et son Orchestre Musette de la Boîte à Matelots. Alongside Guérino's accordion was Baro on solo guitar, with Django and *gadjo* guitarist Lucien "Lulu" Gallopain playing rhythm, violinist Pierre Pagliano, and bassist Tarteboulle.

Even though Odéon advertised Guérino's ensemble as an *orchestre musette* on the record label, the ensemble had stepped out of the confines of musette, also playing tangos and chanson. On these sides, Guérino orchestrated his simple band to create tight arrangements highlighted by dynamic interplay between his accordion, violin, and Baro's guitar. The result were true gems of musette, accomplished pieces far beyond the typical music of the day.

Yet by all accounts, these recordings were just a shadow of the brilliance of Guérino's band with Baro and Django. Odéon's music director—a man remembered only as Le Phoque, or the Seal—insisted that Guérino play an accordion with vibration during this session, and at times the extra harmonizing notes seem to hinder Guérino's jazzy lines. Fellow accordionist Charley Bazin felt these Odéon sides did not capture the excitement of Guérino's sound or repertoire. With Guérino's "dry" accordion, the hot solos of Baro

Ferret, and Django's rhythmic accompaniment, the band was leading the way to a fusion of jazz and musette.

These first recorded examples of Baro's fretwork explode off the 78s in a flurry of arpeggiated notes introducing Guérino and Malha's waltz "Brise Napolitaine." Even as a youth, Baro picked the strings with an aggressive confidence that his later accompanist Francis-Alfred Moerman would remark on, shaking his head in astonishment: "He played *so* hard. I've never seen anyone play the guitar so hard. He attacked it—which he had learned to do so he could be heard when playing in the *bals musette* behind the accordionists." These sides with Guérino captured Baro as a sure and mature guitarist and were the equal of—or stronger than— any recordings of Django to this time.

WHILE DJANGO WAS PLAYING Paris's Boîte à Matelots in autumn 1932, a rising singing star named Jean Sablon first heard his guitar. Sablon was one of a new breed of French singers arriving with the advent of the microphone. Many of the singers of the past sang through megaphones to be heard over their accompanying orchestras, winning renown due to the volume of their lungs and vocal chords; they often were in truth shouters instead of singers. Now, with a mic, Sablon could truly *sing*, and his dynamic, emotional vocals brought him repute, just as Bing Crosby was gaining fans and fame in the United States for similar reasons. Crosby was singing jazzy tunes that you could snap your fingers to, and Sablon, who modeled himself on the American, was striving to bring jazz to French chanson. Inspired by Crosby's recordings with guitarist Eddie Lang, Sablon sought to hire Django.

For Django, his association with Sablon would lift him to a new level. He became known among his fellow musicians as the accompanist of a popular star, earning him recognition and respect. And yet it also provided Django a more basic knowledge as well. Playing in Sablon's suave band, Django learned to polish his shoes and knot his tie.

Sablon was just at the start of his career, but his matinée idol looks and satin voice promised he would go far. Born in Nogent-sur-Marne in 1906 to a family of performers, his father Charles was a composer and his sister Germaine also became a singer. Sablon knew early on that he wanted to sing, so he quit school when he was just 17 to perform alongside Jean Gabin. Even if he had sung like a toad, the mustachioed Sablon could have spent the rest of his life starring as D'Artagnan. By the mid 1930s, any Frenchwoman not already sworn to singer Tino Rossi was swooning for Sablon.

After returning in late 1933 from his first tour of the United States, Sablon and his bandleader, André Ekyan, went to visit Django in his caravan to persuade him to join Sablon's ensemble. Yet when band rehearsals began, Django failed to show. To solve this dilemma, Ekyan—one of the best French jazz saxmen of the time—became Django's chauffeur. As Ekyan remembered, "Jean

Sablon had just bought one of the first Ford V-8 automobiles. He used to let me have it every night to take Django back home, and since I had to collect Django the next day, Jean never had his car!" Thanks to Sablon's automobile and Ekyan's chauffeuring, Django arrived to accompany the singer each day with impeccably shined shoes. It was a concern that was symbolic of Django's growing care over his appearance. He previously had cajoled Naguine into carrying him through the mud of their encampment to keep his shoes from being soiled; gallantry and chivalry came to an abrupt end at *la Zone*. Now, Naguine must have given thanks whenever she saw the Ford arrive.

Django's newfound awareness for his grooming did not begin and end with his shoes. In the past, he often appeared at shows unshaven and grubby, his suits wrinkled and unkempt, sleeves held on by just a few stitches and his shoe soles worn through, all a product of living out of doors in a caravan. Now, along with being Django's driver, Ekyan also instructed Django in the fundamentals of grooming: "I acted as a kind of nursemaid to Django. So as to persuade him to wash his hands, I pointed out to him they were the focal point of the audience's interest. After cutting his nails for him, I bought him a nail-brush and taught him how to use it. At the time he didn't even know what it was for. And when it was time to leave for work, I had to help him get dressed and knot his tie for him to make sure he'd be presentable."

With Django properly buttoned into a tuxedo, Sablon's band began a round of concerts at the type of swank venues where Django once listened to jazz from outside the windows. They played their premiere matinée and evening shows together at the Rococo presented by Jean Cocteau. The Rococo, a hotel cabaret just off the Champs-Élysées, was decorated in glorious boiserie wood paneling lit by candelabras, an elegance far from Django's world.

Sablon and his ensemble then opened at Le Bœuf sur le Toit, the surrealist cabaret that served up shock with each meal. The cabaret was named in honor of Darius Milhaud's radical ballet, first performed in 1920 to the desired affront of the musical establishment. Milhaud's score was accented by jazz as well as latin music and the Brazilian song from which it took its suitably silly title. The "dancers" were clowns from the Cirque Médrano, hidden behind monstrous African masks. And if that was not brazen enough, it was likely the first and only ballet to feature a decapitation. The namesake cabaret opened in 1922 with music, art showings, and theater that was the rage and outrage of the day. It was a venue Django would return to many times.

He was back at Cannes's Bôite à Matelots with Vola during summer 1933, but in winter 1933–1934, he toured again with Sablon. They played dates along the breadth of the Côte d'Azur, sharing the bill for a week in Nice with the brightest star in all Europe, Josephine Baker.

Come spring 1934, Sablon and his ensemble were booked to play London. Getting things in order for the tour, Sablon discovered Django lacked a passport. Nor did he have either his required Gypsy papers or a French identity card. When Sablon accompanied Django to apply for his papers, Django confessed he did not know when or where he had been born. With some strings pulled and a passport finally in hand, the ensemble made ready to leave for London. But another problem loomed. To get to England, they had to cross the Channel. Suddenly, Django the Gypsy did not want to travel. As Naguine remembered, "He was then truly a savage, a wild beast. One would think that he had never traveled anywhere. He was wary of everything." Django refused to fly and confessed a horror of boats. When Ekyan queried him, Django replied mysteriously, "Because there are spies!" When they at last maneuvered him on board the airplane and took off, Django burst into uncontrollable fits of mad, nervous laughter that did not end until they landed.

Sablon, Django, and the band played for three weeks in April 1934 at the swank Monseigneur nightclub in Piccadilly. The Prince of Wales came for the ensemble's first show and then returned every night. Django enjoyed the prestige of traveling with Sablon, and took a liking to fine clothes under Ekyan's tutelage. He began cutting his own fingernails, polishing his nails, shining his shoes, and combing his hair back every time he passed his reflection in a mirror. One evening, Django went along with the ensemble's pianist, Alex Siniavine, who wanted to buy some shirts in a tailor's shop in the Burlington Arcades. Leaving the shop, Siniavine discovered Django too had a new taste for elegance. He had pocketed three silk neckties that caught his fancy.

Django recorded with Sablon numerous times over the years, starting on April 3, 1933, and continuing into 1936. Of all the singers Django accompanied, his recordings with Sablon outshine the rest, reflecting a mutual respect between the musicians for the other's skill. Django made numerous chanson recordings in the early part of the 1930s with singers such as Aimé Simon-Grand, Le Petit Mirsha, Léon Monosson, Jean Tranchant and his wife Nane Cholet, and even Sablon's elder sister Germaine. On most of these, his guitar playing was limited to a supporting role with a perfunctory intro or a solo over a partial chorus displaying little inspiration. In contrast, his guitarwork on many of the sides with Sablon gave dynamic accompaniment to the vocalist. Sablon was a more accomplished singer than most, but he also saw his ensemble as a holistic element and not just as a backing band whose goal was to make him sound better. When recording on January 16, 1934, with Ekyan's band, Sablon held out against the objections of Columbia's music director to give Django a chorus solo on "Le jour où je te vis," the singer's version of Bing Crosby's hit "The Day You Came Along." This became Django's first true solo on record: While it was a simple chorus, it enhanced the aura of the song with sympathetic obbligatos and graceful ornamentation. Django inserted artful arpeggios into the arrangement, bridging verses as well as offering harmonic counterpoints to Sablon's vocal melody. The solo was not the audacious Django of his musette or jazz playing but rather was restrained and stylish, the perfect complement to Sablon's mood.

All of Django's personal wrinkles had not been ironed out under Sablon and Ekyan's hands, however. In April 1934, Sablon and his ensemble were hired to perform at a ski resort owned by restaurateur Louis Moysés at Le Mont-Genèvre, the pass Hannibal crossed to attack the Roman Empire in 218 B.C. Flush with his recent success and newfound air of sophistication, Django decided he needed a new automobile. He coaxed a salary advance from Sablon, then paid it out on a car suiting his image—a Chenard-Wackler racer. Like his old Renault, it was built for just one purpose—speed. The car had no roof or convertible canopy, eschewing even a windshield that might have slowed it down. It did have seats, although these were made of wicker to save weight. Settling in behind the steering wheel, Django donned racing goggles, then he and Naguine set off to meet Sablon high in the Alps.

Sablon awaited Django on the date of their rendezvous, but in vain. He waited another day, and yet another. Finally, as they were sitting down to dinner on the third day, the butler announced Django—who hardly needed any introduction as the roar of his race car preceded his arrival. Django and Naguine had driven their open car through the Alps in a below-zero cold spell. Django was wearing only his tuxedo and racing goggles, and the ever-faithful Naguine's cheeks had turned from cherry to beet red. Django apologized for their delay. After an avalanche blocked the main route, they got lost somewhere in the mountains for a couple days, then ran out of gas and money, a situation Naguine saved by selling homemade lace to buy fuel. But if Hannibal could cross the Mont-Genèvre pass with his army of elephants, then Django could certainly do it in his racing car.

5

Le Hot
1934–1935

IT BEGAN with a broken string.

Django was playing during the summer of 1934 for the rich and famous at the smart Hôtel Claridge's tea dance. Situated at 74 avenue de la Champs-Élysées, the Claridge was one of the most distinguished addresses on Paris's most distinguished boulevard. The hotel was pure glamor, its seven-story façade topped by the columns and pediment of a Grecian parthenon. Django made his way each afternoon through this haughty temple of Parisian elegance on his way to the ballroom, his guitar wrapped in newspaper.

Louis Vola, that tireless impresario, led the Claridge band. Along with Django on guitar and Vola's accordion, the 14-piece band included African American singer Bert Marshall, pianists Pierre Dorsey and Marcel Raymond, guitarist Roger Chaput, trumpeter Alex Renard, saxmen Alix Combelle, Max Blanc, and Coco Kiehn, bassist Francis Luca, Gaby Bart on drums, and violinist Sylvio Schmidt as well as Stéphane Grappelli, whom Vola had hired despite warnings concerning his reliability. The tea dance was a dignified afternoon affair, men in tuxedos waltzing women in crinoline across the marble ballroom floor under crystal chandeliers. It wasn't jazz, yet it was a paying job, and an easy one at that as the band alternated sets with the inevitable tango ensemble. Between sets, the musicians were left with time to kill, a spell usually spent at a nearby bistro with a beer in hand.

"One day, just before we were due to go on, a string broke on my violin," Stéphane Grappelli remembered. "I put on a new one, but couldn't tune my instrument properly because the tango band was still playing and drowned out any other sound. So, I withdrew behind the curtain, where Django and Louis Vola were waiting for our stint. I tuned my violin and at the same time improvised a chorus that just passed through my head. This music seemed to

impress Django because he took his guitar and accompanied my improvisation." Together, they tentatively toyed with Stéphane's melody, trading choruses, throwing in licks they had picked up listening to 78s, copping the stylings
of their American heroes to transport themselves far from the stilted elegance
of the Claridge. It was just Django and his guitar, Stéphane and his violin.
"We took to this mutual game and, every day, when the others left for the
bistrot during the break—I didn't particularly like killing my free time in a
café either—Django and I would find ourselves behind the curtain at the
Claridge improvising whatever came to mind. Sometimes Django would come
up with a theme, sometimes me. Our fellow musicians soon seemed to take an
interest in our daily improvisations. One day Joseph Reinhardt arrived, called
to the Claridge by Django to fill in for him. He was intrigued by our duo,
unwrapped his guitar from its newspaper covering and accompanied us. Now
we were three and had, without intending it, laid the groundwork for the
Quintette du Hot Club de France."

It began with a broken string. And as events transpired, it was only fitting
that the genesis of the Quintette took place behind the bandstand rather than
on it.

STÉPHANE GRAPPELLI grew up an orphan—an orphan living with his father.
He was born on January 26, 1908, at Paris' Hôpital Lariboisière and chris-
tened Stéfano Grappelli. He lived his early years with his family on rue de
Montholon in the Ninth Arrondissemont's Poissonnière quarter. His mother,
Anna Emilie Hanocque of St. Omer, Normandy, died when he was just four,
to be buried in her wedding dress. Stéfano was left alone in the world with his
Italian father, Ernesto Grappelli.

Ernesto was a hermetic Italian Renaissance scholar trapped in the modern
world. He immigrated from his hometown of Nettuno to France when he
was 19 after his father Etienne seduced the local abbess, leaving him em-
broiled in scandal and forcing Ernesto to seek his fortune elsewhere. He had
an Italian love for the arts, especially music, and spent his days sequestered in
the Bibliothèque Nationale translating Latin and Greek writers. Yet Ernesto
lacked patronage to support his scholarship; he taught Italian, sold translations, and sometimes wrote articles for local journals.

Then came World War I. Ernesto, still an Italian citizen, was drafted into
the Italian army in 1914. To care for Stéfano, he turned to the avant-garde
American expatriate ballerina and choreographer Isadora Duncan, about whom
he had written an article. Ernesto begged Duncan for a scholarship for Stéfano
to live in her Temple of the Dance of the Future at her Château de Bellevue.
Stéfano suddenly found himself in a Belle Époque wonderland of poets, musicians, and dancers. Duncan's students were known as the Isadorables, and
robed in a Grecian toga, Stéfano danced over the lawns to Debussy's *Prélude
à l'après-midi d'un faun*.

This idyll soon was shattered. The war encroached, forcing Duncan to flee France and turn her château over as a military hospital. Stéfano was left behind. Ernesto now had no choice but to entrust his 6-year-old son to a Catholic orphanage. "I look back at it as an abominable memory," Stéphane wrote, recounting his life from ages 6 to 10 in the orphanages with the horror of a Hugo novel: "This place was supposed to be under the eye of the government, but the government looked elsewhere. We slept on the floor, and often we were without food. There were many times when I had to fight for a crust of bread." Another time, he ate flies to try to sate his hunger. When his father returned from the war, he found the boy who had once danced like a faun was now an emaciated waif.

Ernesto moved his son back to their garret apartment in Barbès, and took up his old life of studying. Sick of all things Italian after his time in the army, he dragged his son to the city hall and with two witnesses pulled off the street, had him nationalized as a Frenchman. On July 28, 1919, Stéfano became Stéphane.

After the sounds of the guns, Ernesto now immersed himself in the tranquility of music once more. There may not have always been money for bread, but he did find a few sous to buy tickets to the cheap seats at the Concerts Colonne.

Around 1920, Stéphane found a new fascination. Ernesto pawned his suit to buy a three-quarter-size violin for his son. This dwarf instrument became Stéphane's focus—and a substitute for a father. As Stéphane remembered, "My father saw a three-quarter violin and he got the idea to buy that and give it to me—'to amuse me,' he said. We never knew I would do my profession with it. Suppose he didn't go that day to that street! Tis *fatalité*."

Ernesto sent his son to proper violin lessons, but Stéphane soon gave these up; he preferred to learn in his own fashion. "My first lessons were in the streets, watching how other violinists played," he recalled. "The first violinist that I saw play was at the Barbès métro station, sheltered under the overhead métro tracks. When I asked how one should play, he exploded in laughter. I left, completely humiliated, my violin under my arm." Practicing in the streets and bistros, Stéphane taught himself to play. "Finally, I was able to play more or less correctly the 'Java' of Mistinguett, without doubt the first morceau that I played in my life."

On December 31, 1920, Ernesto enrolled his son at the Paris Conservatoire Nationale. From busking in the streets, Stéphane was now studying harmony, ear-training, and solfeggio. In 1923, he graduated with a second-tier medal.

During Stéphane's final year at the conservatory, Ernesto announced he was marrying Alsatian matron Anna Fuchs and moving to Strasbourg. Stéphane was invited to join them, but he despised this new wife. Choosing to stay in Paris, Stéphane was separated by choice and chance from the one person with whom he had ever had a close relationship. Ernesto promised to support his son, but Stéphane knew better than to rely on his father. At 15, he was again on his own, busking full time on the streets to survive.

One day, Stéphane's busking became an audition. An elderly violinist overhead the youth playing and invited him into the pit orchestra at the Théâtre Gaumont accompanying the silent films. Playing six hours every day over a two-year period, Stéphane honed his skills performing snatches of songs, alternating Mozart with light opera and popular melodies.

During orchestra breaks, Stéphane ducked into the musicians' favored brasserie, Le Boudon. There, a "machine box"—an American Multiphone protojukebox—was stocked with wax-cylinder recordings, including Stéphane's favorite, "Tea for Two." One afternoon, he paid his five sous and pushed the wrong buttons. A foreign song came out of the speaker: He had stumbled across Louis Mitchell's Jazz Kings playing "Stumbling." "I was spun upside-down," Stéphane recalled. "This song absolutely haunted me; I used to go every day to listen to the same tune." This music was so new it mystified him: Reading the record label, he thought "Jazz Band" was the odd name of the performer.

Mitchell's Jazz Kings were soon followed by the music of George Gershwin, whose "Lady Be Good" became another favorite. Then, Stéphane ran across recordings by Louis Armstrong and Bix Beiderbecke imported from the United States. As Stéphane said simply, hearing Armstrong "changed my destiny."

Jazz violinists to emulate were few and far between, however. Stéphane was performing in the orchestra at the Ambassador in 1928 when Paul Whiteman headlined with Joe Venuti. Even though Venuti played mainly commercial jazz themes and rarely improvised, Stéphane was impressed by his jazzy bowing as he played Armstrong's "Dinah." Stéphane experimented, creating his own style. "At the beginning, when I started to play my own way, people thought I was playing out of tune, because they were used to the strict melody," he recalled.

Stéphane also experimented with piano when he had the chance. The keyboard's simplicity aided him in visualizing the music and the piano's sound cut through an ensemble while a violin was drowned out. In 1928, Stéphane simply packed away his violin and became a pianist.

At the time, Stéphane was sharing an apartment with fellow violinist Michel Warlop. Conservatory trained, Warlop made a fine living playing classical concerts. And yet he yearned to play jazz, admiring the apparent ease with which Stéphane improvised. Warlop tried to swing his playing but his rigid conservatory technique inhibited him. Stéphane, on the other hand, was envious of Warlop's income. This in part fueled his switch to piano, opening doors to paying jobs.

At this time, Stéphane became acquainted with a musician who would play a starring role in his life. Known simply as Grégor—or as he preferred, the "sublime" Grégor—he led a big band called, in fittingly humble tribute to himself, Grégor et Son Grégoriens. Stéphane was enchanted by the man, as was most everyone: "Grégor was a phenomenon," Stéphane remembered. "He had a sense of spectacle, showmanship, and theater." Grégor, whose real name was Krikor Kélékian, was an Armenian born in Turkey. Forced to flee during a racist pogrom, he traded on his prowess as a boxer. Making his way to Western Europe, he reinvented himself as a dancer, and by accident, Grégor soon became a bandleader. Swept away one evening by his own brilliance after a dance number in Amsterdam, Grégor stayed on stage to lead the house orchestra with acrobatic flourish. His antics impressed two members of the audience, directors of the Casino de la Forêt at Le Touquet-Paris-Plage. They beckoned Grégor to their table and told him they had to have his band. Grégor never batted an eye. He promised to bring his show to the casino but with an even better band—never mentioning that the band he had led was not his, nor that he lacked one of his own. In Paris, Grégor rushed to the musician's bar, Tabac Pigall, and hired himself an orchestra. They did not have time to practice, but Grégor was not concerned—his own dash would dazzle the crowd. Showmanship was Grégor's true gift, or as he pronounced, "I serve people soup and make them believe it's chocolate." Grégor became a French version of Paul Whiteman, and his big band a Conservatoire National de Jazz. Over the years, its ranks included the crème of French jazzmen: saxophonists André Ekyan and Alix Combelle, trombonist Léo Vauchant, trumpet player Philippe Brun, Stéphane's friends Mougin and Warlop, and soon, Stéphane himself, playing piano.

While playing with Grégor, Stéphane again picked up his violin. Late one night in Nice in 1929 after the band finished its set with Argentine tango crooner Carlos Gardel, the champagne was flowing when Grégor mentioned he heard that Stéphane played violin. Stéphane tried to dodge the question. But after a couple drinks, Grégor had Stéphane improvising "Dinah" on a borrowed violin. "I started to play 'Dinah,' very gauche," he recalled, "because when you go for three years without playing the violin you can't use the trick. Piano you can stay on top of without playing, but the violin is an awfully difficult instrument. Then I started to play and, you know, to play an instrument is like swimming: you never really forget." Stéphane's jazz delighted Grégor, and the bandleader immediately transformed his pianist back into a violinist.

Sadly, Grégor's star soon fell. Paying the bills for an all-star jazz band touring Europe was draining his bank account. Then, in 1930, he was involved in a mysterious automobile accident involving a fatality; he retreated to South America to avoid jail. Grégor's departure in 1930 left Stéphane and his bandmates without work. The former Grégoriens were reconfigured under the leadership of pianist Alain Romans and saxophonist Ekyan, who put together a true jazz band to play at Le Croix du Sud in Montparnasse.

There, in autumn 1931, Stéphane was improvising on his violin when his eyes met those of an unsavory character in the audience staring him down. Le Croix du Sud was a hot spot for fledgling French jazz fans—"It wasn't just all of Paris that came to Le Croix du Sud but the whole world," Stéphane said. Some nights the audience included everyone from Jean Cocteau to Jean Sablon to Jacques Tati. But this one audience member did not appear to appreciate Stéphane's playing and looked as though he preferred to see him outside at the point of a stiletto. "This young man with the very hostile look resembled none of the other guests who came regularly to that place," Stéphane recalled. "You would rather have said he was a gangster straight out of an American film. He had skin the color of *café au lait* and greasy hair, black as coal. His upper lip was topped by a thin black moustache in the shape of a circumflex. He really didn't inspire confidence.

"All at once, he started to move in the direction of the band. I had a bad premonition and instinctively took a step backward—I came within a whisker of falling off the bandstand.

"The young man came toward me and, awkwardly, proceeded to speak to me in strange-sounding French: 'Monsieur Drappelli, I believe?' he began, standing before me. It was only later that I realized it was difficult for him to say his G's.

"'Yes,' I answered, and asked him what I could do for him.

"Then he told me—with his left hand hidden as deep as possible in the pocket of his trousers (which were too large) while his right held a cigarette-butt—that he was a musician too, and was looking for a violinist who played like me.

"'And what is your name?' I asked.

"'Django Reinhardt!'

"The name meant nothing at all to me. But I told him that I seemed to have seen him somewhere, though I didn't know where. He answered that he was sometimes in Paris with his brother Joseph, and they played or begged together in restaurants. Then I remembered in fact seeing them in a restaurant, when they asked me for a little money."

It was hardly an epic first encounter.

Django invited Stéphane to the Porte de Montreuil and the caravan Django called home. "We jammed all afternoon," Stéphane remembered. "We played 'hot' purely for pleasure." Django was intrigued by Stéphane's violin playing, but both were booked in other bands and they went their separate ways.

It was not until three years later at the Claridge in 1934 that Django and Stéphane met again. As Stéphane stated five decades later, "My life started when I met Django. Because in those days, before him, I was a musician, playing here, playing there; but I realized when I was with Django, we can produce something not ordinary."

DJANGO AND STÉPHANE continued to jam behind the bandstand at the Claridge. Sometimes Vola joined in on bass, other times Chaput or Nin-Nin. It was a novel sound—string jazz. Up to this time, jazz was horn music, along with the occasional piano. Guitars were mere rhythm instruments, violins were for Mozart.

Rumor of the duo's jams soon spread, and a budding jazz fan named Pierre Nourry made his way to hear the backstage music. This was far from the seedy Pigalle nightclubs the youth was used to. He entered the Claridge ballroom with trepidation, knowing he was out of place in this world, skirting the waltzing dowagers and dotards. Nourry cared little what they thought of him. He was pure energy, and flush with fascination for the arcana of jazz, he became fixated on music and musicians. Nourry was studying at l'École Centrale but got his true education in the jazz clubs, listening to Louis Mitchell, Billy Arnold, and Sidney Bechet. He was an aficionado of American jazz—played by African American musicians—and was astonished to find musicians in the heart of Paris on the main artery of the Champs-Élysées who were neither American nor black but measured up to the best. Impressed by Django and Stéphane's improvisations and the unique music they created on two atypical jazz instruments, Nourry invited his jazz mentor Hugues Panassié to listen.

Panassié was the didactic leader of an in-group of French jazz enthusiasts seeking to promote jazz in France. Yet "leader" was too mild a term for Panassié, and Panassié was never mild. In truth, he was a jazz dictator, the self-chosen Pope of Jazz, as chagrined fans later labeled him. Panassié was raised in a château and lived his life in a castle in the clouds. Born in 1912, he was the son of Louis Panassié, an explorer-engineer who discovered Russia's vast manganese deposits. Louis left his son a fortune, allowing Hugues to devote his energy not to the tedium of earning a paycheck but to exploring his love for the new music. He lived in his family's Château de Gironde in the distant Midi-Pyrénées, but that didn't hinder his interest in African American music. Panassié discovered jazz in 1926 when he was 14 and recovering from polio. He was left with a paralyzed leg and the need of crutches, so his father presented him with a saxophone as compensation for not being able to run with the other children. He then booked lessons in Paris with French saxman Christian Wagner. Soon the sax was forgotten and the sessions with Wagner became lessons in living—who blew the best cornet, who were the members of the jazz family tree from Buddy Bolden to King Oliver to Louis Armstrong, all the important things in life. With money to purchase jazz records by air mail from the United States and time to haunt the Parisian clubs where Josephine Baker, Bechet, and other stars were playing, Panassié became the closest thing to an expert on jazz France could boast. He was befriended by white Chicago clarinetist Milton "Mezz" Mezzrow, then playing at Paris's L'Ermitage Muscovite, and Mezzrow became Panassié's jazz mentor—as well as éminence grise. By the time he was just 18, Panassié was writing a column for the French magazine *Jazz-Tango-Dancing*, spreading the good word on the new music.

Panassié's musings drew a cabal of jazz fans like disciples to an upstart creed. In 1930, a youthful radiotelephony enthusiast named Jacques Bureau approached him to start a jazz radio show. Born in 1912 in Meudon, Bureau was the son of a Parisian industrialist, but remembered the day in 1925 when his world was changed forever by jazz. His father brought home a record of Paul Whiteman's orchestra and the whole household—from his mother to the maids—was swept away, dancing to the infectious music. To Bureau, jazz suddenly infused his life: "I viewed jazz as a three-dimensional liberation of music." Bureau also became fascinated by physics and the brave new world of radio. He built his own short-wave and lying awake in his family's house in the Paris suburbs, he tuned in to a jazz radio station in Schenectady, New York. He recalled first hearing Bix Beiderbecke and discovering Armstrong on the nighttime transmissions: "Beiderbecke, what a revelation! It was music from beyond! I quickly learned the difference between Whiteman and true jazz. Whiteman was a condiment to give taste to the sauce, Armstrong and the others were the red hot peppers!" Because of his son's interest in radio, Bureau's father arranged an interview for his 18-year-old with Lucien Lévy, who in 1917 invented the superheterodyne radio and later started Paris' pioneering Radio L.L. station. Looking for something to fill the blank airwaves, Lévy invited Bureau to broadcast a weekly jazz show. Afraid to lose his opportunity if he admitted that his feeble collection included only 30 records, Bureau contacted Panassié and the two began sharing discs with each other and ultimately all of Paris over radio.

Bureau and Panassié became best of friends through jazz, yet a more unlikely duo was difficult to image. Bureau was a contrast of interests: He started studies at the Institut National Agronomique and was decades later at the vanguard in researching artificial intelligence. He was also drawn to the surrealist movement and was a committed Trotskyite—at least for a couple of youthful years. Panassié, on the other hand, was a staunch monarchist, to the far right of the right. But he was also ironically enamored with Soviet cinema, and the two went to Parisian premieres of revolutionary films such as Eisenstein's *Battleship Potemkin*—where Panassié handed out to the communist comrades photographs of the Bourbon heir to the throne and delivered an impromptu royalist rant during the intermission, waving his crutches wildly in the air. Panassié was excessive in everything he did. Whether it was politics, cinema, or music, he viewed the world in extremes, from hyperbole to damnation: "He knew only words such as marvelous, wonderful, hideous, rotten!" Bureau remembered. "I was completely the opposite. I found jazz to be a kind of mediocrity balanced with some prodigious strokes of genius that illuminated the whole." Disparate as they may have been, together they fell in love with jazz.

Bureau's jazz show and Panassié's column soon caught the attention of two students from Paris's Lycée Saint-Cloud—15-year-old Jacques Auxenfans and 16-year-old American expatriate Elwyn Dirats. Both were still in short pants, but that didn't stop them. In 1931, they wrote to introduce themselves to Panassié, requesting the honor of a meeting to unveil bold plans. In summer

1931, the two met Panassié and Bureau at La Coupole in Montparnasse. Their idea, they explained, was to join forces in forming a jazz club to share records and promote concerts in Paris with the ultimate goal of becoming an international club turning the world on to jazz. It sounded like nothing less than a crazed plot for global domination, and Bureau and Panassié laughed at the students. When Dirats promised the use of his father's commercial hall as well as the after-hours services of two typists and all the stationery they could desire, Bureau and Panassié became interested. In autumn 1931, Dirats, Auxenfans, Panassié, and Bureau founded the world's first jazz club.

It was christened Jazz Club Universitaire as Dirats and Auxenfans believed it would appeal only to students. Yet it soon grew beyond any of their dreams. The club was not a legal entity registered with city hall, as required by French law, and thus could not charge for public events. But as the Jazz Club Universitaire drew more adherents—up to 20 members at its peak—the club was soon reorganized and registered. Panassié also decided the club needed a more evocative name: he recommended the Hot Club, and so it became.

The Hot Club was announced in October 1932 in *Jazz-Tango-Dancing* with its manifesto spelled out in the November 1932 issue in a curious melange of Trotskyite verbiage with an evangelical religious tone. By disseminating their self-proclaimed "propaganda" for jazz through Bureau's radio show, articles in *Jazz-Tango-Dancing*, and concerts, the club vowed to "First, organize the enthusiasts of jazz hot; and second, by spreading the word about jazz, aid it in becoming appreciated, defend it, and help it conquer the place it merits among the movements of artistic expression of our times." Whether they were surrealists or classicists, Americans or French, Trotskyites or Bourbonists, the Hot Club organizers united in jazz and viewed their heart-felt goals as nothing less than a crusade.

BEING A JAZZ FAN in Paris in the 1930s was like being a Christian in Imperial Rome, in the words of one Hot Club acolyte. Jazz was so new, so novel, that it inspired adherents like a revolutionary political cell or a secret religious cult. Or an addictive opiate.

One fledgling fan, Pierre Gazières, became a prisoner of jazz, in Bureau's words. Gazières lived and breathed only jazz. He eventually lost his job in his devotion to the music and found it difficult to speak or even think about anything else. He boasted an enviable collection of a hundred or so records, jealously garnered from American doughboys, mined out of the flea markets' bric-a-brac, or ordered at dear price from the United States. Gazières knew by heart the solos to all his records, playing the 78s on his gramophone until they were so worn out, the sound was nothing but the static of the needle on dulled acetate. Bureau remembered Gazières spinning records for him: "When a record of Bix Beiderbecke or Duke Ellington was playing, I just heard *pchiiii*, but I could see that Gazières was hearing the music even though there was none!" For jazz fans such as Gazières, the Hot Club became a refuge, a sanctuary, a high church.

The Hot Club was a uniquely French idea. Organized unions and societies of all kinds appealed to the gallic mind-set, and French fans rushed to join the jazz club, mailing in their 25-franc fee—a substantial amount in that day. The members were industrious in lecturing, writing, and philosophizing on jazz, taking a freeform music and organizing a bureaucracy to analyze and catalogue it. In 1934, Panassié published, *Le jazz hot*, a shrewd examination that was the first history to single out African Americans as the prime innovators of jazz over the supposed advances of Paul Whiteman and other white players. The Hot Club issued membership cards and continued to publish *Jazz-Tango-Dancing* with its new *Bulletin Mensuel de Hot Club Français* first appearing in the July 1933 issue, read primarily just by themselves. Yet a small cadre of French jazz confreres eventually numbering up to 350 members blossomed around the club. They all made pilgrimages to a tiny record store owned by the Alvarès family known as La Boîte à Musique at 135 boulevard Raspail in Montparnasse. Here, the Hot Club enlisted African American pianist Freddy Johnson as its musical director and organized its first concert, on February 1, 1933. For the show, Johnson and Panassié rounded up expatriate jazzmen to jam in the store's cellar, including Garland Wilson, singer Louis Cole, and composer Spencer Williams. It was like New Orleans reborn on the Seine.

Tentatively descending the cellar steps to a jam session one day in 1933 was a callow commercial artist named Henri Pierre Charles Delaunay. Born January 18, 1911, he was the son of Orphist painter Robert Delaunay and designer Sonja Delaunay-Terk. Charles was a sort of forsaken masterpiece of the artist couple: They lived solely and soulfully for art, and Robert almost completely ignored his son in favor of his palette. "I always regretted that I did not have a true father," Charles wrote later. "My father did not live beyond his art." Charles grew up surrounded and forgotten among the progressive Bohemians of Paris—Stravinsky and Mayakovsky, Tristan Tzara and Blaise Cendrars, Chagall and Picasso. Graduating from the Lycée Carnot, Charles found work painting publicity posters that were beautiful blends of a commercial sensibility infused by pure lines and a bold eye for design. Charles Delaunay would certainly have gone far as an artist, but jazz got him first.

Robert Delaunay had a gramophone and disparate collection of jazz records that he never quite understood, grew bored with, and cast aside. Charles inherited these records—78s including Jelly Roll Morton's "Black Bottom Stomp," Duke Ellington's "East St. Louis Toodle-Oo," and others by Ted Lewis and the omnipresent Whiteman. Inspired by these recordings, Delaunay bartered his poster work to a record company for discs. He carefully listened to the firm's whole catalogue before choosing. What he found were licensed American recordings by Frank Trumbauer, Beiderbecke, and Armstrong, recordings that erased his artistic ambitions. Just as Robert Delaunay and the other Modernist artists were returning to fundamentals—basic geometric forms and primary colors—and to non-Western art such as African sculpture, jazz signaled to Charles a revolutionary reworking of music, cutting it loose from hidebound tradition and setting it free. He now had a modernist art of his own.

One day, he came to La Boîte à Musique, where he shyly asked for a copy of Ellington's "The Mooche," which he heard over a radio broadcast. The clerk invited Delaunay to the cellar jam, and when he arrived on March 29, 1933, Delaunay was overwhelmed by the vigor and warmth of the Hot Club—including Bureau, an old school friend who, unbeknown to Delaunay, was also a jazz fan. "To describe the impression I got from this very first jazz concert ever to reach my ears remains utterly impossible," Delaunay remembered. "I was glued to my seat, paralyzed by emotion to the point that the guy next to me became uneasy and carefully inquired whether I was pleased by 'that sound' and feeling well." For Delaunay, finding the Hot Club was like finding a family. And in turn, the members came to know him affectionately as Charlot, a nickname shared with Charlie Chaplin.

Delaunay was a painfully thin man, yet he had a handsome, aquiline face with a friendly smile and eyes that sparkled with warmth. Joining the Hot Club on July 1, 1933, and issued membership card number 228, Delaunay immediately offered his services. Bureau vouched for his old friend to Panassié, and Delaunay fell in alongside Nourry, working for the Hot Club with devotion. Although he was not one of the founding members of the club, Delaunay would come to have the strongest influence on the organization—as well as on French jazz and the future career of Django.

THE HOT CLUB first discovered Django through Nourry. In turn, Nourry immediately invited the club's arbiter on jazz, Panassié, backstage at the Claridge in 1934 to pass judgment. Nourry also brought Delaunay to the Claridge to witness a jam, and Delaunay described it as though he had entered into enchantment: "At the Claridge, we walked across the dance floor—which was glowing in the limelight shining on the Argentinean tango ensemble—to access an unused backroom that served as a lounge or dressing room for the musicians during their break. There, in a corner, four men were playing a music suffused with a melodic verve, refined improvisations, and efficient rhythms. Our ears were used to the aggressive sounds of brass horns and the rudeness of drums, and this music gave us the impression of returning in a dream through many centuries of history to the court of some distinguished nobleman. Louis Vola dominated the situation from the height of his string bass. Around him were two guitarists: Django Reinhardt and Roger Chaput. Stéphane Grappelli had left the piano and taken his violin from its case. They repeated their minor arrangements that served as intros or codas to standard songs or their own compositions. They played truly for fun, without any thought of creating a band. Several other musicians had come by to hear them play and they too could not resist the charm of the music. Django and Stéphane swapped choruses with each other, each of them visibly happy to discover the inventions of their partner."

Excited by their discovery, Nourry and Delaunay sought to share it. Nourry introduced Django to the elite jazz fans of the Hot Club at one of the jams at La Boîte à Musique in autumn 1933. Django's entrance into the cellar at first went almost unnoticed. Carrying his guitar wrapped in newspaper, he was dressed in a dark suit that was grubby, shapeless, and wrinkled, looking as though he had lived and slept in it for months. Obviously shy, he masked himself behind a façade of coolness. He kept a distance from the *gadjé* jazz fans, standing alone and aloof, reticent in his conversation when introduced. "I never saw Django smile," Dirats remembered. "He was polite but never exactly friendly, like a guest. We were pals with the black musicians that we were having fun with, but I don't remember that type of relationship with Django. The Gypsies kept to themselves." When it was Django's turn to play, he simply sat down, tuned up, and launched into a song by himself. He played a Gypsy flamenco piece and then jammed with the makeshift band on some jazz themes. Dirats and the other Hot Club members were intrigued.

Nourry then enlisted Django to play at a formal concert on Sunday afternoon, February 4, 1934. Nourry coordinated a band entitled for the event as the Orchestre Sigismund Beck, composed of bassist Beck, American trumpeter Frank "Big Boy" Goodie, Freddy Johnson, drummer Billy Taylor, and Django—announced as "Jungo Rheinart" in *Jazz-Tango-Dancing*. The concert was held at the Salle Lafayette in the Poissonnière quarter. The band played all-American jazz standards—"I've Got Rhythm," "Nobody's Sweetheart," "I've Found a New Baby," "Japanese Sandman," and more, songs that soon became the backbone of Django's repertoire.

Django received effusive accolades for his playing—albeit in the club's own magazine. Bureau spared no superlatives in proudly praising the Hot Club's prodigy: "One must say Django was the revelation of the soirée. He is a curious musician, with a style resembling no one else's. Yet this does not hinder the public from understanding him and applauding his solos. This white guitarist crafts small, strange musical phrases, bizarre constructions built according to the resources of an extraordinary fantasy; phrases that have an air like nothing else, and bear a delicacy, smoothness, and unity that leaves listeners dumbfounded. Every one has heard guitar solos that are insipid, but that was not the case for these! In comparison to the style of Big Boy—which is strong, violent, and direct—the lightness and freshness of Rheinart's playing was delightful. We now know that Paris has a great improviser!"

With his success, Django was taken under the wing of the Hot Club. Bureau was particularly charmed: "Django was totally illiterate. He was nil, a blank slate. He was a child. I told him stories about anything in history and he looked at me saying, 'Oooh!' He loved when somebody told him a story." Spending evenings at Pigalle's Brasserie Boudon, Bureau described dinosaurs from his school studies, leaving Django speechless with amazement and fear. Django paged through Bureau's textbooks, gazing in wonder at paintings of Tyrannosaurus Rex, oohing and aahing. His eyes grew large with astonishment as Bureau drew a picture of a Diplodocus. "He would not believe me when I told him about dinosaurs that were 25 meters long. 'You're stuffing my head with nonsense,' he'd tell me, 'you're making this up!' He was a child, a marvelous child, amazed at everything. He was a virgin spirit: He had only pragmatic things stored in his head—the things of daily life, money, food, all that you would find in a Gypsy encampment."

Others too remembered Django's questions—queries to which any school-boy knew the answers. As Stéphane recalled, "He was an intelligent man, always looking to increase his knowledge—even though he couldn't read or write. One day we were walking along chatting when, all of a sudden he asked me point blank: 'What is geography?' He had thoughts and points of view that were so funny, he'd stop you in your tracks openmouthed." Said a later friend, Henri Crolla, "I loved him deeply, not only as a musician, but even more as a man because I love children and Django, deep down, had the purity of a child." Yet many felt his lack of education—especially in music—was the secret to his genius. As one of his later accompanists, Hubert Rostaing, recalled, "His lack of formal education helped him keep a kind of innocence. Probably this was part of his extraordinary musical expressiveness. He'd burst out laughing and slap his thigh when he'd taken a good chorus. There was no pretense in that—it was quite logical. He'd played well and he was happy as a child would be."

Yet opinion was divided in the Hot Club concerning Django's music. The all-important, self-important Panassié was impressed by Django's guitarwork but Django was not black and he was not playing "real jazz." Panassié remained unconvinced. Instead, he championed Stéphane's violin jazz: "If anybody asked me which European soloist came nearest to the greatest hot musicians, I think I would reply: Stephane Grappelly. He has given me some of the greatest musical thrills of my life . . . he is hot from head to foot." Dirats marveled at Django's music, but was hesitant to pronounce it jazz: "At that time, the guitar was only a rhythm instrument and there were few soloists. Django's style was brilliant for the day, but hadn't reached his full sophistication. There was virtuosity, but I don't believe at that time there was that kind of depth of feeling of a black musician. Going up and down the scales with no feeling behind it was not the jazz I loved. Django developed this feeling later. I was impressed by Django only because of his novelty: He was pioneering something, and that was of great interest."

Even Bureau, despite his applause in the club magazine, had reservations about Django's playing. Bureau was unsure of the string jazz sound—jazz to him was horns—but he did not discriminate due to the color of the musician's skin. "I was hesitant about Django's jazz because it was so shrill and had a Viennese character. If there's one thing jazz detests, it's Central Europe, that's certain. Jazz isn't Gypsy music; it's different. Jazz is a stronger music, and Django didn't know much about jazz at this time."

DJANGO'S MUSIC found converts in Nourry and Delaunay. And they saw something more in Django—opportunity. The idea came to them after Duke Ellington performed at Paris's Salle Pleyel in July 1933. The concert hall was packed, sparking an epiphany for Nourry and Delaunay: Money could be made from jazz. By turning the Hot Club into a professional organization to sponsor concerts and sell records, jazz could become profitable. And in Django, they had a musician they could promote.

This was far from Dirats and Auxenfans's original plans. Dirats felt the passion for music was being replaced by Nourry and Delaunay's commercial plans, and already in its first year, the dissension that would hinder the Hot Club throughout its existence racked the membership. "Up until then, we were not professional promoters," Dirats remembered. "We were just guys who happened to enjoy the pleasure of listening to those musicians who otherwise in their professional life did not have the opportunity to do their thing, to perform with the depth of feeling that 'soul music' has. I cannot pass judgment on Nourry and Delaunay and their motives, but obviously they found that money could be made." By January 1934, the newsletter laconically noted Dirats and Auxenfans had departed the club. The original Hot Club was now recast by Panassié and Nourry as the Hot Club de France, filing with the Préfecture de Police and entered in Paris's *Journal Officiel* on March 26–27, 1934. By incorporating, the club could for the first time charge money for tickets to its concerts. The Hot Club de France was now a business.

Delaunay was also ascending the club's hierarchy. When Bureau left for his military call in 1934, Delaunay assumed his role. As Bureau remembered his childhood friend's ascension, "The Hot Club de France became a bit boring to me. It required a lot of administration. We were speaking only of business and not of music anymore." And this is where Delaunay excelled. "Panassié was never a good director. He was president but he was incapable of even writing a letter," Bureau said. Delaunay, on the other hand, was assiduous in correspondence, meticulous in making lists, and prodigious in collecting jazz records. "He had the spirit of a butterfly collector," Bureau recalled. "He had to have every butterfly and was not happy if one was missing. . . . I was not meticulous: I had passion for the music, but not for paperwork." Now, Nourry, due to his tireless organization and promotion, was named secretary, and Delaunay was his aide-de-camp. With Dirats's departure, the club's office was moved to Nourry's family residence and with military efficiency, Nourry enlisted his mother and sisters to paste up concert posters, stuff envelopes, and stamp letters.

It was the first coup d'état to splinter the Hot Club de France. It would not be the last.

Nourry and Delaunay now rushed to organize their next concert featuring Django. He was on the bill for a Bal des Élèves—student's concert—on March 3, 1934, at Nourry's École Centrale, sharing the stage with Goodie, Garland Wilson, and vocalist Alberta Hunter. The April 1934 *Jazz-Tango-Dancing* was once again enthusiastic about its own show: "It was the living end when André Ekyan, Jungo Reinhardt, his brother, and Al Romans joined Big Boy's band . . . it was delirium incarnate, delirium that lasted long into the night."

Django's success thrilled Nourry, and he took the next step forward. In August 1934, Nourry chaperoned Django and Nin-Nin into the Publicis Studios, a small recording studio for amateur musicians. Nourry paid for the brief session out of his own pocket, anteing up 80 francs to gamble on Django's talent. To back the two guitarists, Nourry tracked down Juan Fernandez of Martinique, a bassist who played at several Hot Club jams and for Freddy Johnson and His Harlemites. Together, the trio waxed test acetates of the Dixieland classic "Tiger Rag," the Henry Creamer–Turner Layton confection "After You've Gone," and the lovestruck American ballad "Confessin'." In addition, Django and Joseph alone recorded a separate take of "Tiger Rag."

Django and Nin-Nin's playing on the Nourry test acetates burst forth with youthful exuberance. Nin-Nin's bouncing rhythm was as impressive as Django's improvising. His restless rhythmic chords urged Django on, and he responded with flowing melodic passages, dazzling arpeggios of notes, and even quotes from classical music that resonate with irreverent humor within the jazz themes. These tests showcase better than any later commercial recordings the rapport of two brothers from ten years of playing together around the campfires of *la Zone* and busking in Paris cafés.

Nourry was pleased with the results. He sent copies of the acetates to those he considered the world's greatest jazz critics—Panassié, John Hammond in the United States, and Jost Van Praag and Niesen in the Netherlands. Panassié remained cool; Hammond was unimpressed. The Dutchman admired the music, but that was all.

With the help of Hot Club regular Michel Prunières, Nourry next introduced Django to Spanish guitarist Andrés Segovia. Prunières's father edited the staunch classical music establishment's *Revue Musicale* and organized a reception for the Spaniard. At Nourry's coaxing, Django and Nin-Nin arrived with their guitars and played a few jazz themes for Segovia. But Segovia was never a jazz fan, nor was he generous in sharing accolades with fellow guitarists. The Spaniard turned his back on Django.

Nourry's test recordings had failed and his arranged introductions led nowhere. Still, he was undeterred. "Despite this setback," he said, "I'd already grown convinced of Django's talent."

LOUIS ARMSTRONG arrived in Paris in autumn 1934. Dressing sharp and toting his trumpet, he had chosen France as a hideout: He was on the run from the gangsters controlling his career in the United States. In France, it was a different story. Armstrong was met with a fanfare deserving of the second coming.

There were certainly jazz musicians before Armstrong, but after he blew his horn, even his predecessors were following his lead. He became the pied piper of jazz, his 1925–1928 recordings with the Hot Five and Hot Seven hailed as turning points, shifting jazz from raucous polyphony to a soloist's art. To Panassié, Bureau, and their followers, Louis Armstrong *was* jazz.

Panassié and friends fêted Armstrong, showing off their record collections, and named him the honorary figurehead of their club. Won over by such devotion, Armstrong was soon in tow to Paris's jazz clubs. Then, despite his polite refusals to play, he could resist only so long and bounded onto the bandstand to blow his chops. The Hot Club aficionados were in heaven.

Nourry and Delaunay now arranged to introduce their jazz find to Armstrong. Panassié opened the door to the introduction, playing for Armstrong the sole recording on hand of Django's guitarwork: Jean Sablon's "Le jour où je te vis" with Django's short solo. Armstrong showed no particular enthusiasm for the playing, but agreed to meet Django as a favor. One evening in 1934, Django and Nin-Nin were shepherded to Armstrong's apartment. With Nourry and Delaunay leading the way, they knocked on the door and the king of jazz himself opened it, his head wrapped in a silk stocking to hold down his hair: They had arrived in the midst of Armstrong's toilette. After hasty introductions, Armstrong apologized that he was in a rush to dress for dinner and not to mind him. Django and Nin-Nin stood awkwardly with their guitars, waiting for their host to ask them to play. But Armstrong had other things on his mind. He rushed through the apartment searching out his shirt, seeking his suitcoat. Finally, realizing an invitation to perform was not forthcoming, Nourry and Delaunay persuaded Django to play, certain the sound of his guitar would catch Armstrong's ear. Nin-Nin and Django launched into song, sweeping through endless choruses, Django playing at his peak for his hero. Armstrong appeared again, but it was only to fetch his tie. Django dived into yet another chorus, beads of sweat standing out on his forehead. Only once did Armstrong shout from his dressing room, "Very good! Go on!" Django was mortified. As Delaunay remembered, "It was an utterly dejected little delegation—the two brothers, Pierre Nourry, and I—that made its way down the ill-lit staircase."

On another night, fortune turned Django's way. Late into morning, the telephone rang with African American singer Bricktop on the line telling Django and Stéphane to hustle down to her cabaret in Pigalle—Armstrong was there and raring to blow. It was five in the morning when they arrived. Without preamble Django took a seat alongside Armstrong. Stéphane remembered: "There was no discussion to decide what key they'd play in or what tunes they'd choose. Louis began and Django followed him in the twinkling of an eye." Armstrong blew his horn and then sang in that gravelly voice that soothed so many souls. As Stéphane stated, "It was a revelation. All of us were simply entranced."

With Django's success at the two Hot Club concerts and now with Armstrong's benediction, the club leaders began discussing the idea of a jazz group made up of French musicians with Django as its focus. Nourry envisioned promoting the ensemble under the aegis of the Hot Club: It was an opportunity to spread the word about jazz as well as to promote French talents in the jazz world that was overwhelmingly dominated by Americans.

But before Nourry, Delaunay, and the Hot Club could mobilize, Django and Stéphane were already forming their own band based on their jams backstage at the Claridge.

IN THE BEGINNING, the Quintette was a quartet. In their impromptu jam sessions during summer 1934, Django and Stéphane were joined by two Claridge bandmates—guitarist Chaput and bassist Vola. The musical interludes during breaks from work became a rite, and soon the quartet was also jamming after hours at l'Alsace à Montmartre, a Pigalle brasserie where Parisian musicians met for a swan song before heading home for the night. But one evening, Stéphane sensed reticence in Django's playing: "I could see something was worrying Django. And when I asked him what the trouble was one day, he replied: 'It doesn't matter all that much. It's just that when you're playing, Stéphane, you've got both Chaput and me backing you, but when I'm soloing I've only got one guitar behind me!'" Stéphane could hardly complain. As he described playing with Django, "Having Django accompany me was like having a philharmonic behind you." So, Django's brother Nin-Nin was brought on as a second rhythm guitarist. The four were now five.

The ensemble was still just an after-hours diversion, however. Django and Stéphane were not looking for bookings nor did they seek to record their improvisations. Again it was Nourry who stepped in with dreams of releasing several sides on a known label in the hopes that the records would launch the band and validate his discovery. At the established Odéon label, Delaunay knew artistic director M. Dory due to his work painting posters. Delaunay asked the firm to risk a test recording session. Dory agreed to the audition, and on October 9, 1934, Nourry and Delaunay herded the full ensemble into the Odéon studio. Along with Django, Nin-Nin, Stéphane, Chaput, and Vola, the ensemble also included for the day singer Bert Marshall from the Claridge band; Django told the others that the vocals would make for a more "commercial" recording.

Still, the band lacked confidence in their music. They met one afternoon at the cabaret Chez Florence to rehearse, then on the assigned day, piled into two taxis and set off for the studio. As Delaunay remembered, "Nobody was quite sure what they were going to record, but when Chaput found in his pocket the sheet music of a recent American hit, they took rapid advantage of the short journey to rehearse it."

In the Odéon studio, Django and the band encircled the single mic and began to play. Their jazz sounded a sour note with the engineers, however, who began discussing the din they were recording. Django overheard their disparaging remarks and, his pride assaulted by two mere technicans, decided he'd had enough. He packed up his guitar to leave. "Only with the greatest difficulty was he persuaded to stay until the two test sides had been recorded," Delaunay said.

In the end, the test acetates of "I Saw Stars" and "Confessin'" delighted Django and the band as they listened to themselves playing for the first time. That delight was quickly dispelled. Odéon's directors ruled on the band's audition, informing them that "After deliberation, our administrative committee has found that your band is far too *modernistique* for our firm."

Modernistique was the point of their music, and Django and Stéphane kept faith, even when others did not. Their Odéon auditions of "I Saw Stars" and "Confessin'" were true jewels. The arrangements were inventive and intricate, and the interplay between Django and Stéphane was dynamic, hinting at the musical connection the two shared. For his solos in both songs, Django created improvisations that dashed headlong from the subtle to the extravagant, all highlighted by glissando chromatic runs from one end of the fretboard to the other. *Modernistique* was the perfect word for the band—yet it was also the band's condemnation. They weren't just a rehash of the vaudeville jazz of Joe Venuti and Eddie Lang. Stéphane had been wowed by Venuti when he saw him at L'Ambassador in 1928 and Django was likely influenced by recordings of Lang's single-string playing, but the Quintette sought to play true jazz with hot improvisation. Asked what he thought of Lang, Django was succinct: "Very limited." Stéphane further recalled Django saying simply that "there was nothing to be learned from Lang." Django and Stéphane may have been inspired by Lang and Venuti early on, but they had left their music far behind. Yet for now, the Quintette's eccentric string jazz could not find a home. "No recording label wanted us," Stéphane remembered. "The formula was new: a jazz band 'without drums nor trumpet,' as we said. It was completely original." And completely noncommercial, in the view of the record companies.

Nourry continued to believe, however, even after two failed recording sessions. He thus changed his tack, arranging for Django and band to play their premiere concert. The ensemble was unveiled on Sunday morning, December 2, 1934, at the École Normale de Musique of the Université de Sorbonne's Centre Malesherbes. Yet Django and Stéphane's ensemble was so new they did not even have a name: Show posters announced them simply as *un orchestre d'un genre nouveau de Jazz Hot.*

When the premiere concert was set to begin, however, Django was no-where to be found. Seized by stage fright, he was hiding out in his caravan. Stéphane, Nourry, and the other musicians were thrown into a panic. They held a quick conference and appointed Nourry to go after Django. He jumped into his car and raced off across Paris to *la Zone*. At the caravan, Nourry found a dejected and discouraged Django who refused now to play. Not knowing what else to do, Nourry first tried encouraging Django, building him up with soft words. When this failed, he took on a military manner, ordering Django to grab his guitar and get in the car. As Delaunay remembered, "We did not yet know Django's shadowy and unforeseeable character . . ."

With Django hustled on stage by Nourry, the nervous ensemble took up their instruments and shakily launched into the first song. In the end, Django and the ensemble hit all the right notes with the audience, as Panassié re-counted: "The first concert by the Quintette, on 2 December, was a grand success. The hall was full and, from the first morceau, one sensed that the band was in form and was going to impress."

Pleased by the concert, Nourry broached the subject of a band name. The Hot Club had discussed the dream of an all-French jazz ensemble for some time. As early as March 1932, *Jazz-Tango-Dancing* editor Léon Fiot wrote, "Our idea is to form an orchestra of hot jazz composed only of the best French musicians, and of course they will be devoted to hot music, or to help its formation." The Hot Club even gave its name to sponsor an earlier band, the Hot Club Orchestre composed of Freddy Johnson, Big Boy Goodie, Arthur Briggs, and others that played a club concert. Now, Nourry won permission from Panassié to stamp the Club's approval on his new ensemble. "I was a little dubious about giving the name of the Hot Club de France to the group," Nourry remembered. "Stéphane was none too keen on it; Django, on the other hand, was agreeable . . ." Thus, for its second concert on February 16, 1935 at the École Normale de Musique, the ensemble finally had a name, billed as "Django Reinhardt et le Quintette du Hot Club de France avec Stéphane Grappelly."

WITH THE CONCERT SUCCESSES, Nourry was emboldened to again arrange a recording session for Django and the ensemble. He talked with Pathé-Marconi, but the music director there wanted jazz played on brass. Eventually, Nourry convinced Raoul Caldairou, the director of the Société Ultraphone Française. Ultraphone was a German label that made its name recording Eastern Euro-pean Tziganes music. But when the French branch was established in 1930, it quickly began recording hot jazz in Paris, including visiting American singers and bands such as Adelaide Hall, Freddy Taylor, and Grégor et Son Grégor-iens. The newly named Quintette could fit well into the label's growing ros-ter. Caldairou may have first heard the Quintette at its premiere concert on

December 2, 1934, and been impressed by the music. Whatever the case, it was Nourry's third try to validate his find and it appeared he had finally found a suitable label.

Before the session took place, Django and Nourry squabbled with Ultraphone's Caldairou over contract terms. The disagreement likely began with Django brazenly asking for a small fortune, and Nourry, new to negotiating contracts, innocently passing on Django's requests to the label. Caldairou was shocked by the exorbitant demands. Django may have banked too much on his own pride in his talent, or more likely he was simply a neophyte with regard to the established rates and royalties of the industry. Either way, while it may have been the first time Django demanded outrageous sums for playing his guitar, it certainly wouldn't be the last. Finally, Caldairou offered an ultimatum:

Paris, le 26 décembre 1934.

Monsieur Pierre Nourry
15, rue du Conservatoire
Paris

Cher Monsieur,
I shall not attempt to conceal that I am somewhat taken aback by the astronomical pretensions of the musicians in your Quintette.

You are unaware perhaps that the normal fee currently paid to first-class jazz soloists never exceeds 150 francs for each three hour session at which six sides are generally made.

On that basis, the demands of the three supporting musicians far exceed the usual fees. I am not speaking of Grappelly.

The maximum conditions I can envision are as below:

1. For the three accompanists (two guitars and one string bass) a one-time payment of 30 francs per side.

2. For Grappelly, a one-time payment of 50 francs per side.

3. For Reinhardt, a royalty of 5 percent and 50 francs royalty advance on each side recorded

In view of the hypothetical commercial value of the planned recordings, you understand that I cannot commit my company to paying recording fees that mean there would be no profit even when 500 records have been produced.

I rely on you to give your artists a more realistic vision of the fees they can expect to receive, and I ask you to accept, *cher Monsieur*, the expression of my distinguished sentiments.

Société << Ultraphone >> française
Signé: Caldairou

Django had little choice but to accept.

Early on the foggy winter morning of December 27, 1934, Stéphane, Chaput, and Vola climbed into Vola's small car along with their violin, guitar, and string bass and made their way to the ensemble's first commercial recording session. For the group to have gasoline for the journey, Delaunay had to lend Vola one hundred sous.

Ultraphone had scheduled the recording session for nine, running until midday; the studio was reserved for the label's stars in the afternoon. But before the Quintette could make its date, they had to find Django. Vola steered his car into *la Zone* until they came to a large Romany encampment. Here at last they found Django's caravan. Stéphane and the others roused Django and Nin-Nin, collected their guitars, and turned around to head back into Paris. Stéphane was quickly learning the reality of working with Django: He had to take matters into his own hands. "For Django, it was always an act of pure martyrdom to get out of bed in the morning," Stéphane remembered. "Each time that we were going to record, I would go at seven in the morning to his bedside, where I truly had to drag him out of bed—along with many promises and, if necessary, threats—and I had to make him understand that without his presence the rendezvous would be canceled. Each time it was an incredible drama."

Accompanying the Quintette to the session were Nourry, Delaunay, and Panassié, who had returned to Paris from his château for the publication of his book *Le jazz hot* and to hear Armstrong. Yet the Hot Club elite were not there simply to watch the recordings, but as auteurs. In their conceit, they were on hand to tell the musicians how to make jazz. They no doubt viewed themselves in an exalted role as producers as well as the band's impresarios.

A retired organ factory in Montparnasse served as Ultraphone's studio. The building was a monstrous yet unimpressive wooden shed; inside it looked like the cluttered backstage wings of an abandoned provincial music hall. The band unpacked and tuned up while two engineers dressed like doctors in white laboratory coats hovered around them. They oriented the single mic to best capture the ensemble, positioning Django and Stéphane standing and close in to capture their solos, with the rhythm section seated and farther away to balance the sound. They recorded directly onto a wax-acetate matrix—quaintly called *une galette* after a Breton buckwheat crêpe—which the engineers retrieved from a refrigerator when they were ready to record. As the needle tracked the music, an engineer swiped away the swarf from the virgin groove. "The recording sessions of this time appear prehistoric today," Stéphane recounted. "We played in a circle around only one mic. There were only eight matrixes, so there was thus no question of starting a song again as many times as we wanted. We had to play two morceaux of three minutes each for each 78-rpm record. Everything was incredibly simple. . . . We prepared arrangements of the song heads right before playing them. It was incredible! When I think that these discs became so famous!"

The ensemble began its session with "Dinah," the ubiquitous American jazz theme by Harry Askt. The song had been a hit across the ocean in the homeland of jazz for Louis Armstrong, then for Ethel Waters in 1926 and Bing Crosby with the Mills Brothers in 1931. Now, the Quintette recorded an instrumental version played solely on strings. Panassié remembered the session—also recounting his own part in the recording: "After several wax tests, they wanted to record the final version. The musicians played excellently but one of them made a mistake and it was necessary to start again. As Django and Grappelly were completely improvising, the new version was different. I was pleased with this take, as Grappelly appeared to me even more inspired. But as soon as he had played the last chord, Django bumped his guitar against a chair, which produced an ugly noise. The engineers came out of their booth and said it was necessary to start again because of this inopportune sound. But I feared the musicians had run out of inspiration and insisted they keep the last take, assuring the engineers this noise would hardly be noticed." Panassié coerced Caldairou to release this take, choosing hot improvisation over recording perfection.

The engineers also had difficulties capturing the ensemble's sound: Django and the others simply played too loud. Django was used to strumming and picking solo lines with all his strength in order to be heard above the din of noisy *bals musette* and jazz clubs. Over the years, his strong attack on his acoustic guitar became part of his style and he could hardly alter it now. After the band had waxed "Dinah," Panassié remembered, "The Ultraphone director came to say they could not continue to record the orchestra at such high volume as it would make defective records. For the following songs, it was preferable to decrease the volume. Alas, this is what they did, and this is why the three other recorded sides from this day—'Lady Be Good,' 'Tiger Rag,' and 'I Saw Stars'—sound so much weaker than 'Dinah.' The solos from Django's guitar especially suffer from this lack of volume." If Panassié had his way, he would also have controlled the recording equipment dials.

Panassié saw his auteur role as essential to save jazz from the record company philistines. While Django and the Quintette listened with pride to the playback of their first commercial side, one of the Ultraphone engineers drew Panassié aside. The engineer asked *sotto voce* why the musicians had "changed" the music from the version they played on the wax tests. Panassié laughed: "The band's improvisation had been such that this excellent man had not realized that the musicians had continued to play the same song." The inspired improvisations that jazz fans understood as the heart and soul of the music confounded the Ultraphone engineers.

Behind Django and Stéphane's improvisations, Nin-Nin and Chaput played rhythm in a style that became known as *la pompe*—the pump—for its fierce up-and-down beat. Their chording was based on the typical *bal musette* accompaniment, striking each beat with a percussive strum, any sustain choked off by dampening the strings immediately after the downward strum. Adapting this musette rhythm to foxtrots and jazz numbers, the *pompeurs* imitated stride piano accompaniment in the style of Fats Waller and James P. Johnson. Django and the other Gypsies hit the first and third beats with bass notes, accentuating the second and fourth with chords. Each beat was crisp and percussive, a combination of a guitar's chords, a bass's line, and a drum's beat, creating a full band's sound with a minimum of instrumentation. The sound of *la pompe* was proscribed as light and dry, an ideal rhythmic accompaniment to a violin, accordion, or, as the music developed, a solo guitar. This basic *pompe* was then accented by syncopated half-note fills and rhythmic triplets like strummed versions of the Gypsy flamenco *rasqueado*, which *flamencos* played with a quick unfurling of their fingers across the strings. Among the Gypsy jazz players, this device became known as "shaking a bunch of keys." To drive the harmonic chords, Django, Nin-Nin, and the other *pompeurs* added tremolo chords, echoing the sound of balalaïkas. While the rhythmic *pompe* was based in the banjo playing of the *bals*, it flourished in the Quintette into a complex rhythmic style that was unique—swinging and hot and charged, but also at times limiting and cumbersome.

On the foundation of the *pompe* rhythm, Django's skills of improvisation shone. His two fingers pranced through precise chromatic runs, flourishes of diminished arpeggios and minor-seventh scales, hit intriguing intervals, proudly unreeling his trademark riffs, turning the song inside out. His solo may have relied too much on tricks, but it was fresh and it was stylish. He no longer wanted to play Gypsy music, yet his jazz bore his Romany signature heard in the romance of the glissandos, the colorful hues of the chromaticism, the glitter of the diminished arpeggios with their odd intervals adding rhythmic punctuations, and above all in the virtuoso display of improvisation. He proved he had assimilated the music of Louis Armstrong, had acculturated himself in black jazz, and was now playing it his own way, returning it enriched. He had stepped far beyond the self-conscious, stilted jazz of Venuti and Lang. This was not the "Dinah" of Armstrong and Chicagoland jazz halls nor Josephine Baker's 1926 comic cabaret rendition. The Quintette recreated Armstrong's song on its 26 strings, making something new and original. And Django's playing gave sound to the spirit of Jazz Age Paris. His lines of acoustic guitar notes were pure rapture, effervescent and evanescent, floating away with an unbearable lightness and transience of the moment, their fleeting beauty almost unbelieveable. The genius of all his future music was in embryo in that one solo.

AFTER THE ULTRAPHONE RECORDING SESSION, the future looked brilliant to Django and the Quintette. They pocketed their fees from the session and left the studio in an ebullient mood, still inspired by their music. Walking through

Montparnasse on that rainy Parisian morn, they could contain themselves no longer. They turned into the courtyard of a typical workers' apartment block and unpacked their instruments. There, with the inner walls serving as a natural amphitheater, Django and the Quintette began to play one of their *modernistique* jazz tunes. Soon, apartment windows were unlatched as people stuck their heads out to see who was making music on this gray day. The sound of the guitars, violin, and bass reverberated through the courtyard, up seven stories to the highest apartments as children, housewives, and pensioners listened. And when the song came to an end, the impromptu audience rained down centimes on Django and the Quintette.

6

Djangology
1935–1936

WITH THE RELEASE of the first recordings by the Quintette du Hot Club de France, Django saw himself as a star. After the band and its impresarios left the Ultraphone session on December 27, 1934, to stroll in fine spirits up the boulevard Saint-Germain, Django disappeared into a haberdashery, only to reappear moments later sporting a brand-new broad-brimmed American fedora—half gangster cap, half cowboy hat, all childhood fantasy made real. "As white as snow, this magnificent hat made a shocking contrast with his swarthy countenance, unshaven beard, open collar, and shapeless suit," Charles Delaunay remembered. "He had undoubtedly made his long-held dreams come true by buying a real Stetson, made in the United States, which swallowed up every last bit of the fee he had just been paid!" This did not concern Django: He expected to soon be earning much more. And with the bright white fedora cocked jauntily over one eye, he was Louis Armstrong. Duke Ellington. Django Reinhardt.

These first records signaled a turning point in Django's life. He had never believed himself ordinary, a man like any other. Now, these recordings were a recognition of his talents, a validation from the *gadjo* world. His gift had been cast in wax, a monument to his musicianship. As Delaunay stated, "He became aware of his importance, and almost unwillingly began to think of himself as one of the prominent figures of the non-Gypsy world. . . . Until then he had remained a typically grimy Gypsy whose physical charms and natural dignity distinguished him from his fellow Romany. But his total lack of good manners, his attire, and above all, his wild and whimsical savage nature made it difficult to introduce him to people of polite society. . . . In the space of a few months, he acquired an elegant bearing, decided to dress in the approved manner like everyone else, and sought to be smart and refined."

Along with his debut recordings, Django's transformation was inspired by a romance. He and Naguine were then encamped in a Montmartre hotel and Django was playing nights at Stage B in Montparnasse. Here, he met one of the nightclub's taxi girls. In contrast to the dark Manouche women, this Frenchwoman had glamorous golden hair shining like a movie star's mane. Django was carried away in love, Naguine forgotten. As Jacques Bureau recalled, "When Django started to have some money, started to have some success, he didn't know what to do. He was with the angels in heaven! He lived life like a dream." Now, he moved in with the blonde B-girl, and she took up where Jean Sablon and André Ekyan left off in grooming him. She taught Django table manners, reproved him when he wore his brilliant red socks and hiking boots with his black tuxedo. Taking a cue from Armstrong, he dressed in dapper style, his pants ironed to a knife's edge crease, that blinding white fedora tilted just so. It was Pygmalion risen again, yet with roles reversed. "The strange new life Django led with the B-girl had effects that were as enduring as they were beneficial," Delaunay remembered.

But the affair itself did not last, and after several months, Django was back at the loyal Naguine's side in their hotel room with their pet monkey.

The Quintette's recording of "Dinah" won Django and Stéphane renown—even though it was primarily just within the small but devoted world of French jazz fans and at least one taxi girl. The indefatigable Pierre Nourry mailed out copies of the 78s to European jazz critics, yet inevitably the first review of the Quintette's first recordings appeared in the club's own *Jazz-Tango-Dancing*. The review was not the cheerleading rave that might have been expected, however. Instead, it expressed many aficionados' ambiguous feelings toward this new string jazz. "Do you want to know my sincere opinion concerning these four sides: they are far from ordinary," the anonymous review began in a tentative tone. "Sadly, the combination of instruments grows a bit tiring in the long run. Django Reinhardt reveals himself on these four sides to be truly an exceptional guitarist in his technique as well as his style. Don't forget that the guitar is from all points of view a completely disagreeable instrument exclusively reserved for rhythmic accompaniment in jazz bands. If it is possible, as Panassié says, 'to play hot on any instrument'—and I am certainly of this opinion—it is still undeniable that the melodic resources of the guitar are meager due to its sonority. In any case, Django uses all of the guitar's resources and all its strings in creating swing that is surprising and intense."

Others were even less sure of the new sound. Wealthy young American recording impresario John Hammond was far from enthusiastic. His comments in Britain's *Melody Maker* began with an apologia: "When the first four sides by the Hot Club Five were released, I was probably one of a very small minority not over-impressed. To be sure, there was at least one exceptional chorus in 'Dinah,' and some particularly astonishing guitar virtuosity on each disc, but still I could not see what the tremendous uproar or acclaim was about. Hammond continued, praising Stéphane but dismissing Django: "It is Grappelly who is the real star of the band, even more so than the amazing gipsy Django Reinhardt. His fiddle playing has a bite and vitality, which places it in a class of its own, for there is little copying, for once, of Venuti's tricks and clichés. His tone has a vibrancy that reminds more of the golden days of Eddie South than any other fiddle star. Grappelly's phrasing is always near perfection, and his technique more than ample. . . . Reinhardt would be magnificent except that single-string guitar pyrotechnics are bound to become fatiguing in the long run." Even to an enlightened critic such as Hammond, jazz was still horn music propelled by drumming. And guitars were just for wooing maidens on balconies.

Yet other critics across the Channel were over the moon about the Quintette, the beginning of a fascination among English fans. The British Rhythm Circle's *Swing Music* magazine reviewer was enthralled: "They are not only sensationally surprising in the highest degree, but represent something original, yet completely satisfying, in the art of hot rhythm. The most remarkable thing about these French discs is that there is no aping of Venuti and Lang. These boys have the style, the technique, the personality, the tone and attack, and above all the sense of hot playing, to enable them to dispense with all imitation. Every side is just grand swing music from start to finish." A review in *The Gramophone* was also charged: "Here we have a guitarist with a technique which has to be heard to be believed, but that is only one aspect of his attractions. A superficial hearing is all that is necessary to enable one to realize that in him we have an artist who not only has ideas of his own, but good ones. I don't think it is an exaggeration to say that even Ed Lang had not such a host of material up his sleeve, or the knack of sustaining one's interest so grippingly by being able to twist his phrases about in such an unexpected and intriguing manner."

But the critics' rantings and ravings meant little to Django—he couldn't read them anyway. In his own eyes, his star was already shining bright above the rooftops of Pigalle.

IF A SOUL SOUGHT SIN, Pigalle was the place. While Les Halles—with its vast food markets—was the poetic belly of Paris, Pigalle was its penis. The red-light district unfolded like a stripper slipping silk stockings from her legs: Starting in Pigalle at rue Fontaine, it ran in a long, smooth tease to place Blanche and up the flank of Montmartre on rue Lepic to the summit of la Butte at place du Tertre. In Pigalle, the pursuit of happiness became the eighth deadly sin. The quarter was a carnival of brothels and dubious hotels, clubs where one and all were members, and bars that descended in stature from neon-crowned cabarets to dark underworld dives. Dance halls leaned on innocent-looking street corners, but the cobblestones often needed to be washed clean of bloodstains come day. From the Bal Tabarin to the Moulin Rouge, it was the nocturnal realm of dancing girls and madams, pimps and procurers. And jazz musicians.

New Orleans had Storyville, Paris had Pigalle. It was here that Django first came upon Billy Arnold's Novelty Jazz band and here that jazz continued to flourish. Bars and restaurants hired jazz bands, whether to perform for the high society who came to dance or simply to accompany the striptease's contortions. And more than just jazz, Paris was a melting pot of world music—the finest tango *orquesta tipicas* outside Buenos Aires and Montevideo, Tzigane bands serenading the Russian cabarets, and other bars with bands playing West Indian and latin beats driving fashions for dances from the beguine to the zamba, the exotic to the erotic.

In Pigalle and Montmartre, the distance from heaven to hell was mere footsteps—and perhaps all an illusion at that. The Cabaret de l'Enfer reigned on boulevard de Clichy next door to the Cabaret du Ciel. A wayward soul entered hell's realm through the gape of Satan's fanged mouth. Guarding the doorway stood a diminutive demon, stirring the embers of a brazier and cackling at the falling angels, "Enter and be damned—the Evil One awaits you!" The interior was indeed an inferno. A cauldron was suspended over a fire: Hopping within were six musicians sawing away at selections from *Faust* on violins, pixies prodding them mercilessly on with pitchforks. Then the maitre d' made his entrance, Mephisto in person, mocking and insulting his customers' foolishness. Redemption for hell's habitués was found at heaven's *boîte*. Heavenly beings served drinks as a band of angels plucked harps, offering grace to those who had found their way. The two nightclubs were billed as *cabarets illusionistes*, and Baedeker's guidebook for Paris tourists simply warned the unwary not to venture hereabouts—or to abandon all hope if they did enter within.

Surrounding Heaven and Hell were gambling dens and billiard halls, fortune tellers' stalls and circuses, thieves' markets and theaters, drugstores where any drug was available and rooms where one could get fixed. Walking these mean streets were pickpockets and flame eaters, riffraff and aristocrats, lesbians and homosexuals, drunks and hashish smokers and imbibers of absinthe lost on their own heavenly clouds. It was all one grand illusion.

Through the thousand and one magical nights, the windmill above the Bal du Moulin Rouge turned without ceasing, like hands on a giant clock patiently counting down to perdition. In Paris, all roads led to the Moulin Rouge, the world's most famous and infamous cabaret bar none. It was billed as The Premier Palace of Women, a promised land of forbidden flesh, a temple of the taboo. And inside was a euphoria of legs. The Moulin Rouge was the undisputed cathedral of the divine dance of the cancan—gams kicked high in the air in black stockings, garters, and frills, unveiling a paradise of petticoats. It was over the top, outrageous—and just what Paris desired.

Above it all stood one woman. Josephine Baker had become the Ebony Venus of Parisian nightlife. She arrived in Paris from the United States with the black vaudeville show *Revue Nègre* in 1925, back when Django too was first discovering jazz. Baker led the fanfare of *le tumulte noir*, dancing in nothing but a smile and a skirt of bananas. She strolled down the Champs-Élysées with her pet leopard Chiquita on a leash. And she sparked a cult of style among French women. Baker was the apotheosis of the noble savage, and Parisiennes emulated her dark beauty with gold-painted fingernails, hair curls held in place by Bakerfix pomade, and a rage for sunbathing to copy her caramel-colored skin—or at least the annointment of tinted walnut oil to fake it.

For French men, it was something more.

Troy had its Helen with her face that launched a war. Egypt had Cleopatra with her nose that brought the Romans to their knees. Paris had Josephine Baker, whose butt was worshipped by all, a symbol of the Jazz Age in tempo to the times. One of her worshipful lovers, Georges Simenon, eulogized Baker's derrière: "Hers is, without question, the world's most famous and most desired butt. A butt so famous, so desired that it might well be an object of adoration, enveloped in dense billows of incense burned by the lust of thousands. It is a photogenic butt. The silver screen captures its firm, sweet contours, its lascivious quivers and wild convulsions. We have seen it wreathed in bananas warmly glinting of gold. We have seen it studded with pink feathers of delicate hues, bringing out the bronze of the flesh. We have seen it nude. But most of all we have seen it so taut, jutting so far out from the torso in a staunch gesture of defiance that it becomes a being apart, with a life of its own, far from Baker's face and eyes, comically crossed in stupor. What a synthesis! A synthesis of animal delight, as young and alive as jazz. . . ."

JAZZ WAS BLACK to most French fans. In Pigalle and Montparnasse, people came to hear the black bands and their music. Django and the Quintette proved themselves on their first records, yet as good as they were, there were no jobs for them in those infamous Pigalle dives. For the French—whether they simply sought to dance to jazz or were true disciples such as the Hot Club members— a band made up of Gypsy guitarists and Frenchmen was not the real thing.

African American musicians were in great demand and reaped great pay, but the story was different for Django, Stéphane, and other French musicians. Ultimately, the livelihood became so dire that eventually Louis Vola and Roger Chaput would leave the Quintette.

French nightclub owners scrambled to hire black bands—whether they were truly good musicians or not—instead of the rising French bands of Django, André Ekyan, Alix Combelle, and others. The French seemed to believe that all blacks had jazz in their blood. Bert Marshall sang with E. E. Thompson's all-black band in 1926 at l'Abbaye de Thélème, and believed they got the job only because of their skin color: "There was a lot of pro-black prejudice in Paris. If you were black, they thought you were great even if you were terrible. . . . You know, the band was so lousy that when we went on stage we had to pretend to play while the pit orchestra played for us and we just mimed to it." The craze for blacks spun so far out of control that some Frenchmen were forced to perform in blackface. Delaunay himself, an amateur drummer, wore blackface at one venue. He accompanied Benny Carter's band as impresario to a Zürich concert as late as 1938 where the contract specified an all-black band: lacking the group's usual black drummer, Delaunay donned blackface and took up drumsticks for the show.

Throughout the 1920s and early 1930s, so many African Americans thronged to Paris—musicians, *faux* musicians, and just plain tourists—that the United States' largest black newspaper, the *Chicago Defender*, sponsored a correspondent based in "The Harlem of Paris"—Pigalle and Montmartre. The quarters were dotted with bars owned by blacks, including Josephine Baker's Chez Joséphine, drummer Louis Mitchell's nightclub called simply Mitchell's, and boxer Eugene Bullard's Le Grand Duc. Like Chicago and Harlem, Paris was alive with African Americans blowing jazz.

As early as 1922, French musicians voiced their woes at the hands of *le péril noir* to President Raymond Poincaré, who demanded a solution before the Assemblée Nationale. Finally in 1936, Paris passed a municipal law limiting the number of foreign musicians in a band to 30 percent of the French musicians. The law was strengthened to 10 percent in 1939. Many blacks devised schemes to bypass the law, becoming instant "part owners" of a bar and thus exempting themselves from the rule's mathematics. But severe penalties ensued if they were discovered: Trumpeter Arthur Briggs was caught in such a fraud and expelled from France for a time in the late 1930s.

For the individual members of the Quintette, the 10-percent law was a boon, and finding work as sidemen in other bands became easier. Beyond the sporadic concerts organized by the Hot Club itself, however, the Quintette did not play any gigs together until summer 1935. In between the Hot Club concerts, the bandmates went their separate ways, playing in various pick-up groups formed to perform at nightclubs or in the Russian cabarets and *bals musette*, where the Ferret brothers were also picking their guitars.

For Django, it was the same story—yet worse. African Americans booked berths to Paris to revel in France's freedom from racism. But while no color barriers existed for blacks, entrenched barricades were erected against Gypsies. To many, they were untouchables, itinerants trespassing on French soil, outsiders encamped in a separate and unequal world. The French eyed them with dark suspicion, watchful over their chickens and cutlery, keeping their sons and daughters locked away, fearful of age-old tales of Gypsy child robbers. Django bore an imperious sense of his own worth and faith in the music that came from beneath his fingers. Still, the cabaret owners heard not the beauty of his song but saw the color of his skin and slant of his eyes.

Even after the release of the Quintette's first recordings, Django could only find work as an accompanist for African Americans, rather than as leader of his own group. With the introduction afforded by the Hot Club concerts, he was now in demand among bandleaders and getting a chair as a sideman became easy. Django joined Arthur Briggs's band performing at Stage B for a four-month-long stand starting in November 1934 with Freddy Taylor, Combelle, and Stéphane. Briggs remembered working with Django: "When I was asked to form a band, I hesitated in approaching Django. Not only was I unable to offer him a large fee, but everyone I'd spoken to about signing him on warned me against it. 'You're crazy, old friend,' Louis Vola said. 'Django will never be there for work. He comes only when he feels like it.' Nonetheless Django accepted the terms I offered him on condition he could play as he thought fit. He even dropped a gentle hint he might have to be away accompanying Jean Sablon, for instance, or out on the open road in his caravan. But to my great astonishment Django rarely failed to turn up and in the long run I had nothing to reproach him with."

Yet Django was still only a sideman; the African Americans were the stars. And a jazz band led by a guitarist was far from anyone's mind. Cabaret owners were dubious of hiring Django as a soloist or bandleader based as much on the fact that he wasn't black as that he was a Gypsy.

On stage, Django made beautiful music.

Off stage, he was a pariah.

DJANGO WAS NOT ALONE in pioneering hot jazz guitar in Paris at the dawn of the 1930s. An Argentine creole named Oscar Alemán was also in the city, playing his own style of guitar behind Josephine Baker, Taylor, and others. Although French fans were ambiguous concerning guitar jazz, with both Django and Alemán working in Paris, the city was the capital of jazz guitar at the time.

Oscar Marcelo Alemán came into the world at the ends of the Earth as far as jazz was concerned. He was born on February 20, 1909, in Resistencia, the capital city of the Argentine Chaco, a region in the center of South America cursed as the Green Hell for its humid swamps and sweltering brushlands that was Eden only for the thriving caymans, mosquitoes, and jaguars. Alemán's father, Jorge Alemán Moreira, was a Uruguayan of Spanish ancestry; his mother, Marcela Pereira, a Toba Indian. They formed their family into a folk troupe to escape El Chaco, and by age six, Alemán was dancing alongside his six siblings at Buenos Aires's Teatro Nuevo and touring Brazil.

In 1920, when Alemán was just 11, his family was torn apart by tragedy. After Alemán's mother died of illness, his grief-stricken father killed himself in 1921. Alemán and his siblings were orphaned onto the streets of Santos, Brazil. Far from home and abandoned by his elder brothers, Alemán survived as a shoeshine, newspaper boy, hotel bellhop, street dancer, and boxer. He slept where he found shelter and ate what he could beg, suffering malnutrition that gave way to calcium-starvation and rickets that haunted him throughout his life.

Alemán soon returned to the life of a minstrel in the *tavernas* of Santos, giving up prizefighting to save his fingers for playing the cavaquinho, a four-string Brazilian instrument akin to a ukulele. Wandering the port city, Alemán met in 1924 Brazilian guitarist Gastón Bueno Lobo and formed the duet Los Lobos, alternating between Hawaiian and Spanish guitar and cavaquinho, and recording for the prestigious Argentine Víctor label in 1928.

Los Lobos were soon discovered by Harry Flemming, a flamboyant tap dancer and impresario as well as part-time prizefighter and full-time womanizer. Flemming was then leading his *Bluebirds* show, a take off on the wildly popular Parisian black revue *Blackbirds*, complete with comedians, singers, dancers, and 16-piece orchestra. Los Lobos signed as a Hawaiian guitar duo and sailed for Europe in 1929 to perform across the continent.

Flemming and his troupe of American musicians introduced Alemán to jazz. As Alemán remembered, they "showed me the meaning of improvisation, of playing according to the feeling one has at the moment." Flemming and the others also played jazz recordings for Alemán. "I always liked Brazilian music, but I think even then I liked American harmony better," he said. "My idol in those days was Eddie Lang. I used to buy his records, on which he was accompanied by a pianist and later with Venuti and his group." Yet as strong as the jazz influence was on Alemán's playing, Brazilian music always remained his foundation.

In 1931, while performing at Madrid's El Alcázar cabaret, Alemán received a letter from Josephine Baker inviting him to Paris to become one of her 22 Colored Baker Boys. Even though he could not read music—trumpeter Bill Coleman joked that Alemán couldn't decipher a note as grand as a piano—Alemán soon became the band's director, leading the ensemble in 1932 at the Casino de Paris in the revue, *La joie de Paris*. Crossing paths with Duke Ellington during his 1933 European tour, Alemán was offered the guitar chair in the band—a move thwarted by Baker, saying, "Where in the world will I find another man who is able to sing in Spanish, French, Portuguese, and Italian, who can dance and play guitar, who is black, and best of all, is a great companion."

As one of the Baker Boys, Alemán likely first met Django either in Paris in the early 1930s or in Nice in winter 1933–1934 where Baker shared the bill with Jean Sablon. During December 1934, when Django's unnamed band played its premiere, the Hot Club de France also sponsored Alemán in a concert at the Salle Lafayette. By 1935, both Alemán and Django were fixtures on the Parisian scene. Alemán performed and recorded with Freddy Taylor and His Swing Men from Harlem as well as the bands of clarinetist Danny Polo and Coleman; he also continued to play frequently in Madrid. Django filled in for Alemán in Taylor's band for a month-long run at La Villa d'Este in March and April 1935, which *Jazz-Tango-Dancing* reported on: "La Villa d'Este continues its matinées and evenings with great success. The Freddy Taylor band is always simply remarkable. This formation gives the greatest satisfaction in every formula—hot, sweet, attractive, vocal, etc." Alemán, meanwhile, was leading his own nine-piece ensemble at Django's old haunt, Paris's La Boîte à Matelots, then renamed Le Chantilly. Louis Armstrong jumped in with Alemán while he played his "My Man," jamming through thirty-two choruses. Delaunay also recalled hearing Alemán there: "I remember Alemán when he played Le Chantilly, rue Fontaine, perched on a high barstool, bent forward and wrapped around his guitar, moving to the rhythm and strumming with a flamboyant flourish the chords of his guitar with his nimble fingers, wearing fingerpicks on his thumb and his first finger. Oscar was a small *bonhomme* with copper-colored skin—a *métisse*, as we said—sharp and quick as a monkey, always ready for a joke. . . . Alemán was a natural, and just his presence in an *orchestre* was immediately felt by the tonalities and swing he infused into the rhythm."

Alemán and Django's styles were as different as it was possible for two guitarists to be. This was partly due to the way they approached guitar as well as their backgrounds. Whereas Django used a plectrum and just his two working fingers for the majority of his fretting, Alemán picked and fretted the guitar with all of his fingers, aided by a banjoist's thumbpick. The Argentine played an American-made National tricone metal-bodied guitar. Picking this guitar with his fingers gave him a compressed, percussive sound, mellower in tone than Django.

Alemán's style of jazz was rooted in his background as an all-around entertainer. Not only did he play guitar, he also danced and sang, and his music—like the earliest jazz—was inspired by dance rhythms. With his background in Argentine music, Alemán introduced latin rhythms to his jazz decades before it became popular. Yet above all, he picked his guitar with an intense sense of swing.

In his accompaniment, Alemán often played harmonic ostinato figures—short single-note phrases to back the melody—instead of the Gypsies's *pompe*. In comparison, Django's sound was at the same time baroque in his Romany sensibilities and more modern in his lines and phrasings syncopated over the chord changes. Django also prided himself in his virtuosity, which was much admired among his fellow Gypsies; Alemán was all about the melody and rhythm. In his guitar playing, Django copied the melodic lines of Romany violinists and cymbalom players as well as Armstrong's trumpet—much as Charlie Christian and T-Bone Walker in the United States would borrow from horn players in creating their single-note solos. For his part, Alemán, with his fingerpicking, played a fuller array of notes, harmonizing and even orchestrating his own melodic lines. As Alemán commented concerning Django, "He used to say, 'Jazz is Gypsy,' and we argued over that. I agreed with many Americans I met in France who were of the opinion Django played very well but with too many Gypsy tricks. He had fine technique in both hands, or rather in one hand and a plectrum, because he always played with a plectrum—unlike me, as I played with my fingers. There are things you can't do with a plectrum—you can't strike the treble strings with two fingers and play something else on the bass string. But I admired him and he was my friend. . . . I appreciated him, and I believe the feeling was mutual."

This shared admiration was evident in an incident. One evening after Alemán finished the night's show with Baker, he and his bandmates were having dinner at Pigalle's La Cloche d'Or when one of Django's bandmates ran in. Django had an emergency, the bandmate told Alemán: "Old friend, can you help us? Django broke all his strings! Can you give us a set?" Contrary to Django, Alemán always carried several spare sets, an obvious necessity for playing gigs. Now, he quickly dug them out. "Here! Give them to Django and say '*Bonsoir*' for me." Several nights later when Alemán dined at the same restaurant, he asked the waiter for his bill, only to be told, "No, nothing, Monsieur Oscar. Django paid for your dinner. It was in thanks for the strings the other night."

Despite Alemán's pioneering guitarwork and good jobs in good bands, he lacked the sponsorship of Delaunay and the Hot Club. While he recorded several times in Paris in bands lead by Taylor, Coleman, and Eddie Brunner, it wasn't until December 5, 1938, in Copenhagen, of all places, that Alemán first was able to record as a frontman—and then only four sides that could just as easily have been lost to jazz history. He followed this with four more sides cut in Paris on May 12, 1939, for Delaunay.

These meager sides were masterpieces. Accompanied by Danish violinist Svend Asmussen, Alemán's versions of the standards "Sweet Sue" and "Limehouse Blues" were hot jazz swinging with a searing intensity. The tracks also showcase Alemán's qualities as a bandleader in their tight arrangements and close interplay between musicians. Alemán is all over the songs, unleashing fierce and fiery solos, augmenting Asmussen's violin lines with counterpoint and harmonic vamps, playing hide-and-seek behind the others, throwing in surprising riffs that sing and dance. Yet it was Alemán's solo pieces—"Nobody's Sweetheart" and "Whispering"—that truly astonished. These sides exhibited all of Alemán's influences, blending tinges of Brazilian rhythms with jazz melodic moods and a smart sense of ornamentation with surprising improvisation to create unique and eccentric interpretations.

These eight sides were the sum of Alemán's jazz recordings as a soloist and bandleader prior to World War II, whereas Django would have the opportunity to record hundreds of sides as accompanist and frontman. Due to the color of his skin as well as his prowess with a guitar, Alemán was in high demand in the high-class jazz bands of Paris, but Django, as a nominal Frenchman, won the all-important backing of the Hot Club in promoting French jazz. The discrepancy between Alemán and Django's careers in these formative years illustrated how essential the Hot Club was to Django's fortunes. Without Nourry and Delaunay serving as his svengalis, Django might have gone nowhere.

THE QUINTETTE was largely kept alive by the Hot Club in the early years of 1934–1935. Yet even in its heyday, the ensemble existed primarily on records. While the group played concerts and tours together at times, the total number of live shows that the full band performed was small in comparison with the prolific number of recorded sides it eventually released. And the ensemble was always a sporadic group anyway. The members of the Quintette played together for a recording session here, a concert there, but more often they went their separate ways, performing with other groups, recording behind other musicians. Thus, the band's personnel changed from session to session: One day, Chaput might be playing elsewhere and Gusti Malha was invited to take his chair; another day, Nin-Nin may have fought with his brother, and Baro Ferret was found in a café en route to the studio. Delaunay explained: "For a long time the celebrated Quintette was in reality a fiction and its survival depended on the sporadic activity of the officials of the Hot Club de France. In fact each of the Quintette's members worked in a different club, and a concert, recording session, or overseas broadcast was needed to bring the five musicians together." Hugues Panassié echoed this: "The Quintette's was an ephemeral existence."

The Quintette got together to play a concert on February 20, 1935, sponsored by the Hot Club de Nancy in eastern France's Meurthe-et-Moselle region. It marked the band's first show outside Paris and they were thrilled by their spreading fame. Arriving by train, Django gazed out the window and was stunned to see a large crowd awaiting them—an impression reinforced by Stéphane and Vola, who told him in jest that they were all fans out to greet the band. This seemed only right to Django and he went pink with pride. But as he descended, he was chastened to learn the crowd was actually there to meet a church dignitary arriving on the same train.

The Hot Club de Nancy organizers treated the Quintette to a gala feast and then set them up in the concert hall. Yet only 20 diehard enthusiasts came to hear the band, further proof that the Quintette's fame had not traveled far beyond their own horizons. Following the dismal turnout and after paying the musicians' fees—including that of Django, who had begun to demand a fee in keeping with his vaunted sense of self-importance—the concert organizers had to sell their hard-won record collections to cover expenses. Django may have been the darling of Parisian jazz fans, but in other parts of France he was still only known by the gendarmes for parking his caravan where it was forbidden.

In his business dealings, Django continued to rely on himself alone—a lesson learned from his Gypsy upbringing. He accepted the Hot Club's sponsorship, but he never considered himself bound to the club. He used the Hot Club when he needed, preferring the freedom of dealing in his own horse-trading fashion and falling back on Nourry and Delaunay when the time was right and the offer lucrative. This was proven on Saturday, February 23, 1935, when Nourry and Delaunay organized the Hot Club's most ambitious and prominent concert to date, starring Coleman Hawkins and held in the grand Salle Pleyel. Django agreed to play the show, accompanying Hawkins and fronting the Quintette. But he was playing for money, as he made clear when he demanded an insane sum, as Delaunay remembered. In the end, Django nearly bankrupted the Hot Club.

The arrival of Hawkins in Paris eclipsed the auras of the city's own stars. Hawkins didn't invent the saxophone—Frenchman Adolphe Sax did—but Hawkins gave the instrument its soul. Along with Lester Young and Ben Webster, he was one of the fathers of jazz saxophone, his lyrical tone inspiring the adoption of the horn in jazz bands everywhere. Hawkins proved himself with Fletcher Henderson in a nine-year stint at New York's Roseland, playing the bandleader's stylish arrangements with his impeccable hornwork. Then, in March 1934, Hawkins sent a wire to Jack Hylton in London stating simply "I want to come to England." Hylton replied with an offer the next day, and Hawkins set sail for London to declare his independence from the confines of dance bands. He arrived in Paris in February 1935 on tour with Hylton's orchestra and was immediately ruling over the city's jazz scene. Here, Hawkins discovered Django and came to jam with him when he played with Arthur Briggs at Stage B. As Alix Combelle remembered, "One evening, Hawkins came and sat in with us, and stopped playing only when the club closed." Stéphane recalled the same night: "Hawkins would improvise for an hour and a half on 'Sweet Sue.' We played from ten until four in the morning for ninety francs, but we had a whale of a time."

The Hot Club's planned show with Hawkins was not only a concert, it was a duel, a joust for honor within the Parisian jazz world, signaling another division among Hot Club devotees. With Panassié back at his château, Jacques Canetti—the radio broadcaster who turned Delaunay on to Duke Ellington—usurped editorial control of *Jazz-Tango-Dancing*, and under its aegis, won the confidence of Louis Armstrong to serve as his impresario in France. Angered by this domination of the American star, Nourry and Delaunay latched on to Hawkins. Now, the Salle Pleyel concert was to display the Hot Club's mettle and unveil their new, rival magazine, *Jazz Hot*. But come show day, their plans were in disarray.

Next to the Opéra, Salle Pleyel was Paris's most distinguished concert hall. Just off l'Étoile, it was a fancy address in a fashionable quarter. The hall was a Grecian temple in Art Moderne mode, the blue-blooded domain of classical music. Yet with Hawkins's sax and Django's guitar, the hall would now reverberate to jazz.

The Hot Club distributed tickets to music stores and other venues, yet when the doors opened, only a handful of fans arrived to sit scattered throughout the immense hall. Further, the first issues of *Jazz Hot* as well as the concert program were delayed, so publicity did not get out and it seemed doubtful they'd have copies for the magazine's own debut. Nourry and Delaunay were distraught. Finally they had no choice: They opened the concert doors to any and all, with or without tickets, and slowly the hall filled with more than 1,200 people. At the last moment, a breathless deliveryman arrived with the first printing of *Jazz Hot* and programs so they could be distributed during intermission.

The organization may have bordered on disaster, but the concert itself was a grand success. Hawkins was backed by a band led by Arthur Briggs and including Django, Stéphane on piano, tenor saxman Castor McCord, Fletcher Allen and Peter Duconge on altos, trumpeter Noël Chiboust, drummer Billy Taylor, and bassist Sigismund Beck. Hawkins and his compiled band took the stage first and played an array of jazz standards—"I Got Rhythm," "Avalon," and "After You've Gone." To Delaunay, Hawkins's music was otherworldly: "Coleman Hawkins was similar in build to Louis Armstrong, yet he passed by you almost unnoticed. He revealed little about himself, but his conversation showed a subtle and profound intelligence. As much as the playing of Armstrong corresponded perfectly with his physique and allure, the style of Hawkins contrasted with the self-effacing attitude he adopted in life. When he improvised, it was as though it liberated a formidable strength long contained, like energy let loose from a dam. His eyes closed, his eyelids heavy, an obstinate look on his face, his head down low, his shoulders hunched—it was as though he was embracing his saxophone with all his body and he seemed to have forgotten about the rest of the world. He gave birth to sorrowful, sumptuous arabesques of swelling notes, each one carved out like a jewel, their harmonious combination creating the most priceless of necklaces."

Following Hawkins, Django was joined by the Quintette, playing "Tiger Rag" and two other tunes, then backed Freddy Taylor. *Melody Maker* stated simply that "The three pieces given by this little ensemble were perfect and brought the house down." Django's first recording session may have satisfied his ego, but the Salle Pleyel concert found him an audience.

Yet all was not well backstage. When they tallied their take, the fledgling impresarios came up short. Gross receipts for the show totaled a meager 18,000 francs. While this was an immense sum for the Hot Club compared to any of its past concerts, it paled with recent Paris shows by Duke Ellington (70,000 francs), Louis Armstrong (40,000 francs), Freddy Johnson (35,000 francs), and Cab Calloway (27,000 francs). It also did not cover expenses. After paying for the hall, Nourry and Delaunay settled up with the musicians, including Django's insane fee. Now, the Hot Club was 6,000 francs in arrears. Hawkins, thrilled by the concert, offered to forgo his fee but was paid anyway by Delaunay and Nourry, who wished to remain on good terms with him for the future. Django did not extend a similar offer to his friends.

To make up the difference, Nourry organized a benefit reception at his parents' apartment with music by Briggs and Big Boy Goodie to repay the club—a sort of "rent party," as a chagrined Delaunay joked. But revenues again fell short. In desperation they approached Hawkins with a scheme to record him and buff up their tarnished image.

On March 2, 1935, Nourry and Delaunay entreated Django to join violinist Michel Warlop's band accompanying Hawkins in a session at the Salle Chopin for Gramophone. Along with Hawkins and Briggs, the ensemble included the pride of the French jazz world—Django and Warlop, Stéphane on piano, and French hornmen Pierre Allier, Guy Paquinet, André Ekyan, Noël Chiboust, and Alix Combelle. Together, they cut three sides, yet with mixed results: a lackadaisical "Blue Moon," upbeat "Avalon," and half-hearted "What a Difference a Day Makes." The fourth side was an intimate, world-weary "Stardust" featuring just a quintet made up of Hawkins, Django, Stéphane, a bassist, and a drummer. The two records were released to recoup some of the Hot Club's revenue and reputation, although Panassié—who had been left out of the whole project, always a source for sour grapes—was dismissive.

In the end, the Hot Club redeemed itself—although Nourry and Delaunay didn't try to organize another concert of such scope for a long time. For Django, it was another horse trade with the *gadjé*, and regardless of friendships, each side had to look out for its own interests.

THROUGHOUT 1935, Django and the Quintette reunited in the recording studio for several sessions. Yet the results were uneven. Sometimes they were unfocused and unexceptional; other times they were recordings that made history. In these early sessions, Django and the Quintette were still searching for their sound.

The Quintette's first records for Ultraphone proved enough of a success that the firm called them back for a second session, on March 6, 1935. This time, the Quintette brought along vocalist Jerry Mengo as the bandmates were still unsure of their own commercial value and felt they needed a singer's appeal to sell records. Of Italian origin but raised in England, Mengo was a university student who played drums in his spare time. He sang on covers of

"Lilly Belle May June," "Sweet Sue," and "Continental" while the band played a fine instrumental version of "Confessin'." Yet the session proved remarkably unremarkable due chiefly to the uninspired choice of over-played songs and Mengo's syrupy singing. "Lilly Belle May June" featured Mengo crooning for his "old plantation home"—pure blackface jazz, corny and artificial in any context but especially so when played by a French band. Django and the Quintette seemed to realize the ridiculousness of the situation, bursting forth from the vocal chorus into a quick-pulsed jam as if they were trying to distance themselves from the rest of the song.

In late April, the Quintette returned to Ultraphone to record four more sides: Fletcher Allen's stately "Blue Drag," "Swanee River," "Ton Doux Sourire" ("The Sunshine of Your Smile"), and "Ultrafox." *Jazz-Tango-Dancing* proclaimed "Blue Drag" the best recording by the band so far. A slinky swing tune, its dark undertones created a glorious late-night mood.

Yet it was in "Ultrafox" that the Quintette found its sound. This song was Django's first original composition to be recorded, although the band boasted a number of other originals among its live repertoire composed by Django, Stéphane, and perhaps Vola. "Ultrafox" was named in tribute to the Ultraphone firm's budget label Ultravox. Django's melody was likely built up from Quintette jam sessions, a lighthearted jazz ditty riding atop a bouncing rhythm line. While Stéphane's opening chorus had a classical air to it, Django's following solo was pure jazz: He played with laidback charm and inventive tricks. The music was above all happy and alive—Django and Stéphane were obviously enjoying themselves. Regardless, the review of "Ultrafox" in *Jazz-Tango-Dancing* was dismissive. "'Ultrafox' is a relatively less successful recording for the Quintette: I couldn't find any qualities in it. Maybe it was the last recording of a long and tiring session, which would explain the lack of brio and rhythm on this song." Or maybe even the Hot Club jazz stalwarts were still not ready for Django and Stéphane's concept of string jazz. When the Quintette covered a recognizable American standard, it was palatable, but when they played something new, it was disconcerting; even aficionados couldn't understand what Django and Stéphane were trying to craft. "Ultrafox" may have not been the hottest jam or most distinctive melody Django and the Quintette ever recorded. But it was all their own.

Still, Django and Stéphane were not in control of the Quintette's recorded sound or its choice of repertoire. Nourry and Delaunay were trying to shape the band to their own ideas of jazz while Ultraphone's Raoul Caldairou was seeking recordings of pure commercial value. The result was a long series of covers of American standards—many of which were already timeworn tunes, yet they were songs French fans knew by heart and the uninitiated might recognize and buy. In late June 1935, the Quintette returned to Ultraphone, this time enhanced with a horn section led by Briggs and featuring trumpeters Alphonse Cox and Pierre Allier and trombonist Eugène d'Hellemmes with

Baro Ferret replacing Chaput on rhythm guitar. The repertoire was more of the same: "Avalon" and "Smoke Rings," followed by "Clouds" and "Believe It, Beloved" featuring just the Quintette. Back at Ultraphone on September 2, 1935, they waxed "Chasing Shadows," "Some of These Days," and "I've Had My Moments"—all forgettable popular songs that the musicians termed *soupe*, tunes with flavor but little substance that went down easy and caused no one indigestion. In the last of these numbers, Django sounded so bored he led the Quintette into a high-speed jam halfway through, breaking away from the ennui of the melody.

In September 1935, the Quintette's exclusive contract with Ultraphone ended, opening the door for myriad recording sessions with a variety of labels, including Ultraphone as well as Gramophone in 1936. The large British Decca label, successful in licensing the band's Ultraphone recordings for England, also jumped on the bandwagon. Django had a great admirer at Decca in recording manager Harry Sarton, and when Sarton took over the firm in October 1935, he continued to license releases and record new material. Typically cut at the Polydor studios in Paris, the Decca sides began also to be released on Decca in the United States, both usually listing the band as "Stephane Grappelly and His Hot Four." Yet Decca was even more controlling than Ultraphone in its commercial choice of material, seeking out popular tunes to cover and eschewing Django's originals; it was 1938 before Decca recorded one of Django's own songs. For the Quintette's first Decca session on September 30, 1935, the band with Baro's taut rhythm cut W. C. Handy's "Saint-Louis Blues" and a hot but unissued "Chinatown, My Chinatown," followed by several sessions in October with "Limehouse Blues," "I Got Rhythm," "China Boy," "Moonglow," and Ellington's "It Don't Mean a Thing."

Django and Stéphane's string jazz was beginning to ring true with critics. In its review of "Saint-Louis Blues," *The Gramophone* raved, "The greater part of the record is played by Django Reinhardt and it is a triumph for him. He tells in simple poetry everything that Handy must have felt and meant when he wrote this melody. I might add that the performance is also a superlative example of guitar technique, that its phrases are jazz idiom at its best, that it swings and so on, but one mentions these things only when they are an end in themselves. Here they are a means to the end which is summed up in one word—Artistry." Not everyone was impressed. A review in England's *Swing* found nothing worthwhile in the Quintette's recordings and told the world so in a curmudgeonly tirade: "Lack of space makes it impossible for me to say all the very rude things I have in mind. 'St. Louis Blues' has its points. The other ["It Don't Mean a Thing"] is one of those great unplayables. It doesn't mean a thing."

As with "Ultrafox," it was at the finale of the September Ultraphone session when a last side was needed to fill out two 78s that Django was again allowed to record an original. "Djangology" was a catchy melody with all the grace of Fats Waller's "Honeysuckle Rose." It began with a baroque intro, Stéphane's violin matching Django's guitar note for note in a teaser building tension before leaping doubletime into the melody. Django's theme was a repeated riff in descending arpeggios, a tune displaying a maturity in his composition skills beyond "Ultrafox." And then came the solos, inspired tours de force, improvisations ornamented by stylish accents that marked the song as the band's best recording to date. With "Djangology," Django and the Quintette created a simple jewel.

IN SUMMER 1935, Django began playing a revolutionary new guitar built by Henri Selmer & Compagnie of Paris. The quest for volume was the Holy Grail of guitar construction in the 1930s as jazz guitarists sought instruments to slice through the sound and fury of a jazz band. Selmer's modèle Jazz guitar excelled here. Featuring steel strings that were louder than traditional gut strings, it was built around a unique resonating soundbox hidden within the outer body to boost the guitar's volume while retaining the purity of tone. It's unclear whether Django was given his first modèle Jazz guitar by Henri Selmer for promotion or if he purchased it, but once he began playing a Selmer, he swore by it the rest of his life.

Italian luthier and classical guitarist Mario Maccaferri designed the Selmer guitar. Apprenticed at age 11 to luthier Luigi Mozzani, Maccaferri learned to build violins, mandolins, and guitars, including Mozzani's special steel-string guitars and his lyre-guitar, akin to a diminutive harp. But Maccaferri did not solely devote himself to lutherie—he was also studying music. Graduating from the Accademia di Musica in Siena, he toured Europe in 1923, playing concerts and earning plaudits from critics. At the time, Maccaferri and Andrès Segovia were lauded as the two luminaries of classical guitar.

In 1928, Maccaferri immigrated to London to establish a lutherie in the back of a furniture shop. Here, he crafted a prototype of a novel gut-string guitar, which he showed to the managers of Britain's largest music shop, Selmer's London branch. Impressed, Henri Selmer immediately charged ahead in producing Maccaferri guitars. Django began using the Selmer-Maccaferri gut-string guitar, but soon Maccaferri launched a louder steel-string version that proved perfect for jazz.

In the quest for volume, guitarmakers were experimenting with inventions and innovations ranging from bold to bizarre. Believing bigger was better, American makers Gibson, Stromberg, Epiphone, and John D'Angelico vied to build ever-larger archtop guitars. The race was won by Elmer Stromberg's massive Master 400 with its 19-inch lower bout, a guitar so immense some players couldn't reach around its body. In California in 1927, Austro-Hungarian immigré John Dopyera unveiled the most radical, complex, and expensive solution.

Dopyera's National tricone was a metal-bodied guitar fitted with three stamped-aluminum resonating cones serving as crude speakers amplifying the strings. Due to its volume, the National became the instrument of choice for Oscar Alemán and other jazz guitarists. Further inventors built electrically amplified guitars experimenting with everything from gramophone needles to crude radio transmitters to capture string vibrations. In 1933, visionary Lloyd Loar was ousted from the staid Gibson firm and sparked his own Vivi-Tone Company, offering the first commercial electrically amplified guitar. But the technology was still exotic and acceptance slow. Vivi-Tone was bankrupt months after it was founded.

Maccaferri's answer was ingenious. Taking a cue from mandolin construction, his guitar had an arched soundboard glued to the sides under pressure, aiding his patented interior soundbox in amplifying the volume. This volume was especially pronounced in the treble registers, giving the guitar a tone that cut through the powerful voices of accordions and horns. In addition, the body featured a cutaway, allowing guitarists facile access to the upper frets. A short fretboard extension ran out over the soundhole, offering a wider palette of notes with a full two-octave range on the high E string alone.

The first Selmer guitars were made in 1932 and shipped to England, where they were eagerly promoted by Chappie D'Amato, Hylton's guitarman. By mid 1935, the French guitars were finally available in France and Django played his first riffs on a Selmer.

Previously, Django tried a variety of other guitars. Following Poulette Castro, he used one of Paris-based Spanish luthier Julián Gómez Rámirez's steel-string guitars. Photographs show him playing other instruments, including a large-bodied steel-string made by Arthur Carbonell, a Valencian luthier working in Marseille. And even after Django began using a Selmer, he also played jazz guitars built in the Maccaferri style by other Italian luthiers who established ateliers in Paris in the late 1930s, including Bernabe "Pablo" Busato and Sicilian émigré Antonio Di Mauro. Busato's instruments were faithful to the Selmer in style and quality. Di Mauro's family crafted guitars in Paris for decades, working alchemy on their inexpensive instruments to create a magical sound.

Still, it was the Selmer guitar that Django made famous and that helped make him famous. Later in 1936 or 1937, he began playing a revised Selmer with a small oval soundhole and a longer neck with 14 frets to the body, offering him an even greater array of notes. In the late 1930s, Django and Selmer joined in a promotional arrangement, likely a handshake agreement whereby Selmer provided Django all the guitars he required in exchange for his endorsement. Django reportedly visited the Selmer shop and tried out every guitar as soon as they arrived, picking and choosing the best-sounding ones for himself. The Quintette members were also given Selmers, although legend has it their guitars were only on loan. Django was pioneering jazz guitar on a pioneering jazz guitar, and after he began using a Selmer in 1935, it was rare to see a French jazz guitarist—Gypsy or *gadjo*—play anything but a Selmer, both for the guitar's jazz qualities and in emulation of Django.

IN SUMMER 1935, the Quintette finally found stable work—at least for a time. Like Louis Armstrong's epochal Hot Five and Hot Seven, the Quintette had existed primarily on records. Now, it was booked for a succession of concerts and nightclub stands. Still, none of the members yet believed they could make a living from the music they loved; as Vola said bluntly, "Nobody had confidence that the band could go anywhere." And as such, Django and the others viewed their Quintette in fun and jest. They took their music seriously, but saw the band as one big practical joke.

Django's sense of humor came alive on the bandstand. For a laugh, he tried to trip up the staid Stéphane and his bandmates. When Stéphane asked for the next song, Django might reply with a play on words based on a well-known title, calling for "Pédéraste et Médisante," a crass alliteration on Debussy's *Pelléas et Mélisande*. Another time he'd announce "Madame Django," then charge off into "Lady Be Good," launching into the song and leaving them to catch up.

This playfulness doomed the band at one venue. While Django and the Quintette recorded together in six sessions during 1934 and 1935, they only played three dates up until June 1935. Now, the Quintette united with Baro Ferret at the request of chanteur Jean Tranchant for a concert on June 13 at Salle Rameau and again on June 15 at Salle Pleyel. For the second show, Tranchant explained to the hall electricians he wanted a theatrical extravaganza spotlighting the band during their solos, then turning on him while he sang. In addition, the light was to change colors to match moods with his songs. All went well until they come to Tranchant's "Attila! Es-tu là?" Vola remembered the event: "Tranchant asked for the lights to be changed from blue to red to green and so on. While this was happening, the Quintette was in the dark. Django was intrigued by the changing colors. Stéphane had his back to the audience, bent double with silent laughter. Nin-Nin was cleaning his fingernails with his plectrum. But Baro had his eyes fixed on Grappelli, and after restraining his mirth for a while, finally burst out into an enormous guffaw that ruined the whole performance." Always striving to promote "his" Quintette, Nourry convinced American impresario Irving Mills to stay in Paris an extra day to hear them. Mills was not amused by the band's faux-pas, and castigated them in *Melody Maker*, "It is not enough to be an artist, one must be a gentleman too."

On July 5, 1935, the Hot Club sponsored a Quintette concert at Salle Lafayette, after which the ensemble began a month-long run at the new Les Nuits Bleues cabaret in Montmartre, inaugurating its opening. The premiere drew a fashionable crowd—but not Django. When their leader failed to arrive, one of his bandmates hustled over to his hotel, where he found Django resting quite peacefully. No amount of cajoling or reasoning could get him to budge: Django was in bed and set on staying there.

Through autumn 1935, the Quintette was again without work, forcing Django and his bandmates to find other paying gigs. In January 1936 as the

Spanish Civil War was erupting, the Quintette made its second foray outside of Paris, sharing the bill with Benny Carter for three concerts in Barcelona. The bandmembers were playing in a variety of ensembles and regrouped for the Spanish tour; telegrams were sent to Stéphane in Monte Carlo, and he flew to Barcelona to join the ensemble. The tour began at the Cinema Coliseum on January 29 and 30 and continued at Musica Catalana on January 31 and February 1, taking the stage after the Orquesta de Hot Club de Barcelona. In the end, the Spanish tour was a resounding success—especially compared with the Nancy trip—and the Quintette played double the concerts scheduled. As Stéphane remembered: "We had a magnificent reception marked by all the warmth and enthusiasm the Spaniards are capable of. After each concert, hats rained down onto the stage as though it were a bullfight. It was marvelous!" Yet when the applause ended, a surprise awaited the musicians: The concert organizer had departed with the proceeds. The band was paid an advance of 3,000 francs before leaving Paris, but now the balance of 4,000 francs plus their travel expenses were gone. Django, Carter, and their bandmates pooled the money in their pockets to afford train tickets home, with one lone Catalonian sausage to slice up between them to quell their stomachs on the long journey back to Paris.

Throughout the remainder of winter 1936, the Quintette played together only sporadically. On March 28, 1936, the Hot Club organized a concert at the Salle Pleyel featuring Herman Chittison accompanied by Django, Big Boy Goodie, and others. On June 5, another Hot Club concert at the École Normale de Musique featured guest star Garnet Clark and the Quintette. In the spring, the band regrouped to play at Bricktop's Montmartre cabaret.

In summer 1936, the Quintette again went its separate ways. Django was booked to play in Romanian pianist Marco's band at Saint-Jean-de-Luz. Émile Savitry recalled the season: "Django left his guitar with Marco and promised he'd be there on opening day. When it arrived, Marco was a trifle anxious, for he'd had no news of Django for several weeks. The train from Paris arrived without him. The tea dance was just about to begin when to everybody's surprise an enormous coupé lurched to a halt outside. The door opened and in walked Django!" This time, he had bought a monstrous Peugeot—with a roof. "Django had come with his wife and brother, but if he'd bought a car he had neither spare strings—those famous metal strings he loved so much—nor a plectrum. And his brother, who usually looked after such details, had also forgotten all about them. Inevitably one or two strings broke and by the time the season was drawing to a close Django had already been playing for a week with only two strings on his guitar! He'd forgotten his plectrum too, so he worked the whole season with a tooth from a comb—the large one at the end. How he could manage to play at all with a tooth that was so pointed and so difficult to get a grip on I've never been able to understand."

Marco booked a room for Django in Saint-Jean-de-Luz' best hotel, but Django could not stand the feel of the luxurious carpet beneath his bare feet.

Instead, he found a humble room with bare wooden floors. When the season ended, Django and Naguine packed up their car and pointed it back toward Paris. As Delaunay remembered: "He left just as he arrived, at the steering wheel of his big Peugeot, without a driving license, absolutely uninsured, and not giving a damn—but with an enormous cap shading his eyes, a deep suntan, and his red silk scarf around his neck."

DJANGO BELIEVED in enjoying his newfound success. Snow-white fedoras, lavish feasts that cost him everything he earned, bets on billiards, or decrepit automobiles that shone in his eyes—all was part of Django's reward. Money was flowing in as fast as Django could pick his guitar. And after years of living without, Django now flaunted his good fortune. A friend described Django's pride in his prosperity: "Whenever Django had money, he bought himself a car. He loved cars! And when he was broke, he smoked cigarette butts but he was never unhappy. When he was broke, he simply stayed home and Naguine went on the scrounge for money. And when he had money again, he bought champagne—he was the grand seigneur!"

On a day he was flush after a big show, he decided to buy yet another automobile. English jazz harmonicist Max Geldray remembered: "In a showroom window he saw a most luxurious and extremely expensive car. He entered and demanded the price. I always saw Django either dressed in the sharp zoot suit fashion, or literally like a tramp . . . and this happened to be one of his tramp days. The salesman eyed him superciliously and named the astronomical price. Django proceeded to spray francs all over the shop and drove the car away. He traveled into the country, entertaining his many friends lavishly as he went. Finally he ran the car into a tree and wrecked it completely. He had to wire to the office in Paris for enough money to take the train back."

For Stéphane, it was all too much. Like Django, he had grown up desperately poor and yet as a result, was now cautious with his earnings—to the point of being chastised as so tight it would later lead to disputes within the Quintette. Stéphane shook his head over Django's profligacy: "After seeing a George Raft gangster film, Django would act rather like a gangster when he came out of the cinema. He loved the big bankrolls gangsters pulled out of their pockets, and when he had money he'd tie the bills up in a rubber band and take out the entire wad paying for coffee or cigarettes. He could never be bothered to go and put money in a bank. He'd just have this wad, hundreds of thousands of francs sometimes, usually noticeably smaller in the morning than the evening before."

When his pockets turned up nothing but lint, Django fell back on his hatful of tricks. A gang of his unsavory Romany cousins would take a table at a Parisian restaurant to the consternation of the frowning staff. Django would then arrive with his guitar in hand and wander the tables playing requests. The other diners shrank away from this unkempt Gypsy, but after a few notes his music would win them over as he unreeled timeless Tzigane melodies ripe with emotion. Realizing they were being serenaded by a true musician, the diners dropped francs into his hat. Then came Django's *coup de théâtre* that bowled over everyone from busboy to boss. He'd set aside his guitar, smooth down his collar, and seat himself with his Romany cousins to order a feast of the best food and wine available.

Yet beyond Django's sense of theater, the *gadjé* simply could not comprehend his lack of concern over finances, a seemingly blind faith in surviving the future whatever it might hold. At times, Stéphane was lost in dismay and disbelief: "We had no work and I was offered a private party engagement by a rich industrialist, so I accepted immediately. I found Django in his little Montmartre room. He went there when he couldn't be bothered going back to his caravan. So I told him about the job, but he said he preferred to stay in bed. As I left, Naguine asked me for five francs to buy some sugar! He had not a penny in the house, yet he turns down a substantial sum of money!" To Django, money was nothing more than a validation of his talent, the symbol of recognition. As a Manouche, the *gadjé*'s francs were foreign to him, a necessity of living, but not the sign of true wealth. One friend remembered, "This is not to say he is a stranger to folding money; from time to time it finds its way to him. But then he has a hard time holding on to it for more than two days." And as Delaunay said, "What fortunes he threw away! . . . Money, the modern deity, had not the significance for Django that our society attaches to it. He had little difficulty in making it and even less in spending it."

True wealth to the Romanies lay in a different currency after generations on the road. France's francs or Germany's marks were worthless when you were forced to keep moving from nation to nation; real estate had no value if a pogrom burnt it to the ground. Their capital too had to be moveable. Some Gypsies hoarded gold, which kept its worth no matter where they traveled; as the wise Romany saying went, Gold never rusts. Others put their pride in their horses, assets that could be bartered anywhere—a transportable wealth that also provided transportation.

True wealth to Django came in more tenuous terms, in something difficult to count—in enjoying life. Money gave him a certain freedom, but not the true freedom of the road. He was always enamored with nature, whether it was fishing or simply playing music around a campfire under the stars. Family fêtes, clan feasts, Manouche baptism parties—all brought a chance to celebrate. In Paris, Django was now performing every evening as well as matinée shows with the Quintette or other groups. As much as he loved to make music, the routine and pace grew tiresome, and Django needed the freedom of the road to restore himself. Thus, some nights he simply didn't show up for gigs. A billiards game might beckon, a Gypsy wedding promising food and music might await, or he might simply be tired from the never-ending round of recording sessions and concerts and wish to stay abed. In the end, the lure of a night's pay was not enough; it simply got in the way of enjoying the finer things.

Some nights, Django sent the loyal Nin-Nin in his stead. Other times Baro sat in for him. Oscar Alemán took Django's chair one night when Django went missing after playing half a show. Alemán was recuperating in a Pigalle bistro after playing his own gig when one of Django's bandmates dashed in. The musician beseeched Alemán, "Oscar! Come quick! Django's disappeared! We've been looking for him for an hour, and in five minutes we must go on to play the second part of the show. If you don't sit in for him, all is lost! It's a night of bad luck as our trumpet player got sick and had to leave too! You simply must come save us!" Without delay, Alemán grabbed his guitar. The band hurried to take their seats and jumped into the first morceau. The ensemble played its usual repertoire, its new guitarist never missing a beat.

During intermission, Alemán stepped across the street for refreshment— where he found Django, arms and legs entwined with those of a woman, staring deep into each other's eyes. Alemán was stunned. "What are you doing here?" he demanded. "Your bandmates were looking for you everywhere, and I've been playing in your place for more than an hour!"

"I am with my fiancée, as you can see," Django answered, nonplused by Alemán's sacrifice.

"Your fiancée! You're not fooling me!" Alemán said. "I know Naguine— and she'd scratch your eyes out if she found you here!"

"Okay, okay," said Django, quickly brought down to earth by the mere mention of Naguine's wrath. "Don't say anything to anybody. Go back and play in my place and you can have my fee for the evening—all of it! I give it to you."

Shaking his head, Alemán returned to play out the night, never speaking a word about Django, who spent his evening in love in the bar across the way.

Throughout autumn 1936, Django was scheduled to play numerous recording sessions as a sideman—a lucrative but boring role for a budding star. So, as soon as he could, Django, with Naguine, packed up their caravan and hit the road, making for the Midi to visit fellow Romanies. As Stéphane remembered, "He could never stand town life for long, and was always running off to the country to fish or visit a gypsy camp. He would say: 'I'll be back in three or four hours,' and return three or four days later . . ." This time, Django's vacation left his Quintette in the lurch. Delaunay had booked them to play in Zürich on November 28, 1936, for a Jungle Night ball organized by Zürich University's Italian students at the showhall Au Bord du Lac. Sharing the bill with the Quintette was Fletcher Allen with Freddy Taylor's former band, the Swing Men from Harlem. Delaunay and the Quintette took the train from Paris to Zürich, where they expected to meet up with Django. Before leaving town for destinations unknown, Django promised Delaunay he would catch a train from Lyon—and to prove his goodwill, he even charged Delaunay with carrying his guitar. The Quintette arrived in the Zürich station and waited. Train after train arrived from Lyon, Geneva, or other points from where Django could have departed, but he was not on any of them. Starting to worry, Delaunay queried a ball organizer concerning their predicament, but the organizer was unforgiving, saying "If Django doesn't play, we don't pay the band for the trip here—or back!"

After the last train arrived without Django and the start of the ball loomed, the bandmembers were in a panic. "We held a quick council of war," Delaunay remembered. "Grappelli saw me standing there with Django's guitar in my hands and shouted out in jest, 'Delaunay will replace Django!' Under any other circumstances, we would have all laughed, but the situation was serious and a decision had to be made. No one had any other suggestions—Stéphane's idea was the only one on the table. Without knowing how, I was stuffed into a black tuxedo and bowtie and found myself catapulted out onto the stage under the limelight without even having a moment to catch my breath!" The Quintette kicked off the show, Nin-Nin playing the solos while Delaunay mimed the lines. As a stunned Delaunay stated, "I had never played guitar in my life!" At one point, he accidentally struck the strings during his double act, letting loose a cacophony of discord. After that, he was careful not even to pretend to pretend to touch the strings until the show was over. The ovation was sincere and the deception a success.

Throughout that autumn, Django was on the road. On December 10, 1936, the Quintette played at La Gala du Jazz Française at Paris's École Normale. Where their bandleader was, none of the Quintette knew.

Django had been sighted, however. The Hot Club's *Jazz Hot* was assiduous in listing where musicians were appearing on the French jazz scene. That autumn, the magazine reported that "Django Reinhardt was seen on Route Nationale number 7, at kilometer post 489, close to Lyon."

7

Swing
1937

HE WAS THE TOAST OF PARIS as 1937 dawned. From Bricktop's to Salle Pleyel, jazz fans and high society alike saluted his music. No longer was he the Gypsy pariah; his guitar wooed the audiences and smoothed his way. As the poet Jean Cocteau declared, his guitar spoke with a human voice.

Django's records were being released in France, England, Japan, even in the homeland of jazz, the United States. The Rothschilds paid him to perform at their soirées, movie stars danced to his music, royalty lined up to shake his magical hand. The Countess Anna de Noailles was so moved by his song she exclaimed, "This Gypsy is worth a Goya." They told his story like a fairy tale on the café terraces and in the fashionable salons, just as it was repeated in reverent tones among jazz acolytes. He was spoken of in awe as a child prodigy who never grew up, an idiot savant of jazz, a noble savage let loose in cultured Paris. His life was on its way to being mythologized. In the city of Josephine Baker and Picasso, of the sacrilege of *Le Sacre du Printemps* and alphabetical anarchy of *Ulysses*, of Expressionists, Cubists, Dadists, and Surrealists, of Georges Simenon writing an instant novel on command in a glass box, of black balls and drag balls and gay balls and nude balls, the city where both Lenin and Hemingway hatched their plots, it seemed only natural that this Gypsy jazz guitarist would fit in. His was the kind of modern fairy tale that Paris loved—even demanded—of its celebrities.

In the eyes of all, Django was romance incarnate. The cabarets were a world of theater and artifice, but when the show was over, the sequined costumes hung on hooks, and the greasepaint wiped away, Django was still the real thing. He was cloaked in an aura both mystical and mythical, surrounded by superstitions of Romany curses, Gypsy passion, and music so masterful it was almost other-worldly. At times, he played the part. Like an oriental prince in his white tuxedo, he breathed mystery. Django was innately regal and infinitely proud. Olive skinned, with dark almond-shaped eyes capped by arched eyebrows, he carefully cultivated a mustache more perfect than anything Hollywood could ever have conceived. He shyly hid his famous deformed hand in his pocket with the nonchalance of a musical Napoléon and only smiled when he played his jazz. At other times, he was a typical Gypsy of *la Zone*, dressed in a bum's cast-off suit. Around his neck was wrapped still the working-class red scarf while on his feet were a monstrous pair of hiking boots that he propped up on a stump of firewood or a Louis XIV table with equal concern. Invited to dine with the King and Queen of Belgium, he ate his salad with his fingers—yet did it with such charismatic elegance it seemed natural. Django was an uncensored man. Whether he was in the palace of his caravan or the hideout of a seedy Montmartre hotel room, his bed was his throne. He lay on his back, smoking forever, picking melodies from his Selmer, the notes of the improvisations drifting skyward in arabesques. He would rather escape to the open road or an all-night Gypsy fandango than play a command performance for the Prince of Wales: he played only when he wished and the spirit so moved him. He lived a dichotomy, moving with a near-schizophrenic change of face between two worlds—the make-believe of the sophisticated Parisian cabarets and his real world of the caravans of *la Zone*. Yet he was always still Django.

He was pleased by the *gadjo* world's adulation and money, but after the applause died away into the absolute of the night, there was only one thing left—the music. Above all, he lived for the music. Django and the Quintette's early records, concerts, and nightclub shows laid the foundation for their fame; 1937 was the year their success came true. It was Django's most prolific year, the year in which he created his legacy.

DJANGO SPENT New Year's Eve 1937 in jail.

With the new year had come new troubles. As the eldest, Django commanded grave respect from his younger brother in accordance with Manouche tradition. Yet Django took this to extremes. Nin-Nin was not only his junior, he was also his sideman while Django played the solos in the spotlight. This situation went back to when they were boys busking in the flea markets or playing for change in the cafés. Their duets formed a strong bond between the duo; Django adored his brother and for Nin-Nin, Django was the greatest musician in the world. Yet as Django's fame grew—especially in his own mind—he forced further roles on his kin: Nin-Nin was to be the faithful bearer of Django's guitar, the storehouse of spare strings, the porter of plectrums. Django began to look down on Nin-Nin as a vassal, elevating his own sense of grandeur.

Above Caravans encamped in *la Zone* just outside the Porte d'Ivry to the southeast of Paris in the year of Django's birth, 1910. While Paris was hailed as the City of Light, the squalor of *la Zone* was a city of blight. This image was taken by tireless documentary photographer Eugène Atget.

Right Django at age thirteen in 1923 or 1924, dressed in dapper style and holding his six-string banjo-guitare as if it were a weapon to wage war for his ambitions. (Alain Antonietto collection)

Left   Poster by artist Paul Colin advertising Billy Arnold's Novelty Jazz Band. Arnold's African American ensemble introduced Django to the wonders of jazz during its stand at Pigalle's l'Abbaye de Thélème in 1926.

Bottom Left   With his newly cultivated mustache, Django stands like a proud prince. His first wife, Florine "Bella" Mayer, is next to Django at right. Bella's sister, Philippine "Petit Sœur" Mayer, is beside her with their mother, Josephine Renaud, at front. A family friend, Marie Dumoulin, stands at left. (Mayer-Renaud family collection)

Bottom Right   Portrait of Django the young jazz guitarist, circa 1934.

Advertisement for the first concert by the as-yet-unnamed Quintette du Hot Club de France, featuring the five founding members—"Jungo" Reinhardt, Joseph Reinhardt, and Roger Chaput on guitars, violinist Stephane Grapelly [*sic*], and "Vola" on bass. The first show took place at 10 on a Sunday morning—hardly a grand debut.

Advertisement for the Quintette's first releases on La Voix de Son Maitre from a session on May 4, 1936. From left, Stéphane, Nin-Nin, Django, bassist Lucien Simoens, and Pierre "Baro" Ferret.

The Quintette on stage during their first English tour, in mid-1938. From left, Stéphane, Eugène "Ninine" Vées, Django, Nin-Nin, and Roger Grasset. (Stéphane Grappelli collection)

A publicity portrait of the
Quintette, taken for their first
English tour. From left, Nin-Nin,
Django, fourteen-year-old Beryl
Davis, Stéphane, Ninine Vées, and
Roger Grasset. (Stéphane
Grappelli collection)

Django the star.
During the Occupa-
tion, Django was at
his peak, and portraits
like this were sold
throughout Paris to
be pinned to fans'
walls. This portrait
was signed by Django
for an American GI's
friend back home,
guitarist Fred Sharp.

Baro Ferret and accordionist Gus Viseur's landmark band that led the way from old-time musette to swing musette starting in 1939. From left, René "Challain" Ferret, Baro, bassist Maurice Speilleux, Viseur, and Jean "Matelo" Ferret. (Scot Wise collection)

Django's Nouveau Quintette in 1940 featuring clarinet and drums as modeled after Benny Goodman's small swing groups. From left, clarinetist Hubert Rostaing, drummer André Jourdan (who joined the band after Django fell out with Pierre Fouad), Django, Emmanuel Soudieux, and Ninine Vées. (Alain Antonietto Collection)

Business card for La Roulotte–Chez Django Reinhardt in the heart of Paris's red-light district at 62 rue Pigalle.

Django's caravan-serai La Roulotte–Chez Django Reinhardt just after the Liberation in 1945. Two GIs on the prowl for a good time examine the topless Romany maiden on a white stallion next to the caravan-styled entrance. (Duncan Schiedt collection)

CONTINUED ON NEXT PAGE

Top Left Baro Ferret's *bebop valses* were eccentric and unique music unlike anything anywhere. They were also much admired by Django, Baro's best friend and arch rival. Baro likely wrote most of his *bebop valses* during World War II but did not record or publish them until between 1946 and 1949. He later rerecorded them for Charles Delaunay's Vogue label in 1966.

Top Right Django in the promised land, trying out his new Gibson electric guitar during his U.S. tour as special guest soloist with Duke Ellington and his orchestra in autumn 1946.

Right Ever the loving father, Django shows Babik how to play guitar. Négros Reinhardt looks on from the doorway of the family's new trailer camper parked outside Paris at Le Bourget in 1950. (Alain Antonietto collection)

Bebop at Club Saint-Germain. Django made a triumphant return to the Paris jazz scene with his new musical foil, alto saxman Hubert Fol, during a stand starting in February 1951 at Boris Vian's landmark club in Saint-Germain-des-Prés. (Alain Antonietto collection)

After Django's death, Nin-Nin packed away his guitar in homage to his beloved brother. It was not until the mid-1950s that he again began to play. Here, he performed in 1959 with Gitan Étienne "Patotte" Bousquet (left) and Gérard Cardi at Marseille's notorious bar, Au Son des Guitares.

Django's legacy. Babik (center) and Lousson (center-right) jam with fellow Romanies in the Clignancourt flea market in 1959. Although he never recorded commercially, Lousson was a fine guitarist on the cusp between his father's jazz and a more modern American style. He performed in Pigalle cabarets during the 1950s and 1960s following Django's death. Babik later recorded a number of albums before his death in 2001. (Alain Antonietto collection)

In character, the two brothers were darkness and light. Django sought refinement and elegance. Nin-Nin was down to earth, never quite comfortable
in evening dress. Django rarely smiled, Nin-Nin loved to laugh. Masking his
shyness, Django could be cold, even haughty, whereas Nin-Nin was warm
and friendly. Django couldn't be bothered to wear a watch or troubled by
time while Nin-Nin was dependable to death. Django was handsome, charismatic; Nin-Nin was the accompanist, always following the leader. In photographs, Nin-Nin's character showed. Beneath his immense bushy eyebrows,
his eyes rarely met the eye of the camera. His brow often appeared furrowed,
and under his mustache, his mouth was hesitant. Yet as a guitarist, Nin-Nin
was one of the best accompanists on the Paris scene. He had a strong sense of
harmony, fleet fingers, and a sure feel for rhythm. Yet all too often Nin-Nin
was left jilted on the bandstand, forced to sit in for his famous brother—and
then playing with such grace that few were aware of this Romany sleight of
hand, attributing it all to Django's genius.

Django's definition of brotherly love and his disappearance before the
Zürich concert now provoked Nin-Nin. On New Year's Eve 1937, the
Quintette was dining at Django and Naguine's hotel along with other Gypsy
cousins and the inevitable monkey. Food was plentiful, spirits were high, and
there was wine for all. Emboldened by drink, Nin-Nin stood up to Django
and laid down his own law: He was no longer going to take Django's treat-
ment. For Nin-Nin, this was an emancipation proclamation, a revolt against
the tyranny of his brother. For Django, it was nothing but disrespect. No one
remembers who threw the first blow, but soon the brothers were battling
around the room, swinging wildly at each other, careening into furniture,
crashing into walls. The other members of the Quintette jumped into the fray
to separate them before they drew their knives. Someone ran for Négros, and
only their mother's authority quieted the brothers. But it was too late. The
gendarmes arrived and Django, Nin-Nin, and the rest of the Quintette began
1937 in the local police station.

When they were set free, Nin-Nin marched off to find other work. He
would marry a Gypsy woman from the Adel clan and have a son, Kuick
Reinhardt; thus, Nin-Nin needed the pay of regular gigs to provide for his
family. He was quickly hired into Aimé Barelli's big band and Alix Combelle's
Jazz de Paris ensemble; he then recorded alongside trumpeters Bill Coleman
and Philippe Brun. But it wasn't long before Nin-Nin and Django settled
their dispute and Nin-Nin was back at his brother's side. As Stéphane stated,
"If it had not been for me, his brother would have left us 20 times. It was my
duty to end the hostilities between them each morning after a disagreement,
so that Joseph would be back in the evening for work. For two days or more,
they would not speak to each other, until something made them laugh. Then
everything would be patched up over a glass of wine or a meal." At least for
the time being.

In the meantime, Django was forced to find new rhythm guitarists, which he did first in Baro Ferret, then Django's cousin Ninine Vées and newcomer Marcel Bianchi. Born in 1915, Vées followed the path of Django to the guitar. Like Django, he learned from his own father. Vées's style was rustic yet charming, mirroring his person. Like Nin-Nin, he felt most at home in *la Zone* and was never comfortable in a tuxedo or the cabarets. When he wasn't playing guitar, Vées labored with Nin-Nin dealing scrap metal. It was a tough way to make a living, but perhaps easier than with music.

Bianchi was a Corsican born in Marseille in 1911. Given a mandolin at seven, he was leading a band in the sailors' dives of the Old Port by 17. Fascinated by the Hawaiian guitar style the sailors brought back, he taught himself to play a guitar laid flat in his lap, recreating with a steel bar the sweeping wails and plaintive tremolos of the far-off islands. Cheering his music, the sailors dubbed him Le Mascotte—the Charmed One. But when Bianchi heard the first records of Django and the Quintette in the mid 1930s, he was stunned by their virtuosity. He wore out the 78s, deciphering the choruses on his guitar like a secret code. Arriving in Paris in 1937, he entered an amateur jazz contest organized by Charles Delaunay. In the audience was none other than Django, who was impressed by this Corsican, exclaiming, "But he plays like us!" As a new rhythm guitarist was needed in the Quintette's eternal game of musical chairs, Bianchi was hired.

All was not harmonious within the Quintette, however. Django's antics—from his self-important aura of stardom to his unexplained disappearances—were a continual source of antagonism. Sometimes it seemed Django was a success in spite of himself. But a combination of the low pay of life as a sideman and Django's exacting musical demands conspired against keeping a stable roster. As Delaunay stated, "For a long time, the trouble with the Quintette was that they didn't have sufficient engagements and bookings to be able to pay all the musicians. Django didn't care because as long as he could live in a caravan it made no difference. But the others had families—they had to make a living." The problem was worst with bassists. Django's regard for bass players was low—they did little anyway beyond plucking out a bottom line to his flights of fancy. Many bassists were far from accomplished musicians, and one bad note would send Django into a silent fury. "He couldn't stand wrong notes—they would traumatize him," Stéphane remembered. "A wrong note had the same effect as an insult to him. He couldn't bear the mediocrity of certain accompanists. And despite his dreamy and peace-loving nature, he became violent and even sarcastic with them." Bass players shuffled through the Quintette like cards dealt in a game of belote—Louis Vola, Sigismund Beck, Roger "Toto" Grasset, Eugène d'Hellemmes, Wilson Myers, Lucien Simoens, and a nameless queue of others who played one-night stands and were then forgotten. Vola left for better pay in Ray Ventura's big band, les Collegiens. Other bassists played one evening or one recording session and were not asked back, fired, or far worse, given Django's infamous evil eye and dared not show their face again. It was then up to Stéphane to find a replacement as Django wouldn't lift a finger to help. "All the difficult jobs, it was me doing it," Stéphane moaned. Often before a show, he had to dash to Tabac Pigall, the bistro and musician's hangout that doubled as a makeshift employment agency. Here, Stéphane could always recruit a new bassist—even at the last minute before the Quintette took the stage.

The motley parade of bassists finally ended in 1938 when 19-year-old Emmanuel Soudieux tuned up his instrument for a Quintette gig. Born in 1919, he earned a living in Parisian musette and tango bands, but dreamed to the sound of jazz. Soudieux was an elfin figure, a happy-go-lucky boy lost behind the bulk of his bass. Django heard him play one night, then asked him, "What are you doing tomorrow?" Soudieux replied, "Nothing." To which Django stated simply, "Good, you'll come play with us." And with that, Soudieux was part of the Quintette. In his youthful ardor, he was more than willing to accept Django's dictates on pay and playing—an ideal combination for success. But Soudieux soon proved himself worthy beyond these basic requirements. Performing with Django one night while playing "Dînette," he struck a novel counterpoint bassline to Django's solo. The bass obbligato caught Django's ear and he spun around in his chair to give Soudieux a rare, beaming smile in appreciation. That smile stuck with Soudieux and he stayed faithfully at Django's side for the next 11 years, enduring as one of Django's longest-lived musical partners.

Yet the Quintette was not always a cohesive ensemble. While seeking Django's musical approval, Soudieux fended off Stéphane's intimate advances. Soudieux also remembered a deep-seated cultural division between the Quintette's Gypsies and gadjé. During the band's second trip to England, Baro taught the naïve Soudieux to play poker and in the process, lifted a healthy weight from Soudieux's wallet. Then one day, Soudieux realized the rest of his earnings from the tour had been stolen: He long suspected Baro as the pickpocket. "Baro was a great guitarist," Soudieux remembered, "but he was also a gangster." Lacking funds for a ticket home, Soudieux was stranded in England for some two weeks after Django and the rest of the band left for France.

Even with a solid bassline, there was above all the rivalry between the Quintette's lead duo. Django and Stéphane were great music partners, foils to each other's improvising. But Django's wiles drove Stéphane to exasperation and he certainly needed great forbearance to suffer Django's extravagances. As with Nin-Nin, Django and Stéphane were near opposites in character, mixing at times like nitro and glycerine. Django lived for his whims, carefree and caring less. Stéphane was steadfast and earnest, a dandy delicate in dress, always punctual, eternally professional. Growing up in poverty, Stéphane counted every sou to the point that many considered him uncharitable; Django was profligacy personified, ready to share his last centime with friends in need. When they played their music, the duo were in harmony, but the duet often came to an end off the bandstand. Like children, they could be envious, hard-headed, spiteful. Sometimes they couldn't stand the sight of the other; at other times, they were the best of friends. Naguine explained: "Django adored Grappelli—but only for his music. Django stated that Grappelli was the greatest violinist that ever existed and he adored him for this. But as a comrade, as a man, he did not like him." And as Vola remembered, a simple event could set them off: "There was much jealousy between them. Grappelly, when he played in a cabaret would take five, six, ten choruses and . . . sometimes Django would get so mad he'd drop his guitar and go across the street for a drink, and then I'd have to go and fetch him back." The spotlight was never large enough for the two of them.

Things came to a head during a radio broadcast for CBS's "Saturday Night Swing Club" transmitted to England and across the Atlantic, where it was relayed coast to coast in the United States. The program was a showcase for jazz greats, the Quintette following past performances by the Original Dixieland Band, Fats Waller, Billie Holiday, Duke Ellington, Tommy Dorsey, and Benny Goodman. For the broadcast on June 13, 1937, the Quintette was playing at Bricktop's club The Big Apple, where Django and company served as house band for several months, backing Bricktop herself during her nightly turn on stage. To time the live performance for America, the Quintette had stayed up all night after playing their regular show, and not until 5:40 A.M. was the broadcast ready. Radio technicians hovered around the band, fussing with microphone positioning and running serpentine coils of cables outside to a radio van, stumbling over Django and the other musicians, exasperating them with repeated sound checks. Nin-Nin was back on rhythm guitar alongside Gusti Malha with Vola on bass. Playing for the first time to an American audience, Django was shaking with anticipation of turning the United States to his music, and this was transmitted to the band, who was on a nervous edge to do their best. Django was anxiously fiddling with his guitar while Stéphane readied his fiddle. "The atmosphere between the Quintette's two chief protagonists was far from ideal," Delaunay remembered. This night, catastrophe seemed inevitable.

At long last, all was ready. The show's New York host, Paul Douglas, introduced the Quintette, but started with Stéphane before mentioning Django. Then the countdown came and the silent point of a finger to the announcer in Paris, Edward R. Murrow, who erroneously introduced the first song, "Djangology," as a composition of Stéphane's. At the band's introduction—mentioning Stéphane prominently and giving him credit for Django's namesake composition—Django went white with anger and rose to his feet. He always considered the Quintette *his* band, and this was a slight heard around the world. "The band, not knowing what to do, stayed silent," Delaunay recorded. "Signs were made begging the other musicians to start and while the broadcasting was going on they convinced Django in undertones that it was all a mistake and amends would be made later in the program. Django returned to his place in a fury, glaring at Stéphane even though it was in no way the latter's fault. He could hardly be held responsible for the American announcer's error." Such a mixup was hardly surprising—and perhaps intentional—as the Quintette's records were released at the time on Decca in England and the United States as "Stephane Grappelly and His Hot Four," with Django's name in the small print below. Still, Django was enraged, which showed in his playing. Radio audiences, not knowing of the bandstand battle, heard only a blazing version of "Djangology," followed by "Limehouse Blues" and "Bricktop"—which Murrow introduced as "Breakup" and again gave Stéphane top billing. Throughout, Django's guitar playing was fierce, his hurt pride seething. "Following this incident, Django addressed not a single word to his colleague for weeks on end," Delaunay said. "I am disposed to believe Django bore Stéphane a grudge about it until his dying day."

Whether they were playing hot jazz in the heat of anger or sweet melodies in harmony, the two men's approaches to music echoed their personalities. Whereas Stéphane's playing was suave and smooth, Django's was sharper, more dissonant. Like Louis Armstrong, Stéphane's violin improvisations came out of the melody while Django's were built up from the harmony, imitating Bach, Django's favored composer; as Delaunay stated, "Django was never concerned with melody—it was always suggested by the chord sequence." Stéphane was grounded in classical technique as well as popular songs and chanson; Django was always wandering, exploring. Together, despite personal differences, they resolved each other's styles, creating music greater than the mere sum of the notes. As Stéphane remembered of their music and their relationship, "Often it was just the two of us playing together because the rest of the musicians were incapable of following us."

DJANGO, STÉPHANE, and the Quintette were on the verge of falling apart under the strain of their own genius throughout 1937. Yet at the same time, Delaunay was at work behind the scenes on a project of his own that would all but ensure the Quintette's success—the creation of his own jazz record label, baptized Swing. When against all odds the label was finally launched, Swing became largely focused on Django. Of the 180-odd Swing sessions Delaunay produced from 1937 through March 1947, 28 featured Django and the Quintette and resulted in the release of literally hundreds of sides on the label and under license to other firms during these ten years alone. In addition, Django served as accompanist at 36 additional Swing sessions during this decade. Never before in the short history of jazz had one label been so devoted to one artist.

The Swing label was Delaunay's vision realized. He and Pierre Nourry had already transformed the Hot Club into a business in 1934 to promote concerts. When Nourry was called up by the French navy and later moved to Algeria in the mid 1930s, Delaunay took over as secretary general. Delaunay stepped up another rung in the club hierarchy when Jacques Bureau was called to military service in 1934. That same year, with assistance from Panassié, Delaunay published his *Hot discography*, the world's first jazz account book. In 1935, the Hot Club was organizing the Fédération Internationale des Hot Clubs with Panassié as president and members from as far afield as the Hot Club of Cairo and American jazz buff Marshall Stearns's Yale Hot Club and United Hot Clubs of America; as Delaunay dreamed, "Such an organization in the postwar chaos in Europe would help bring about peace and under-standing between men of good will." Then Panassié retreated to his Château de Gironde, returning to Paris only for rare occasions; with war looming, he remained cloistered in the provinces. Panassié was all pomp and no circum-stance, as Bureau remembered. Delaunay took over handling all club affairs, from the menial to the grand. It was a job he was ideally and uniquely suited for—Delaunay was a rare blend of an artist and accountant. The record label was the next logical step.

With the success of Django and the Quintette's Gramophone sides, Delaunay wrote in January 1937 to Jean Bérard, the new Gramophone label director at Pathé-Marconi, to suggest creating a jazz line under his control to produce recordings and license American releases for France. To Delaunay's great surprise, Bérard approved his proposal, and the two met to discuss the project on February 6. Pathé-Marconi would provide studios, engineers, and record-pressing and distribution services; Delaunay and the Hot Club would have a free hand in selecting artists and repertoire. Thus was born Swing, the first record label in the world loyal solely to jazz.

Delaunay's whole being became focused on the project. On a scrap of pa-per, he sketched out a design for the label's logo with a stylish Art Deco "S." He then named Panassié as Swing's artistic director, although he reserved ownership of the label for himself. In the short term, the arrangement with Panassié proved invaluable to Swing, as Panassié's connections aided the fledg-ling label in contracting musicians and licensing American sides. But in the long run, this relationship was doomed.

Delaunay began work as soon as the agreement was sealed. Coleman Hawkins was back in town, and Delaunay immediately organized a Hot Club concert at Salle Chopin-Pleyel on April 23, 1937. Yet both Delaunay and Panassié were hoping for more. They dropped hints to Hawkins that during his five-year sojourn in Europe, his recording legacy was lapsing and he boasted little of quality on disc to show for his prolific time away from home. So, on April 28 in the Studio Pathé, Hawkins tuned up with Django for a session. Yet this was not going to be just another routine jam with Hawkins blowing his sax in front of the Quintette. Delaunay and Panassié had a novel concept:

Alongside Hawkins, they lined up fellow American Benny Carter and the best French sax players, André Ekyan and Alix Combelle. Backing them were Django, Stéphane on piano, bassist d'Hellemmes, and African American drummer Tommy Benford.

Carter—back in Paris from London after his English work permit expired—was charged with creating arrangements for a handful of songs. In the end, he failed to come through, to Panassié's chagrin. So, settling down in the studio at nine in the evening, they began jamming on "Honeysuckle Rose," etching out an arrangement on the spot in half an hour with Hawkins and Combelle on tenors, Carter and Ekyan on altos. After running through the song several times, they made wax tests, the engineers having trouble balancing the sound of four horns around the single mic. Finally ready, the sax quartet jumped into the song, creating a master in just one take. The four saxes slid through the melody with the grace of a big band, their assorted timbres working together to form a perfect whole. Charging into the first chorus, Hawkins blazed away on an opening riff leading into a passionate solo. The song then wound up with a dialogue between saxes and Django's hot guitar. Yet these brief lines, as eloquent as they were, highlighted a persistent problem for Django: While he played his acoustic guitar with all the strength he could muster, it sounded thin next to the power of brass. It was as if he was playing pianissimo while the horns were swinging fortissimo. Still, it was a glorious take.

Yet by the time the quartet cut "Honeysuckle Rose," the night was growing old and they quickly recorded three standards to cap the session. "Crazy Rhythm" was played off the cuff, followed by a sultry "Out of Nowhere" and a raucous "Sweet Georgia Brown" that fell back on a New Orleans-style head before jumping ahead into swing solos. Behind the horns, Django strummed out his four-beat rhythm so forcefully his guitar resonated like a Dixieland banjo.

Delaunay was thrilled. He selected what he believed were the best tracks—"Honeysuckle Rose" and "Crazy Rhythm"—and released them on flip sides of Swing No. 1. The other two tracks he deemed unworthy of release, although Gramophone later issued them. With characteristic modesty, Hawkins dismissed the session, "The records are really just 'jam sessions,' nothing very musical." Delaunay disagreed—as did French, and later American, jazz aficionados. Delaunay would go on to release a formidable discography of Swing 78s, but Swing No.1 by Coleman Hawkins and his All-Star "Jam" Band remained the best-selling record ever issued by the label.

WITH HIS FIRST RELEASE, Delaunay established a reputation. Now, for Swing No. 2, he turned to a series of sessions with Django and the Quintette.

Following the strong sales of Decca's licensed Quintette recordings in England, the British arm of the Gramophone firm asked Bérard to produce 18 sides by Django and the band. Bérard sought Delaunay to organize the session. These recordings would be released on the English Gramophone label as well as His Master's Voice, featuring as its logo the famous white dog quizzically listening to the sound of his master's voice from the gramophone horn. Gramophone/HMV boasted a thorough distribution network throughout Europe and would prove to be essential to the success of Django and the Quintette in the coming years. And out of these sessions, Delaunay would save two select cuts for his own label.

As with many of Django's early sessions, the label dictated the material. On March 3, 1937, Gramophone/HMV sent a list to Bérard of 14 tunes as well as "two guitar solos from Django Reinhardt, choice of titles to be left to the artist." Panassié was outraged, as usual. "It was an annoying habit of record companies," he stated, "as if it were not better to leave to the interpreters a certain latitude in the choice of the morceaux they recorded. This forced musicians to interpret pieces they did not like, and the label was then astonished to have poor records, lacking inspiration." When he was read the list, Django grimaced. During recent gigs, he and the Quintette had developed more original compositions that he hoped to record. The label curtailed this, but offered a compromise: The list's most irksome songs could be replaced by Django's selections and with Delaunay's connivance, the song list was shuffled. Delaunay now scheduled the ensemble at the Pathé studio for the first of four sessions, starting on April 21 and continuing on April 22, 26, and 27.

While the Quintette may have been in danger of breaking apart, the sessions were magical. Django and Stéphane were backed by the rhythm section of Vola with Baro and Bianchi on guitars. Together, these two guitarists created the tightest, most propulsive, and at the same time most innovative *pompe* accompaniment of all the early Quintette recordings. Their rhythm drove Django and Stéphane to a complicity of new inspiration. Over the four sessions, the Quintette recorded 22 songs, only one of which was not issued. As usual, they ranged from covers of American jazz standards and pop tunes—such as a rousing "Rose Room," "Body and Soul," and "Ain't Misbehavin'"—to a handful of originals. Some songs were recorded smoothly, requiring just 15 minutes from wax tests to master. Others required well over half an hour to get right. Among the most troublesome was "Mystery Pacific," an original composition. It was a typical train tune, the type of imitation cut by jazz and blues bands everywhere during the railroad's heyday, but from Django the train ride was a tour de force. In "Mystery Pacific," the train starts out, gains speed, runs along the track, and then crashes—part of Django's childlike sense of humor. As Panassié remembered, "This piece, played at any pace, required virtuosity on behalf of the musicians, and it was sometimes one, sometimes the other that made a mistake during the execution. I don't know how many times they had to start this piece over, but at least the final wax was excellent." The song was fueled by Django's furious picking, in one chorus offering a gorgeous modulation of repeated phrases in ascending half-note intervals building tension that erupted in a stunning crescendo. Here, as in other songs throughout these sessions, he perfected his glissandos into thirty-second-note chromatic runs, translating the slides of Gypsy violinists into a trademark ornamentation.

On the other end of the spectrum was "Tears," based on an old Gypsy tune, "Muri wachsella an u sennelo weesch." Django fingerpicked the song, creating a mournful minor-major melody against a backdrop of descending harmonic chords that moved along like a New Orleans funeral parade. Django and Stéphane's interpretation was unique in jazz—a Gypsy song harmonized with jazzy diminished, minor sixth, and minor seventh chords, casting a dark mood, bittersweet and melancholy.

Django's powers of harmonization also shone on the Quintette's interpretation of Franz Liszt's "Liebestraum No. 3." Delaunay was fascinated by the relationship between classical music and jazz, and this was the first of several fusions he produced with Django and Stéphane. Here, Django harmonized Liszt's melody with the chords from "Basin Street Blues," the New Orleans jazz classic penned by Spencer Williams and made immortal by Armstrong. While HMV requested this song—no doubt at Delaunay's urging—the company directors surely never dreamed of this result.

The last pieces to be recorded were the two guitar solos requested by the label. The choice of these solos was left to Django, but when the time came, he didn't have any songs in mind—nor did he even want to make these recordings. As Panassié remembered: "Django did not want to fulfill this demand. He had never made recordings like this and did not know what to play. Finally, Delaunay said to him: 'You have only to improvise something, it will surely go well.' Django abruptly decided what to play and nodded to the engineers he was prepared. He asked me to take out my watch and signal to him when he was approaching the third minute of the recording, so he could ready himself to finish his interpretation at the appropriate time. And thus was recorded this admirable solo, entitled, justifiably, 'Improvisation,' which escaped from the frameworks of jazz and into the Andalusian Gitan spirit. Django was completely absorbed with the inspiration of the moment, launching out in a succession of phrases and harmonies, each more beautiful than the ones before. Standing two steps away from him, I attentively followed the movement of the second hand on my watch. Fifteen or 20 seconds before the three-minute mark, I raised my hand to signal Django he had to finish soon. Without outward emotion, he continued his improvisation a few more seconds and then brought it to a conclusion so logical I would have sworn he had it all studied and prepared. All of the people in the studio considered this improvisation so perfect they begged Django not to listen to this master [as it would ruin it for pressing], believing that he could never replay it so well. Django went along with our advice, and this small masterpiece was thus recorded in only one take." Forced on the spot to create an instant melody for his "Improvisation," Django dropped from jazz back into the mysticism of some of the first music he had ever heard or played—the Gitan sounds of the Midi.

From these sessions, Delaunay set aside two jewels to be issued as Swing No. 2, Django and the Quintette's "Charleston" and "Chicago." Far from Django's Gypsy meditation of "Improvisation," these songs were themes for dances then in vogue in the distant United States. Yet Django and Stéphane jammed on them as though their hearts beat to an American foxtrot rhythm.

FOR DJANGO, music—like life—was all one grand improvisation. He was renowned for his impromptu guitarwork, whether in his solos or in crafting compositions. In the studio as well, the song harmonies and arrangements he dictated to the Quintette were often on-the-spot improvisations.

To record this music, the first dilemma was to get Django to show up. Panassié listed the hazards in overcoming this deceptively easy stage: "It was never possible to assure we'd have Django's services. He always agreed to come, but it was folly to hope he'd arrive at the studio on time. Most of our sessions were in the morning between nine o'clock and noon. Django didn't go to bed until six or seven in the morning, and there was always the question of awakening him and then if he'd have the strength to quit his bed. I had to send someone to awaken him, but never before eight in the morning. He had to be awakened as gently as possible, and then Django would not want to budge. So, my envoy then went to the nearest café to fetch him a café crème and croissants. Django could then be enticed to sit up in bed to eat breakfast. This was the first step down the road to success. Then Django would ask for some music on the radio, and my friend would toy with the tuning dial to try and find music to please Django. Finally, after many yawns and every delay or excuse possible, he'd accept his fate and get up to do his toilette and dress. There was no question of hurrying him; everything was a compromise to his mood. At long last, he'd arrive at the studio at 10:15, and we'd have lost forty-five precious minutes—yet Django's playing was so good that he compensated for any time we lost."

Once in the studio, Django and the band needed to determine what to record. Whether the song list was set by the label, producer, or more rarely, left open to the band, one musician or another often needed to be taught the tune. Then, an arrangement had to be crafted. Django usually jumped into a song on the spur of the moment, directing each musician in his role. At times, he illustrated the harmonies for his accompanists by performing his pieces on guitar and then simply whistling the accompaniment for the band to learn their part. Django's later bassist, Coleridge Goode, was amazed at the unsophisticated way he worked in the studio and the novelty of his ingenuous approach to arrangements: "It was very difficult—almost impossible—to organize Django. . . . We didn't have any sort of pre-rehearsals; it was all put together in the studio. Stéphane and Django would decide what they were going to record, and then when we got to the studio, decide on who played what, when, and where. It was all head arrangements and such. But the musicians were good musicians, and this is what good musicians can do."

Ready to record, Django now had to cater to the engineer's needs. Recording was a black art rather than a science, and Panassié described in detail the trials of Django's recording sessions of the day: "The engineers must find the ideal sonic placement for each instrumentalist around the single mic, which is not easy as every band has its particular sound balance. Once the musicians are placed, the engineers listen to them from the control room. Contrary to the sound in the studio, the engineers can hear the musicians through the mic, as one will hear them on the disc. While the musicians warm up, the engineers move them around to the best spots in relation to the mic based on the first test. Then, the musicians must play the piece in its entirety while the engineers judge whether it is the desired length: It must last at least two and a half minutes but less than three minutes twenty seconds for twenty-five-centimeter 78rpm discs. The engineers also examine whether the band must play a passage fortissimo or pianissimo for sound quality. Therefore, the abundant improvisation in jazz is an additional difficulty for the engineers as they will never be able to plan completely for what will occur during a take. A saxophonist who played a soft solo during the first test might play with more force during the second, modifying the sound. Moreover, the musicians must approach the mic when they're preparing to solo. But they do not always go to the exact place assigned them. Sometimes it is necessary to set on the ground a handkerchief or some other object indicating the place where they must stand."

Since they were improvising, each new take almost always differed from the one before, either in whole or in details. As one of his later bassists, Pierre Michelot, remembered of Django's sessions, "When he set down a second take, it was truly a second song because it departed so completely from the first that it was a different piece."

Not surprisingly, Stéphane's approach to recording was solemn and serious—sometimes too serious, and he needed a bit of artificial inspiration to oil his playing. As Panassié remembered cutting the Gramophone/HMV sides, "During the sessions, Stéphane was 'supported' by frequent absorption of glasses of Cinzano, one of his preferred aperitifs. There was a bistrot next door to the studio, and one of his friends marched back and forth unceasingly, carrying fresh glasses of Cinzano. In the end, it was more convenient to buy a bottle. It was set on the piano and Stéphane could serve himself his frequent glassfuls. While he had a good many glasses, he was never drunk and I never saw him lose control of himself. At most, he was a little merry toward the end of the last session, when he said to me with his Parisian street accent: 'I must send a letter of thanks to Monsieur Cinzano.'"

For Django, recording was like painting, the studio his atelier and the wax discs canvases upon which to create. Panassié described this artistic process with astonishment: "Django recorded with great esprit. He dashed off the most daring improvisations and completely modified his solos from one test to another. You had to see him listening to the wax tests: When he heard one of his own lightning-like phrases, he leaped up, stupefied, crying with joy—a child astonished at his own brilliant exploits." The engineers were amazed by Django's pleasure. Most bands were concentrated and serious when they recorded, listening to their wax tests with a concerned air, endeavoring to tighten their interpretation until they considered it perfect. With Django, each wax test was a new song played with spontaneity and he intensely lived each phrase, each note. As Panassié remembered, "Django's joyous outbursts after hearing some of his phrases were not of pride or conceit: Django listened as though it was another musician—he didn't know that he was capable of this, he was sincerely amazed when he heard the phrases that he had played. He played them without planning them; they had come from some unknowable region of his subconscious. Listening, he laughed and repeated his favorite expressions: '*Oh, ma mère!*' or '*C'est n'est pas possible!*'"

"WITH MY GUITAR in my hands," Django once said, "I am not afraid of anyone—neither the Pope nor the President of the United States." Without his guitar, he was a humble man, at times even timid. His aloofness and cool demeanor were masks, shielding his shyness, hiding his identity as an outsider in the *gadjo* world. He rarely uttered a word when he was not among friends; as Soudieux remembered, "Django never spoke in public. He didn't dare open his mouth." On stage, he would never dare speak, and one bandmate likened him to Harpo Marx. Romany remained his first language and he never spoke French perfectly, retaining his Manouche accent as well as a slight lisp. When asked questions by radio interviewers or journalists, he was strictly a yes and no man, rarely explaining himself, never effusive. Yet with his guitar, he was a different person. His guitar joked and jested, laughed and cried; it was serious and sublime, eloquent and heartrending. As a Gypsy he had long learned to hide his feelings and fears from the *gadjé*, but in his music he played in phrases like torrents, an outpouring of emotion. With his guitar in his hands, he was pure poetry.

Django's lack of education and illiteracy remained an embarrassment to him. He eschewed the métro as he couldn't read the station signs, pretended to read menus and contracts—all the games an illiterate person plays to hide his shame. And most amazing of all, Django never became a member of the French Société des Auteurs, Compositeurs et Éditeurs de Musique simply because he couldn't pass the vaunted union's written test.

Stéphane, his greatest friend and fiercest enemy, taught Django the basics of spelling in the long hours they spent together between shows and on tours. "There was a chink in his armour," Stéphane said. "Sometimes he was intimidated because of his lack of formal education, though you had to know him well to discern this. As you would expect, he was not keen on people knowing that he could neither read nor write. In the first days of the Quintette he was often shown a contract which he would eye for some time before nodding his acceptance. He was not a man who found it easy to ask advice, and he would sometimes okay an offer without even showing it to me. That was one reason why we had a few catastrophes at the beginning. Later on most of the letters came to me, and I tried to arrange the work for the group. Even so, two signatures were needed, and after a time I said: 'Look, Django, when we sign a contract it is miserable for you having to put a cross.' (It was a funny cross too.) 'I think it will look brighter if you sign your name.' At once he was enthusiastic to learn—so long as we kept it a secret—and I began showing him the letters of the alphabet. As it was a difficult matter for him, I taught him just the capitals. I will not say that I taught him to write; but I certainly showed him how to sign his name. We began, naturally enough, with 'Django,' and took so long on the word that I said: 'Never mind the 'Django'—'D' will do just as well.' At first he was insistent on the whole name; he really liked the name Django, said it sounded nice (he never liked me to call him Reinhardt, always Django). Finally, he got tired, too, and agreed with me that 'D' would do. That was all right. The great job came when we started on 'Reinhardt.' It is a complicated name and spelling meant nothing to Django anyway. Still, he was a painter who could remember a shape, and at last he got it. Once he had, there was not enough paper in the room to satisfy him. Everywhere I looked I saw 'D. Reinhardt.' It was a relief, because few things were ever more difficult than getting that man to sign his name. And it was worth the effort, because in his face I saw such pleasure."

Still, signing his name was a struggle. To hide this indignity, Django often merely wrote a "D" and an "R" followed by a long squiggle. And when he had to sign a hotel ledger, he usually commanded one of his bandmates such as Soudieux to do it for him.

Following his first spelling lessons, Django now began to sound out words and write a purely phonetic French. Stéphane remembered his progress: "He regularly asked, in odd moments at the theatre, how he should put certain sounds down on paper. Correct spelling did not worry him, but he was interested in being able to write phonetically. '*Dis, Grappelly,*' he would say, 'what does so-and-so mean?' 'How would you write this down?'" Just as he improvised music, Django was improvising spelling.

Now, when fans pressed him for an autograph, Django was happy to oblige. But learning to sign his name caused new problems. After playing a gala at the Scheveningen Kurzaal during a Dutch tour in July 1937, Django was besieged in the theater hallway by hundreds of fans. As it was so difficult for him to sign his name, he was writing out autographs for more than an hour before he made good his escape.

DURING 1937, Django labored during much of his days in the confines of the recording studio. Yet his nights were spent among high society in the most celebrated cabarets of Paris. Django and the Quintette's novel string jazz—too *modernistique* when first played only a few years before—was now the rage. Throughout the year, the band was in demand, performing night after night.

The City of Light was infamous for its nightclubs: some catered to homosexuals, some were renowned for their music, others were known for their food, and many were known for their women. Yet Parisian society was famed for its fickleness and nightclubs came and went like meteors through the skies. One month, a new cabaret would overflow with crowds. The next, it was the haunt of ghosts.

And then there were the entertainers. The street singer that looked like a starveling sparrow, Edith Piaf. Ménilmontant's Maurice Chevalier, who made it big with a straw hat and a song. Mistinguett, who refused to sing a song in a minor key as she feared it made her face sag. At Chez Florence, the crowds came to see African American singer Florence Embry Jones, dressed each night in a skin-tight evening gown of gold, her head crowned by sprays of orchids. Poet Langston Hughes, who washed dishes in the kitchen, described her as a glorious tigress, "a brownskin princess, remote as a million dollars."

Django played all the best cabarets. Following the New Year's revolt of Nin-Nin, the Quintette performed a long stand at the Don Juan, a short-lived Montmartre club owned by Charlie Chaplin's former wife, Lila Gray. Starting in May and running for two months, Django held forth at Bricktop's The Big Apple in Pigalle. Bricktop was Ada Beatrice Queen Victoria Louise Virginia Smith, a sparkplug of an African American woman, her mustard-colored skin topped by the frazzle of brick-red hair that inspired her nickname. It was reliably reported her singing could take 20 years off a man's life. At The Big Apple, the party lasted until dawn—and often beyond. Bricktop was fond of Django and he of her. He dispensed with her usual nickname and affectionately christened her Minou—Pussycat. As Bricktop described Django: "He was already famous when he came to work for me. At least, he was famous for being hard to work with. When I told friends I was going to hire him, they said, 'Bricky, you're out of your mind. If he doesn't like the color of your dress, he'll walk out. If he doesn't like the way a client is looking at him, he'll walk out.' As a matter of fact, Django did walk out on me twice. Once he had to go bail out a gypsy gal who'd gotten arrested, and the other time he had a toothache! . . . when people asked why he worked so well with me and was so temperamental with everyone else, he'd flash a spectacular smile and say, 'Because she's a girl and has nice surroundings.'" At The Big Apple, the Quintette often accompanied African American singer Mabel Mercer, another one of Django's favorite singers, for whom he later named his composition "Mabel."

After playing his regular gig, Django usually ended the night at the Pigalle club Swing Time, run by Ekyan. Here, the musicians played until daybreak. Combelle recounted the impromptu sessions in spring 1937: "When the last customers left and the doors were locked, we'd start to play. . . . These were real jam sessions. They were not fake ones, set up to please someone, or to try to recreate something. At these jams, we were really creating something. It was a jam session like you just don't have anymore. . . . We weren't out to cut each other, only to create the best possible ambiance, in a sincere and pure spirit. There was one evening when our jam session was truly extraordinary. I'd been playing for about an hour and had stopped . . . because I was enjoying myself more listening than I was playing. It was going like a bomb! It was simply incredible! Each player was in their best form. The atmosphere was amazing. And everything was a success, as sometimes happens only once in an artist's life. I know that for me, that session just couldn't have been better. I'll never forget it. At last, Django was the strongest of us all. I remember that at one point they began to play a pop number—the young musicians play it today as a classic—'I Won't Dance.' It's a tune that modulates incessantly and is very difficult. They'd chosen it just to see how far each of them could go with it. They were amusing themselves playing it in a variety of different keys. And I remember quite clearly that Bill Coleman was the first to give up. It was fantastic! After Bill, it was Hawkins. Only Benny Carter and Django were left. Benny played in almost every key with typical relaxation, without once giving in. But Django was indifferent to the key: He played just as well in any key without once making a mistake. He was truly unbeatable. In the end, we all took our hats off to him that night. A general outburst of laughter hailed his exploits. It was just beyond us. What was so unusual about Django was that he just couldn't play out of tune or stumble in any way. Music came naturally to him. The right notes and the right chords seemed to fall naturally from his fingers."

In July, Django and band embarked on their second foreign tour, traveling to the Netherlands. They played concerts in Den Hague and Amsterdam, where they jammed with Hawkins, Carter, and Freddy Johnson. In autumn 1937, Django and the band played a long stand at the Casanova, then headlined a Hot Club concert at the Salle Gaveau on October 20 before a packed house of 1,100 people. An American fan described the show: "While playing, Django, who always seems to have a broad grin on his face, sways from side to side, keeping time as it were to the infectious rhythm. Grappelly, looking very smooth and suave cocks his heads to one side, and smilingly lures forth bewitching melodies from his singing violin; the plump Vola contentedly plucks away on his sonorous bass, while Joseph Rheinhardt [*sic*] and Ferret, with absolutely expressionless faces, plunk out a most solid rhythmic background on their guitars. Each number was received with prolonged applause. The smoothest and most elegant, and yet one of the very hottest treatments of *Tiger Rag* I have ever heard was included during which the entire audience rose to its feet, loudly cheering." Panassié christened the show simply "the finest jazz concert I've ever attended." Afterward, the band left for Belgium where they performed on October 30 at the Brussels Palais des Beaux-Arts sponsored by Le Jazz Club de Belgique. From there, they returned to the Netherlands, where their earlier tour had won them fans. By November 7, they were back in Den Hague as guest stars at a Dutch amateur jazz contest, Stéphane serving as judge. When the Flanders tour reached its finale, Django and the Quintette reluctantly returned to Paris. Delaunay reported they spent all their pay enjoying themselves during their travels: "Our prodigals were broke as usual without a sou in their pockets, trying in vain to work out how they had spent so much money on a few days' holiday."

For Django, it was all a moveable feast eaten during a life on the move.

THE NIGHTCLUBS of Paris also offered a nocturnal world of various other vices. From wormwood-spiked absinthe that was readily available in many cafés to cocaine that was only slightly more difficult to procure, the pleasures were there for the seekers. Opium dens awaited in back alleyways, ether could be procured from disreputable pharmacies. But marijuana and hashish were the fetish of choice among many jazzmen. With French colonies in Indochina, a steady supply of the miracle leaf was plentiful, and as early as 1835 the Club des hashichines was founded in the capital, Baudelaire poeticizing its praise.

On November 25, 1937, Django and the Quintette recorded a tune titled "Viper's Dream," a slinky and sinuous jazz stroll, a melody so moody it was almost a caricature of jazz. Yet this was not simply another sublime theme; it was what was known fondly among American jazz musicians as a reefer song. *Viper* was Jazz Age slang for a smoker of marijuana, and the song's composer, Fletcher Allen, was a prolific viper—as were Louis Armstrong, Cab Calloway, Freddy Taylor, Charlie Christian, and many other American jazzmen. Violinist Stuff Smith waxed "You'se a Viper" in 1936; Sidney Bechet recorded "Viper Mad" in 1938; even Benny Goodman cut "Texas Tea Party" in 1933. And Fats Waller—when he wasn't singing about "Ain't Misbehavin'"—composed his own "Viper's Drag" in 1934, featuring the joyful lyrics, "The sky is high and so am I."

Marijuana empowered jazz from the beginning, and it was little wonder that it also now fueled jam sessions on French bandstands. Yet to some, these roots of jazz were too much. In its 1936 exposé "Dope Cigarette Peddling Among British Musicians," the prim *Melody Maker* reported with puritanical outrage, "The time has come for light to be thrown on an astonishing situation which is likely to become a serious menace to the jazz world on two continents. This concerns the 'reefer' or dope habit which is spreading rapidly amongst musicians, and has been going on comparatively secretly for a number of years." Intrepidly tracing the marijuana plague from New Orleans to Chicago to New York and then across the ocean, the magazine blamed it all on a certain unnamed "celebrated hot clarinettist" who "has sent supplies to coloured musicians touring Europe." This was undoubtedly Mezz Mezzrow, who proudly admitted his reefer habit: "To us a muggle [a marijuana cigarette] wasn't any more dangerous or habit-forming than those other great American vices, the five-cent Coke and the ice-cream cone, only it gave you more kicks for your money." Yet to condemn Mezzrow alone simply showed how out of touch *Melody Maker* was with the real jazz world. As Bill Coleman told of the jazzman's life in picturesque Paris: "Freddie 'Snake Hips' Taylor and I lived in the same hotel and Freddie was hip to gage, as marijuana or reefers were called. I went to Freddie's room and it would be like walking into a London fog. The windows were closed and reefer smoke would be so thick that you could cut it with a knife." Quintette bassist Soudieux served as tour guide to visiting American musicians, driving around the capital in his automobile with the marijuana smoke so dense they could hardly see out the windows to view the Tour Eiffel or other sights. Soudieux summed up the times succinctly: "All the American musicians smoked marijuana."

"Viper's Dream" was a hazy jazz ode to marijuana, followed by Allen's "Blue Drag," another reefer song waxed by Django and the Quintette in April 1935. Yet while he recorded inspired versions of these two reefer songs, alcohol and marijuana were never essential influences on Django's music nor a needed freedom to allow him to improvise. Django certainly was no prude, yet he typically drank little—only the odd aperitif and the usual wine at dinner, less than most every French person around him. He was never known as an over-indulger, which made him stand out in the jazz milieu in which he lived. And he was certainly not a viper, as marijuana and drugs in general were taboos for the Manouche. Django likely chose to wax "Viper's Dream" and "Blue Drag" due to their catchy melodies, and the meaning of the titles was probably lost in translation. As Stéphane stated, "Music was enough for us— we'd often get drunk with it."

IN AUTUMN 1937, the Exposition Internationale opened its doors in Paris and some 34 million people rushed to see with their own eyes the latest advances of civilization. The Tour Eiffel was lit from toe to top, a "televisor" set turned on, the Palace du Réfrigération displayed the glories of the latest household invention, and the Spanish pavilion unveiled Picasso's *Guernica*—a warning to the world even as Nazi flags flew before the German Pavillion and red banners before the Soviets'. For jazz fans, there was just one reason to visit, and it was not to see the refrigerator: The Exposition heralded the return of violinist Eddie South to his beloved France, and Django was soon back at the side of his favorite violinist. South's first performance was at the Club aux Oiseaux—a birder's group—in the Exposition's Pavillon de l'Élégance. Panassié also hurried to hear South, but the Club aux Oiseaux was a better spot for bird calls than jazz; he had to wait impatiently until they could rendezvous that evening in a Pigalle bistro to discuss a recording session.

Wasting no time, Panassié and Delaunay escorted South into the studio with Django on September 29, and this series of recordings became the pinnacle of South's career. As Panassié stated, "South had an admiration for Django that knew no bounds. I was accustomed to the admiration the blacks had for Django, but South exceeded most of the others. Or rather, it was not admiration: Eddie was, one could say, musically in love with Django. . . . I even believe that South was jealous of Grappelli's position with Django in the Quintette." As Delaunay stated simply, "In the presence of Django, Eddie South played like he never played before or after."

In a simple trio with just Django and bassist Wilson Myers, South crafted a sentimental blues improvisation. Django's accompaniment was stately. He offered solid blues chords with off-beat strides and jazz-inflected turnarounds that were innovative and evocative. Django likely learned to play the blues from American recordings—perhaps Lonnie Johnson's 1928 and 1929 duets with Eddie Lang, who played in disguise as Blind Willie Dunn. South also may have taught him these simple yet stylish accompaniments. Or he may have intuitively created the harmonies, hitting on the blue notes by ear.

This blues was followed by a laidback take of "Sweet Georgia Brown." South performed with fluidity and fluency, accenting his bowed riffs with pizzicato exclamation points. As French trombonist Léo Vauchant remembered of South's playing in Paris clubs at the time, "He could play a fast tune but he didn't like it. He liked to expose the real beauty of a tune and whatever notes he added were just gems. . . . Eddie South concentrated on the beauty of tone and the feeling—never went for the tricky stuff." This time, South was thrilled by the take, exclaiming, "That's a ride, man!" Panassié had to decipher this for an inquisitive Django: "*Ça, mes amis, c'est une promenade!*" Something didn't quite swing in translation.

Against South's wishes but at Panassié's insistence, South then joined Stéphane and Michel Warlop in a violin trio on "Lady Be Good" and duets with Stéphane on "Dinah" and Django's "Daphné." Django composed this melody while listening to Stéphane tune his violin in octaves and named it for a mutual English friend, Daphné de Stafford. This simple yet sweet melody became one of his most enduring themes.

An experiment of Delaunay's capped the South sessions. Delaunay explained his vision: "The idea came to me from hearing how the jazz improvisations resembled certain pieces of baroque music, notably those of Johann Sebastian Bach." Now, he sought to record a jazz improvisation based on Bach's Concerto in D Minor. South thought the idea ridiculous. Grappelli was noncommittal but willing to play the piece for pay. Django, though, was intrigued. As he couldn't read the score, Delaunay loaned him copies of the recording by Yehudi Menuhin and Georges Enesco, and Django transcribed a harmonic accompaniment by ear. Django always loved Bach: "The harmonies, that's what I love best in music—this is the mother of all music," Django said. "And that's why I love Johann Sebastian Bach: the harmony is the foundation of all his music." Now, here was Django's opportunity to play Bach.

Django was eager when the second session started on November 23. Delaunay passed out copies of the score to South and Grappelli, dictating his arrangement: Django would introduce the song with several measures from Louis Armstrong's "Mahogany Hall Stomp," then the violins would quote Bach's theme before launching into improvisations. Yet things did not transpire as Delaunay envisioned: "The violinists were very reserved, as if they were afraid of committing a crime of high treason. . . . I asked the two violinists to play improvisations simultaneously as freely as possible yet remaining faithful to the original music. For the first take, at the moment where the two soloists should have abandoned the sheet music, South and Grappelli continued to read and play from the music despite all my gesticulations." Panassié agreed: "We listened to several more wax tests but none of them satisfied anybody. A long parlay took place between the musicians and Delaunay. The clock ticked over another hour, and the engineers pushed us to finish as they were eager to go to lunch. A last test was made, and the musicians played with great swing but without deviating notably from the theme. We decided to keep this wax but to return later to record another version; we could then choose the best to release."

Django and the Quintette were booked to record again on November 25, and Delaunay took the opportunity to bring South back to the studio to revive his experiment before South bid adieu for the United States. This time, after Grappelli and South played Bach's theme, Delaunay stole the scores away from their stands, leaving them no choice but to continue on their own. This time, the results were better. In the end, the two takes were released back to back as Swing No. 18, the straight version entitled "Interprétation Swing du 1er Mouvement du Concerto en Ré Mineur de J. S. Bach," the second as an "Improvisation."

The record was unique in jazz at the time. Just as Delaunay's father and mother painted modern art with an eye on the past, Delaunay heard the roots of jazz in baroque music. With these swing versions of Bach, he conducted his small orchestra in turning his philosophy into music. And while the "Interprétation Swing" and "Improvisation" may not have lived up to the full grandeur of his vision, they were Delaunay's masterpieces as a producer.

AT THE END OF AUTUMN 1937 Django laid down in wax two minor master-pieces that were the high points of his prolific year. He was in the recording studio throughout the fall, playing in 11 different sessions, resulting in 42 released sides. Among these, two originals stood out—"Minor Swing," from November 25, and "Boléro," from December 14. Both were produced by Delaunay: "Minor Swing" was released on Swing No. 23; "Boléro" licensed to La Voix de son Maitre. These two tunes were extremes of Django's varied compositional skills. "Minor Swing" was an unadorned and unaffected jazz melody, a hot riff like Armstrong might have blown. "Boléro" was based on Spanish Gitan rhythms and harmonies yet orchestrated with all the grace of an Ellington arrangement. As such, it was a key song in Django's compositional development.

The melody to "Minor Swing" was sweet and simple. Based on repeated ascending phrases climbing from the root to the minor third to the fifth in the I, IV, and V chords in the key of A minor, nothing could be more basic. Yet Django and the Quintette imbued it with an infectious swing that resonated from the record. It would become one of Django's most covered compositions, a jazz classic, and a Gypsy anthem played around caravan campfires throughout Europe.

On this premiere recording of "Minor Swing," Django was backed by the return of Nin-Nin alongside Ninine Vées. Grappelli's violin sometimes sounded thin—a fault of his propensity to buy cheap violins to save money—yet his lines were lithe with a swing no other violinist could match. Above all, the tune was a tour de force of Django's guitarwork. In this one recording, he flaunted his wealth of licks and tricks. From the start, he played his solo lines over the changes, syncopating his phrasing. He then interspersed deft chord-melody solos into his single-note lines. Jumping into a glissando chromatic run descending from the tip of his guitar's fretboard to the headstock, his two fingers flitted across the neighboring strings before climbing back up the fretboard in a diagonally running diminished arpeggio, ending with ringing riffs of octave chimes. It was a bravura performance, so hot that even his bandmates cheered on the master take when finished.

"Boléro" was an opposite to "Minor Swing." Whereas the swing tune was pure improvisation, "Boléro" was an orchestral piece, carefully conducted to create a mood. While the tight unit of the Quintette recorded the jazz tune, "Boléro" featured the ensemble backed by a small orchestra of three trumpets, two trombones, a flute, and three violins—yet without Stéphane. Django not only composed the piece but arranged it as well. He could hear in his head the multilayered sound he sought, then played on his guitar the melody and various harmonies for the others to reproduce.

Django began the song quoting the rhythmic figure of Maurice Ravel's *Boléro*. The horns then made their entrance playing a mournful melody modulating in ascending half-steps, building tension and anticipation resolved in a flurry of majestic guitar riffs. Underlying the theme, Django's harmony was expressed in the Phrygian mode with its flatted second notes and foundation of ninth chords, some with the addition of sixth notes, creating a flamenco overtone.

In composing "Boléro," Django paid homage to the Gitan music of his child-hood yet was also influenced by the impressionist modal music of Ravel and Debussy, all conducted with Ellington's sophistication. After Bach, Debussy and Ravel were Django's favored composers; they were near-contemporaries of Django and also thoroughly *modernistique*. Stéphane remembered going to a classical concert with Django: "He liked great things. And I believe he expe-rienced them in the way they should be experienced. To see his expression in the glorious church of St. Eustache in Paris, hearing for the first time the Berlioz *Requiem*, was to see a person in ecstasy." Ellington too had long been a favorite of Django's. Only Ellington could compose a gutbucket blues tune like "East St. Louis Toodle-Oo" and orchestrate it into elegance. Django heard Ellington's records as early as 1930, but now perhaps for the first time Django had the experience and skill to fulfill the concepts of jazz that Ellington's music opened to him. Yet despite the varied influences and hom-age paid, in the end, "Boléro" was all Django.

"Boléro" ran almost four minutes and thus did not fit on a standard 78. Gramophone was forced to release it on a 25-centimeter 78rpm record, usually reserved for serious classical music. Panassié was prolific in praising Django's composition. Describing the Quintette's Hot Club concert at the Salle Gaveau on October 20 where Django played the song, he wrote: "How am I to express all the enthusiasm I felt for Django's fantastic 'Boléro.' . . . He is not only a wonderful soloist and accompanist; he is also a very great composer."

"Minor Swing" was pure jazz, but "Boléro" unveiled something more. Django had begun 1937 in jail, spent much of the rest of the year in recording studios and cabarets. He ended it on a high note. "Boléro" displayed ambition beyond jazz, beyond flamenco improvisations, beyond swing interpretations of Bach. It displayed a desire to create music without boundaries.

8

Ruling Britannia
1938–1939

THE SHOWS WERE VAUDEVILLE, pure and simple. The curtains at the English music halls opened for a ventriloquist or burlesque dancer, conjurer or comedian. Once the preliminary acts ended, the rollicking laughter died down. The lights dimmed again and the curtains closed as the audience waited with an expectant hush. The vaudeville was over; the main attraction was anon. From behind the curtains came the first rippling of notes, a guitar with a golden tone creating sounds that glittered through the darkness like stardust. Two other guitars joined in, building a solid, swinging beat. Then came the sound of a violin, soaring above. The red-velvet curtains glided apart and there, grouped center stage, was Django with his Quintette arrayed about him. He sat on a raised dais and made his guitar speak like a ventriloquist, juggling notes in midair, making music like a magician.

One fan remembered a night of the English vaudeville tour in a breathless rush: "A great roar of applause surges from the audience—drowns the music for a moment—and subsides as the jazz *aficionados* of Lancashire settle down to hear the music of their idol—*Django Reinhardt*—the myth; the unbeliev-able and unforgettable; the enigma—a Gallic gypsy mystery. The legend-in-his-time has come to town! [He is] a casual, swarthy, figure hunched over a Macaferri [*sic*] guitar from which pours with an effortless fluency a cascade of rhythmic and incredibly melodious improvisations. There against the contrast-ing background of the elegant slim, white-jacketed standing figure of the vio-linist, Stephane Grappelly, sits this little, rather nondescript looking, figure—dress trousers hoisted carelessly up to reveal a bare leg above the top of a sock; feet clad in what looks like street boots. The legend comes to life; the myth embodied at last to a waiting breathless audiences of devotees. The first number finishes in a roar of adulation (you think: 'Applaud: clap until your hands are sore. He *must* play again, before we wake up, or before he disappears again behind that screen of mysterious anonymity'). Nonchalantly— incredibly nonchalantly—the little French gypsy acknowledges the plaudits with a slight, wry, whimsical half-smile—and sweeps into another number— 'Limehouse Blues' this time—lifted along by the solid, tramping four-in-a-bar of the two other guitars and the deep rubbery thump of a plucked bass. The violin plays the first chorus 'straight', with a cool dispassionate, almost Oriental tone, followed by an incredible virtuoso improvisation—and then it is Django again! Chromatic runs bubbling up from the bass and streaming up, unbroken, through three octaves; great chunky solid mounting sequences of octaves that bring the audience out of their seats; lingering, liquid and tender blue notes of a gypsy pouring out his soul through the negro medium of Jazz! We still cannot believe it!"

Django and the Quintette became known in Paris among jazz fans and cabaret goers, perhaps reaching the pinnacle of fame possible for their music at the time. But on their arrival in England in January 1938, the ensemble found a new, broader audience. They toured the country playing vaudeville stages and music-hall theaters, recorded in English studios for English labels, were filmed for the silver screen, and performed over radio and the new-fangled televisor. They were heralded by music magazines and praised by newspapers, who picked up and repeated Django's Gypsy story like a fairy tale come to life, the child prodigy overcoming grave disaster and herculean tasks to become a genius.

In Britain, Django, Stéphane, and the Quintette became famous.

DJANGO AND THE QUINTETTE's recordings were first championed in London by a dusty little recording studio and record shop called Sound Studios. As early as 1935, owner Morris Levy imported Django's French pressings and played them for fellow aficionados, who passed the word by mouth and through the jazz journals about this Gypsy. Levy later licensed recordings for release on his Oriole label and attempted to organize a Quintette tour of Great Britain in autumn 1935. *Jazz-Tango-Dancing* proudly noted the renown the Quintette was winning in England: "Rare are the records of French jazz that are published in England, but even more rare are those that receive a favorable welcome."

Following Levy's lead, the English Decca label began licensing Quintette recordings, then Gramophone/HMV in an escalating battle for rights to the ensemble. After several failures to organize English concerts, *Melody Maker* magazine and M.P.M. Entertainments finally arranged the debut of Django and the Quintette with their first concert on Sunday, January 30, 1938. The ensemble headlined the gala Swing Music Concert For Musicians at London's Cambridge Theatre. Sharing the bill were an array of musical acts, including

Claude Bampton's Blind Orchestra featuring pianist George Shearing. In anticipation of Django's first appearance in England, the concert was sold out.

Django did not disappoint. As a fan described the ensemble in *Melody Maker*: "The Quintet is curiously static as it plays. The three guitarists, sitting in a widely spaced line with Django in the centre, hardly bat an eyelid. The maestro occasionally cocks an eyebrow in concentration or permits an enigmatic smile to pass across his face, but, except for an almost imperceptible rocking, there is no movement, no showmanship, no gallery play whatsoever. Grappelly, standing, works to the mike with great skill and experience. Unobtrusively he moves to the flank when he is tacit, a polished, good-looking grave-faced sort of fellow who plays like an angel. Louis Vola, the bassist, was a personal hit with the spectators. Once or twice he amused them with a little byplay, but he had already endeared himself to all by his beautiful tone and technique. . . . Credit to both Vees and Chaput, the two other guitarists, self-effacing machines who never take a solo bar but who provide a foundation for their two principles, which is uncanny in its accuracy, aptness and understanding." The magazine could hardly have been more effusive in raving for its own show.

Following the concert, Django and the Quintette recorded at Decca's London studio. In sessions on January 31 and February 1, 1938, they cut a prolific 12 sides for release. Photographs of the session show the five musicians grouped around the single mic, Vées and Chaput—smoking a cigarette as he plays—seated to downplay their rhythm guitars in the mix, Django and Grappelli standing, while a bored Naguine watches. The Quintette recorded a transcendent version of Cole Porter's "Night and Day" in a graceful swinging mood. The session was noteworthy for the flurry of original compositions they waxed—"Souvenirs," "Black and White," "Stompin' at Decca," and the sublimely sweet "Daphné." These originals were all credited to both Django and Grappelli but were likely Django's compositions notated for copyright by Grappelli; as was common practice at the time, the two were often listed as shared authors. But during a take of Hoagy Carmichael's "My Sweet," the session erupted into laughter after Django introduced Vola halfway through the song in a slip of the foreign tongue, "Would Monsieur Solo like to take a Vola?"

When Django traveled to London with Jean Sablon in April 1934, he had been terrified to fly or take the ferry. This time, he was an old hand at crossing the Channel, and the Quintette took the boat without mishap. But traveling around London and staying in the luxurious hotels was another matter for the Romany entourage. Stéphane was constantly forced into the role of etiquette instructor, teaching Django lessons in manners, from common courtesy to explaining which fork to use with which course. Getting into elevators, Stéphane would nudge Django and hiss at him to remove his raven-black fedora as there were ladies present. It was the first time Django's cousin Ninine Vées ventured far into the civilized world from the safety of his caravan. He wandered around London lost, wearing his grand Gypsy hat topping off his swarthy face that seemed in perennial need of a shave. They were booked into the swank Regent Palace Hotel off Piccadilly Circus, and Delaunay remembered the confusion wrought on Vées by staying at a hotel: "Completely out of his element in these strange surroundings, he delighted the rest of the band, who were vastly amused to see how ill at ease he was in the elevators or swing doors. They found it hard to contain their mirth when they saw the smartly attired staff terrified by this sorrowful rustic, who would wander round the corridors for hours on end searching for his room. Because he did not know a word of English and was unable to read anyway, the hundreds of numbers he saw on the doors were insoluble enigmas. . . . When he stood near well-dressed British gentlemen they recoiled in horror and carefully made room for him in the elevators, though the poor wretch had no idea what floor he needed." Django, on the other hand, giggled at the silliness of his luxurious surroundings. He spent his days idly dozing in bed and amusing himself by ringing for the maid, only to laugh at her horrified looks at finding him half naked in bed. In the afternoons, he mysteriously disappeared, only to rejoin his bandmates at the restaurant Gennaro's in the evening. Where he went no one knew—until several days later when one of his armoire drawers was discovered full of cigarette packets. Opening further drawers, they too were stuffed with yet more cigarettes. Django explained: He had found an amusement arcade nearby with games of skill and chance, and his famous deftness of hand enabled him to win a packet of cigarettes almost every time. Amid the glories of London, there could be no greater thrill for Django.

Despite the good music and good times, the tour ended on a sour note. The Quintette was still not a lucrative enterprise—especially for the sidemen— and after the Cambridge Theatre concert, Grappelli pocketed what others felt was more than his share of the take. Chaput challenged him, demanding a fairer accounting. Grappelli turned cold in his refusal. Chaput had had enough. He swung and punched Grappelli in the nose, turned on his heel and with that, Roger Chaput said good-bye to the Quintette forever.

DJANGO AND THE QUINTETTE were performing one night in 1936 at Bricktop's when a towering figure approached Django between songs, pulled his monstrous cigar from between his lips, and asked for the Quintette's "businessman." Not understanding a word of English, Django pointed him to Stéphane.

The man with the cigar was Lew Grade, a former Cossack dancer turned impresario. Born near Odessa in 1911, his Jewish parents fled to England before the pogroms and revolution caught up to them. Grade had been Louis Winogradsky, but in the new world he took a new name. Growing up athletic and strong, he danced the *kaztatzke* and other Russian dances before being crowned by Fred Astaire as the World Charleston Champion in 1926. But by 1934, his knees were worn out and he became an agent, joining forces to create the Will Collins & Lew Grade Theatrical & Vaudeville Exchange. Now he was in Paris seeking acts to represent in England. Hearing of the Quintette, he sought them out at Bricktop's. With Stéphane serving as the band's impromptu "businessman," a deal was agreed to over a drink to tour the Quintette through Britain.

A contract was eventually negotiated between Grade and Parisian agents the Marouani brothers. When it was time to sign, Stéphane advised Django to follow his lead: "I said to Django, 'Listen, Django . . . I will show you the paper, and when I'm reading, if I said OK, remember: OK. I'll give you the paper and you say OK. Understand?'" Stéphane read through the contract and everything was proper. He signaled Django with a simple, "OK." But Django, embarrassed by his illiteracy and put out at not being the business-man, did not follow the plan. He studiously examined the contract he could not read, then pointed to an indistinct paragraph and indignantly said, "I don't like this!" Turmoil broke the negotiations apart, until Stéphane could read the clause that upset Django: It promised the band all expenses paid for round trip first class travel. Stéphane quickly told Django to shut his mouth.

Before the Quintette set sail for England, Grade lined them up with a British female singer under his management. Django and band were playing at Paris's ABC and Olympia, and a singer seemed just the thing to round out their act. Grade duly presented his singer—Beryl Davis, then a mere 12 years old. The Quintette may have been perplexed by this girl who arrived complete with a chaperone, yet they agreed to give her a go. Davis might have been young, but she didn't lack experience. She wore strapless off-the-shoulder evening gowns while fronting big bands in London and performing on BBC Radio, belting out torch songs of love and heartbreak as if she had lived them all. Davis was booed by her first French audiences for singing in English, but then there weren't many jazz numbers in French and she could sing swing with a sophistication that inspired the band to keep her. Davis would sing with Django on and off for the next three years.

For their impending British tour, Grade had the novel idea of booking the Quintette on the English vaudeville circuit. Here, the band with Davis could reach a broader audience than just playing to jazz fans in traditional concerthalls. Yet the plan had its risks. The Quintette was not known among the British public and there was no telling how their music would resonate. To hedge his bet, Grade decided to educate his audience. He hired a movie crew to film a six-minute promotional short entitled *Le Jazz Hot* to be shown in British theaters providing a lesson in jazz appreciation to warm up audiences. The film opened with a symphonic orchestra playing Handel's *Largo* with the charm of a dirge, then the announcer explained the differences in jazz interpretations so no one would be offended as Django and the Quintette swung with all their might through "J'attendrai." If the British harbored any question about the Quintette, Django and Stéphane's jam on the silver screen answered it.

THE QUINTETTE'S FIRST English tour almost ended before it began in July 1938. As Django and Naguine were leaving, Vées asked Django if he had his passport. Django waved him off, reassuring Vées with his breezy response, "No need. They know us over there." Django and Naguine took seats on the ferry, and set off on an uneventful crossing. But when they reached Folkestone on the English shore, the customs agents of course demanded Django's passport. Stuttering with indignation but speaking little English, he and Naguine had no choice but to turn around and take the next boat back. While Django fumed, the tour impresario made the trek to the Continent to collect him and smooth things over with customs. From Folkestone, they set off on a desperate dash north across England to make it to Manchester for their tour debut at the Ardwick Hippodrome on July 2. Their race was in vain. The Quintette played the first shows without Django.

The tour spanned almost four months in vaudeville halls into October 1938. Django caught up to the Quintette and finished out the shows on July 4 in Manchester, then they moved on to the Kilburn State Theatre in London for a gala. They played to a packed hall—including American actor Eddie Cantor, who came up on stage after their set to kiss Django's hand. From there, they performed on July 10 at The Gig Club in London's Wood Green before beginning week-long residencies at theaters in London, Glasgow, and back to Manchester. Playing at the London Palladium, the Quintette shared the bill with American cowboy movie star Tom Mix and Tony the Wonder Horse. While waiting to go on, Django tried his hand at twirling Mix's lasso, then joined Stéphane in turning their attention to Tony, "playing" his penis with Stéphane's violin bow to send him onstage with a dazzling erection befitting a stallion. Stéphane remembered the show with wit: "If all London rushed to see the celebrated cowboy and his horse, I can say without pretension that it was the Quintette that saved the show." With two evening performances daily, it was a grueling schedule of near nonstop show dates. And in between these performances, Decca lured Django and the Quintette into the studios on three occasions, resulting in nine released sides. The schedule was grueling, but the pay beguiling.

As soon as he could, Django worked an advance on his pay from Lew Grade. Then he bought another automobile, which always meant trouble. This time, he purchased an ancient American Buick, a car almost as long as the bar at Maxim's and twice as luxurious. To pilot his prize in style, Django engaged a very English chauffeur.

Django's driver soon became an unwitting partner in crime. One evening, Django disappeared. Naguine set out in search of him through Soho and spotted the Buick parked in a suspicious locale. She found the chauffeur waiting inside and questioned him as to Django's whereabouts. The chauffeur spoke no French, but it soon became obvious he understood all too well both the question and answer. Naguine noticed a club across the way and marched through the traffic and in the door—where she discovered Django sharing a bottle of champagne with yet another woman. Naguine spun on her heel, stalked back to their apartment, packed her bag, and left for Paris.

Now it was Django's turn. Full of remorse, he too began packing for home. He played that night's show with such nervous energy that he roared through "Tiger Rag" so quickly that Nin-Nin's tortoiseshell plectrum melted. Grappelli was beside himself at such charades. Realizing the tour—and their future in England—was ruined if Django abandoned them, he telephoned Paris, searching for Naguine. He finally found her at a Pigalle hotel owned by their friend Micheline Day. Now Grappelli pleaded: "My dear Naguine, you must come back. Django wants to quit everything. He's gone crazy! He doesn't want to play. Come! We have a contract. We just can't drop everything like this! We'll never be able to pay all the money back."

Naguine finally gave in. Never surprised by anything her husband did, she caught the train back to London. The tour could continue. Naguine accompanied Django and the Quintette on the road, watching the adulation for her husband with a sardonic smile.

As pleased as he was by the applause, in the end Django was unimpressed. The Quintette had reached a pinnacle of success playing two concerts daily to cheering English audiences and filling the bandmembers' pockets. They were staying at sumptuous hotels, eating steaks under chandeliers in white linen restaurants, hanging out with Fats Waller, Adelaide Hall, and Spencer Williams at London's swank Nest nightclub. Django saw it all as his due. Yet while the high living went to his head, he was more intrigued by the simple things in life. Walking through the English countryside one night on a respite from the never-ending rounds of concerts, Django pointed up to the sky and said to Stéphane, "Look, they have a moon here, too." Then he ducked into a farmyard, caught a chicken using his best Romany technique, and wrung its neck.

"For supper," he explained.

BACK IN FRANCE at the end of October 1938, Django returned to the open road. Whenever the pace of performing grew too quick, he dreamed of leaving it all behind. On the road, he was reborn.

Django and Naguine set off in their Buick with their new English chauffeur at the wheel. The driver had worked for a British nobleman and was always prim and proper in white livery—which stood out in stark contrast to the surroundings as Django first directed him to the musicians's bistro L'Alsace à Montmartre to show off his automobile. Then they made the rounds of the Romany camps in *la Zone* outside the Portes de Choisy and Montreuil. The Gypsy children swarmed through the Buick spinning knobs, turning levers, dirtying upholstery, tearing curtains, and blowing the horn unceasingly as if it were Louis Armstrong's trumpet playing the hottest jazz. The chauffeur was terrified by Django's cousins—and perhaps saddened to have sunk so low in his duties after serving an English peer. Yet his life was an easy one, his days spent lounging about in front of cafés waiting for hours on end for Django, who was paying him five thousand francs a month—the equivalent of a French government cabinet minister.

After playing two shows at the Marignan cabaret and l'ABC Théâtre, Django hit the road with his fellow Romanies. It must have been a strange sight, the convoy of Manouche caravans stretched out down the roadway in all their color and charm, some pulled by horses, others by cars—and in the midst of them all, Django's Buick driven by his chauffeur who likely wondered which roadmap had led him there. After traveling for a time, they parked at a campground in France's central Allier region where just days before a war between Gypsy clans was fought out at the point of knives, ending in the deaths of several men and the subsequent burning of their caravans as part of the Manouche funeral rites. The campground still looked like a battleground, shocked Gypsies going about their daily lives among the torched cadavers of caravans while gendarmes circled like vultures awaiting the breakout of further vendettas. After nightfall, campfires were lit and the tension increased, strange characters moving through shadows, all watching over their backs for a stiletto out of the dark. It was too much for Django's chauffeur. When daylight came, he begged Django to set him free and caught the next train home. He would certainly have tales to tell his grandchildren around the safety of his own hearth fire.

Django and Naguine continued on. They set out for Toulon with Django at the Buick's wheel and packed in with several Gypsy cousins. Departing Lyon, Django overtook a trolley car only to find himself staring into the headlamps of an oncoming automobile. He swerved off the cobbles into a ditch, threading his way through the trees lining the road. A dazed Django climbed out of the car, and before helping Naguine and her fellow victims, hurried to the trunk to make certain his guitar was safe.

The gendarmes arrived on the scene, and when Django could not produce the driver's license he never had, the whole troupe was arrested under suspicion of having stolen the grand Buick. At the Lyon police station, Django proudly explained who he was and demanded his release. But the gendarmes were not impressed, having heard of neither him nor his Quintette. Now Django began to fret. Realizing he was on his way to jail, he requested his guitar and struck up a song. Rather than play a jazz melody that would fall on deaf ears, he choose a Neapolitan love song. His playing seduced the gendarmes, and he was freed to continue his journey.

IN FEBRUARY 1939, Django and the Quintette with Beryl Davis left Paris by train bound for their first tour of Scandinavia. They traveled first to Copenhagen, then on to Stockholm, and ended in Oslo. The concert series got off to a bad start when the delegation receiving the Quintette placed a garland reserved for distinguished visitors around Stéphane's neck instead of Django's. Still, there were no major problems until the Quintette set off by train for their final shows in Oslo. Awaiting departure in Stockholm Centralen train station, the band's latest bassist, Eugène d'Hellemmes, was searching for a French newspaper to read on the journey. He missed the train, causing the band to miss the concert. The Oslo impresarios had to return the ticket fees to a full audience. As Stéphane remembered, "It was all in the best traditions of the Quintette du Hot Club de France."

The music's pleasures were overshadowed by worries brought to light during the Quintette's travels through Germany. Adolf Hitler's Nazi government had annexed Austria and Czechoslovakia. Django never concerned himself with politics, but suddenly politics were looking him in the eye. Crossing the Franco-German frontier at Aachen en route to Denmark, German border officials collared Django and his bandmates. Germany was not yet at war with France but tensions were high between the nations; the Germans now demanded visas of French nationals. The Quintette members were blissfully unaware of this development—until they were dragged off their train and escorted into a customs office for interrogation. Dominating the proceedings was an immense oil painting of Hitler. By moving side to side, the light reflected off the paint surface and made the Führer's ridiculous moustache appear to quiver. Django first smirked, then erupted in laughter. Yet this was the wrong stage and the wrong audience for comedy. The Nazi officials glared at Django, and Stéphane was forced to smooth things over. Still, in retribution, the Germans confiscated their traveling funds. Allowed to continue on across Germany yet without money or food, they witnessed swastika banners and massing German soldiers in the train stations along the way. It was a sobering journey hinting at what was to come.

BACK SAFE AND SOUND in Paris in springtime 1939, Django's future looked bright with new prospects blooming.

In April 1939, Duke Ellington returned to Paris with his orchestra, and Delaunay took advantage of his arrival to arrange a gala to inaugurate the Hot Club's new home. Although Panassié remained titular president, Delaunay now ruled over the Hot Club, almost single-handedly organizing concerts, running *Jazz Hot*, and keeping up the ever-growing correspondence with jazz fans. It was a herculean task, but it was Delaunay's family.

Delaunay's new Hot Club office at 14 rue Chaptal in Pigalle became the jazz parthenon of Paris. Just a short stroll from the red-light district, it was at once an odd and yet fitting neighborhood for the Hot Club. Rue Chaptal was a residential street filled with schoolchildren's laughter, the street's staunch building facades frowning down on the surrounding bars and brothels. As morning arrived in the neighborhood, it was common to see jazz musicians and prostitutes wandering home as the local residents left for work. By noon, the B-girls and strippers awakened and ventured out for their breakfast or to walk their poodles, crossing paths with the respectable women on their way home with the morning shopping.

The Hot Club's quarters included a library of jazz records and books, meeting room, small garden, and a cellar fit for rehearsals. Across the way was a bistro run by the club's "mother," Berthe Saint-Marie, who watched over her young jazz fans, keeping the best table reserved for them as they arrived for breakfast on their way homeward after a long night. Joining his bandmates and other musicians of Pigalle, Django too stopped in most days, often needing a shave and wearing just bedroom slippers, settling in for a baguette and a café crème.

For the office's opening, Django and the Quintette played on the first floor to an audience including Ellington and his impresario, Irving Mills. The party continued in the cellar and up to the second floor, spilling out into the garden and running through the night. Django hoped this concert would serve as an audition and Mills would sign him to tour the United States. No offer for a tour came that night, but the idea was kindled.

Several nights later, Django was playing for the opening of a new Montmartre cabaret, Hot Feet, a dive shaped like a triangle in the rue Notre-Dame-de-Lorette with just enough room for a piano next to the bar and a stool for Django. Around two in the morning, two African Americans arrived for a nightcap, their entrance arousing great fervor. Concentrating on his guitar, Django hadn't seen them come in nor did he notice the fuss. But the proprietor recognized them immediately as Ellington and his bassman. Django finally looked up from his guitar to see the guests, who gave him a broad smile that sent Django soaring. He greeted Ellington, shaking hands à l'américain. They shared a drink, then Ellington asked Django to play another tune. Overjoyed, Django picked his guitar, his head swinging from side to side, exclaiming to Ellington, "*Ah, mon bon frère!*" Then Ellington sat down at the piano and the two of them improvised a melody, playing together as the light began to seep back into the sky.

Plans were made over their last glasses of wine to travel together to America and play their collaborations in the homeland of jazz. With the New York World's Fair and Hollywood waiting, Django was ready to pack up and leave the next day. But it was not yet to be. Events hinted at during the Quintette's tour of Scandinavia would interrupt their duet.

DJANGO AND THE QUINTETTE divided their time between recording sessions in Paris and London during 1938 and 1939. The ensemble counted five sessions each in the two capitals, but while 38 sides were released from the sessions in

England alone, only 13 were offered in France—five on the Swing label and thus also distributed to Britain. At the same time, three sides were licensed to the United States. It was all proof of how important the English market had become for the band.

Among the sides was one of Django's most beautiful solos, cut in a trio with his friend and rival Baro Ferret and backed by bassist Soudieux. The song, "I'll See You in My Dreams," was part of a prolific Quintette session overseen by Delaunay in Studio Pathé on June 30, 1939. Django's solo was alive with a simple beauty.

Django's fellow musicians heard this finesse. Delaunay and Panassié were lining up Swing sessions with American jazzmen who toured Paris, and all of them insisted on having Django in their rhythm section. "Every great coloured musician who visited Paris asked for Django when I offered him a recording date," Panassié remembered. "It didn't take me long to realise that any time we did not have Django in the rhythm section, or at least two good coloured players, the session was unsuccessful."

When Ellington returned to Paris in April 1939, Panassié and Delaunay knew the bandleader was under contract but they quickly grabbed some of his distinguished sidemen. Panassié cornered cornetist Rex Stewart and invited him to record for Swing. Stewart protested he was unprepared, yet Panassié persisted, suggesting he handpick a band from out of Duke's orchestra. He also promised to bring Django. "I was dubious but consented," Stewart remembered. On the Ellington orchestra's second night in Paris, Stewart heard Django play in Pigalle in a battle of guitars with Henri Salvador and Oscar Alemán. This jam left a lasting impression on Stewart: "The air was electric, the champagne flowed and the magic of the moment is firmly etched in my memory." With the strains of Django's guitar still in his head, Stewart was inspired for the session.

On April 5, 1939, Stewart, clarinetist Barney Bigard, and bassist Billy Taylor made their way to Studio Pathé with great expectations for Stewart's first session as a leader. Arriving at the venerable studio, Stewart was crushed to see how dilapidated it was: "We looked at each other and couldn't figure how in the world anybody could record in a setup like this. But it was too late to back out, so we unpacked our horns . . ." Stewart's skepticism was renewed. He tried to beg out, saying he had no written arrangements. The Ellingtonians spoke no French and Django's English was limited to hip jazz phrases such as "Yeah, man!" and "Come on!" Panassié waved this off, telling him Django could hear anything once and play it. "And, to the amazement of the three Americans, that's just what happened," Panassié said. "They had only to show him one or two special chords on the piano, here and there and, for the rest, we were able to record the tunes immediately." Stewart now launched into a song: "Deciding not to waste time, I began to blow a simple blues for Django to learn. Django spoke little English, if any, but there was no strain of communication between us. . . . I was unaware of his virtuosity and quick ear. To my astonishment, he proceeded not only to play the blues but to embellish them with an evocative gypsy quality." The makeshift band taught each tune to Django, rehearsed once, and then waxed five sides in quick succession.

Stewart was proud of the sides cut: "One of the most intriguing facets of the recording business is the element of chance. Actually, it is like a crap game loaded with a larger amount of misses than hits. Many a proven artist, with a string of hits behind him, can sometimes be humpty-dumped off the popularity throne overnight by a neophyte. Conversely, a newcomer can rise from coffee and cakes to champagne and filet mignon in less time than it takes to write about his success." This session was pure champagne. Lacking a drummer, clarinetist Bigard confiscated a pair of wire brushes, discovered a decrepit snare drum, and added the rhythm. Yet even the makeshift drummer soon lost track of the time. Finally, he confided to Panassié, "Django's playing is so beautiful that I almost forget to play, just listening to him."

AT THE END OF JULY 1939, Django, Naguine, and the Quintette set off again for England on their third visit in two years. Yet this tour—and Europe in general—was doomed.

The band's arrival set the tone for the tour. They piled into Grappelli's miniscule Peugeot 201, left Paris to catch the ferry, and arrived in Folkestone in the midst of a blackout drill. The town—and all of England—was cast in darkness. As Stéphane remembered, "All of the streetlamps were out, it was forbidden to use our headlamps and we had to drive by the light of the moon. It took us four hours to drive to London and by the time we arrived we were completely worn out. We began the tour the next day, but the mood was sinister. They were already painting the windows of our dressing rooms dark blue for future blackouts." It was an ominous opening note.

As with their mid-1938 English tour, Lew Grade organized this one, featuring week-long residencies at the Moss Empire Theatre chain in London, Liverpool, Glasgow, and Aberdeen, often playing at least two shows nightly. The band again began each show from behind the theater curtains that parted to reveal them in their white evening dress. They began with "Djangology," moving on to their newly recorded "Hungaria" and "Minor Swing." Then Beryl Davis sang the slow tunes "Wishing," "Don't Worry About Me," and a plaintive "The Man I Love." The band offered a finale of "Deep Purple" and typically played an encore of an enthusiastic "Running Wild." The shows ended with much "palm-pelting," *Melody Maker* reported.

Throughout this second English tour, the Quintette was at peak form—and its popularity had never been higher. Yet behind the scenes, the mood of the country seemed to have affected the mood of the band. Django and Stéphane were butting heads, their spirits capricious and contentious. If the other band members talked and laughed with Stéphane, Django gave them the evil eye. If they went out with Django for a drink, Stéphane turned his back on them. The only time they seemed to agree was when they were making music.

The band hoped to continue on to India and Australia—truly a world tour. Yet it was poor timing. During the English tour, blackout rehearsals continued each evening and at intermissions, lobby chatter quickly drifted from music to events on the continent. A feeling of foreboding lurked in the air.

Then, while the Quintette was playing Glasgow's Empire Theatre, the Nazi blitzkrieg overran Poland on the quiet Sunday of August 20. War in Europe seemed certain. Back in London on September 3, the musicians prepared to start another week's run at the Kilburn State Theatre. They were taking a well-earned break in their London hotel when air-raid sirens broke the morning apart. Stéphane heard the sirens, but it was Django's calls from the street below that startled him.

"So, are you coming then?" Django shouted up at him. "I'm gone!"

"Where are you going?" Stéphane yelled down to the street.

"But it's war!" Django shouted back, surprised and exasperated.

Stéphane had not heard the declaration. He called: "What do you want me to do about it? I'm not Chamberlain. I can't stop it."

But Django was in a panic. He had one foot in the door of a waiting taxi and no more time for conversation: "If you don't come down immediately, I'm off without you!"

"Alright, go on then!" Stéphane jested, thinking Django was joking.

He should have known better.

Django quit England then and there. He, Naguine, Nin-Nin, and Vées slammed the doors shut in the taxi and directed the driver to Victoria Station. Here, they caught the next train to Paris and what they believed was the safety of home.

Hearing the taxi roar off, Stéphane realized it was not a jest. He dressed and caught a taxi of his own, hurrying off in Django's wake to talk sense. But by the time he reach Victoria, Django's train was nothing but red lights in the distance.

Impresario Lew Grade then sent Soudieux off to Paris on a mission to retrieve the fugitive in the hope of reviving the show schedule. But as the bassist caught the boat-train to France, war was truly on.

And with that, the grand world tour was scuttled. In his haste, Django left behind his clothes, belongings, and guitar. Yet Django wasn't the only one to desert London. With rumors of impending bombardments, Beryl Davis fled the city at the same time, her father piling her into the family car and racing for the safety of northern England. The band had been booked for a full schedule of dates, starting with another show on September 4 at the Kilburn State Theatre in London. But the Quintette without Django was not the

Quintette. Stéphane was a star—especially in England—but Django and his guitar were the soul of the band to the fans. Even Stéphane realized this, and Grade was forced to cancel the following month of shows.

Stéphane was exasperated beyond words. He decided to stay on in London, a city he enjoyed and a country where he had many fans. Perhaps he felt safe in England as war loomed and was willing to live there for as many years as the war might take in a self-imposed exile from France. He was also fearful of being called up by Mussolini's army in a draft, as his father had before him. Yet more than anything, he was weary of Django's wiles and the roller coaster existence of the Quintette. And during the past weeks, he and Django had hardly been able to speak to each other. As Stéphane stated, "What troubles he gave me. I think now I would rather play with lesser musicians and have a peaceable time than with Django and his monkey business." No longer would Stéphane and Django have to share the spotlight. Within just a short time in London, Stéphane found a slot in Hatchett's Swingtette, a dance orchestra under the direction of Arthur Young at Hatchett's Restaurant in Piccadilly. And soon after, with Grade's assistance, he hooked up with Beryl Davis and pianist George Shearing.

Stéphane's decision to stay in London while Django and the rest of the band fled to France was his way of giving notice. The Quintette du Hot Club de France was no more.

9

Nuages
1939–1944

FOR DJANGO AND FOR JAZZ, World War II was the best of times and the worst of times. When Adolf Hitler and his National Socialist Party took power in Germany in 1933, the very foundations of their ideology were aimed at someone like Django Reinhardt. He was a Romany and a jazzman—the first a crime against Nazi beliefs in racial purity, the second a degenerate affront to decency. Hitler inherited a legacy of German anti-Gypsy laws stretching back centuries, and even before he set out to rid his Third Reich of Jews, he began rounding up, sterilizing, and deporting Django's people; in the end, some 600,000 Gypsies throughout Europe would perish. And in the jungle rhythms and blue notes of jazz, the Nazis, led by Hitler's propaganda minister Josef Goebbels, heard music threatening German cultural greatness, an international conspiracy of American-Judeo-Negro decadence destroying the minds and morals of Germany's youth. Jazz more than any other art form—from other questionable styles of music to even the despised Cubist painters—symbolized to the Nazis the overarching evils of depraved races and corrupt modernism. Between being a Romany and a jazz musician—the first a birthright, the second something he could not live without—Django appeared to be a marked man.

Yet during the war years, Django flourished. It was a grand paradox in a dawning era of paradoxes. In spite of Goebbels's crusade against jazz, the war heralded a golden age of swing in Europe, jazz reaching a pinnacle of popularity of which its earlier fans could never have dreamed. Jazz was happy music and sad music, outlawed music and protest music. And in France, the most celebrated star became Django Reinhardt. The German Occupation forces loved to hear him play his guitar in the requisitioned cabarets of Paris while the people of France fell in love with his wartime song "Nuages"—Clouds. In a single composition he captured the woes of the war that weighed on people's souls—and then transcended all in a melancholy melody both bittersweet and nostalgic, floating above like the heavens the song was named after.

WHEN DJANGO RUSHED BACK to Paris in September 1939, ending the Quintette's second English tour, he found few things changed. In France, these days were known as the False War. On the café terraces, few among the French believed a German invasion possible; the impregnable Maginot—that long borderline of bunkers and gun emplacements like an armada anchored on land—would deter the Nazis. A strange sense of security prevailed as Paris bathed in the golden sunlight of a glorious autumn. Maurice Chevalier remembered the days: "Of course we understood that terrible things were happening in Poland and Austria. But Parisians don't really care about anything but Paris." Yet many of the African American expatriate musicians in France heard the warning, booked berths on the next ship from Le Havre, and sailed for home. Cabaret owners were left with empty bandstands, and they now called for the French entertainers on whom they had earlier turned their backs. Django immediately found work in an ensemble organized by Alix Combelle and André Ekyan performing at Jimmy's Bar in Montparnasse, a club that before featured just blacks. In the band alongside Baro Ferret and bassist Emmanuel Soudieux was African American pianist Charlie Lewis, one of the few who opted to stay in his beloved Paris rather than return to Jim Crow's America. Django was also back in the studio several times during winter 1940, playing sessions organized by Charles Delaunay in ensembles fronted by Combelle, Arthur Briggs, and Philippe Brun as well as under his own lead. Paris seemed far away from war.

Yet the Parisian jazz world was slowly falling apart. Delaunay read Hitler's *Mein Kampf* and feared for the future of all Europe. His mother was Jewish and he could foresee what that meant. He hid his jazz records away in the cellar at rue Chaptal, then went to the U.S. consulate and applied to emigrate to the United States. When asked if he was Jewish, he cautiously said no. His visa was refused. Now he—as well as Ekyan, Brun, and others—were drafted into the French army, Delaunay serving with the 401st Company in charge of an anti-aircraft emplacement defending Paris. Despite his duties in the army, he heroically found time to keep up Hot Club correspondence, wrote articles for *Jazz Information* magazine in New York, and published a new book, . . . *de la vie et du jazz*. Released in 1939 as war loomed, this book preached Delaunay's musical metaphysics: Jazz was the essence of life and essential to life. His new work was part prose poem, part typographical fantasy, all singing the praises of jazz as the great art of a new age. The coming years were to challenge Delaunay's philosophy in ways he never dreamed.

On an eerily calm Sunday, May 12, 1940, Django, Delaunay, and the rest of Paris listened to the news with horror: The Germans were invading France, crossing the Meuse River through Belgium and circumventing the Maginot. Within days, refugees flooded the capital from the northeast, fleeing the Nazi advance. Still, no one believed Paris could ever fall. But as the Germans encroached on the city, millions evacuated to the safety of the south. They abandoned Paris any way they could. Django and Naguine fled Paris for the Midi, followed by Nin-Nin and the other Romany of their clan. On June 3, German Luftwaffe airplanes appeared over the capital, dropping some 1,100 bombs, veiling the city in clouds of black smoke from burning fuel storage tanks. The next day, the last of the British Expeditionary Force abandoned the continent in anything that would float from the seaside town of Dunkerque. France was suddenly alone in her defense. Within days, the French government disappeared from Paris and the army collapsed. It was a debacle. On June 14, Paris capitulated, and German soldiers marched in victory down the Champs-Élysées.

As the Occupation began, Django and others returned hesitantly to Paris, where an uneasy truce reigned. Bricktop had locked up her cabaret and abandoned France, moving on to open a nightclub in Mexico City. Charles Lewis changed his last name to Louis in a vain attempt to hide among the Parisians. Josephine Baker and Arthur Briggs also decided to tough it out in France—how bad could things get? Marcel Bianchi was interned by the Germans; when freed, he immediately left for the safety of neutral Switzerland. Louis Vola boarded a boat bound for Argentina. Oscar Alemán fled to Spain to find a ship home to Buenos Aires. Crossing the Franco-Spanish border at the town of Irun, German guards halted him, confiscating his two National tricone guitars on which he had played such wondrous jazz lines. The steel-bodied, nickel-plated instruments were deemed essential to the Nazi effort and were to be melted down and made into weapons of war.

For Django, France was now a prison. He and the other Romanies stayed off the roads and went into hiding in the depths of *la Zone* or within the provincial forests and mountains. Django feared for his life, yet he had nowhere to run.

THE NAZI ZEAL against jazz was summed up in an exhibition inspired by Josef Goebbels's propaganda ministry. Organized by Nazi cultural watchdogs in 1937, the exposition's poster and catalogue featured on the cover a savage black-skinned musician bearing an unmistakable resemblance to a monkey tooting on a saxophone. He wore a top hat and tuxedo in a caricature of respectability while on his lapel was a carnation blooming with the Jewish Star of David. Scrawled across the bottom in letters that screamed off the poster and catalogue were the words *Entartete Musik*. The message was shouted out as shrill as one of Louis Armstrong's famous high C notes from his trumpet: Jazz was degenerate music.

Goebbels knew the power of music. An amateur pianist, he was enamored with Wagner and Bach—but not Delaunay's Bach. As self-proclaimed arbiter of culture, Goebbels was quick to vilify swing: He denounced it as *niggerjazz*, *jazzbazillus*, cultural bolshevism, and modernism, this last a special enemy of the Nazis as the recent history of modern German was sapped of the age-old folk strength. Underlying all the propagandistic posturing, Goebbels feared jazz and its potency. Jazz made people dance, not goose-step; laugh, not salute; sing, not hail Hitler. It was an ideological challenge to fascism, the antithesis of everything Nazism stood for. And Goebbels was right. By the 1940s, the Allies began using jazz as their own propaganda tool on the Germans, with radio broadcasts of swing by Major Glenn Miller's U.S. Army Air Force big band and others as a demonstration of freedom and democracy in action.

After Hitler became chancellor of Germany on January 30, 1933, Goebbels took control of Germany's radio airwaves even before seizing the newspapers. He foresaw the power of the new medium of radio as a propaganda tool and sought to bend it to the Nazi will. Goebbels unveiled on November 15, 1933, the Reichsmusikkammer, a ministry devoted to propagating proper German music and silencing the undesirable. Goebbels named composer Richard Strauss as president, and the ministry soon began issuing lists of "unwanted" music. Jazz songs dominated the lists. Under Goebbels's command, German radio director Eugene Hadamovsky banned the broadcasting of jazz on October 13, 1935. His action was for the nation's own good: Hadamovsky explained that the new Nazi government wished to prevent "a nation of Germany's high cultural level from seeking indefinite sustenance from an *Hottentot kraal* without doing irreparable damage to its soul." And when the United States entered the war, Goebbels outlawed selling and playing all American jazz records. Swing was a force so strong it had to be controlled.

As much as he despised jazz, Goebbels stayed his hand in ever banning it outright. Jazz and sweet dance music was the rage in German homes as well as nightclubs, as popular among the nation's housewives as with German soldiers and the military High Command, who threw *reichsmarks* like confetti to buy champagne in Berlin's cabarets. Goebbels understood the insidious art of propaganda like none other, and he knew he would never win over the masses to Nazism if he deprived them of their favored dance music. Thus, jazz was both an enemy of the Reich and at the same time essential to the war effort; it was escapism from everyday life and wartime worries, a needed opiate for the people. And with Goebbels's vaunted German troops as crazy for swing as mere mortals, jazz built the morale of soldiers in their foxholes on the front. As Goebbels astutely advised a conference of his radio officials in March 1933, "Never be boring. Avoid dreariness. Don't put your convictions on the turntable. Do not think you can serve the Nazi Government best by the sound of blaring marches evening after evening." With this in mind, the Reichsmusik-kammer gave its grudging nod to select German and European bands to play jazz that was neither American nor too hot. Playing concerts in German caba-rets as well as entertaining German troops were Jack Hylton's orchestra and Belgian bandleaders Fud Candrix and Stan Benders's big bands. It was jazz with the Nazi seal of approval.

Jazz came out of hiding in Paris within days after the German Occupation. Restaurants and cabarets pulled the boards down from their windows and unlocked their doors as both French civilians and German soldiers rushed to quench a newfound and insatiable thirst for diversion to relieve the fears of war. Some of the cabarets were requisitioned by the German High Com-mand for officers or soldiers, but other restaurants—particularly the fanciest cabarets—continued business as usual. During a visit to a depressed Paris on July 23, 1940, Goebbels ordained that the capital was to be its old self, the City of Light even amid the darkness of war, alive with gaiety to show En-gland a symbol of the new Europe ruled by the Reich. The Nazis sought to soothe the French with a stable supply of bread and ample entertainment in the form of circuses, music, and movies—films that were "light, trivial, and, if possible, stupid," according to Goebbels. They were all distractions to aid the French in forgetting the war.

More than just propaganda lurked behind Goebbels's decree. Paris was to be the Wehrmacht's brothel. Goebbels planned that every German soldier would have a chance to come to Paris as a reward from wherever they were stationed in the Reich's growing realm. His slogan was soon on the lips of all troops—Everybody Once in Paris. The city was still a moveable feast, but now the table was set just for the Germans. And to make their dreams of Paris come true, there had to be wine, women, and even jazz.

Everyone—soldiers and civilians alike—were now calling for jazz in the capi-tal's cabarets. Delaunay more than perhaps anyone was awed by the sudden love of swing. "Jazz—until then the province of a small minority of enthusiasts—was stirring up interest and excitement amongst the public at large. It was an event without precedent," he remembered. "Almost overnight, jazz records began to sell in the thousands—the public craved 'swing,' whether in the established music halls or the illegal dancehalls that opened throughout the city. 'Swing!' The word was magic. It became the rallying cry for young people everywhere and they spoke of nothing else. It had to be swing!"

The golden age of jazz had invaded Europe.

Back in Paris after fleeing to the Midi, Django heard this clamor for jazz. Like other French entertainers, he first had to appear before the German Propagandastaffel, the official censorship bureau. With divisions overseeing French press, radio, cinema, theater, publishing, and musical performances and recording, the Propagandastaffel had three goals: to censor anti-German or pro-Jewish, Masonic, or communist messages; gather intelligence on the

French people's mood; and spread Nazi propaganda. Never before had such an efficient system of censorship and propaganda been established. Possibly helped by his Germanic surname and surely by his fame, Django had to submit his song programs to the Propagandastaffel for approval before every concert so it could control the playing of degenerate music before the first notes were struck. And the ministry had its spies, with the Gestapo and SS to enforce its decrees. Django then began a long stand on October 4, 1940 at the landmark Cinema Normandie on the Champs-Élysées playing sets between Nazi-approved films for a crowd composed of a mélange of French civilians and German military. For Django, it was a coup. He performed day after day for large audiences on one of the city's most visible stages. It was a platform that could launch him to new heights.

And yet offstage he still fretted for his life.

DJANGO UNVEILED at the Cinema Normandie in 1940 his Nouveau Quintette du Hot Club de France, a new ensemble based on a new formula. The old Quintette had been influenced most by Louis Armstrong and his flavor of New Orleans and Chicago jazz. Now, Django sought to swing. He styled his Nouveau Quintette on the small combos of Benny Goodman, doing away with the all-string sound and heavy-handed *pompe* rhythm. He strived for a sonority that was light and airy, held to earth by a drummer, Egyptian Pierre Fouad. Django was not giving up on music just because Stéphane was no longer at his side. Instead, he found a new second soloist, clarinetist Hubert Rostaing.

Django first met Rostaing when Combelle left the band at Jimmy's Bar, recommending Rostaing as his replacement. Born in Lyon on September 17, 1918, Rostaing had studied music at the conservatory in Algiers, where he lived much of his childhood. He formed a dance band when he was 18 to tour the cabarets of the Mahgreb from Morocco to Tunisia, then ventured on to Corsica, Luxembourg, and finally Paris before returning to the White City. Rostaing came back to Paris in 1940—terrible timing with war breaking out and ideal timing as jazz was booming. A baby-faced young man of just 22, he performed at Mimi Pinson's cabaret. Then, shortly before the German invasion, Baro Ferret approached him as Django's emissary. "Django wants to hire you," Baro announced: "Go see him." Rostaing was giddy to be summoned by a jazzman of Django's stature. He hurried off to Jimmy's Bar, where Django was sitting in state, dapper in his evening dress. Catching sight of Rostaing, Django beckoned him to be seated and said, "Come, my brother! Let's have a drink." Rostaing remembered their "discussion" of terms: "I had one, two, three drinks—and still Django didn't say anything. By the time I'd got to my sixth glass, I was completely wiped out. Finally Django said simply, 'Good, you'll start tomorrow then.' And not a word had he said about hours or conditions!" Rostaing might not have been an accomplished musician, but he was inexpensive to hire and easily influenced in his playing, all key attributes for Django.

The next night, Rostaing arrived at Jimmy's armed with his tenor sax. Django counted off the first number and then looked to his new horn player, calling out, "Play, brother!" Rostaing faltered. He tried his best to honk out a solo, yet he didn't even know what a blues was—although he was doing his best to learn, then and there on the bandstand.

Rostaing played tenor sax alongside Django for just ten days. Then, one night he carried his clarinet to alternate on a tune. When he started playing the clarinet, Django stopped. "Don't ever put down that instrument," Django said to him, then picked up the song again. And with that, Rostaing became a clarinetist.

Django warmed up his Nouveau Quintette with rehearsals in the Hot Club cellar, then they headlined for several months at the Normandie before playing Ciro's, the Olympia in Bordeaux, and then the Semaine des Vedettes de l'Écran, du Disque et de la Radio at the Salle Pleyel from Christmas Eve to New Year's 1941. Django continued through 1941 with matinées and tea dances at the Avenue, the Folies Belleville, back to the Normandie, Moulin Rouge, ABC, and Alhambra. At the same time, he was playing through the night at the swankest cabarets Paris had to offer—Chez Jane Stick, Montecristo, Impératrice, Doyen, Le Nid, and Paris's celebrated Olympia for two weeks in September 1941.

Nighttime in the capital was wilder than ever, charged by the sounds of swing. Paris was under blackout orders—the streetlamps were painted blue, leaving the city's streets cloaked in eerie darkness. But inside the cabarets, all was aglow. On leave from the front, German soldiers overran the nightclubs while the officers annexed the Russian Casanova and Shéhérazade cabarets, where the Ferrets performed. From his seat on the bandstand, Django looked out over audiences of occupiers in their mouse-colored uniforms. These were the Nazi minions that were interning Django's people to halt the spread of the *zigeunerplage*—Gypsy plague—and had proscribed jazz, yet here they were paying him to play, shouting out requests for American jazz, tune after tune.

After Django and his Nouveau Quintette opened at Chez Jane Stick, the club was packed each evening with Wehrmacht generals as well as those among the French who weren't about to let the good times end just because of a war. Actress Danièlle Darrieux, her husband, Dominican diplomat and playboy Porfirio Rubirosa, and their clique arrived early each evening and stayed late to applaud Django's jazz.

After hours, Django and his ensemble played covert concerts arranged by Delaunay and other fans like Rubirosa. These *concerts clandestin* were held in homes and cellars and known in strangled Americanized French as a *surprise-partie* or *pot-luck*. Other times, they played in bars or dance halls with the shades drawn and lookouts posted for German soldiers. People danced with abandon to forget the trials of the day and as if there was no tomorrow—which given the times, was all too possible. Fouad remembered a secret soirée played by Django and the Nouveau Quintette at Chez Jane Stick: "After the German patrol passed by and we believed the coast was clear, the tables were pushed back and the dancing began. As soon as the alarm was given, the tables were set back in place and everything became orderly again as though by enchantment." But getting home after the curfew was another problem. The last métro train running each evening was jammed with musicians, entertainers, and their fans hurrying homeward. Other times, Django and his ensemble braved the patrols. As one of Django's wartime managers, Madame Boyer-Davis, remembered, "None of the musicians had a pass, and we used to have to hurry home in the snow, hiding in the doorways at the least sound of jack-boots on the cobblestones. One night, though, we ended up in the Saint-Philippe-du-Roule police station. Since the gendarmes wouldn't believe we worked in a cabaret because we had no passes, Django, Gus Viseur, and the rest of the musicians started to play. But it didn't end with a mere demonstration. They went on until dawn, encouraged by the police, who marked the beat by clapping their hands. By the time we left, we were all buddies and as thick as thieves. And, better still, our new friends explained to us how to go about getting official passes."

Django and his Nouveau Quintette returned to play between films at Paris's Olympia, then on to the Germans' requisitioned Moulin Rouge. Here, Django performed on a three-tiered stage shared by Ekyan and Viseur's bands featuring all the Ferret brothers. Backstage, Django and the other musicians had long spells to kill while the films ran, time they spent shooting billiards and drinking at a café around the corner. Bored, they began a new game in their dressing room, drawing a target on the back of the door to lance with their knives. "While one of us listened closely to hear if anyone was coming, we'd all take turns throwing knives at the target," Fouad remembered. "You had to throw pretty hard to make it stick in the wood. After a fortnight there were an incalculable number of holes, and in time they grew into cracks between anything from 10 to 30 centimeters long. When we were finished, you could see daylight right through the door! It was lucky the job finished when it did, for when we left the door was ready to fall apart. I imagine that when the manager went to open it after we'd gone it most likely came away in his hands."

Despite the war, times were good, and Django was making money as fast as he could strum. The new swing sound of his Nouveau Quintette was inspiring Django's playing: He was pleased by his young band's tight performance and the modern tone of the clarinet. Stéphane was a more formidable musician with ideas of his own that led to great music, but these new bandmates stood in awe of Django and were uncomplaining in following his lead in song arrangements or accepting his dictates on pay. It was a trade-off, but one

Django was willing to make. Now there was no question who was the star in the spotlight. Proud of his music and band, Django was even punctual in making dates.

Then trouble arose. Django led his ensemble to play at a Romany wedding, but when it was time to leave for work that night, Django didn't want to quit the party. Rostaing, Fouad, and the others finally left for their contracted job, leaving Django to glower over their infidelity. Several days later, playboy Rubirosa hired Django and his band to perform at a soirée at his home in Neuilly. On the outs with his Nouveau Quintette bandmates, Django hastily organized a new band for the occasion with Nin-Nin, pianist Eddie Barclay, and others. Yet when he arrived at Rubirosa's party, he was astonished to find Rostaing, Fouad, Soudieux, and his own cousin Ninine Vées there as well. In a fury, Django set aside his Selmer and refused to play. The other musicians bore no grudges against each other; they joined forces and were in top form. While Django fumed from a corner, they jammed as they rarely had before—"I don't think we'd ever played better in our whole lives!" Fouad boasted. Django cast an evil eye on them, but the band of friends launched into a new song, riding higher than the one they just ended. Still Django sat out. Finally, he could bear it no longer. He swallowed his pride, grabbed his guitar, and jumped in. The party continued through the night, the morning dawned, and they played on until ten the next day when all the guests finally dragged themselves homeward. And still Rubirosa would not let the musicians stop. An amateur guitarist and one of Django's greatest fans, he urged them to play yet another tune, and they jammed on their last song for more than an hour before wearily but regrettably packing away their instruments.

DJANGO ALSO HAD a strange new audience yearning to hear his music during the war years. This crowd first materialized as if from nowhere, taking seats at a concert on December 19, 1940, at the Salle Gaveau when Delaunay organized the Hot Club's premier Grand Festival de Jazz with Django's Nouveau Quintette and the ensembles of Combelle, Viseur, and Noël Chiboust. Delaunay awaited his usual audience of jazz aficionados, including those wearing German uniforms, but to his astonishment, the hall filled to overflowing with this new crowd—fresh-faced French teens hooked on swing. Delaunay could not believe his eyes: "I was witnessing the sudden and extraordinary explosion of popularity of jazz in France." This crowd of youths was derisively dubbed *les petits swings* by the French press. But these teens soon had a better name for themselves. In love with the scat singing of Cab Calloway that they transliterated as "Zazouzazouzazouhé," they called themselves *les zazous*.

To *les zazous*, swing was a lifestyle. Inspired by Calloway's zoot suits, *les zazous* dressed the part, or at least as well as they could given wartime deprivations. They wore their hair long, hanging over their neck in the back and puffed up into a proto-pompadour on top. Boys grew moustaches in the style of Django, carefully cut circumflexes accenting their top lip. Baggy pants and long suit coats covered high-collared shirts and brilliant vests, adding a splash of color to the gray of wartime. Serving as jaunty canes in the mode of the English gentleman, they were never without a long-handled umbrella, come rain or shine. But the symbol of the *zazous* was their shoes—ideally two-tone black-and-whites with wooden soles as thick as they could hope to balance atop. They were young, they were dandies, and they were cool. But most of all, they swung.

Yet *les zazous* were more than just jazz fans with fashion sense. To them, swing was a political stance. Even their sunglasses were a sign of protest, the dark-blue lenses mirroring the blue-tinted windows of Paris's blackout in a cynical statement against their parents' generation and all it had wrought. Their elders, the Vichy ministers, and the occupying Germans were suitably outraged by *les zazous*. Standing for a staunch vision of old-fashioned French values, the Vichy government was on many fronts the conservative equal of the Nazis, and as Vichy Education Minister Abel Bonnard stormed, *les zazous* stood against the nation of France for a society of individuals. *Les zazous* whole-heartedly agreed. They were a proud flourishing of a rebellious youth culture, and their love of jazz was inspired in part because the Vichy and Nazi powers frowned on it; similar swing youth movements were alive in Belgium and even in Hamburg, Germany. As Delaunay noted, "Jazz had the flavor of forbidden fruit." To *les zazous*, swing was freedom. And if they couldn't have freedom, they could at least have swing.

Les zazous inundated Delaunay and his Hot Club. At the outbreak of the war, the club counted 350 members; by spring 1941, it swelled to 5,000. Noon each day at the rue Chaptal offices resembled rush hour in the métro, the Hot Club packed with *zazous* straining to hear the music and listen to Delaunay's wisdom concerning its history and style. Yet Delaunay and the true believers kept their distance from *les zazous*. Delaunay did not know quite what to make of their excessive enthusiasm and doubted it was more than a passing fad. At concerts, *les zazous* did not sit respectfully in their seats and contemplate the music as though it was a church sermon. Instead, they were sacrilegious zealots. When a song began, they rejoiced, jumping up and down, dancing in their seats and aisles, throwing paper airplanes and cheering with Indian war cries they copped from American westerns. It was a bacchanalia, an orgy of youthful exuberance—and it was all expressed in the music.

Yet just as jazz's golden age in Europe was dawning, the music also found new enemies, many of whom spoke with a venom that must have made Goebbels proud. "Jazz and swing are the scourge of New Europe," proclaimed *Paris-Midi* journalist Walter Rummel, while venerable French music critic Casadesus led a cry to "send jazz musicians to the slave galleys." The fascist French collaborationist group Les Jeunesses Populaires Françaises took matters into their own hands with *les zazous*. Armed with razors, the junior fascists went on the prowl. Trapping *zazous* on the streets, they forced them to the sidewalk and publicly shaved their heads. Goebbels's Propagandastaffel was not about to let *les zazous* take jazz too far. As the Gestapo warned one Hamburg swinger, "Anything that starts with Ellington ends with an assassination attempt on the Führer!"

Delaunay, however, came up with his own rules to this game: He cheated. With wit and wisdom far beyond the comprehension of the fascist bureaucrats, Delaunay simply translated the titles of American jazz songs into French, and these camouflaged tunes were stamped with the Propagandastaffel's approval for play. Thus, the old Dixieland warhorse "Tiger Rag" became "La rage du tigre," which, Delaunay explained in a century-long stretch of the truth, was based on an ancient French quadrille. "Honeysuckle Rose" bloomed anew as "La rose de chèvrefeuille" and "Sweet Sue" was now "Ma chère Suzanne." Some American songs were simply translated into French, "Sweet Georgia Brown" becoming "Douce Georgette," while others were transliterated into gibberish as "I Got Rhythm" became "Agatha Rhythm." And most famously, "St. Louis Blues," named for the city, was christened "La tristesse de Saint Louis" in an ironic double entendre summing up the era. In a subtle twist of wording, Delaunay's canard conferred sainthood on Louis Armstrong—a feat most fans would have applauded.

And now, Saint Louis was blowing the blues for the fate of jazz in France under the Occupation.

EVEN UNDER THE OCCUPATION, Django's own muse was alive and well. The war brought restrictions and deprivations—there was suddenly a shortage of that French lifeblood, red wine, while turnips and rutabagas were all the feast most could look forward to, and there was never enough coal to heat apartments. Yet the Occupation did not deter Django from composing new songs that were some of his finest, richer than ever in elegant melodies and opulent harmonies. Inspiration came to him even in these dark times, and to the musicians who shared the bandstand with him, it all seemed magical.

In 1941 while playing tea dances at Le Doyen, Django often gazed out the bay windows into the beauty of the trees along the Champs-Élysées, finding inspiration for a new melody. He turned to his band, including Rostaing, and said, "Let me start. You come in playing very softly and when you've got the tune, Hubert, then, you join in too." This spontaneous song—languid and light, an airy flight of fancy—was christened "Lentement, Mademoiselle."

Another day, sheer happiness moved him. Django and his bandmates were dining at a favorite restaurant near L'Étoile. With good food—always a relative term during the Occupation—and a glorious evening in the restaurant garden, Django was taken by an urge to hum. His humming soon turned into onomatopoeic scat singing mimicking Armstrong, and before the band knew it, Django had formed the joyous melody of "Swing 42." They played the song that night at Chez Jane Stick.

When Django was inspired and the music was flowing, there was no stopping him. Fouad remembered that the tea dances at Le Doyen became jam sessions: "We took little or no notice of the clientele, made up for the most part of old dowagers who could hardly have found our music interesting. You had to understand Django. When he was pleased with his band, he was serious. He made a list of the morceaux he wanted to play and passed it to Rostaing. This list was really only a basis, because when everything was going well, Django no longer took any note of it. He counted out the tempo and you had to guess by the way he tapped his foot what tune he had in mind! What we really needed was clairvoyance, because the least hesitation on our part annoyed him. If he seemed pleased, we were supposed to know what tune it was that he wanted to play. And when he wanted to play there was no halting him." Playing at the Folies Belleville, the band was in top form and Django launched into "St. Louis Blues," continuing to improvise on the melody chorus after chorus for 45 minutes. The audience grew bored, putting their overcoats on and heading for the door with disgust twisting their faces. Yet Django simply did not care, and only the manager's storming onto the stage and interrupting the music could rein him.

On another day, the band was playing with the Cirque Médrano at the Alhambra when someone forgot Django's guitar. Carrying his guitar was his bandmates' responsibility, but without a guitar there was no music. Happily, the Fratellini clowns had a guitar—a metal-bodied toy with wire strings they used to hit each other over the head. Django didn't care. He took the metal guitar, tuned the wires as best he could, and played it as though it were his Selmer. When the evening was done, the pads of his fretting fingers were cut through, blood running down his digits. But Django had made music on a clown's toy guitar.

Invited to a soirée at a titled lady's salon, Django was to perform for guests along with Andrés Segovia. Django arrived some three hours late—and again lacking his guitar. Segovia, who had years earlier turned his back on Django, now turned up his nose at this gauche behavior. He refused to lend Django his guitar, so someone rushed off in a taxi to get Django's Selmer. Finally, Django was ready to play. He improvised a melody with his plectrum before switching to play with just his fingers as a coda. Now Segovia was enchanted. Humbled, he politely asked Django, "Where can I get that music?" Django simply laughed and shrugged off his request. "Nowhere," he said. "I've just composed it!"

Soudieux remembered another one of Django's improvisations that did not survive. During a train ride through the French provinces, Django took up his guitar. Looking out the window as the country rolled by, he whistled an improvised melody, strumming and picking out harmonic chords and accents to accompany himself. The tune caught Soudieux's attention, pulling him out of a daydream. He listened as the melody and harmony were created and could not believe what he heard—for Soudieux, it was an ethereal instant, a moment of transcendence: "It was simply the most beautiful melody I ever heard, bringing tears to my eyes." And just like it began, in a moment Django's song ended and was gone.

Inspired by Django's intuitive composing, Soudieux summed up his admiration for him in a simple description: "Django was music made man."

IT WAS ANOTHER SONG—a simple, apolitical melody—that became the ersatz anthem of France during the Occupation. Paris was suffering cups of imitation coffee made of roasted chicory or grilled acorns while Parisiennes were painting their legs with the seams of sham silk stockings. But the people happily embraced this song as their own. The melody seemed to come to Django from out of thin air, as his amazed bandmates remembered. He called it "Nuages."

Django rehearsed "Nuages" with his Nouveau Quintette in autumn 1940 and first recorded it on October 1 in his return to the studio following the invasion. For the date, his ensemble featured Rostaing, Nin-Nin, bassist Francis Luca, and Fouad. It was a short but epochal session. The band played with an intensity and brilliance and force as if it were their last session on earth. They cut just six songs, only two of which were released at the time—"Rythme futur" and "Blues"—neither of which bore the word "jazz" in the title or were immediately identifiable as swing by Nazi censors.

"Rythme futur" was a futuristic composition summing up Django's anxiety and fears of the past year. Nin-Nin played *la pompe* like a panzer rolling over the rhythm with Django's melody line the staccato stutter of a machine gun. Echoing the horror of Picasso's *Guernica*, "Rythme futur" was war orchestrated into jazz, a fully human commentary on the terror of the times.

If "Rythme futur" was war made song, "Nuages" was a melody of peace. This first recording began with an intro more Stravinsky than swing. Django's theme was delicate and understated, a sublime run up and down a chromatic scale with modulations in notes and time structure at each pass. Much like Debussy's 1897 nocturne *Nuages*, Django's composition was an impressionistic melody, the chromaticism coloring the song in a rainbow of tones.

This October recording of "Nuages" was not released at the time. From 1940 through 1944, Delaunay recorded 270 sides, almost half of which included Django. Yet many of these sides were not released then, ironically due not to the Propagandastaffel but to wartime shortages of materials for manufacturing records.

Django was also unhappy with the October "Nuages" take, and returned to the studio on December 13 to record again. This time, the Nouveau Quintette was augmented by Combelle on clarinet, creating a duet with Rostaing that reinforced the airy sound of the melody. "With a single clarinet, Django could not get the effect he was after: It was just a typical quintet sound," Combelle remembered. "Now, with two clarinets he had the makings of an orchestra at his disposal and even succeeded in giving the impression of a much larger group." And this second version of "Nuages" was played at a slower pace, enhancing the melody's rapturous beauty.

"Nuages" struck a chord throughout France. This soft, bittersweet tune was easy to whistle, speaking to Parisians in these gray days of ration cards, curfews, and blackouts. The melody was laconic, at once sad and mournful, yet also evoking a dreamy nostalgia for the way things were, a mnemonic password inspiring a remembrance of things past as real as Proust's madeleine. Django debuted the song during the Semaine des Vedettes de l'Écran, du Disque et de la Radio at the Salle Pleyel and the crowd's subsequent cheers reverberated through the grand hall. When he started another song, they forced him to stop and replay his new melody—and then play it again. In all, he performed "Nuages" three times in a row and still the crowd was not satisfied. With its release as Swing No. 88, all of Paris seized upon "Nuages" and more than 100,000 copies were sold. It was more than just a hit song. "Nuages" was truly a paean.

Jacques Larue wrote words to Django's melody, and Lucienne Delyle sang them in her 1942 recording; soon other European musicians rushed to cover the song in their repertoires and recordings. In 1946, Spencer Williams used Django's melody in his "It's the Bluest Kind of Blue." "Nuages" was adopted as an American jazz standard, perhaps the sole European jazz melody to earn such honor.

Overnight, Django became a national hero. With the swing-crazed public of France, he was a household name, a star on the level of Maurice Chevalier or Sacha Guitry. His portrait was for sale in news kiosks and shops everywhere, deplacing the old images of Tino Rossi and outselling those of Suzy Solidor. His image appeared throughout Paris on posters pasted to the walls announcing his next concerts, which often sold out within 24 hours.

And with the royalties from "Nuages" and the increased bookings the song's popularity brought him, Django was suddenly a wealthy man. That this good fortune should come during the war when so many others were doing without did not force Django to hide his newfound wealth. Instead, he and Naguine set up camp in a luxurious apartment on the Champs-Élysées. They ordered new suits and dresses from tailors. And while others ate rutabagas, they sliced into filet mignon. "Nuages" made Django richer than even he could ever have dreamed.

THE FLIP SIDE of "Nuages" on Swing No. 88 was "Les yeux noirs," a Gypsy melody played for as long as anyone could remember in France and tracing the Romany route back through Eastern Europe. It too was a simple theme, one of the first songs struck up around caravan campfires when the Gitans in the Midi or the Manouche in *la Zone* unpacked their violins and guitars. Along with "Tears"—which he had hidden behind an English title—"Les yeux noirs" was one of the few Gypsy songs Django ever recorded. This version, cut at the same December session as "Nuages," was like a bayonet charge through the tune, a virtuoso showpiece of dazzling runs and dizzying arpeggios, translating a Gypsy melody into a jazz jump.

The song was released with ironic timing. While Django was living on the Champs-Élysées and accorded unofficial protection by the Nazis due to the jazz he played, other Romanies were being rounded up as part of the Nazi's racial cleansing.

Hitler bore a deep hatred for Gypsies. A rumor circulated Europe explaining Hitler's vehemence against the Romanies, a story sounding more like a Grimm brothers fairy tale than fact: Before he came to power, Hitler visited a Gypsy fortune-teller and asked her to predict his future. She duly gazed into the mists of her crystal ball and examined his palm. At last she spoke. She predicted great power for him. But she also foresaw a sudden fall, more rapid than his rise. This infuriated Hitler, and according to the tale, he decided the only way he could break the evil spell of this Romany augury was by exterminating the Romany people.

On his rise to power, Hitler and his Nazis put German racial scientists to work on the Gypsy issue years before they concerned themselves with Jews, homosexuals, or the disabled. In studies and conferences devoted to protecting the Aryan race's purity, Gypsies were labeled immoral, a plague on Germany. Dr. Johannes Behrendt spoke for the Nazis in his 1939 article "The Truth About the Gypsies," writing, "They are criminal and asocial and it is impossible to educate them. All Gypsies should be treated as hereditarily sick. The only solution is elimination. The aim should therefore be *elimination without hesitation* of this characteristically defective element in the population." Scientists offered their own ideas on solving the Romany menace: The establishment of Gypsy ghettos or deportation of Gypsies to Abyssinia or Polynesia was recommended. The newly founded SS proposed herding Romanies onto ships that were to be sailed out into the ocean and sunk.

From 1933, German Gypsies were doomed. The Nazis barred Romanies from cities, shuttling them into settlement camps. Nazi doctors began sterilizing Romanies as early as 1933. And German Gypsies were required to wear a brown triangle sewn on their chest marked with the letter "Z" for *zigeuner*, German for "Gypsy"—a precursor of the yellow Stars of David pinned to Jews.

On November 5, 1942, SS leader Heinrich Himmler's proposition to exterminate Romanies, Jews, and others won Hitler's approval, and the Nazis began sending German Gypsies to their deaths in the new camp at Auschwitz. An estimated 20,000 French Gypsies soon followed them to German and Polish death camps, where 18,000 of them were exterminated.

In France, the new Vichy government was quick to follow the Nazi example in establishing anti-Gypsy laws. Under the supervision of Vichy's Ministry for Jewish Questions headed by Xavier Vallat, French Gypsies were rounded up starting in autumn 1940 and sent to internment camps where they provided slave labor for French farms and factories. France soon had 20 large internment camps and numerous smaller ones, including the major camp at Linas-Monthléry, just outside Paris. Some 30,000 French Gypsies would be interned during the war. In fact, the Vichy forces were so vehement in fighting their perceived "Romany scourge" that they shocked some German officers.

Yet in Paris, Django was flourishing. Never did he have so much work or live in such sumptuous surroundings. Just as the Germans permitted jazz in Paris, they allowed Romany musicians to continue to play—and paid to come hear them every night. German soldiers even made pilgrimages to the Hot Club, including Luftwaffe Oberleutenant Dietrich Schulz-Köhn, who became such a regular at Delaunay's offices he lent the jazz club legitimacy in the eyes of the High Command. As Schulz-Köhn remembered, "The officers of the Club liked me coming there, especially in uniform as sometimes they were raided by the Gestapo. They found the place full of letters, magazines, records with labels—all in English and this was no laughing matter at the time. So they could use me as a signboard to prove their innocence and reliability." A longtime jazz fan, Schulz-Köhn even had himself photographed outside of the Cigale nightclub standing in full uniform alonside Django and other jazz musicians—a German officer, a Romany, four blacks, and a Jew.

One afternoon while Django was performing at a Le Doyen tea dance, a stranger arrived and asked the maître d' for Django. "I want to speak to the so-called Django Reinhardt," the stranger announced.

"Why do you say, 'so-called'?" Django's bandmates queried.

The stranger was indignant: "Don't try to trick me. I've just come back from a prisoner-of-war camp where I stayed six months with Django Reinhardt. The sign here advertises 'Django Reinhardt,' but I came to see the real one."

The sad truth was that in an internment camp somewhere in France or Germany, one of Django's Gypsy cousins had faked his identity in the desperate hope of saving his own life.

Yet Django's life had never been better. He signed on with a new manager, impresario Jules Borkon, replacing his informal business relationship with Delaunay. Borkon was a true hustler, keeping the Nouveau Quintette booked and the money rolling in. Django soon cast off Borkon when Parisian booker Eugène Grumbert promised better things, then later worked with Madame Davis-Boyer. With his success, Django became more capricious than ever.

He enjoyed being a star and demanded preposterous fees, sums that served to satisfy his ego more than anything. When Borkon asked him how much he wanted to perform, he'd reply, "How much does Cary Grant or Tyrone Power get? I want the same as them!" In Django's eyes, there was no difference between himself and the brightest stars of Hollywood. To bring Django down to earth, Borkon sometimes had to bargain with him for days to arrange a simple booking.

At the same time, Django was often mean in paying his bandmates. Recording for Swing one day, Fouad asked Django how much he was to be paid as a sideman. Django replied: 350 francs. Yet Fouad knew from Delaunay that accompanists typically earned 400 francs. An argument ensued, but Django would not give. So Fouad craftily changed the conversation to billiards, inspiring Django to ask, "My brother, let's play some billiards tonight after the session." Fouad queried Django on how many points he'd give him, to which Django, in his vanity over his pool playing, offered Fouad more points than even the best poolshark could afford. As they settled up at the end of the evening, Fouad had won 300,000 francs off Django. The fifty francs difference in pay for the session now meant nothing.

To Django, money was a symbol of his worth, but little more. Money was to be spent, and he never bothered to save a sou. Returning from a tour to Brussels in April 1942, Django bore a gold watch on each wrist while Naguine had golden bracelets dangling from her arms, ankles—anywhere there was room for them. The rest of his earnings he gambled away. As bandleader Fud Candrix remembered of Django's ascension, "He loved shiny things. When he was in Brussels during the war he walked around town wearing a cowboy hat, a red scarf with white polka dots, white leather shoes and a shiny bright blue suit. Obviously everybody stared at him, but he did not do these things to attract attention. He was just like a child wearing a costume—it was a game to him." Yet he had no head for figures, and Fouad remembers often being paid more than Django promised due to Django's deep-seated generosity. As another of his later sidemen said, "Django had a heart of gold." This generosity extended to everything Django had, which was all part of the communal life of the Manouche. He and Naguine's apartment on the Champs-Élysées became a hideout for his Romany cousins, and food was always on the table, even during the days of deprivation.

Django's pride at being a star led him to experiment with his stagecraft. He always begrudged Stéphane and now Rostaing: They could stand while playing their instruments in full view of the audience whereas he had to play sitting down to hold his guitar. While performing on the Côte d'Azur during September 1942, an idea came to him. He dreamed up a support that held his guitar in a playing position so he could stand to lead his band. The apparatus duly arrived from Selmer, but after several performances, the new toy was left in a corner and Django returned to his chair.

This setback did not diminish Django's dream of spectacle. He found new inspiration when the Nouveau Quintette performed with the Cirque Médrano in summer 1943, as he watched the acrobats and trapeze artists performing their derring-do in the heavens of the circus tent. Approved by the Propagandastaffel, the circus was one of the favored public performances and had its own golden years during the Occupation as German soldiers and French civilians alike thronged to the shows rich in escapism and fantasy. Now, Django envisioned being lowered to the stage perched on a luminous star as he played— a fitting reflection of his own stardom, after all. Egged on by his bandmates, Django had a star built by the circus hands. "It'll be *très américain!*" he pronounced with pride. Yet when the star was ready and Django was set to rehearse the stunt, one of his bandmates joked that the rope holding the star looked none to strong. Django was now seized by fear and no amount of cajoling could get him onto the star.

In the end, he arrived on stage less spectacularly, riding a dolly just centimeters above ground on the safety of steel rails.

DJANGO WAS NOT THE ONLY GYPSY jazzman whose star ascended during the war. Nin-Nin and the Ferrets were also prolific and profiting from the love for swing that infused all types of music in Paris, from the glamor of the Russian cabarets down the alleys to the *bals musette*.

Nin-Nin and his guitar were in great demand. He continued to back Django at sessions and shows, but was also a cornerstone of Aimé Barelli's big band and Combelle's Jazz de Paris before finally organizing his own ensemble, the Orchestre Swing Jo Reinhardt, which first recorded in March 1942. Nin-Nin returned to the studio in December 1943 alongside violinist Claude Laurence—the nom de jazz of writer-musician André Hodeir—to cut four sides, including two of his own compositions, "Un peu de rêve" and "L'œil noir." On Nin-Nin's premiere sides, he proved himself a confident and stylish soloist, without Django's flash but with a lyricism all his own. His original compositions were intriguing tunes, their complex melodic lines of dark intervals creating a distinctive blue mood. Nin-Nin even wrote one song— "Mélodie au crépuscule"—so ethereal in its poetic evocation of twilight that Django appropriated it into his own repertoire. Nin-Nin was not simply walking in his brother's famed footsteps.

Sarane Ferret also launched his own jazz ensemble. Other Gypsies refrained from taking a solo in Django's presence for his musical brilliance was too strong. Sarane alone was undaunted as he believed himself Django's equal. He at least had the temperament of a bandleader and with the Occupation's call for jazz, Sarane organized his Swing Quintette de Paris.

Just as Django found a worthy foil in Stéphane, Sarane met violinist Georges Effrosse. Yet Effrosse's tenure with Sarane was short-lived. The Nazi occupiers applauded Django and the other Gypsies' swing, allowing them safe passage through Paris. But Effrosse was Jewish, and even though his violin could play jazz during these golden years of swing, he was a marked man. Effrosse tried to hide his identity to escape the Nazis' wrath, but to no avail. In 1944, he was herded up by the Germans with other French Jews, interned at the Drancy camp outside Paris, then packed into a railroad boxcar, and shipped off to the Dora concentration camp, where he perished.

Matelo Ferret was also leading a jazz ensemble on nights he was not backing an accordionist at a *bal musette* or playing in the Russian cabarets. Others heard the magic in Matelo's guitarwork as well, and in 1943, he was invited into the Paris Pathé studio. Matelo's Sixtette boasted an avant-garde lineup in its use of drums, clarinet, and vibraphone years ahead of even Django. Matelo played with a verve and joi de vivre telling of his age. The sides were marked by tight arrangements and vivacious interplay, breathing new life into Django's "Swing Guitares" and "Swing 42" as well as Matelo's own "Le Rapide," a Romany train song. "Le Rapide" stood out from Django's swing numbers as a startling step forward to a modern jazz sense. The song was highlighted by Matelo's audacious solo, which jumped from furious arpeggios to syncopated chords. If Django's jazz signaled a revolution in music akin to that of the Impressionists in painting, Matelo's music was Cubism—angular sounds, odd intervals, and jutting syncopations. In these first solo recordings, Matelo displayed early on his love for adventurous harmonies and off-kilter beats. It was a bold beginning.

During the Occupation, a new Gitan guitarist also arrived on the Paris scene, appearing like an apparition one day out of *la Zone*. He was 14-year-old prodigy Jacques "Montagne" Mailhes. Remembering the debut of Django, Delaunay kept an eye on him.

Montagne learned to play from his uncle, banjoist Gusti Malha. With Delaunay's guidance, he assembled an ensemble with two Gypsy cousins—guitarists Djouan Sollero and Noye Malha—and Polish Jew Léo Slabiak, a classical violinist newly enchanted by jazz. The three Gitans first met Slab—his nom de jazz—at a 1940 contest at the Salle Gaveau organized by Delaunay. After a quick rehearsal, they stole the show. Montagne and Slab then formed their own Swing Quintette de Paris and began playing Parisian cabarets. When a German officer invited them on a tour of the Fatherland, Slab diplomatically turned him down. Django too heard of Montagne, and came to one of the band's rehearsals. Yet when Montagne saw him, he was too frightened to play. Django pretended to leave, then hid in the shadows to listen to the boy's impressive fretwork.

Montagne and Slab's Swing Quintette sadly lasted but a short time and never recorded. Montagne was growing up too fast. He not only played music beyond his age but smoked cigarettes, drank, and chased women, living the musician's life of late nights and little sleep. Slab remembered that the war and his life as a musician turned Montagne into a "savage animal." In 1942, just two years after his debut, Montagne died of consumption at 16. He was buried with his guitar cradled alongside him in his coffin.

A new musical development was also startling Paris, and Baro Ferret— along with Sarane, Matelo, and their cousin René "Challain" Ferret—was in the vanguard. This revolution was inspired by Django and his jazz, but he took little part in playing this music.

In 1938, Baro had teamed with accordionist Gus Viseur, who amused himself by toying with the sacred musette songs of the elder generation: Sometimes, he swung the notes, other times he improvised over the timeworn themes, playing his own novel melodies and wide-ranging harmonies. Viseur's creativity caught the fancy of Baro.

Just as guitars ran in the Ferret family, accordions were the heart of the Viseurs. Yet while playing musette in dance halls, Viseur's ear was tuned to jazz. Joining forces, Viseur and Baro boasted the hottest band in all the *bals*, and alongside the favored musette waltzes and javas, their ensemble played swing. With Viseur, Baro founded a new music, swinging the rhythm and adding a new feeling to the stately old music. Out of their collaborations came swing musette.

In summer 1938, Viseur made a pilgrimage to the Hot Club to play a surprise audition for Delaunay. Yet Delaunay detested accordions. With their quavering tremolo dripping with sentimentality and the rigidity of musette, accordions symbolized everything old fashioned in Parisian music. "There was nothing more execrable to me than an accordion," Delaunay swore. Yet when Viseur began running his fingers across the buttons, Delaunay was transfixed and hurried to record this new jazz. Viseur idolized Django and had created an accordion style as free of the past as Django's guitarwork.

Viseur and Baro were prolific from 1938 through the early years of World War II, waxing waltzes and swing tunes with one foot in the old world of the *bals*, the other foot keeping time in the new world of swing. Their swing musette was light and cool, breathing a jaunty air. Baro's solo guitar proved an ideal contrast to Viseur's accordion. Where Viseur played sweeping, full chords and rich scales, Baro's notes were quick and incisive, stabbing like a stiletto. As Delaunay wrote in *Jazz Hot*, "I have no hesitation in saying that we have in Viseur a musical phenomenon on the order of Django Reinhardt." Delaunay also applauded Baro: "We can say that this record contains another revelation in the person of Pierre Ferret, whose guitar solos are so reminiscent of Django Reinhardt." By then, there was no higher accolade.

Yet for Baro Ferret, it was not enough. He was renowned as the *second* best guitarist in Paris, but his own stardom was eclipsed by the brilliance of Django. In the mid 1940s, Baro set aside his Selmer guitar. He was not one to be runner-up, so he conceded the fight and turned his hands to other business. He had backed Django on some 80 sides, but in Django's presence he was

forever the accompanist. Baro would pick up his guitar at times over the coming decades to play the odd date, record a few brief yet brilliant sessions, and
jam after hours in the series of bars he owned, but he was largely finished as a
musician by 1943. With the Occupation came the lure of a lucrative underworld, a black market in everything from finding food to procuring women.
In Pigalle, gangsters were aristocracy, and Baro went into this shady business
with the same brilliance he had brought to music.

Baro left as his musical legacy a series of final waltzes that stepped beyond
any of Django's music. These tunes were created during the war years but
recorded later, in 1946. They were unique, eccentric compositions that fit no
musical category then or now. They would later be labeled *valses bebop* in an
attempt to describe their avant-garde form.

Baro's earliest *valses bebop*—"Panique," "La folle," "Dinalie mineure," and
"Turbulente zoë"—were recorded with accordionist Jo Privat at his side. These
were not waltzes to which to waltz. Moving in 3/4 and 6/8 time, they stretched
the boundaries of the term. The melody lines led by Baro's virtuosic guitar
playing took surprising turns down dark alleyways and into dangerous
backstreets. Odd harmonies followed the theme like an ominous shadow, Baro
adding stabbing chordal accents and startling obbligatos behind the accordion—precursors of bebop rhythmic accompaniment. The results were impressionistic songs of a strange, unnerving atmosphere, a reflection of Baro's
own character and his frustration over his place in jazz behind Django. They
were surrealism put to jazz, unlike anything else ever recorded anywhere.

Baro's *valses bebop* won Django's everlasting admiration. And yet Baro remained so daunted by Django's playing that he set down his own guitar. Baro
and Django remained best friends, recognized on the Paris jazz scene as the
two premier guitarists—a recognition that had also made them rivals. In later
years, Baro confided to his nephew, Gitan guitarist René Mailhes, the reason
he packed away his guitar and turned to other métiers: "Technically, Django
did not scare me. It was his mind. He had ideas that I would never have, and
that's what killed me."

DJANGO WAS MOVING on to new ideas. During the war years, he began thinking big—a big band, the pinnacle of jazz in the American style. His fascination for playing with an orchestra was not only due to the sound he could
achieve and the boost to his ego of having a big band behind him. Django was
also drawn to composing and arranging more intricate and adventurous music. The symphonic lineup provided him new powers.

During a session on March 22, 1940, at the Studio Albert, Django found
his first opportunity to arrange his songs for a big band. The session was
organized by Delaunay and included an all-star lineup of the best of the French
jazz world—or at least those who were still alive or available: four trumpets

led by Brun, Ekyan on alto and Combelle on baritone sax, three trombones, pianist Charlie Lewis, a rhythm guitar, and bassist Soudieux. In various ensembles, they recorded Django's arrangements of "Tears," "Limehouse Blues," "Daphné," and "At the Jimmy's Bar." "Tears" was an incredible transformation of the simple Gypsy melody into orchestral jazz with delicate interplay syncopating the horns. "Limehouse Blues" presented a tour through jazz history, beginning with a languorous intro before launching into choruses harking back to the polyphony of Louis Armstrong's Hot Five and ending with a modernistic modulation of horns moving ever upward. And yet Django played less guitar in these songs, almost as if he were rationing his notes. But he punctuated his phrases with an affluence of big-band might, signaling a new understanding of his music and the possibilities of orchestral arrangements. The music was not just about him any more, not just a showpiece for his guitar, but a full, multitimbred work of art. These were bold statements, a thorough reinvention of Django's now-antiquated string jazz.

The session was released under the sobriquet Django's Music, shielding its swing from the eyes of the Propagandastaffel—although those who knew saw Django's name in lights. Playing with a big band may also have been a way for Django to make swing more palatable to the Nazi censors, a smoothing out of the wild freedom of jazz in the symphonic approach, music more akin to their beloved Wagner or martial marching bands. For Django, his big band was the realization of a vision. He readily picked up the baton and attempted to style his arrangements like his other hero, Duke Ellington.

In crafting his arrangements, Django was able to hear in his head the textures for the full orchestra, but he couldn't write them down. He could, however, sing and whistle them—or better yet, pluck them out on his guitar. Delaunay remembered the time-consuming, exacting process of Django's arranging his big band's performances: "He would call the musicians together and play the parts for them one by one—the violins, the five trumpets, and so on, sometimes as many as 70 parts." During rehearsals, Django's renowned musical ear could pinpoint one musician in his big band playing one wrong note. He would halt the proceedings, correct the player, and start over again.

At other times, Django had one of his bandmates transcribe his arrangements. For this exhausting work, he turned to his new clarinetist, 19-year-old Gérard Lévêque, who came to Paris to perform in an amateur band contest and wound up in Django's Nouveau Quintette. Days after arriving in the capital, Lévêque moved into Django's apartment, where the clarinetist was employed as transcriptionist. As Lévêque remembered, "Every night we used to go off to the cinema or music hall and once we got back, Django would lie down and spend the rest of the night playing. We'd stop to eat and drink, but that was all. He'd play each instrument's part on his guitar and I'd get it down on paper. That's how we did the scores for 'Belleville' and 'Oubli,' which Django recorded soon after with Fud Candrix's band."

Django's skills at harmonizing his melodies came through during his sessions cutting "Nuages." Combelle detailed Django's powers of arranging: "In 'Oiseaux des îles' [another song recorded at the same session], Django hit on a wonderful device. I remember that in the release we played a series of chords, which is normal enough. But what was so extraordinary was that we didn't play two of the main notes of the chord. He had us play only the two least important notes. And the most curious thing of all was that though we didn't play the two main notes, you could hear them all the same, by force of association as it were. Only Django would have thought of it!" As Stéphane described Django's sense of music, "I believe that he heard more music than a full orchestra was capable of playing."

Django and his Grand Orchestre Swing made their debut at the Salle Pleyel on Sunday, February 2, 1941. For the first part of the show, Django performed with his Nouveau Quintette. Then, the Grand Orchestre Swing took their chairs behind the curtain. Delaunay described the show: "For the first time, Django was to conduct a large orchestra. This, we knew full well, was one of his wishes come true. . . . Then came the warning three knocks and up went the curtain. At that precise moment, however, Django, who had never before led an orchestra in public—and with a baton, if you please—was seized by stage fright and refused to go on. In the end we had to push him on, and if I remember right he made his appearance walking backward! And all this trouble despite his magnificent white dinner jacket, splendidly complemented by his shoes with their yellow buttons."

After the Salle Pleyel show, Django and his big band played a stand at Paris-Plage, a new cabaret near place de Clichy. Royalties from "Nuages" and the opportunities afforded by the Occupation provided Django the money to pay a big band and keep it together—for a time at least.

He performed another series of concerts on April 3–5, 1942, at the Salle Pleyel with Candrix and his band. Reedman and bandleader Candrix had proved to the Nazis that he could be trusted to swing just right and was hired for long stands in Berlin as well as for the Wehrmacht's troop-entertainment program. The Salle Pleyel shows led to a Belgian tour, Django playing the Palais de Beaux-Arts in Brussels on April 16–18 with Candrix and Stan Brenders's Orchestra.

Django reached the height of his big band recordings at the tour's end a month later in the Société Belge du Disque's Sobedi Studios in Brussels on May 8, 1942, with Brenders's 23-person orchestra, including a four-violin string section. Django recorded eight sides, including an orchestral version of "Nuages." As Lévêque remembered of Django's work with the Belgian big bands, "Used as he was to playing with the Quintette, a group that was compact enough but fairly limited from the musical viewpoint, he took great delight in hearing a big band with brass and saxophone sections, and violins into the bargain at times. It not only gave him an incentive to play but suggested countless ideas to him for orchestrations. He came upon fresh possibilities, all kinds of combinations of sounds, voicings that were out of the question where the Quintette was concerned."

Django's Music recorded again at Paris's Studio Albert on March 31, 1942, with 13 musicians under his direction. Django's new compositions best displayed his new ideas. "Nymphéas" flowed with the flavor of Debussy punctuated by the *wah-wah* horn accents of Ellington. Ricocheting between classicism and the modernity of jazz, "Féerie" was brought to a head by a drum solo. Back to back, they were minor masterpieces without antecedents in Django's work.

And yet Django's most ambitious undertakings were the musical pieces he did not record. While his favored musicians remained Armstrong and Ellington, his main interest in 1942–1943 was classical music, especially modern composers Debussy and Ravel. Django dreamed of writing a full symphony and he picked out his ideas for the orchestra on his guitar while Lévêque tirelessly transcribed note after note, page after page. Django's vision was truly daunting. Jean Cocteau promised to write a libretto for a choir, which totaled between 80 and 300 singers depending on Django's fantasy of the moment. It was to be a production beyond anything he had ever attempted before.

Django's symphony was entitled *Manoir de mes rêves*—Castle of My Dreams. The image and musical theme came to him in a reverie. Sleeping soundly one night, he dreamed he was in a grand château lost in the midst of a never-ending forest; it was midnight and he was playing on a large pipe organ the music that became *Manoir de mes rêves*. Now he labored to transcribe the music heard in his dream.

Django and Lévêque worked for months on the score even as its premiere was being talked about around Paris. Laboring through the nights, they finished just days before the scheduled concert. But as with many of Django's plans, organization was not part of it—he trusted to fate that things would fall in place. When Django and Lévêque delivered the score to conductor Jo Bouillon at l'ABC Théâtre, they were greeted with disappointment. Bouillon was overwhelmed by the modernistic music and its daring harmonies: He paged through the piles of manuscript and declared it unplayable. Bouillon may have feared as well that the Propagandastaffel would react against such modernity, costing him his vaunted position—if not his life. Cocteau had also not written his libretto as Django had not thought to send him the synopsis; thus, the choir's portions were far from ready. And there may have been technical problems with the score itself as Lévêque confessed he did not possess the musical skill to notate all of Django's complex ideas. In the end, *Manoir de mes rêves* was never performed. And to add to the disappointment, Django's original score was misplaced.

Django did not fret. He instead returned to the themes of *Manoir de mes rêves* in recording a distilled version of the symphony several times in the coming years with his various jazz ensembles. He first cut the melody on

February 17, 1943, backed by Ninine Vées on guitar with a bass-and-drum rhythm section. His *Nouveau Quintette* again featured the coloring of two clarinets, played by Lévêque and André Lluis, yielding a sonorous tone evoking the strains of an organ by starlight. The rhapsodic theme was punctuated by Vées's subtle *pompe* and Django's tender obbligatos, creating a sublime piece that may have been more stunning in this simple setting than it ever could have been performed by a chamber orchestra. As Stéphane described Django's mind-set, "Like Ravel or Berlioz, he was truly a composer who imagined a composition down to the smallest detail. If he was above the other musicians he played with, it's precisely because he thought like a composer. When he went into the studio to accompany, say, Jean Sablon, he didn't merely play specific chords or notes, but an orchestral structure. The key to his style was that he was an orchestra in reduction."

From his symphony, Django next turned to creating a Mass. He wished to write a religious work for his fellow Romanies as early as 1936, a piece to be played during the pilgrimage to Les Saintes-Maries-de-la-Mer. The pilgrimage continued as normal in May 1941 and 1942, but was suppressed by Vichy in 1943. This may have played a part in Django's determination to focus on his Mass during 1943 and into 1944. As he described his inspiration, "My people are savagely independent, private, and proud of our traditions, so we need a Mass of our own, written in our language by one of our own. I hope that my Mass will be adopted by my people throughout the world and that it will be consecrated at our annual gathering at Saintes-Maries-de-la-Mer."

In composing his Mass, Django was overwhelmed by his musical illiteracy, as he explained: "It's true that I cannot distinguish an F from a C on a page of music. However, we Gypsies, we have an instinct for hamonies which we compose as improvisations on our instruments. To put together my Mass, it's essential to have a good musician who is able to pluck my notes out of the air and transcribe them onto paper. In my Quintette I have Gérard Lévêque who can do this task." With Lévêque again loyally transcribing, the composition took shape. Django was writing his *Messe des Saintes-Maries-de-la-Mer* for organ, presenting new problems to Django's mind. But despite long nights picking out the notes on his guitar for Lévêque and studying the structure of masses, Django became discouraged. After almost 18 months of work, he abandoned the project.

Even with the Mass incomplete, Django was asked to record it at the church Saint-Louis-d'Antin. A radio van arrived on the appointed day, but no one else. Léo Chauliac, the pianist in Django's big band who was to play the organ, had also gone missing. Django was still in bed with a cold compress on his forehead to ward off the effects of too much drink the night before—and he was intent on staying there. Not pleased with the Mass, he told Lévêque, who had come to find him, "I don't give a damn."

A second recording session was arranged sometime in 1944 on the famous pipe organ in the chapel of L'Institution Nationale des Jeunes Aveugles, a school for the blind. Django had to be dragged to this session, but eventually the recording was made although not released at the time. The Sacre Cœur's organist was amazed by the Mass, stating that never had he heard a piece that respected the canons of harmonization so faithfully yet revealed such originality. He then asked Django where he had studied and what other works of this type he had composed. One can imagine Django simply turning back to his guitar with one of his rare smiles.

FROM FAR AWAY across the ocean in Chicago, the jazz journal *Down Beat* reported in its June 15, 1942, issue that Django was dead. This report symbolized the gulf between the American and French jazz worlds during the war: There was nothing in the United States but rumors about the French jazz scene and no news or recordings of recent advances in American jazz coming across the Atlantic to France. Now, Django's American fans mourned their loss. But the rumors were wrong. Django was alive and well and at the peak of his popularity.

And perhaps he was too successful.

In September 1942, the Nouveau Quintette left by train for the Côte d'Azur, performing in Lyon and then Nice, where Django won 345,000 francs one night at the casino only to lose 365,000 the next. Dressing in grand elegance like the perfect aristocrat, he had beautiful women on his arm and money to throw around. Touring the Riviera, Rostaing said that Django became more unbearable than ever: "By the time we set sail for Algiers we'd had just about enough of him. There was no doubt about it, Django had too much money." He was capricious about what concerts he'd play, contract or not. In Algiers, he refused to play matinées; he was bored by the crowd and had a big bankroll bulging in his pocket. "He had no desire to work," Rostaing remembered, "and so he went back to France and left us in Algiers. I remember we eventually took the last boat; the day after, the Allies landed in North Africa. We linked up with Django again on the Riviera but the place was crowded out with Italian troops and all the clubs were closed. After a few days we were flat broke. The only thing we could do was to get back to Paris. With our last few francs we booked third-class seats and sat in our compartment munching away at sandwiches." As they glumly ate, Django strolled by, his nose in the air, bound for first class. He did not even bother to greet his bandmates.

Back in Paris, Django and Naguine moved into another luxurious apartment, this time on the rue des Acacias, suitably near the Arc de Triomphe. His fame and his fortunes were at a zenith, yet when Rostaing asked for a raise, Django refused him. Rostaing packed his clarinet and left in disgust.

While the rest of Paris was starving, Django rarely did without. As Lévêque remembered, "Despite the restrictions he never went short. He had plenty of cash and went out every night before getting down to work." As a Gypsy, working around the system was nothing new to him. While other guitarists in Paris couldn't even find guitar strings, he proudly boasted that he could break as many strings as he wished and always have replacements. Django had Baro Ferret to turn to for black-market goods. And, almost as a form of tribute, an offering to his music, his Manouche cousins brought him hedgehog caught in the countryside. When Ninine Vées appeared one evening in 1942 with a hedgehog fresh from its burrow, Django had it cooked at the cabaret Le Nid where he was performing. Settling down at table to eat his delicacy, other customers were perturbed at the sight of what they perceived to be the latest in wartime rations. "But what's that you're eating?" they asked him in horror. "It looks like a rat!"

"But of course it's a rat," Django replied. "And it's very good, too!"

From 1943, the Occupation worsened. Nazi Germany's zenith came in summer 1942 when it ruled most of Europe and was preparing victory celebrations in Russia and Africa. Then the tide turned: Von Kleist's army was defeated at Stalingrad and Rommel's Afrika Korps was halted at El Alamein. The about face in Germany's fortunes brought new cruelty. In Paris, food and wine were in ever shorter supply and of poorer quality. A black market in cigarette butts began; others tried smoking anything from dried nettles to Jerusalem artichokes to toasted sunflower leaves. Bicycle-taxis and automobiles converted to burn wood plied the streets, following the new German street signs. Shop windows and shelves were barren, pâtisseries displaying fake cakes made of frosted cardboard as they had nothing else to show. Shoe stores sold real boots made of cardboard and wood in place of leather. With the winter insidious in its cold, people searched factory ash heaps in hopes of uncovering a single nugget of coal. Once-chic Parisiennes stuffed old newspapers inside their sweaters to keep warm. Weary now after three years of Nazi rule, French resistance grew, and the Germans were ruthless in reprisal.

While Panassié hid in his provincial château, Josephine Baker volunteered for the Red Cross, then secretly served the Gaullist resistance, before fleeing to Algeria where she was made a lieutenant in the French army for her service. Arthur Briggs and Charlie Lewis were both rounded up by the Nazis for the twin crimes of being black and American. They were each sent to internment camps for four years.

Delaunay was using the Hot Club as cover, gathering intelligence to be transmitted to England. Unable to publish *Jazz Hot*, he issued a clandestine one-page *Circulaire du Hot Club de France* for the faithful. He traveled France organizing concerts and lecturing on music—all sanctioned by the Propagandastaffel. But in each town he visited, Delaunay made contacts among the growing resistance and carried information on German troops and defenses back to Paris. He fed the details to a British Special Operations Executive contact, whom he called by the code name "Pauline," yet also knew from peacetime as his childhood friend Pearl Cornioley. Trained in England by the SOE, Cornioley parachuted back into France in 1943 to relay dispatches. Delaunay also hid behind a code name. He was known as "Benny" and his network was "Cart"—all in honor of saxophonist Benny Carter.

The Nazis were on Delaunay's trail, however. In October 1943, the Gestapo raided the Hot Club, turned the offices upside down, and hauled Delaunay and his secretary Madeleine Germaine off to Fresnes prison. Held for a month and interrogated at one session for five and a half hours, Delaunay held firm. "It was my grandest day," Delaunay recalled. "They wanted to know where to find our [resistance] leader. I was fortunate enough to understand enough of the German that was spoken preparatory to each question to have time to work out the best possible answers. Never have I talked so much or so well." A message was routed to him from his secretary that she too had not talked, and Delaunay relaxed, knowing if he could hold out the Gestapo had nothing on him. Finally he was freed, the Gestapo trailing him in hopes of tracking down their mastermind. Delaunay managed to pass a warning, and the leader fled to the United States. Delaunay's secretary and the Marseille Hot Club president were not so lucky, both perishing in German gas chambers.

Jacques Bureau used his radio expertise to fight the Nazis as well. He worked with the British in Lebanon, spending long hours scanning airwaves for German transmissions, then tracing their locations to plot bombing runs or commando raids. Slipping back into France with a transmitter, Bureau was in turn tracked down by the Germans and spent the rest of the war in Fresnes prison. To retain his sanity and dream of better times while surrounded by brick walls and barbed wire, Bureau sang to himself the solos from his favorite Bix Beiderbecke recordings. He knew Bix's cornet improvisations by heart, and now they saved his sanity, allowing him to create a fantasy world that he could travel to in his own mind, far from the Nazi jail cell.

Others in the Paris jazz world also served the resistance. Violinist Léo Slab hid his Jewish background behind a false identity, but while playing with Jacques Montagne in Nice, he was collared by gendarmes and drafted into Vichy's military service. Sent to a camp in the Jura Alps, he spent endless days chopping wood. He appealed to the military board, stating he was a classical violinist and woodcutting endangered his hands. Miraculously, he was freed. Slab made his way back to Paris but found the situation too dangerous for a Jew. He went into hiding, setting aside his violin and taking up a machine gun to fight with the Maquis in eastern France for two years until the war's end.

With the Nazi's declared war on Gypsies, some among the Romany also fought back. Manouche Jean Beaumarie and his brother served with the resistance, only to be captured and hanged. Armand Stenegry—who would become better known as guitarist and singer Archange—led Gypsy guerrillas in partisan raids backing the Normandy invasion, exploits that won medals from the British and Free French forces.

Django, meanwhile, continued to play his guitar. As the most famous jazz musician in Europe, he was trapped in the spotlight and could do little but play his music—or *not* play. Django may have been enraged by the Germans but he was not engaged in the resistance. The Nazis were enslaving French workers, shipping them to Germany, and forcing them into the *Service du Travail Obligatoire* in factories. The same fate awaited French professional musicians: As German musicians were drafted into the military, French and other European musicians were conscripted to entertain German soldiers and civilians. Monsieur Verner served as one of the Nazi's official agents, offering booking services for musicians on their way to Germany to serve their musical enslavement. When the German *Kommandantur* in Paris requested that Django bring his Nouveau Quintette to perform in Berlin for the Nazi High Command, Django held him off. Soon, the request was repeated, becoming insistent. Still, Django delayed. He asked for an impossible fee, which the Germans refused to pay. But the exorbitant fee was pure cover; Django had vowed never to venture into the heart of the Third Reich. Now the Nazis grew angry, reminding him it was compulsory to comply with their request. This time, Django simply disappeared.

Being in the spotlight saved him from the fate awaiting other Gypsies, but Django began to sweat under the glare. He sought peace to finish his Gypsy Mass and also feared for his and his family's lives. While on tour in Belgium in April 1943, he visited Liberchies in search of his birth certificate, allowing him to marry Naguine under French civil law on June 21, 1943, in the town of Salbris in the Loir-et-Cher region, with Django's new impresario Eugène Grumbert and the town's bookseller Marcel Rouffie as witnesses. The idea of the wedding was Naguine's; in these uncertain times, she fretted she would lose Django for good. Now, she was pregnant with their first child.

Following the *Kommandantur*'s demands that he tour Germany, Django, Naguine, and Négros slipped out of Paris in September or early October 1943. Django somehow acquired enough of the priceless gasoline coupons to fill the tank of his old Buick automobile, and they took off. Django had been fishing many times in the Savoy. He also knew the Hoffman Gypsy family who were weathering the war near the Franco-Swiss border in the spa town of Thonon-les-Bains on the Lac Léman shore. From here, Django planned to escape to the safety of neutral Switzerland.

Django's hegira soon went awry. His Buick guzzled more gas than he had ration coupons for and the tank went dry in the town of Annecy, 60 kilometers from his destination. Exasperated by yet another automobile failure but ever resourceful, he simply sold the car and parlayed the take into train tickets. Arriving at last in Thonon, Django and family moved into the Hoffman clan's encampment in the park of Crête.

Django was anxious to act. The Hoffmans introduced him to some acquaintances, the Corfu family, scrap-metal dealers who drove their truck across the border daily and offered to spirit Django and his family into Switzerland for a fee. On the appointed night, Django, Naguine, and Négros hid themselves in the truck piloted by the family's daughter, Jacqueline Corfu, to make the journey. They set off, confident customs officials would wave the truck through as usual. But this night was different. The truck was halted and a quick search uncovered Django and family. They were sent back to France with a stern warning.

Django returned to Thonon to prepare a new plan. While he waited, he joined the Hoffmans in performing at the town's Savoy Bar. Introduced to the owner, Django discovered his fame did not extend to far Savoy and the barman offered him a pittance in comparison to his Parisian fees—just 1,500 francs a night. Still, Django needed the money to pay for his escape. At the Savoy, he played accompanied by the Hoffman sons and their violinist father. The Hoffmans had been playing Hungarian melodies and classical pieces while dressed in traditional Tzigane garb; now, on Django's lead, they eschewed the Romany costumes and turned to jazz. After a short time, Django notified Lévêque and drummer André Jourdan to catch a train south and join him. Soon, the Savoy was crowded each evening with jazz-loving German soldiers, fellow Gypsies, Thononais fans, and even a group of *zazous* who had fled Paris.

Django found lodging in the outskirts of Thonon at villa Souroff, a magnificent mansion owned by exiled Russian General Alexander Souroff on Lac Léman. Here, even amid his war worries, Django went fishing. He also found ready billiards opponents at the Café du Général and countless poker games at which he gambled away his escape funds. One night during an ill-starred poker session, he lost everything and on the last deal, had only his Selmer guitar to ante up. Happily, he won the hand.

Django soon moved his family to a small house at 18 rue du Chablais, close by the Savoy Bar. They often dined at the Restaurant Savoisien, whose owners, the Mingard family, were resistance members with an arms cache hidden in the cellar. Django also found work playing lavish parties for the rich Schwartz family, whose château in the village of Amphion was named La Folie, a play on words of *feuillée*, or "leaf-covered" from the mansion's wooded acreage, and *folie*, or "folly" due to its ostentatiousness. Inspired by these fêtes, Django composed the melody "Folie à Amphion," which he would record in 1947. Yet the Schwartz parties came to a tragic end. Denounced by their gardener's son to the Gestapo as Jews, they were deported and soon perished. The Gestapo took over La Folie.

Fear for the fate suffered by the Schwartzes and countless others hung over all France, and after a month in Thonon, Django made his move. He failed at crossing into Geneva to the west and confidants warned him of the impossiblity of crossing Lac Léman to the north as it was patrolled by Nazi

E-boats. The only hope was to hike over the Alps and into Switzerland to the east with the aid of a mountain guide. One night in late October or November 1943, Django, the pregnant Naguine, and Négros set out to meet their guide at a café. Django's existence in Haute-Savoie long fueled rumors that he sought to flee France, and when German soldiers at a nearby table overheard their conversation that evening, they were arrested. The troops hauled them to headquarters, were Django was searched. Found carrying a membership card from the British Performing Rights Society, he was deemed a spy as well. They were imprisoned for the night in the Hôtel Europe, then marched through Thonon under armed guard. Watching this pitiful parade, townsfolk proudly believed Django was with the resistance. Django, however, was in despair, thinking his end had come.

A miracle arrived in the unlikely form of the German *kommandant*. He was a jazz fan, and when he came to question his new prisoner, he was astonished. "My good Reinhardt," he said, "whatever are you doing in this fix?" Django promised not to try to escape again, and was freed. Now, as he left German headquarters, the townsfolk viewed him with suspicion as a collaborator.

Django was more fearful than ever and despite his promise, decided to set off for Switzerland on his own just days later; Naguine and Négros would join him shortly. After paying his guide a 500 franc fee, they left under cover of darkness on November 24, 1943. The guide led him through the forests of Veigy and with Switzerland in sight, pointed out to Django the route across the border's no-man's land. Django was dodging his way through a three-meter maze of barbed wire when Swiss soldiers discovered him near kilometer marker 185 outside the town of Gy. Django explained who he was, but this was not enough to gain him sanctuary. The guards interrogated him: Was he a political prisoner? A Negro? A Jew? Switzerland did not give refuge to Romanies. The soldiers instead gave him a meal, then led him back the way he came. Unable to find safe passage through the barbed wire, he was forced to climb over the barbs in the dark rain. He knocked at the door of a Savoyard farmhouse in the early morning hours, and the farmers awoke to find him covered in scratches and caked in mud from head to toe. After yet another respite, they directed him back to Thonon.

Django now called it quits on his folly of escape. Chastened, he retrieved Naguine and Négros, and they returned to Paris.

BACK IN PIGALLE, Django and Naguine apprehensively set up camp in a charming little villa in avenue Frochet around the corner from place Pigalle. They now had two fears—the Nazis, with their war on Romanies, and the Allies, who were bombing Paris nightly in their war on the Nazis. Django's new home was close to the cabarets, but more important, it was nearby the métro station that served as a bomb shelter. Built into the base of the Montmartre

Butte, Pigalle métro was one of the deepest and safest shelters in the city, and Django often dashed under the Guimard archway to dive down into the depths even before the air-raid sirens sounded. As the nighttime bombing increased, it became his home away from home.

Avenue Frochet was a rare corner of the countryside within the city, one of the last vestiges of the rural town that was once Montmartre. It was one of the most secret—and beautiful—of Parisian streets, a world away from the surrounding city. The street wound uphill, laced by trees hiding small chalets and villas, garden plots and patios. Here, Django and the pregnant Naguine settled in, far from their luxurious apartment on the Champs-Élysées. The house, like many in Paris, bore no central heating, so to ward off the record winter cold, Django broke up and burned the excess furniture piece by piece. When the furniture was consumed, he cast an eye on the flooring in an upstairs bedroom. "So, what do you think of that?" he asked Émile Savitry, who came to visit. "It's pine. We should get a nice blaze out of it!" Meanwhile, the roof leaked prodigiously and the laundry Naguine hung on lines strung throughout the house never quite dried. Yet while they lived without heat, they never wanted for food. Whatever his whim, a boy appeared as if from nowhere and Django gave his orders. The boy returned carrying an enormous box that opened to reveal monstrous hams, fresh baguettes, and great blocks of butter—all black-market merchandise more valuable than gold. Django had money and he had contacts in the underworld, including Baro Ferret. Before he excused the boy, Django sent him back for a satchel of the best true coffee available, worth a king's ransom.

Django left once again in March 1944 with his Nouveau Quintette to tour France. They appeared at the Knickerbocker in Monte Carlo for a week, then continued to Toulon, Bordeaux, Biarritz, and through the provinces. By the end of this stint, Django refused to perform any more shows: He was out of clean shirts. Playing one-night stands, the band was never able to do its laundry, and Django now revolted against another show. One of the organizers roused a storeowner to buy a shirt, paying with his own ration coupons. Even then, Django was recalcitrant and the band had to beg him to play. The ensemble continued north to a finale in Chartres. It was a grueling trip and by the time they returned to Paris, Django was happy to settle into a long stand at Le Bœuf sur le Toit, where he fronted a ten-piece big band. On opening night, Django was again missing. By ten o'clock, cabaret owner Moysés—who boasted a long history of suffering Django's wiles—was pacing the floor. He swore to everyone he would never hire Django again, promising to fire him as soon as he did appear. Just then, a tribe of Romanies swarmed into the swank club with Django, who took the stage as if nothing was amiss, unreeling his beautiful arpeggios to soothe Moysés.

On June 6, 1944, the Allies invaded France at Normandy, and two days later, on June 8, Django and Naguine's first child was born. Django was then

34, Naguine a year younger. They named their son Jean-Jacques, but affectionately called him first Chien-Chien and later Babik. He was a cheerful,
plump baby, born to news of hope and the promise of better days as the Allies
began slowly pushing the Germans back. Django and Naguine's Romany cousins filled their villa to celebrate Babik's baptism. Through the days, Django
was at home tending his newborn. Madame Davis-Boyer, his manager and
neighbor on avenue Frochet, remembered visiting the couple: "Naguine had
not the slightest idea of how children should be brought up. The first time I
went to see the baby I recoiled in fear when I opened the door, thinking the
place was on fire. There was so much smoke inside you couldn't see a thing.
When I got near the bed I saw Naguine sitting up nursing the baby and at the
same time smoking like a chimney. Moreover, Django and all the visitors who
crowded into the tiny room were smoking too. When I explained to Django
that the child was in danger of suffocating, he immediately forbade anyone to
smoke anywhere near the baby." Django had been a father before, but he had
been preoccupied with the trauma of his burn injuries. Now, the force of
fatherhood filled his heart. Even music became secondary to his son.

During the nights of spring 1944, when he wasn't protecting Babik in the
bomb shelter, Django joined forces with hostess Lulu de Montmartre in running his own cabaret. As Delaunay explained, "Aware of his new duties as
head of the family, Django decided to lead the uneventful life of a middle-
class businessman and was beginning to organize his new home on a rational
basis." The grand cabaret at 62 rue Pigalle was redecorated and relaunched as
La Roulotte–Chez Django Reinhardt. Towering above the street, the façade
featured the bas-relief of a caravan pulled by a bucking white stallion ridden
by a topless Gypsy beauty proclaiming, "You're invited into his caravan." Yet
Django's was truly only an honorary title, an inducement for people to visit
the club of France's jazz hero; Django's role in running the club was to play
his guitar and lead the band. La Roulotte was a raffish dive. A murky cavern of
a room, its tables were hidden in shadows, and the goings-on were equally
shady. "It was a strange atmosphere at La Roulotte," Delaunay remembered.
"After curfew, the doors were shut and drinking went on into the early hours
of the morning. . . . The most unlikely people rubbed shoulders there: you'd
hear as much English as German spoken. 'That's Commandant K of the Gestapo,' someone would whisper. 'And they're British agents at the table over
there on the left.' In turn, the band was asked to play 'God Save the King' or
'Bébert' or 'Lili Marlene,' the favorite tune of the German officers."

Throughout summer 1944, Paris was on edge. Rumors of liberation were
whispered, yet the Nazis were fiercer than ever in quelling resistance. The
monuments and bridges were packed with explosives destined to leave Paris
in ruins if the Allies overran the city; Hitler only needed to give his order. A
thrill of anticipation gave way to a pall of dread. Django was running La
Roulotte and staying close to home and baby Babik. On August 19, Gaullist

underground fighters seized police headquarters on the Île de la Cité, sparking clashes between the resistance and Germans throughout Paris. Air raids rocked the city, and Django spent most nights in the Pigalle métro, cradling Babik in his arms, trying to comfort him and sing him to sleep. On Thursday, August 24, the Allies broke into Paris, led by a Free French tank corps. Battles raged at every city crossroads as bakers and butchers, shopgirls and old women arose against the Nazis. Hitler gave the order to blow up Paris and burn it to the ground, but instead Wehrmacht General Von Choltiz spared the city and surrendered. Still, the Luftwaffe bombed Paris one last time in spiteful revenge, sending Django and Naguine to huddle with their son once more in the métro. The next day, General Charles de Gaulle arrived at the capital's Hôtel de Ville and spoke his famous words, "Paris outraged, Paris broken, Paris martyred, but Paris liberated!"

Babik could finally sleep in peace.

10

Échos de France
1944–1946

THE HARDSHIPS OF THE WAR YEARS could be read in Django's guitar. For the whole of the Occupation, he owned just one Selmer with the small oval soundhole, and during those four years the guitar suffered. The silky varnish polish on the spruce top was all but worn away by play, the soundboard scarred by the fierce action of Django's homemade tortoiseshell plectrum and the brush of his arm across the bass bout. Finally, just patches of polish remained in out-of-the-way corners. With the soundboard collapsing from the torture of playing, Django had wedged a matchbox cover under the bridge to keep the strings from buzzing on the frets. The neck too was ravaged by the passage of Django's two fingers traversing the pitted ebony fretboard uncountable hundreds of times each night, millions of times in the past years, a well-traveled path on the road to making music. The Selmer was wounded and worn—earning the affectionate nickname Gypsy guitarists gave their instruments: *une gratte*, literally "a scratch," as scratching the strings was their slang for playing. Django now had a case to protect his instrument, but it too told of their journey. A case was known in descriptive jest as *un cercueil*—a coffin—and this one looked as though it had been exhumed. The stylish black leatherette covering had long since parted company with its plywood soul and the closing clasps given up the mechanical ghost. String was wrapped around the case to be tied and untied each time Django raised the guitar from the dead. The case's handle had broken and been replaced with a length of twisted wire. When an English fan looked down his nose at this famous guitar and its case, Django simply shrugged his shoulders and said, "*C'est la guerre.*"

The war was over, but its echo resonated. A new army invaded Paris in summer 1944—American GIs. This was a liberating army, but the effects of 1,533 days of German Occupation were still felt in barren store shelves and grim faces on the gray streets. The city awoke as if from a nightmare to celebrate; as Naguine said in her usual understatement, "When the Americans arrived, it was craziness—it was amazing!" As night fell on Liberation day, Paris was one grand party. Long-hidden bottles of champagne were popped, GIs found welcoming mademoiselles, and the young and old danced across the cobblestones. After the past four years, any future looked bright. In place of turnips and rutabagas, the GIs brought K rations and SPAM, which may have been an insult to French cuisine but was a balm for starved stomachs. The soldiers in turn were hungry for a good time in "Gay Paree." After a quick looksee at the landmarks, the GIs aimed their sightseeing at Pig Alley, searching for wine, women, and swing.

To many, swing meant just one thing—Django.

Staff Sergeant Charlie Byrd was one. From the backwaters of Chuckatuck, Virginia, he had learned to play blues and bluegrass on a guitar at age eight, sitting at his father's side on the veranda of the family's crossroads country store. When he was ten, he heard one of Django's records and Virginia suddenly seemed just a small spot on the globe. Arriving in Paris as a U.S. Army band musician in 1945, his private mission was to search out Django. Curious about the rumors of Django's death, Byrd first went looking for Joseph Reinhardt. He found Nin-Nin in La Roulotte, Django's louche Pigalle caravanserai, filled now with grateful Romanies out of hiding and platoons of GIs on a mission for a good time. Nin-Nin was playing his Selmer fitted with an electric pickup through an amp in a small combo of a sax, rhythm guitar, and bass. During a break, Byrd introduced himself and asked after Django in pidgin French and simplified English. Django was indeed alive and well, Nin-Nin told him; at the moment, he was performing somewhere on the Riviera. A disappointed Byrd returned to his table for the next set and the next beer. And then in walked Django, followed by an entourage of sinister-looking Gypsies, one of whom proudly toted his guitar. Plugging in his own electrified Selmer, Django joined Nin-Nin's group and the night came alive. Byrd discovered he wasn't the only soldier in the bar looking for Django as a queue of men in olive drab formed to shake his hand. Django was friendly and gracious with each one, grinning and nodding at the English he didn't comprehend, smiling for snapshots, scrawling his hard-learned signature on portraits and bar napkins. Those who could pick some guitar were all invited to sit in for a song, and Byrd too took his turn at Django's side. He unpacked his gleaming D'Angelico archtop—the Cadillac of lutherie—to jam alongside Django and Nin-Nin on their war-weary Selmers, the GI from rural Virginia trading riffs and lines he learned off Django's 78s back home with the man who made jazz guitar.

Other GIs found that Django was the brightest star, eclipsing other talents in a large galaxy of Parisian Gypsy guitarists. The United States led the world in jazz played on horns and piano, but Paris was then the capital of jazz guitar.

First Lieutenant Herb Caen of the U.S. Army Air Corps also searched out Django, but found a surprise. In Django's place at La Roulotte was another guitarist billed as "Django's cousin"—Matelo Ferret. Caen sent a dispatch about his eye-opening discovery to *Down Beat*:

> On the tiny bandstand facing the bar sit two characters holding beat-up guitars they must have won in a crackerjack box. Behind them, leaning on a bass fiddle, stands a long, tall joker wearing thick glasses and an expression to match. One of these gitbox gees is wearing a tuxedo that must have been Simonized—how else could it shine like that? The other, in a sad sack suit and dirty fingernails, turns out to be Django's cousin—Jean Ferret by name, and very fitting, too. . . . Ferret plays a la Django as far as style is concerned, but for my francs the kid has a few tricks of his own that The Old Master has yet to conceive. His technique is flawless and his staying powers are incredible. Twenty consecutive choruses of any standard tune are strictly par for this guy's course, and he was breaking par all night. There isn't a position on the frets that M. Ferret fails to negotiate. His long fingers race back and forth from the box to the keys in one, long black blur—and even with his dirty fingernails, he plays as clean as Goodman on the clarinet. His ideas are as innocent of cliches as a newborn baby whose first word is "Antediluvian." . . . After M. Jean Ferret's performance, there was just nothing left to say on six strings.

Knowing the power of swing as well as Josef Goebbels, the American armed forces quickly enlisted Django and his compatriots to entertain the troops. He played nights at Bal Tabarin to rowdy crowds of GIs and their newfound *chéries*. During the evenings of September 24–26, 1944, Django was one of the headliners at l'Olympia Théâtre for a series of Liberation variety shows staged by the Army's Special Service Office and United Service Organizations. With Jack Hylton as master of ceremonies, the Fred Méle orchestra, and act after act of can-can dancers, it was a revival of the Paris of old. During their Olympia premiere, Django and his Nouveau Quintette were waiting in the wings when a GI walked by, did a doubletake, and then rushed up to grasp Django's hand. It was Fred Astaire, who was also on the bill. "I know who you are!" Astaire exclaimed. "I heard you at the London Palladium in 1938 or 1939!" The band's jams at the Olympia were greeted with all the enthusiasm the victorious army could muster, and clarinetist Gérard Lévêque remembered one wild concert when the ensemble's drummer failed to show and their rhythm spun out of control: "We got by all right so long as we were playing down tempo, but when we went into 'Tiger Rag,' our final number, things began to go haywire. Django was very nervous and broke a string just as he was starting his solo. He turned to his brother, doubtless thinking to borrow his instrument; Nin-Nin latched on to the tempo as best he could and broke a string himself. Then Django had another string go, followed by a third. Beads of sweat stood out on our foreheads. There was only one thing to do, and that was to leap into the fray myself at this breakneck tempo and finish this 'Tiger Rag' off as well as I could." The GIs roared their approval.

For their second evening at the Olympia, Django forgot his guitar—a common if incomprehensible occurrence. He usually had a Gypsy cousin as a lackey to carry his Selmer, but that night, the American Army mobilized. A GI and a Jeep were ordered at Django's disposal to fetch the famous guitar.

LIKE THE REST OF FRANCE, Django now sought a return to the unattainable past of the prewar years. Much of the country was reduced to rubble and the French needed to rebuild on all levels, from reconstructing homes out of the war's wreckage to razing the black markets and resurrecting a food supply. Even the government had to be recast. In the Assemblée Nationale, the Gaullists battled the communists for the future of France—there were even fears of civil war breaking everything apart once more. The wounds of the war still seethed and the scars would take years to heal. Innocence had been lost before, yet it now seemed gone forever.

The natural reaction was to search out scapegoats. The Occupation left a stain on France and now the French sought to scrub their country clean. In a fervor to hunt down German collaborators, the country joined together in a feverish purge that erupted in mob melees, lynchings, and painful trials of the French soul. Politicians and fascist sympathizers were jailed or guillotined; authors and artists were denounced; courtesans as well as everyday Parisiennes who fell in love with German soldiers were paraded through the streets with shaven heads and spit upon for their *collaboration horizontale*. Among the popular entertainers, Maurice Chevalier was blacklisted for singing on German-run Radio-Paris with too much esprit. Chanteuse Suzy Solidor dared to mouth the words to "Lili Marlene." Tino Rossi was locked up in Fresnes prison—although one of his devoted female fans offered to be shot in his stead. Even Edith Piaf was suspect: she had traveled to Germany to entertain French prisoners. Django's success too was questioned. Some labeled him a collaborator who performed for German soldiers; others heard a message of resistance in the melody of "Nuages." "It is clear that the majority of our stars are more or less tainted," French diarist Jean Galtier-Boissière wrote. Yet blame was not easy to fix. *Boulangers* could bake their baguettes with a clear conscience, but if you bought your bread with pay from playing a guitar for the occupiers, did that brand you a collaborationist, or were you just working to survive?

Django shrugged off any collaborationist accusations. As a Romany, he was on the fringes of French society anyway and he easily escaped the purges. Newly coined French slang for surviving the street mobs and official trials was *se dédouaner*—literally, to get through border customs. In his travels, Django paid little attention to national boundaries and had a long history of getting *around* customs.

It was less easy escaping the dire economic times. Record labels had little money for sessions and producers couldn't fund concerts. In all of 1944, Django recorded just once, cutting two sides for Delaunay's Swing label. One side was his new composition "Artillerie lourde"—Heavy Artillery—a four-minute-plus orchestral piece performed by his 12-man ensemble Django's Music. In the spirit of Tchaikovsky's *1812 Overture*, Django's theme was a symphony of war. Yet this was a happy song of deliverance, a victory parade down the Champs-Élysées with all the brash swagger of a brass horn section. Over the marching bass riffs came the light sound of Django's guitar, rising above like the delirious cheers of the crowd. "Artillerie lourde" was topical, but it was not released at the time; perhaps neither Delaunay nor Swing's parent company Pathé-Marconi had the finances to bankroll Django's celebration of liberation.

The rest of Paris was ready to celebrate, however. The *bals musette* and cabarets reopened and were packed each night with dancers. But this revival was short-lived. In October 1944, De Gaulle's provisional French government banned dancing in the capital's cabarets: Too many French families were in mourning to allow such levity. De Gaulle next shut down all nightclubs, starting January 16, 1945. In an effort to cash in on the demand to dance, the musicians union decried the ban as prudery, yet De Gaulle was famed for nothing if not standing firm: his ban remained. Public dancing was not allowed again until April 1945 and the German surrender—and even then organizations of deportees and prisoners-of-war objected. For Django, there was simply no cabaret work. From the bountiful days of the Occupation, times were now lean.

There was, however, a new army with which to collaborate. At sites throughout France, the American army set up rest camps for soldiers, and Django found constant work performing for the troops. After the shows at l'Olympia Théâtre, Django and his Nouveau Quintette were hired to play for Free French soldiers in Toulouse. Returning to Paris, he found a rare job for the summer at Bal Tabarin, but his good fortune was cut short by the Gaullist dance ban. Django and his ensemble now returned to the Midi army camps for a short tour. The Nouveau Quintette journeyed back and forth crisscrossing the Côte d'Azur from Monte Carlo to Marseille, playing at camps, hospitals, and army-requisitioned theaters. The band's base was the Hôtel Rose-Thé at La Ciotat, a rehabilitation center for French soldiers. The pay was minimal but food and lodging were guaranteed. Django, Naguine, and Babik were provided a grand apartment in Bandol complete with the rare luxury of an indoor bathroom. Basking in the Riviera sun with the war at an end, they could almost believe that life was returning to normal.

Yet the stability of the tour was soon upset. While passing through Monaco, Django lost all his earnings from the Midi dates in the Monte Carlo casino. Luck then caught up to him in Cannes where he ran into one of his Romany cousins who had an automobile to pull his caravan; he offered Django and his family a ride back to Paris in style. The car was on its last legs, though, and they suffered flat after flat with its bald tires. Finally, the trip came to a sudden halt when the engine threw one of its weary connecting rods. Stranded on the side of the road, Django telephoned his newfound GI friends at Bandol and an American soldier with an Army towtruck came to their rescue.

Django was next approached by French entrepreneurs who were opening a large cabaret and had to have him as their headliner. Django was down on his luck but never low on pride: He demanded 10,000 francs a day to play at a time when laborers were lucky to earn 1,500 francs a month. To Django's pleasant surprise, his price was accepted. After he performed for just a couple nights, though, the gendarmes padlocked the cabaret and arrested the owners; their enterprise was funded with black-market penicillin. Django was never paid a sou of his grand sum. In the end, he had to steal away from Bandol in the night to escape local toughs he owed 100,000 francs from bets on a game of boules.

Django and Naguine ventured on to Marseille looking for work in other U.S. Army camps. Again their fortunes turned. An American officer hired Django to play—and also promised he could arrange a tour to the United States. Django was overjoyed. He had long dreamed of performing in the homeland of jazz, and with Delaunay, made plans that always had to be aborted for one reason or another. Now, with the war over, the dream seemed to be coming true. When the officer unwisely asked Django what he wished to be paid, Django's reply was characteristic: "As much as Benny Goodman gets!" As no commercial air or ship service was reestablished to the United States, the officer told Django he would find him a berth in a submarine. Shuddering at the thought, Django's dream became a nightmare and he was rudely awakened once again.

Now he scrounged together some money to buy yet another car and set off on the road with Naguine and Babik—this time with a spare wheel and jerry can of gasoline. Stopping for the night by a stream, Django caught a fish for dinner. Naguine looked doubtfully at the scrawny trout that also seemed to be suffering wartime deprivations. Django, however, was elated: "Let's stay here, Naguine. There's fine fishing!" Restlessness soon outweighed the prospects for angling and they hit the road again. When Django's car inevitably broke down, they were overtaken by the traveling Cirque Bouglione, home of the famed Italian clown Achille Zavatta. The circus workers repaired Django's car, refilled his jerry can with gas, and provided him with a gaggle of old tires. For several days, Django, Naguine, and Babik traveled within the motley convoy of circus caravans, finally arriving back in *la Zone* in October 1945.

His plan to play a handful of shows in the Midi had turned into a six-month picaresque adventure.

DJANGO'S VISION of venturing to America remained indistinct, yet now America had come to him. While playing his stint at the Bal Tabarin in summer 1945,

Django and his Nouveau Quintette were often joined on stage by a succession of American musicians. Django met members of Major Glenn Miller's U.S. Army Air Force big band during the bandleader's concerts in Paris at the end of 1944. Serving as a traveling musical ambassador for the Army and a propaganda machine for the Allies, Miller recruited the best jazzmen in uniform to staff his high-profile ensemble. The band traveled with a crew of singers and even a string section to perform for troops at USO concerts in both the Atlantic and Pacific theaters of war. When their Paris shows ended for the evening, Miller's musicians migrated to Django's gig and sat in. One evening, pianist Mel Powell jammed with Django, trading choruses until finally Powell simply closed the keyboard lid to listen to Django's improvisations. Other nights, reedman Michael "Peanuts" Hucko and trumpeter Bernie Previn joined Django. Many evenings, Django's ensemble was staffed with men in olive drab.

Hearing these jam sessions, a group of French jazz fans worked magic to get them on record. Known as the Jazz Club Français, the association was one of several rivals to Delaunay's Hot Club. Delaunay was likely not happy to have *his* star record for them; Django, however, could not resist. From there, the intrigue thickened. Miller's musicians were officially "employees" of the USAAF and served under the armed forces' labor laws. They were not permitted to record commercially—even Miller couldn't budge the brass to lift a ban on releasing sides the band cut for HMV in England. Thus, the session with Django would have to be recorded on the sly. The band was listed on the label as Jazz Club Mystery Hot Band with the musicians cryptically named only by letter: U. Saxo clarinette, V. Trompette, W. Piano, X. Guitare, Y. Basse, Z. Drummer. Behind the monograms were Hucko, Previn, Powell, Django, Josz Schulman, and McKinley, respectively. In case their identities were revealed, the band was officially unpaid—although the club slipped each of Miller's musicians some francs on the side. On January 25, 1945, the mystery band cut four inspired sides more akin to Louis Armstrong's polyphonic jazz than Miller's polished swing. Their version of Benny Goodman and Chick Webb's "Stompin' at the Savoy" was recorded far from New York, but still Django played as if he was truly stomping out the beat in Gotham.

Django met up with another U.S. Army orchestra while performing for the military camps in spring and summer 1945. The 35-piece European Division of the Air Transport Command Band was directed by Sergeant Jack Platt, a former high school music teacher who enlisted the Army's brass at the Camp Lee, Virginia, recruitment center to allow him to organize a big band. When the ATC was transferred to Alabama in 1943, the band found its cornerstone in trumpeter Corporal Lonnie Wilfong, an arranger who wrote two charts recorded by Jimmy Lunceford's orchestra. After Glenn Miller's plane disappeared into the English Channel in December 1944, his band disbanded and the ATC orchestra took over as the Army's chief touring outfit. It set out to play concerts in Italy, Greece, Scandinavia, France, and soon Germany, backing performers such as Bob Hope and Jack Benny.

Wilfong had long been a fan of Django. In 1939, he bought a ticket and made a pilgrimage to Paris in a vain attempt to meet him. Now, Wilfong again sought to find him. As the ATC Band traveled France playing USO shows, Wilfong ran across posters for Django's past concerts in each city they passed through. Yet Django eluded him like a wraith. Finally, serendipity played a hand. One night in a Cannes army camp, Wilfong and the ATC Band were performing when a man with a battered guitar appeared out of nowhere and asked if he could sit in. It was none other than Django.

Back in Paris in October 1945, Wilfong renewed his friendship with Delaunay, whom he first met during his 1939 trip. And through Delaunay, Wilfong found Django again. He invited Django to come along on October 26 to the makeshift Armed Forces Network studios at Orly to perform with the ATC Band in a broadcast. Wilfong hurriedly sketched out arrangements for Django and the band. In Django's honor, they dedicated the show to him.

Delaunay organized a recording session for his Swing label on November 6 with Django and the ATC Band playing Wilfong's arrangements of Django's "Swing Guitares," "Djangology," "Are You in the Mood?" and "Manoir de mes rêves." Like Miller's USAAF outfit, the ATC Band was banned from commercial recording. But Delaunay was a wily veteran of dealing with the military mentality. To make the recordings, he again played with words, much as he had done in outwitting the Propagandastaffel. Delaunay conspired with Platt and Wilfong, and released the session's four sides under the disguise of "Django Reinhardt and his American Swing Big Band."

Django performed with the ATC Band members throughout winter 1945. He was recorded at the AFN studio on December 1 playing with a three-man rhythm section from the larger band in what was termed the Franco-American Quartet. He also performed two numbers with the AFN's alto saxman Leslie Lieber, who played virtuoso slide whistle on "Sweet Sue." During these sessions, Django borrowed a bandmate's trombone and after finding his embouchure, picked out a solo by ear. He also joined the full ATC band for a December 8 recording session broadcast in the United States on the "NBC Bond Day" show as a war bond drive. With the U.S. Army's backing, Delaunay next organized a benefit concert at Salle Pleyel on December 16, 1945, to raise money for French war orphans. Django and the ATC band lent their services, and the concert was broadcast on the AFN, BBC, Radio Luxembourg, and Radiodiffusion Française, the French national radio network. It was one of only a handful of public concerts by Django in all of 1945. Like his recording sessions that same year, the bulk of his music was played for Americans, whether they were in France or, via radio hookups, the United States.

More and more, Django believed his destiny lay in America.

JUST BEFORE PARIS'S church bells sounded midnight one eve in October 1945, the telephone rang at the Hot Club offices. When Delaunay answered, an English operator was on the line: "Hello Paris? This is London. Do not hang up!" The line went silent for a moment as Delaunay waited in wonder, then the voice of Stéphane Grappelli came to him from across the Channel. It was six years since Django and Stéphane had said a hasty *au revoir* on a London street as World War II was declared. Since then, there had been little news of Stéphane beyond a letter reprinted in the revived *Jazz Hot* asking in a panic if the news of Django's death were true. Used to speaking English rather than French now, Stéphane was so thrilled by the call he could hardly express himself. When Stéphane asked for news of Django, Delaunay said, "Don't *you* hang up, my friend! I'll pass you to Django now!" Django happened to be at Delaunay's office when the call came and he eagerly took the receiver. Yet as momentous as the occasion was, he could think of nothing to say. Stéphane too couldn't form words to express his excitement. Delaunay remembered their conversation: "The two could not find more than a word to say. Django, hearing Grappelli's voice, burst into crazy, uncontrollable laughter. And when it was his turn and Django asked Grappelli for his news, it inspired a prolonged outburst of hilarity from Grappelli. And, interrupted by roars of laughter, so this historic conversation continued between Paris and London."

Django and Stéphane communicated best through music, and Delaunay, ever the impresario, took the opportunity of this phone call and following letters to arrange a resurrection of the Quintette. As Django and Stéphane were now signed to different labels—Decca and HMV, respectively—Delaunay negotiated an arrangement between the two firms as well as with Stéphane's manager, Lew Grade. He also sowed the seeds of publicity for the reunion by arranging for Django to broadcast a series of seven shows for the BBC. The first was broadcast from Paris on January 4, 1946, on the BBC's "Kings of Jazz" program. As *Melody Maker* reported, the broadcast brought the first sounds of Django's guitar to British listeners since the Occupation.

On a fogbound Parisian morning at the end of January, Django and Naguine closed up their rented house on avenue Frochet and prepared to move to London. If he couldn't get to the United States, England seemed the next best thing to Django. Stéphane reported plenty of work, whereas Django knew from experience that jobs were scarce in postwar Paris. So they planned to join Stéphane and see what the future held. To their various Romany cousins, Django and Naguine distributed their bedclothes, kitchenware, and the furniture they had not burned during cold spells. Babik was swaddled against the winter and carried in Naguine's arms; a perambulator they bought earlier had been casually discarded on a Midi beach when they migrated back to Paris. With just one suitcase, a shopping basket filled with Babik's necessities, the novelty of a new thermos, and the essential guitar, Django and Naguine said goodbye to Négros and set off for a new life in London.

They arrived at Stéphane's hotel, the Athenaeum in Green Park, knocking at his door on January 26, the day of Stéphane's thirty-eighth birthday. "I opened my door and there was Django, his wife Naguine, their son Babik, and Charles Delaunay," Stéphane remembered. "I was in tears seeing them again after the terrible ordeals that we survived." There were embraces all around, and then Django and Stéphane picked up where they left off: Django's guitar was unpacked, Stéphane's violin found, and the two tuned up. Not knowing what song to play, Stéphane in jest bowed the first notes to the French national anthem, "La Marseillaise." Django jumped on the tune, and they turned the stately anthem into a jazz jam that moved Delaunay: "Without premeditation it was the national 'hymn' that they chose to play, solemn and impassioned. In a foreign land, these two reprobates displayed the kind of patriotic stand one would never have thought them capable of!" And, along with several other musical compatriots of Stéphane's who were agog to meet Django, they continued to play through the night.

Django and his family moved into a plush apartment in the same hotel. The rooms immediately looked like a Romany encampment with 18-month-old Babik running wild, ringing all the hotel bells that beckoned the staff. During the evenings, Django made the rounds of London's cabarets with Delaunay before sitting in with Stéphane where he was playing with George Shearing.

On the last day of January 1946, Delaunay herded Django and Stéphane to the recording session he arranged at the EMI Abbey Road Studios. The session would be billed as "Django Reinhardt et le Quintette du Hot Club de France" in an effort by Delaunay to revive the past. The rest of the old Quintette—Nin-Nin, Ninine Vées, and Emmanuel Soudieux—planned to join the reunion but could not obtain visas. So, Stéphane rounded up several accompanists, and while the ensemble followed the same formula—adding English musicians Jack Llewellyn and Allan Hodgkiss on rhythm guitars and Jamaican bassist Coleridge Goode—it was the old Quintette in its principals only. Under Delaunay's hand, the band recorded a mix of standards aimed at commercial appeal, tunes such as the Gershwins' "Embraceable You" and Guy Lombardo's "Coquette." The sole original was a riff tune called "Django's Tiger," an opportunity for Django and Stéphane to improvise freely over the harmony. To cap the session, Delaunay asked Django and Stéphane to recreate their impromptu "La Marseillaise." Stéphane led off the melody with somber violin lines full of pomp and circumstance, Goode bowing his bass to add to the grave mood. Then, in two bursts of arpeggios like Bastille Day fireworks, Django jumped into a double-time jam. As Delaunay giddily remarked on their reunion: "From the very first note, they rediscovered the miraculous communion of old as though they had never ceased to play together. Nothing seemed impossible. Stéphane was delighted to have Django beside him once more; his inspiration flowed as freely as ever, his instrument seemed to play itself. From time to time he cast a glance of confidence, of gratitude even, toward Django, who for his part was no less moved to find the man who could best express his ideas playing with him once again."

The English Quintette was back in the studio on February 1, this time to wax four sides for Decca. At the session, Django introduced Stéphane to some of his wartime compositions—"Belleville," "Mélodie au crépuscule" (released in England as "Love's Melody"), and "Nuages," which Stéphane took up as if the melody were written for his violin.

The British music press was abuzz with Django and Stéphane's reunion. Django hoped to fill in his time around the contracted BBC concerts by re-uniting with Stéphane to play London gigs while Grade plotted out a year-long tour that would take them as far as India. But it was not to be. On February 11, Django was struck ill. A recurring abscess in his throat flared up, and he was rushed to the Hôpital Français. There, he was operated on—no doubt to his great horror. While Django recuperated, the BBC programs were can-celled and dreams of an English tour again called off. Finally, after several weeks convalescing and with Babik also sick, Django and Naguine packed up their meager possessions and made the journey back to Paris.

ON HIS RETURN to France, Django found his own nightclub, La Roulotte, locked. The club's closure was symbolic of the depressed economy as a whole. France was bankrupt, and the U.S. Marshall Plan of sharing American abun-dance had yet to show its effects. The young yearned for all things American, from movies to music, fashion to affluence. But the riches of the liberators soon sparked ill will, and gratitude toward the liberators had graduated to resentment. And now, many among the French public who had swung to swing during the Occupation turned their backs on jazz as representative of American culture. La Roulotte's closure was symbolic as well of this backlash against jazz.

A further sign of the era came with the release several months later of the results of Django and Stéphane's reunion. Swing No. 229 featured "Embrace-able You" backed by the duo's "La Marseillaise," which Delaunay cautiously retitled "Échos de France." Django and Stéphane played the anthem hot, but they were playing with fire. "La Marseillaise" had been banned during the Occupation; now, after the Nazis were gone, it had became a near-sacred theme. Delaunay later claimed "Échos de France" was greeted with outrage and officially proscribed after selling just a dozen copies. The truth was more prosaic, but equally telling. While some patriots such as French World War I spy Marthe Richard had condemned the blasphemy of the anthem, there was no governmental decree against the song. Delaunay also reported Swing's parent company, Pathé-Marconi, subcontracted the disc's pressing to the Chatou firm, which refused to press the record again due to its bastardization of the anthem. But all of that may have been a ruse by Delaunay. After Swing

No. 229's first pressing and respectable sales of some 1,800 copies worldwide, sales had slowed to a trickle, so Delaunay made the decision of a good businessman and simply retired the recording. Across Swing's inventory form for "Échos de France" was written "Do not order nor press again."

Jazz's fall from grace hit Django both in finding work and in a greater sense, as a French hero. No longer did his fame shine with the once-starstruck public; "Nuages" was now a song of the past, of times best forgotten. From his zenith during the Occupation when his portrait was pinned on many a fan's walls, he was now near the nadir of his popularity. For Django, proud and vain, it was a painful blow to his self-esteem.

In spring 1946, Django found work at a small Parisian cabaret, Le Rodéo, where he was made nominal manager during his stint. He formed a quintet of young musicians with little experience, a pattern he would follow over the next several years. Yet even with Django as headliner, Le Rodéo too locked its doors, another victim of the constant meteoric rise and fall of Parisian nightclubs. Django was again out of work.

In May, Django tracked down a handful of jobs. He played a concert at Salle Pleyel on May 7 with André Ekyan's orchestra, then he led a reformed Nouveau Quintette in a recording session for Delaunay at Studio Pelouze on May 16. His ensemble was made up of the return of Hubert Rostaing on clarinet and alto sax, pianist Jacques Dieval, bassist Lucien Simoens, and drummer Arthur Motta. Django cut three sides of American pop songs and one new original, "Swingtime in Springtime." But despite the upbeat tempo of the session's songs, Django set aside his guitar when it was finished. As one friend remembered, "He will not play for less than 50,000 francs—1,000 dollars—a night, and since no one in Paris will meet his price he lives in poverty in a miserable Montmartre hotel."

As spring turned to summer, Django, Nin-Nin, and their families packed up to hit the road. They drove Django's latest automobile purchase to rue Chaptal to say *au revoir* to Delaunay, who was on his way to New York in August to license American jazz recordings for release in France. Django give Delaunay some last words of advice with hopes of arranging an American tour, then they set off. Delaunay remembered the car and their departure well: "Django's van was piloted by Nin-Nin, and inside it contained a disorder of suitcases, cooking pans, bald old tires, and some shady-looking accomplices with dark demeanors. Worthy of a 1920s western, the old jalopy vanished in a plume of smoke."

Perhaps as a reaction to his falling fortunes, Django still sought to trade on his faded celebrity. Carrying his fame in his pocket like a switchblade, he declared he had no need for a driver's license. He also delighted in taking revenge on the gendarmes that had been a curse to the Romany his whole life. Django, Nin-Nin, and their families were sitting around their campfire where they had stopped for the night in a village square. Nin-Nin and his family had their caravan while Django, Naguine, and Babik were sleeping in the back seat of their car. Into the light of the fire appeared two gendarmes, both of them red of nose and warmed inside by a bottle of wine. "Out with your identity papers!" the gendarmes demanded.

Django was ready to do battle with such demeaning abuse. The year before, he had played a concert for the Préfet of Troyes, in whose prefecture they were now camped. The Préfet had been expansive in inviting Django to return, and Django now knew he would be under the Préfet's protection. So he feigned innocence before these two drunken gendarmes and told them he didn't have any papers. The gendarmes couldn't believe their ears. They threatened to run Django and company straight to jail if he didn't produce his driver's license or automobile registration. Again, Django taunted them, saying he didn't know what such forms were. The red-nosed gendarmes now figured the car stolen and gleefully rubbed their hands at the tortures they were going to inflict on him.

Looking for further infractions, the gendarmes asked after the rest of party, insinuating Nin-Nin was off tickling trout. Naguine then entered into the fray, opening the car trunk to display a pandora's box filled with Django's collection of fishing tackle—casting rods, fly-fishing rods, long bamboo rods, an array of reels, landing nets, woven-wicker creels, bait buckets, fly wallets. This show of fancy fishing paraphernalia in the hands of a gang of Gypsies inspired new visions to the gendarmes. This swarthy character could be up to no good.

Django was set on enjoying his revenge to the fullest, however, and he was not finished inciting the gendarmes. He now led them on a tour around his car, pointing out all its legal deficiencies, from burned-out brakelights to failed turn signals.

The gendarmes were now foaming with anger. Then one collected himself and asked Django, "So *who* are you?"

"Shhh!" Django replied. "I am incognito."

Exasperated beyond endurance, the gendarme asked again, "But who are you?"

With impressive solemnity, he finally intoned his name: "I am Django Reinhardt."

The gendarmes looked at him dumbstruck. "Django Reinhardt? Who's that?"

Django certainly had not expected this. But his own pride overcame their lack of recognition of his name, and he continued on. "So, have you never heard of Duke Ellington, Benny Goodman, Louis Armstrong?"

The gendarmes were obviously not jazz connoisseurs as the names meant nothing to them. They demanded he pay a fine or go straight to jail.

"Oh no, I will not pay up so you can go drink more red wine with my money!" Django insulted them. "Drag me in!"

This defiance from a Gypsy unsettled the gendarmes, and they decided to go check before cuffing him. They walked away, issuing their final, weak warning, "We're coming back after you. Don't go anywhere!"

Off the gendarmes went, arguing between themselves, casting last glances back at Django and Naguine, the caravan parked brazenly in the town square, and their car with its mattress in the backseat and a trunk full of fishing equipment. They may have asked others at the police station or even telephoned the Préfet of Troyes about this Romany with the strange name. But they never returned to make good on their threats. Django's fame still stood for something.

IN THE MIDST of the glory of springtime in postwar Paris in 1946, a nondescript package arrived by post at 14 rue Chaptal. Addressed to Delaunay, it was yet another batch of records from the United States. Similar packages had nurtured and nourished Delaunay, Hugues Panassié, Jacques Bureau, and Pierre Nourry during the Hot Club's early years. Yet Delaunay was especially thrilled to get this package: He had not heard any new jazz recordings from America for four long years during the war. Delaunay tore open the wrapping with excitement.

Yet this was not just the usual batch of recordings. Inside, was a simple 78 that went off like a bomb.

On May 11, 1945, trumpeter John Birks "Dizzy" Gillespie led his All Star Quintette with alto saxophonist Charlie Parker into a New York City studio to cut two sides for the obscure Guild label—Dizzy's own compositions "Salt Peanuts" and "Hot House." This record, among others, was in the parcel. When Delaunay played it for the first time, he could not believe his ears. "Salt Peanuts" was a riff tune that sounded like musical onomatopoeia of the ages-old street vendor crying his wares punctuated by the hustle and bustle of modern Harlem streets. Now, "Salt Peanuts" exploded off Delaunay's record player. Few among the French jazz cognoscenti had ever even heard the names Gillespie and Parker— before the war, they were both mere sidemen in bands led by Cab Calloway and Jay McShann. The war's isolation left Delaunay in the dark on American jazz developments. Now, this new music—known by the bizarre name bebop—sounded to Delaunay so new, so novel, it was like an immaculate conception of jazz. Breathless with excitement, Delaunay called Django and all his Hot Club friends to hurry to hear the disc. They lined up in the halls and down the stairs awaiting their turn while Delaunay spun "Salt Peanuts" again and again. As Delaunay's friend, critic and musician André Hodeir, wrote in *Jazz Hot* heralding the new recordings, on this black disc with its blood-red labels was "inscribed the future of African American music." Even Django shook his head in admiration and stupefaction as he listened, saying over and over, "They play so fast, so fast."

The music *was* fast. It was also jagged and jarring with daring chromatic colorings and dazzling rhythms that were a revolution against the tedium of life as a sideman and an evolution from the sounds of swing. Bebop was born on the sly in the horn sections of the big bands and in the freedom of after-hours jam sessions. Accompanying bandleaders like Calloway and McShann as well as Earl Hines and Billy Eckstine, Gillespie and Parker built their arsenals of riffs. Gillespie was enamored with the flatted fifth, the ancient Catholic church's "devil's note," the tritone interval that broke the scale in two. He liked the flatted fifth's disarming dissonance in half-diminished chords and arpeggios. Gillespie and Parker also extended their arpeggios and chords, exploring intervals beyond the octave—flatted and natural ninths, elevenths, thirteenths. The notes added new color to their musical palette, new tension to their sound—as well as tension to the movement toward a new jazz.

Bebop coalesced in jam sessions at the Harlem clubs Minton's Playhouse and Monroe's Uptown House and on stage at New York's 52nd Street clubs like the Three Deuces. The jams were part cutting contests, part musical laboratories. Here, bebop bloomed. Walking bass lines and chordal accents from the piano vamped out harmonies. Rhythm guitars or drums played not the four-on-the-floor paradiddle of swing but new rhythmic beats moving the music forward with rimshots and off-center accents. These novel drumming techniques were dubbed "dropping bombs," a wartime term fitting in its irony for the effect they had on jazz.

Gillespie and Parker, along with others such as pianist Thelonious Monk, drummer Kenny Clarke, and trumpeter Howard McGhee, also sought new ways to harmonize old songs. Bored with playing the same changes to the same songs time after time in the big bands, they reinvented the music with exotic new harmonizations, introducing shadings of passing chords and haunting ghost notes. Now, these new harmonies created new songs.

Far from New York, Django had moved in the years since 1940 in some of the same directions as bebop with his Nouveau Quintette. Unconstrained by formal training, the rigors of musical theory, or a role as a sideman in a big band, he had long experimented with melodic extremes. Gillespie's beloved flatted fifth was a recurring tone in Django's playing. His Gypsy sensibility savored minor keys and favored emotional intervals as well as the flatted fifth in diminished arpeggios played over major chords. Django also was well versed in the use of the flatted second or ninth from his flamenco influences and employed a variety of minor scales, including the Phrygian mode and deep-toned harmonic minor scale, even in a straightforward riff tune such as "Minor Swing."

Django's evolving approach to harmonization came alive in "Dînette," a resurrection of "Dinah," the American classic that was one of the first jazz songs he had learned to play. His new harmonies took two directions. First, he was infatuated by the mood of major and minor sixth and seventh chords, adding dark dissonances to enhance melodies. He was experimenting with further minor-major key shifts within songs and adding passing chords—often intriguing diminished chords—to the harmonization. His "Dînette" was spiced by major-minor shifts, major and minor sixth and seventh chords, plus the addition of flatted and natural ninths as well as diminished and augmented chords as passing tones. It was a thoroughly modern "Dinah," and it was all Django's.

Second, his Nouveau Quintette usually featured only his guitar, as in "Dînette"—although he was at other times still backed by his favorite accompanist, Nin-Nin. Django's ensemble sound consciously moved away from the powerful *pompe* and into a looser feel, breaking the rhythm wide open. Accompanying his clarinetist, Django rarely hung on one chord voicing for more than one or two beats. As in the old days behind musette accordionists when his banjo provided rhythm, harmony, and a moving bassline all in one, his rhythm guitarwork now was constantly on the go with ascending and descending chord lines, offbeat and syncopated chordal flourishes, and stabbing accents vamping out the harmony. Django was no longer playing dance music.

Yet even in "Dînette," his ensemble was still a world away from Gillespie and Parker's bebop in velocity and rhythmic inventiveness. Hiring a pianist instead of a second guitarist and working with a drummer created a brighter sound, but for the time being, the Nouveau Quintette's rhythm remained rooted in swing instead of moving to the angry sound of bebop.

Bebop induced anger from another quarter, however. While Delaunay and the Hot Club acolytes were abuzz with bop, Panassié was outraged. He spent the war safely hidden away in his family's provincial château listening to his Louis Armstrong records. Now, a new music had evolved and he was not part of it. While Delaunay raved in letters to Panassié about "Salt Peanuts" and promised to send him a copy, Panassié fumed. By the time Delaunay finally forwarded him the record, it was too late. Panassié may simply have been put out at no longer being the epicenter of French jazz or he may truly have despised bebop. Either way, he denounced the music with all the venom in his bite. "How anybody can call this music jazz is beyond my understanding," Panassié ranted in "The Unreal Jazz," a counterpoint to his landmark book *The Real Jazz*. In his new dialectical diatribe, *La bataille du jazz*, he outlined the evolution of jazz en route to denouncing bebop like a racial scientist proving it a recessive gene. Throughout his writings, he bemoaned bebop as anti-jazz, faux jazz, the death of jazz.

However it was described, bebop was the beginning of the end for the Hot Club de France.

THE MANOUCHE have a saying, *Many children means much happiness*. Naguine was again pregnant, but this time happiness did not arrive with the birth of their second son.

Born in mid 1946, he was named Jimmy in honor of New Orleans clarinetist Jimmy Noone. But this Jimmy did not flourish. He died in the Hôpital des

Enfants Malades just weeks after his birth. Django and Naguine were devastated. Filled with great sadness, Django requested that a full Mass be performed at his little Jimmy's funeral. A dark progression of Romanies from across Paris made their way to the church on rue de Sèvres neighboring the hospital. Amid the glowing light from hundreds of candle flames, the church filled with the somber, grandiose sound of the organ playing Django's requests of Bach, Handel, and Mozart. The infant Jimmy Reinhardt was buried in the Cimetière de Thiais past *la Zone* to the south of Paris.

Among the Manouche, the deceased are not spoken of—*on n'en parle pas*. It is a sign of respect and homage and tribute. Django and Naguine now grieved in silence, and Django's guitar too was quiet.

UNINSPIRED, LACKING JOBS, and mourning his son, Django turned his back on music. The drive to create, the need to express had not left him, however.

The spark of new inspiration came to Django over dinner with pianist and bandmate Eddie Bernard, whose apartment's walls were hung with paintings by Bernard's father. Django asked Bernard *père* if painting was difficult.

"No more difficult than playing your guitar," he responded.

"Good!" Django replied, and he was off on a new project.

Throughout his travels, Django had long been surrounded by painters— both amateurs and true artists. Delaunay continued to draw, following his famous parents. He often spent his evenings in cabarets sitting alongside the musicians and sketching exquisite portraits that were collected in 1939 into a portfolio of lithographs, *Hot iconography*. Roger Chaput was a fine portraitist, and his humorous caricatures—including images of Django and Nin-Nin— appeared regularly in *Jazz Hot*. Following World War II, Chaput grew disillusioned with the hardscrabble life of the musician and moved to Toulon to became a professional cartoonist. Others, such as Pierre Nourry, dabbled with drawing and painting. And among Django's acquaintances were Toulonnais painter Amédée Pianfetti, met during Django's early days in La Rode. Still it may have been his encounter in 1931 with Émile Savitry that proved the most formative in Django's new endeavor, as it had been with his music. Among Savitry's souvenirs of his South Seas travels were his paintings of Maoris and their island life, colorful recreations akin to Gaugin's canvases. And in his atelier in Paris, Savitry continued to paint where Django could watch pictures created before his eyes.

It was Nin-Nin who first took up a paintbrush. In 1935 when the Quintette was starting to make itself heard, Nin-Nin began painting. His pictures were pastoral scenes of Romany life with caravans parked on the edges of French villages, horses at feed, Gypsy women carrying water and building campfires, children and dogs at play. Nin-Nin's hand was sure, his proportions and sense of perspective clear. His vision, meanwhile, was sentimental for olden days at a time when he was living in the heart of the city in a rented apartment on the grimy boulevard de Clichy.

Now it was Django's turn. He set aside his plectrum for a brush, his guitar for a palette. He'd pack up his painter's box and set off up rue Pigalle to wander the narrow streets of Montmartre seeking inspiration. Back home, he'd paint through the evenings by the dim light of an oil lamp, surrounded by the scents of turpentine and linseed oil. He drew scenes of Gypsy life, pastoral reminiscences both documentary and nostalgic, as well as landscapes of the French countryside or sea. His favorite subject was female nudes—a staunch Gypsy taboo. Django's nudes were drawn from memory and perhaps wistful imagination—rarely did he use models—and he amplified their contours and forms, creating voluptuous Odalisques, part Reubens, part Modigliani. Django's images were often candid and straightforward, accentuated by dashes of rich color. Django's paintings also followed the style of Gauguin and Matisse, the modern painters known as the Fauves, or wild beasts, for their fierce love of basic form and brilliant hues.

Django was a Fauve in the true sense. He never studied nor even seemed to have interest in painting technique or problems of perspective. His was a natural eye, and his images were naïve and joyful, like a child's happy creation—in one painting he even added eyes to the face of the sun rising over a landscape. And in his nudes, he rarely showed the figure's hands, perhaps a display of a personal phobia due to his own handicap—or perhaps because he simply couldn't render the hand's intricacies. Nor could Django be bothered by the musty details of art history. He rarely visited art galleries, never went to museum exhibits: While playing a tour in the Netherlands he skipped the collection of Rembrandts at the Rijksmuseum to visit instead a museum of horrors to shiver over guillotines and instruments of torture. The first exhibition of Django's canvases opened on May 14, 1947, at Galérie Constellation at Le Bœuf sur le Toit where he was then performing with his big band. Organized by his impresario of the day, B. Étienne, the show was accompanied by a small catalogue listing Django's seven canvases. All bore simple titles—*Maison, Petit nu, Femme gitane, Château de Moutiers, La Chemise ôtée, Week-end aux USA*. As Delaunay stated, "Django's painting is especially interesting as it was born directly and immaculately from music, and for him, the two arts—music and painting—are thus intimately related." Asked about his art during a showing later in February 1951, Django could only describe his work in terms of music. A radio announcer queried him, "Your paintings, they are in what tonality?"

Django responded without hesitating, "In a minor key."

Why? came the question.

"Because it's more *mysterious*."

For now, Django was a painter rather than a guitarist, prouder of his canvases than his music.

DJANGO'S GUITAR remained silent through much of 1946. Not until September did he perform again, roused from his dolor by the promise of a Swiss tour. He reformed his Nouveau Quintette with Nin-Nin and an ensemble of young musicians, including clarinetist Michel de Villers, pianist Bernard, bassist Alix Bret, and drummer Pierre Brun. In the first week of September, they departed by train for Geneva. From there, they traveled on to perform at Neuchâtel and Zürich, closing the tour with a concert on September 21 at Basel's Stadtcasino. Django, always enamored with the outdoors, fell in love with Switzerland's mountains. Resurrected by this alpine therapy, he bought a complete mountain trekking outfit, including a new pair of hiking boots. And when he returned to Paris, he strutted about in his new gear on the mountain of Montmartre.

Django also had something else to announce. While he lost much of his tour earnings in the Swiss casinos, he also ran into some good luck. In Zürich, he was chased down by a British agent for the prestigious American William Morris Agency who carried an invitation from Duke Ellington to join him in the United States.

Now, Django told Delaunay, he was off to America.

The news of the American tour must have come as a shock to Delaunay. On Django's behalf, Delaunay had attempted to organize concerts in the United States starting in the prewar years in conversations with Ellington's impresario Irving Mills when he visited Paris. Delaunay had continued his endeavors during his first trip to New York in 1939 to correct galley proofs for the American version of his *Hot discography*, published by the Commodore Music Shop in 1940. He traveled to New York again in August 1946 to license American recordings. While there, he had attempted to schedule shows for Django, including a tour with Ellington. But try as he might, Delaunay could not put plans in place. Now, Django himself had negotiated the contract for the American tour, leaving his devoted agent out of the picture.

Django went through agents, managers, booking impresarios, and even fellow musicians like he went through guitar strings: He used them as long as they were in tune with his needs and played them hard until they broke. Django sought Delaunay's services as a manager and agent when and if he needed them, preferring the freedom of doing business in his own horse-trading fashion. This ongoing situation was a frustration for Delaunay, who styled himself as the discoverer of Django's talents. Delaunay's was a heroic yet thankless task. And now Django announced his news with the self-centered innocence of a child boasting of his good fortune and without a thought for the effect this might have on the friend who had worked for years to arrange a similar tour. Django may have invited Delaunay along to act as his interpreter since Delaunay loved the United States and spoke English—or at least an eccentric form of English learned from African American jazzmen in Paris. But Delaunay politely refused the offer, leaving no place for him in Django's plans.

Delaunay was a mild-mannered man who held few grudges, even in the metaphysical battleground that was French jazz. But Django's handling of the American tour was the start of a rupture in their long-standing business relationship and personal friendship that grew over the last years of Django's life. Delaunay didn't often air his grievances in public, yet eight years later, writing his *Souvenirs* of Django's life, the issue of the American tour was still an open wound. He began his account of the tour with these wrathful words as though he was describing Dante's descent into Hell: "Like the sinner who quits this ignoble world to meet his eternal judge, Django Reinhardt arrived in the United States. . . ."

That was not the way Django saw things. He was now off to conquer America. Django planned first to take New York by storm, likely with thoughts of staying in the United States for good with Naguine and Babik joining him later. And he bragged to all who would listen that while in America he was taking time out from playing his guitar to do screen tests for Hollywood's Paramount Pictures. He had heard that actress Dorothy Lamour owned several of his records and was his greatest fan. Lamour would surely want Django as her new leading man on the silver screen.

11

Pilgrimage
1946–1947

To DJANGO, it was the promised land.

Since 1934 and his first disastrous audition for Louis Armstrong in Paris, he yearned to play his guitar in the homeland of jazz, fantasizing of jamming alongside Satchmo on the fertile soil that gave birth to the music, picking out his improvisations with the American greats in the high churches of jazz—the Savoy, Roseland, Paramount, Apollo, Minton's, Monroe's, the Onyx, the Three Deuces. Those reveries had gone unrequited, concert plans thwarted, tour schemes halted by war.

On October 29, 1946, he first set foot in the United States. Django had finally arrived.

He came at the invitation of Duke Ellington. As special guest soloist with Ellington's orchestra, Django would tour the United States from Cleveland to Nebraska, along the East Coast to a finale in Detroit. The high point of the tour would be two concerts at New York's Carnegie Hall, the pantheon of American music.

Yet when the Pan American Airways Yankee Clipper landed in New York from London, it held Django but not his guitar. He left his famous Selmer modèle Jazz guitar behind in Paris, descending from the airplane with only the clothes he wore, unburdened by any luggage. Django hadn't even troubled with a toothbrush.

Instead, he brought his dreams of making it big in America. As he was the greatest guitarist who ever lived, he believed in his innocent hubris the famed American luthiers would offer him their finest instruments like keys to the city. As his records spun magic on turntables across Europe, the renowned American labels would vie with each other for the privilege of recording him. As he was the brightest star in the constellation of European jazz, lucrative concert deals with the best American musicians would rain down on him like stardust. And as Dorothy Lamour was rumored to be his greatest fan, Paramount and other movie studios would rush to exalt him on the silver screen. As he told his drummer Pierre Fouad before quitting Paris, "If I was rich, I would live in New York. I would have a beautiful bungalow—not a skyscraper, just a bungalow—the best cognacs and a wonderful billiards table. I wouldn't do anything, just play a bit of music from time to time so I could become even more rich. I would live like those who own goldmines or oilwells. I would live like Ford, Rockefeller, Rubirosa. In the afternoon, I would go hear the Boston Symphony Orchestra. I would listen to classical music—the melodies they play are so, so beautiful. I would listen to Bach, to Beethoven, to Stravinsky. At dinnertime, I would go to a chic restaurant on the island of Manhattan, a penthouse restaurant at the top of a skyscraper. It would be like owning the whole city. When I ate, I would not be hurried—it is bad for the stomach. During the whole meal I would listen to sweet music. Glenn Miller is good for the digestion. Then, after coffee and a drink, I would leave for Harlem, because dancing too facilitates the digestion. That's why I would go to dance in Harlem to the good swing rhythms of our black brothers." It was all an innocent and idyllic dream. Yet Django believed in it with all his heart.

Django's U.S. tour of 1946–1947 was a pivotal point in his life. His American sojourn included great successes and cruel disappointments. Many—including Django himself—later labeled the tour a failure. And, in some aspects, it was. The feeling that he had failed in the United States haunted his final years.

Yet Django's American travels also inspired him to create some of his most stunning music, and for that reason his time in the United States would be an enduring success.

NEW YORK CITY rose up around him like a fantasy. The skyscrapers were modern-day castles, ramparts of steel and brick and glass soaring heavenward. Like bebop come to life, the streets reverberated in a concatenation of vendors' cries and police sirens, hydraulic hisses, brake screeches, and all the music of machinery. Everywhere he looked were those grand American automobiles he swooned over. And every time he turned his head American women caught his eye like Hollywood starlets strolling the sidewalks. Paris was the capital of the Belle Époque, but New York was in a breathless race to supplant it as the metropolis of the new century. New York was bigger and taller and faster and louder than Paris. It was *modernistique*. In Paris you had to wait forever for a meal to be cooked and served in a brasserie; in New York, it was ready at your beck and call, pushed by a bodiless hand through the gleaming metallic compartments of an automat. Elevators whisked you to penthouse suites in the clouds, escalators lowered you into the depths of subways. Paris was the fabled City of Light, yet the theater marquees around Times Square boasted bigger and brighter lights. And while Paris was war-ravaged and bankrupt, New York's prosperity was on show everywhere he looked. It was all he envisioned—and more.

Yet upon arriving in New York, Django had but one pressing question: "Where is Dizzy Gillespie?"

Told Gillespie was playing in Baltimore, Django was ready to drop everything and venture off to jam with him. Impetuous to a fault, Django seemed to have forgotten all about his scheduled tour with Ellington.

American jazz cognoscenti had not forgotten. Django's debut with Ellington was anticipated with sheer giddiness after *Down Beat* announced rumors. The premier American weekly news magazines *Time* and *Newsweek* dueled to outdo each other in lauding Django. His story made for good copy: Being a Gypsy inspired romantic notions in the big-city reporters, and his mythic rebirth after the caravan fire, leaving him just two fingers to fret his guitar, branded him a freakish genius. *Time*'s capsule biography of Django was pure fairy tale: "Swarthy Django Reinhardt, now 36, is an almost illiterate gypsy who was born in a *roulotte* (trailer) and only recently has succumbed to houses. . . . Django developed a one-finger picking style because his left hand was badly burned in a fire and became useless for chords [*sic*]." *Time* also poked fun at Naguine, noting that "Django's 250-lb. gypsy wife" stayed behind in Paris. *Newsweek* was equally enraptured by the aura surrounding Django: "By legend, he is supposed to prefer living in the open in a caravan with his multitudinous Romany 'cousins,' but in New York City he was outwardly happy at the swank Hampshire House on Central Park South. He speaks almost no English, but even in French is a strict direct-question-and-answer man." Yet, racist jabs and false "facts" aside, any publicity was good publicity.

On October 30, the day after his arrival, Django met up with Ellington where the band was finishing a two-week engagement at the slick Aquarium nightspot. Ellington's career was riding high. With a reputation built on his decades at the famed Cotton Club, he was now touring the world, fueled by his composer's royalties, with a 17-piece orchestra at a time when most big bands had long gone bankrupt. Ellington's orchestra was arguably the finest big band in jazz with original compositions, airtight arrangements, and stellar musicians playing breathtaking solos. At the center was Ellington—handsome, dapper, brilliant, and inspired by a boundless vision of music.

To capture the reunion between Django and Ellington, *Down Beat* sent reporter and photographer William Gottlieb. A great fan and friend of Ellington, at the Aquarium Gottlieb had the run of the club, and he was led backstage to meet Django. Gottlieb asked to take his picture, and Duke's guitarist Fred Guy loaned Django his Swedish Levin guitar as a prop to pick on. Gottlieb remembered: "We didn't communicate very much, as Django spoke very little English. I didn't know much about Django's personality. When I couldn't get a grasp of someone, I'd at least try to focus on something. Now in Django's case, that was easy. The most interesting thing about him were the fingers of his left hand which had been mutilated in a fire in his caravan when he was a young man in Belgium [*sic*]. So I made damn sure when I took my key photograph of him that you could see those fingers. It would have made an impression to have written about it, but it was that much more impressive to see it in a photograph. That was my objective." The images captured Django in the tweed sport coat he appeared in often over the next months as he had little else to wear. With a healthy dose of pomade glistening in his dark hair and the ubiquitous cigarette dangling idly from his lips, he picked at the guitar, using his fire-damaged fingers to help his two good fingers fret a chord. Django studied his guitar with a serene look on his face—outwardly happy to have finally arrived at the center of jazz. The image appeared on the cover of *Down Beat* welcoming Django to the United States.

ON THE EVE of his long dreamed of American debut, Django found himself a guitarist without a guitar. Now, without Nin-Nin to serve him, he was forced to find his own instrument.

That he would play an electric guitar with Ellington was certain. The orchestra was booked in municipal auditoriums and theater halls; no acoustic guitar had the power to project above the band in such spaces. And besides, this was modern America where Charlie Christian had been playing his electric Gibson with Benny Goodman since 1939. Under the banner headline "Guitarmen, Wake Up and Pluck! Wire for Sound; Let 'Em Hear You Play," Christian penned an electrified declaration of independence in *Down Beat* on December 1, 1939. "Guitar players have long needed a champion, someone to explain to the world that a guitarist is something more than just a robot plunking on a gadget to keep the rhythm going. For all most bandleaders get out of them, guitarists might just as well be scratching washboards with sewing thimbles," he wrote. Yet Christian and a handful of others had gone electric and were now being heard. As he stated, "The dawn of a new era is at hand for all these fine guitarists who had become resigned to playing to feed their souls but not necessarily their stomachs. Electrical amplification has given guitarists a new lease on life."

Still, Django had his doubts. Playing jazz on his acoustic Selmer, his sound was musical pointillism, an impressionistic daubing of myriad notes to create an image. With an electric guitar, he had to learn to paint anew using a broader brush, balancing the sustain, volume, and tone. The sound was not sympathetic to his ear. He felt he could not reproduce what he considered the "human voice."

Django's former bandmate Marcel Bianchi was the first in Paris to perform on an electric guitar, in 1944. Nin-Nin soon followed Bianchi's lead, experimenting with a screw-on pickup beginning in 1944–1945. And Django was not a neophyte when it came to electric guitars. He was playing his Selmer with a pickup when Charlie Byrd saw him in Pigalle in 1945 after the Liberation. Paris's Major music shop became guitarists' new hangout and source of the latest pickups and amps, and it was here that Django likely found an American Rowe-DeArmond, a Swiss Bâle, or one of the early French Stimer magnetic pickups to screw onto his Selmer. And during the several weeks of his Swiss tour in October 1946 preceding his venture to America, Django performed electrified.

Yet an electric guitar was not simply a louder version of an acoustic guitar. A whole new instrument, as different as an automobile from a horse, it required new skills and revised technique. Volume was one factor. Django had played acoustic instruments since his childhood in noisy dance halls where loudness was next to godliness. Now, volume was available with the spin of a dial, and he had to adapt his picking hand to a more refined attack. Sustain was another concern. As with an accordion, a plucked note could resonate much longer on an electric guitar than on an acoustic, and flurries of chromatic runs became a blizzard of noise if he didn't dampen notes with the palm of his picking hand. During his performances in France since the Liberation and on the Swiss tour, Django had had the opportunity to adopt and adapt to his electrified Selmer. As Stéphane remembered, "He was like a child with a new toy." Yet when he first took the stage with Ellington, he was still learning the potentials and modifying his playing to the more refined control.

On the Ellington tour Django played an acoustic sunburst Gibson hollowbody L5 fitted with a DeArmond pickup and amplified by a small combo amp. Where or how he got this guitar is not known for certain: Charles Delaunay asserted almost mockingly that Django was forced to pay for it himself. Django may have been given the guitar by a Gibson representative or a William Morris agent may have acquired it for him. It's also possible that Ellington or his musicians aided Django in finding the guitar. Either way, Django acquired this Gibson sometime between his arrival in New York on October 29 and the tour's first show on November 4. Now he was ready to play.

WITH HIS NEW GUITAR and amplifier at the ready and Ellington's Aquarium stand ended, Django and the band boarded a train headed west. The tour opened on November 4, 1946, in Cleveland, Ohio. Promotion for the show began in October with advertisements in the city's newspapers trumpeting the arrival of Ellington as "America's genius of jazz." Posters, handbills, and ads spotlighted the most famous members of Ellington's vast ensemble—saxman Johnny Hodges, trombonist Lawrence Brown, violinist Ray Nance, and vocalists Kay Davis and Marion Cox. No mention was made of Django.

There was a simple reason for this. Contracted to appear on the tour only weeks prior, Django was a late addition to the program. As Ellington remembered, "We brought Django to America, we decided, after all our concerts were all booked and advertised, as Django was available, and I said bring him! So we added him to the concert program, for kicks, this is it. He's a great man, he's available, what the hell, I want to hear him myself, I don't care if anyone else wants to hear him!" The newspaper ads and posters had been drafted before Django signed on. Promoters may have thought about holding the ads and adding Django's name, but they probably decided to save their money: Ellington was the draw, and most folk in the American hinterlands had never heard of this Gypsy guitarist, save for the odd jazz fanatic or serviceman who saw Django play in some Pig Alley dive.

These late preparations for the tour also carried over to the musicians' rehearsals. Because Django was a last-minute addition, he and Ellington had little opportunity to prepare. In keeping with his impetuousness, Django rarely worried about practicing, but Ellington was famous for his strict rehearsals and intricate band arrangements. For the first show, Django and Ellington made hasty preparations backstage before the concert. "They rehearsed only 20 minutes before their Cleveland performance," reported *Time*. "They talked in sign language and monosyllables, since Django understands hardly any English. '*Tiger Rag*—number *un*,' the Duke said, holding up one finger. 'First you play around . . . just a few riffs' (the Duke made guitar-strumming motions). 'Then we give you a chord—wham, you go into *Tiger* by yourself and we start giving you the beat' (the Duke demonstrated on the piano.) 'Understand?' Django grinned enthusiastically. They jammed for five minutes, until one by one the band boys left their cards, gossip and naps to gather around, calling out their encouragement: 'Go to it, master. Yah, yah, yah.'"

Crafting another on-the-spot arrangement, Duke asked Django, "What key do you want to play in?"

"No key," answered Django, confused by the English term "key" yet not wanting to lose face.

"But there has to be a key?" said a puzzled Ellington.

"I follow," replied Django. "You start."

And, famed for his musical ear, Django immediately hit the right key.

He hit the right note with his first American audience that night as well. Contrary to his own impressions, Django was certainly not a household name in the United States, but after each show his name was on every concertgoer's lips. As *Newsweek* noted following the Cleveland show: "The 1,800 people who went to the Cleveland Public Music Hall to hear Duke Ellington on the night of Nov. 4 were completely unprepared for what happened. There had been no advance publicity. And when they found out that the Duke was sponsoring the American debut of Django Reinhardt, that still meant little or nothing except to the heppest cats in the crowd. But when the audience heard and saw, they knew they had drawn something special. With left fingers flying over the frets and right hand plucking at dizzy speed, the dark French jazz guitarist showed that he was a master of his instrument in tone, technique, and musicianship." The Cleveland newspapers were unanimous in their applause for Django. The morning after, the *Cleveland Press* carried an encore of praise: "Duke Ellington came to Cleveland without fanfare and he gave his fans here the greatest treat in the annals of local jazz when he introduced in this country, for the first time, the hottest guitar player in the world." *The Cleveland Plain Dealer* echoed the plaudits: "In the hands of this virtuoso, who resembles the screen's Adolphe Menjou, an electric guitar acquires richer, magical qualities. His digital dexterity was remarkable, in intricate chords that were executed with such technical brilliance that the band musicians kept shouting, 'Go to it, master!'" The *Plain Dealer*'s headline on newsstands throughout the city was unambiguous: "French Guitar Artist Steals Duke's Concert."

Ellington did not worry about any such robbery. Throughout the tour, he enjoyed teasing the unaware audiences: Since Django's appearances had not been advertised, Ellington sometimes brought him out to play without preamble. "I forget what spot I had him in, somewhere in the first part of the second half, something like that," Ellington recounted. "First we'd put up something like 'Honeysuckle Rose,' and people would say, 'I think it *is* Django!' But nobody had said he was going to be there or anything! And then I would say, 'We're going to play, Django is going to state a theme and follow through.' And so we would just hit him with a pin spot and he'd be sitting there, black out the whole stage, he'd state some theme, every night it was a different theme, and none of his stuff was recorded, what a horrible thing. He'd play these wonderful things and just sit there in that one soft spot, and just play and play."

FROM HIS ROOM at Minneapolis's grand Hotel Nicollet several days later, Django wrote a letter home to clarinetist Gérard Lévêque, proudly outlining his tour itinerary. After the Cleveland show, the band boarded a train to Canada, where they played for a dance at Toronto's Mutual Street Arena. The tour then led them back into the United States to play Toledo and Cincinnati, Ohio; Indianapolis, Indiana; Chicago; and Rochester, Minnesota, before venturing to play a one-night stand in Minneapolis on November 13, marking a midpoint in their travels. The tour would continue on to Lincoln and Omaha, Nebraska; Kansas City, Missouri; Des Moines, Iowa; and then a long train ride back to New York City for two concerts at Carnegie Hall; Baltimore, Maryland; Lynchburg and Petersburg, Virginia; Philadelphia; Syracuse, New York; Boston; Cranston, Rhode Island; and a finale in Detroit.

In his letter, Django went on to boast that all of the musicians had magnificent bedrooms and he and Ellington shared *un petit living room*—"it's a bit better than the place Pigalle," he added in jest. He ended the two-page letter stating that he reminisced often with Ellington about the glory days of the Quintette,

requested the address of his brother Nin-Nin, and closed with salutations to
Lévêque and his parents, who often welcomed Django into their home.

This was likely the first letter Django ever wrote in his life, and he was
proud to show off his hard-earned literacy. He wrote in phonetic French
fraught with misspellings, his penmanship that of an unsure child. Scrawling
all his letters in the upper case, they ran ever larger as he gained enthusiasm
for his subject, racing and rambling crookedly across sheets of free hotel letterhead so that he required two pages for the message most people squeezed
into a simple picture postcard.

Django's letter overflowed with his obvious happiness. Yet the fact that he
even wrote the letter carried a hidden message within his innocent words.
While Django had been on the move most of his life, this marked the first
time he ventured far from his own traveling home without his brother, his
wife, or his usual cabal of fellow Romany musicians. His inspiration to write
home came not only from his pleasure in bragging about the tour but also a
growing sense of separation. The distance and the loneliness would soon come
to have an effect on Django that he had never foreseen.

IN FINE FRENCH FASHION, Django found life in America amusing and bizarre.
First, there was the underwear.

Traveling by train across the United States, Django shared a two-berth
compartment with Ellington. On their first night out, Django walked through
the rest of the band's sleeping car en route to the toilet before going to bed.
As he entered, he was struck by a sight that left him flabbergasted: All of the
bandmen sported flowered boxer shorts printed with a beautiful summer's
day worth of blossoms and blooms. Django could not believe his eyes. Then
he could not resist taunting his fellow musicians in the little bit of English he
knew. "You're crazy!" he yelled at his American bandmates in a mixture of
astonishment and prudish French outrage at their lack of class. Forgetting all
about his trip to the bathroom, Django hustled back to his suite to let Ellington
in on his discovery. But when he opened the door to their shared berth, there
was Ellington in his own pair of flowered boxers—and they were even gaudier
than those of his musicians.

The flowered underwear secretly caught Django's fancy, however. When
he returned to New York City at the tour's end, he set out in search of his
own pair—yet was too embarrassed to buy them himself, enlisting instead a
French friend to make the purchase.

On the subject of American women, Django was less prudish. He complained that American females were consistently cold to his charms. This was
a point of honor to Django, and his belief that the puritanical American women
were not enamored by his attention was simply too much for his pride. Chicago guitarist Andy Nelson remembered one instance of Django's frustration

brought on by a joke lost in translation between the jesting Americans and the seriousness with which Django took his love life. Nelson was at a bar with Django and friends after the Chicago concerts, and their waitress was impressed to hear that Django was the world's greatest guitar player. She said she wanted to greet him in French and asked the Americans how. One wag told her to say "*Voulez-vous coucher avec moi?*" Django lit up over this lovely lass. He responded, "*Oh! Oui!*" When it was time to leave, Django refused to go without the confused waitress, crying out in his few English words as they dragged him from the bar, "Oh no, the lady wants me!"

Ellington also remembered Django's fascination with American women. "You had to stay with him every minute because if a chick went by, he'd be behind her," Ellington recounted. "If somebody was coming down the elevator and he sees a sharp chick, oh man! He'd get in the cab with her, Django was too much man!"

Django also had another tack for attracting women: To while away the time on his return to New York, he began painting again and set up a makeshift studio in his hotel room. Painting served as a pastime to ease his growing loneliness. Django found "models" willing to come up to his room to pose. During his time in New York, he was prolific in painting nudes.

Guitarist Johnny Smith recounted another anecdote regarding Django's sometimes skewed sense of correctness: "Django invited me to join him at this club where he was working [following the tour], the Café Society Uptown, a real hoity-toity place. I didn't even have on a tie and he hadn't shaved, and I didn't want to go in but he insisted—I had to be his guest for dinner. So we go into this restaurant and the place was full of people in dinner clothes and looking immaculate. They put us at a table way over in the corner—I guess to get us out of the way. So we sat there and all of a sudden Django picked up his knife and started banging on the table. People started looking around because by now dishes were falling off the table, and waiters ran over to try to quiet him down. They spoke French, so finally we found out the reason for the commotion: he was insulted because all the other tables had a little glass vase with a flower in it and our table didn't. And he just tore up the joint because that was an insult!"

And finally, racism haunted the black band members whenever and wherever they traveled. It may not have been as bad as some black musicians faced in the 1920s and 1930s, when they were forced to enter showy hotels and ballrooms through back delivery doors, eat in the kitchen, and travel in segregated train cars. Yet instances still occurred, at least one of which Django witnessed. As a Romany in France, Django suffered incidents of enduring racism against his own people and quickly perceived and rebelled against any discrimination of his fellow bandmates. Django did not take such insults kindly, whether they were directed against him or his black friends, and this created a unique kinship between a French Gypsy and these African Americans. Drum-

mer Sonny Greer recalled: "I remember one time we played a concert in
Pittsburgh. So he, a French boy, say, 'Come on Sonny, we go have a drink.' I
say all right. So we go in this high-class joint, we stand at the bar, cat don't
pay him no mind. So you know, French hot, so he knock on the bar, 'Service!'
And the guy says, 'I can serve you Mister,' but he wouldn't serve me. 'What'd
he say that for?' Had to drag the guy out of the bar. He wanted to create a
scene. I said, 'Man, it's nothing. Forget it.' He says, oh, a lot of French. I
don't know what he was saying but I know it was hot!"

DJANGO'S MUSIC with Ellington was also hot. For most of the audiences, this
was the first time they had heard a guitar played with such virtuosity. One fan
described the Chicago shows: "The concert started to a standing-room-only
audience. Probably every guitar player in the midwest was in attendance. The
band and music was marvelous. Duke's band was never less than excellent.
Thing was, the band kept playing and playing and no Django. The band played
another song and then another and *still* no Django. We figured Django must
have done one of his legendary 'no-shows,' preferring to play to the pigeons
in Grant Park, across the street from the Opera House. Finally, Duke Ellington
announced, 'Now ladies and gentlemen, the incomparable Django Reinhardt.'
Django came on-stage to thundering applause. He stood while stagehands set
up his amplifier, and hooked his guitar to it. He sat down with his guitar, a
beautiful Gibson L5, I'll always remember that. The band started playing
'Honeysuckle Rose.' They played chorus after chorus after chorus. I told [a
friend] that it seemed like they must have hired him to play rhythm! The
band must have played 12 to 15 choruses. Suddenly, at the point where we
just about gave up on the whole thing, Ellington pointed to his left, toward
Reinhardt, and dropped his arm while announcing over the microphone,
'Django.' At that point, the band stopped cold. Django took the four bar break.
I have never heard more pure guitar in four bars than I heard in that four bar
break. It sounded like an explosion! He hit his guitar and played one of the
wildest chromatic runs I have ever heard. When he finished the four bar break
and started the chorus, 3,000 members of the audience simultaneously jumped
to their feet and cheered."

This Chicago concert was secretly recorded by research chemist and Chicago jazz collector Dr. John Steiner, surviving as the sole known recordings
of Django from the American tour. Steiner was a great Ellington fan, and
made clandestine arrangements with ushers at the Chicago Civic Opera House
to capture the show. He was well-connected and known by all area aficionados as half of the Steiner-Davis record label, so had little trouble getting unofficial permission to set up his recording equipment. His record-cutter was a
monstrous contraption as large as a refrigerator, and Steiner toiled away with
it like a mad scientist in his laboratory, bent over the plates as the music played,

brushing cut acetate from the spinning record as it was recording. He recorded one of Ellington's complete Chicago shows purely for his own pleasure and with no plans to release them. These private recordings were later
commercially released by Delaunay.

Listening to the Chicago recordings with Ellington, one hears a new
Django. He had grown dramatically from the former Quintette soloist, and if
you didn't know it was Django on these cuts, you might not guess it. He
sounded as though he was in complete control of his new electric guitar, so
fluidly and effortlessly did he play. But there's something more to the music,
something startling. Only four tunes were captured—"Honeysuckle Rose,"
two tracks nicknamed "Ride, Red, Ride" and "A Blues Riff," and a solo improvisation. "Ride, Red, Ride" spun off of "Tiger Rag," creating a modern
version of an old classic. It opened with luxurious guitar lines punctuated by
stabbing melodic chords before Django bounced into double-time improvisations played at top bebop speed. In "A Blues Riff," he established a simple
blues head before venturing off to toy with the nuances of the melody, his
fingers traveling over his guitar in aleatoric abandon, drawing spontaneous
applause from the audience and shouts of encouragement from his band members. For "Honeysuckle Rose," one of the Quintette's old favorites, Django's
playing was at its most modern. He was inventive and innovative, even off the
wall in his reworkings of Fats Waller's famous melody. Django's phrasing
had evolved into longer, more expressive lines with new accents and complex
dialogues, as though he suddenly spoke a new language. As Django proved
during the first makeshift rehearsals with Ellington backstage before the opening American tour show in Cleveland, he was not a slow learner.

Django's music also enthralled Ellington and his musicians. Ellington's
star trombone player, Lawrence Brown, summed up the band members' respect for the guitarist: "Ah, Django. That was the first time we ran into a real
terrific guitar player. Django didn't have but three fingers [*sic*]. Yeah, he had
three fingers and he would do impossible things with those three fingers on
guitar. Oh, yes, he really registered with the American audience."

It was the orchestra's venerable drummer, William "Sonny" Greer, who
was perhaps most taken by Django's music. Years later, he spoke of the tour
with sustained fascination: "Something else. He was something else, man.
Django Reinhardt—yeah. . . . I tell you, man, that cat could take a guitar and
make it talk. Nobody played like him. . . . We were playing a concert, I think it
was in Boston. At the auditorium in Boston. So we had about an hour before—
we always got to the place about an hour or so, the band would be relaxed. So
me and him, he was sitting backstage, playing one of the things he used to
play with the Hot Five, a fast thing, you know. So I had some brushes and a
newspaper. So just me and him were playing. He said, 'I like that.' Duke
come in and said, 'I like that.' So as a surprise encore, we did it. Me and him
and Duke was playing a little piano in the back, and the bass. We done it, it

was a big thing. Duke said, keep it. I don't know what it was called, he had some fancy French name for it, he used to play it with the French Hot Five."

Yet it was an incident nearly inexpressible in mere words that showed the effect Django's guitarwork had on even these accomplished musicians. At the start of the tour after Django and Ellington's very first rehearsal of their very first song, Sonny Greer's ear was caught by Django's playing. Stunned by the music, his response was succinct: "Well, fuck my britches!"

STILL, SOME CRITICS and jazz fans were disappointed. Django was performing each night with only Ellington and his rhythm section, not the full orchestra as they expected. But behind the curtains, there may have been several reasons for this arrangement.

Ellington had not planned to hire only Django; he had sought to bring the full Quintette to the United States. He first heard the Quintette in France in 1934, and wanted to introduce American audiences to this French brand of string jazz. Only later, in the early 1950s, did Stéphane discover he and the rest of the Quintette had been offered this chance. Meeting up again with Ellington at the Club Saint-Germain in Paris, Ellington asked Stéphane why he had not accompanied Django to America. "By what mystery had this proposition never reached me? I do not know," lamented Stéphane. The so-called "mystery" was not so mysterious, and Stéphane surely realized that: The underlying reason lay in the competitive jealousy between Django and Stéphane that was a cornerstone of the Quintette. Django was told of Ellington's offer and accepted—for himself. He always saw himself as the star of the Quintette, and here was a chance to prove it.

When Django arrived to play with Ellington, he thus did not have the backing band Ellington expected. Ellington and his arranger Billy Strayhorn were renowned for their meticulous charts and encyclopedic arrangements, yet Django did not read music. Even so, Ellington also believed that "You can't write music right unless you know how the man who'll play it plays poker," and he didn't yet know how Django held his cards. With little time for rehearsals, Ellington made things simple. He presented Django with a portion of his own rhythm section that served as the Quintette. Then, he aimed the spotlight on Django's guitar.

Django's guitar itself was a likely second factor. The setup of the electric hollow-body Gibson and the early combo amp proved volatile onstage in large halls during the Ellington tour. Other pioneering American jazz guitarists like Christian and T-Bone Walker contended with this problem by stuffing their hollow-body guitars with rags to ward off feedback. American reviewers reported that Django sometimes had problems with feedback from the stage, so Django and Ellington may have agreed that playing with less volume in an intimate ensemble best suited their large venues.

Finally, there was the music itself. World War II was the Golden Age of Swing in occupied Europe and Django reached a peak in his popularity. But in America, swing was out among the in crowd. During the war years, Dizzy, Christian, Charlie Parker, Kenny Clarke, and Thelonious Monk were hammering out the rudiments of bebop. By 1946, Ellington's swing was refined by new sounds, including influences from classical music to slave spirituals to the blues. As Ellington boasted, "We stopped using the word *jazz* in 1943." Thus, when Django came to America, his music was behind the times. When they were on stage together, it made sense to highlight Django's style of music by having him play solo, with just a rhythm section. And when Ellington's band took over, the members struck up again what they were proudly calling "modern" jazz.

CARNEGIE HALL was America's high temple of music. If New York was then on its way to becoming the center of the musical world, Carnegie Hall was the center of the center. True to steel-magnate Andrew Carnegie's philanthropic vision, his namesake hall was the biggest and best cathedral to music money could make. It was the stage for Beethoven and Mozart. Not jazz. Yet in 1928, W. C. Handy, the self-proclaimed Father of the Blues, broke the classical music barrier. In 1938, Benny Goodman brought jazz to the hall in a landmark concert both for Goodman and for public recognition of the music. Ellington was one of several bandleaders along with Goodman's integrated band and Count Basie to break not only the jazz barrier but also the color barricades. Ellington first played Carnegie Hall on January 23, 1943. Since that stellar debut, Ellington returned to play an annual show.

And now, in his first time in the United States, Django was to play America's most vaunted concert venue in two shows on Saturday and Sunday, November 23 and 24, 1946.

Django's New York City debut was widely promoted in newspaper ads and posters. The November 23 show was a sellout hit. Ellington was at his best, his band stylishly swinging through "Diminuendo in Blue," "Magenta Haze," a spirituals and work song medley, and "Jam-A-Ditty," his concerto for four jazz horns. These were not lowdown blues or dance hall jazz but sophisticated music that only Ellington could write. And then Django took the stage. *Jazz Hot*'s Jimmy Weiser gave a full report for the fans back in Paris: "The hall was packed out. I can safely say that by far the greater part of the audience was made up of admirers who had waited for this moment for ten years. Duke played as wonderfully as ever and announced Django at 10:30. He had no arrangement to play but was backed by Duke. This was something of a disappointment, for the public had expected to see Django and the orchestra onstage at the same time, nevertheless Django received a great ovation and took six curtain calls."

The second show was fraught with problems, however. Dressed in black tuxedos with tails, the orchestra entered followed by Ellington, who, in his usual refined and polished manner, sat down at his grand piano to rule over his dominion. The first set went like clockwork as always, the band playing as a well-oiled machine under Ellington's command. But when Django's turn came at the start of the second set, he was nowhere to be found. Ellington hastily improvised a program to fill his slot, holding out hope that Django would still appear. Finally, a flustered Ellington gave up and regretfully apologized to the audience that Django was not playing that evening.

Suddenly, at 11 P.M., a taxi roared up to the Carnegie Hall stage door and Django hustled out. His arrival was whispered to Ellington, who, flushed and embarrassed, apologized yet again and announced Django. But Django was dressed in just a casual suit and did not have his guitar with him. Another electric guitar was found and hurriedly thrust into his hands. "They presented a guitar to him. Apparently, he had never played it," guitarist John Pisano remembered. "It was all de-tuned. The strings were totally loose. They introduced Django and he had to tune it up, 'WR-R-R-RANG!!!,' right on stage." Once he was in tune and settled, Django played his usual set and, in *Jazz Hot* writer Weiser's words "brought the concert to a close all the same, amidst thunderous applause."

Backstage, Django apologized profusely to Ellington. He explained at first in his chopped English that he overslept. Overslept? His stint on stage was set for 10:30 at night! Pressed further, he admitted the truth: Lonely for home after his long journey through the American heartland, he met up with French middleweight boxer Marcel Cerdan and reminisced away the hours chatting about their beloved Paris. Suddenly Django looked at his watch, realized how late he was, and dashed to catch a cab. Yet the taxi driver was confounded by Django's pidgin English and escorted him to the far side of Manhattan before Django made himself understood. They screeched to a halt at Carnegie Hall just as the show was nearing its end.

Reading through the radically differing reviews of the second Carnegie Hall show—some raving, others ranting—it's difficult to believe the critics were at the same concert. *Down Beat*'s review of the two nights was downright silly. Under the ridiculous banner headline "Ellington Fails to Top Himself!" the concerts were labeled good but not great—although reviewer Michael Levin then stumbled over himself saying that if anyone but Django and Ellington gave these shows, the crowd would have been in ecstasy. "Part of the trouble was Django Reinhardt. Billed as star soloist, he simply didn't score the expected artistic effect, even though drawing more curtain calls than any other soloist," wrote Levin in tongue-twisted logic. "Reinhardt seemed to have a great deal of trouble keeping his guitar in tune, constantly altering string pitch during his solos, two jump tunes with the band, a blues, an improvisation of his own, *Honeysuckle Rose*, and *Body and Soul* complete with expected double-timing. Reason may have been that Django uses a push string technique, favoring light gut strings, and the saddleback of the guitar he was using was built for heavier strings, thus allowing his fingering to give him the feeling he was out of tune." Levin's blatant lack of knowledge about the guitar in general and Django's playing in particular may have had something to do with his panning the show.

Other critics, however, were entranced and forgave Django's late arrival. New York's *World Telegram* labeled his solos "remarkable." *Esquire* magazine beamed that "At his Carnegie Hall appearance with Ellington, he also suffered from the world's most ineptly balanced sound system, but managed to play more inventive jazz than any other soloist on the program."

Metronome magazine's review, on the other hand, was scathing with a bizarre blend of xenophobic and patriotic zeal: "And, though he was well received, it was obvious that he was nervous and that his performance on this particular evening could have been equaled or even bettered by any one of many dozen top-flight guitarists playing in bands, studios or on 52nd Street. Django did 'Rose Room,' 'Tiger Rag,' 'Honeysuckle Rose' and 'Body and Soul' employing all the time-worn clichés in the book." The reviewer didn't know Django had composed those clichés.

The coldest review came from British critic Leonard Feather, who, with English sangfroid and snobbery, long prided himself on failing to be impressed by Django: "The most talked about item in the concert was, of course, the appearance of Django Reinhardt. To me, Django was a pleasant surprise because I had expected little, but to others he was a big disappointment because they had expected too much. Django seemed to play with much more of a beat than in the old quintet days; needless to say, the presence of the Ellington rhythm section, instead of the French Hot Club's, emphasised this difference. Django also benefitted from the use of an electric guitar. However, as the disappointed over-expectants pointed out, he cannot hold his own as an all-round musician, or as a jazzman with such American artists as Oscar Moore, Barney Kessel, Church Wayne, Mary Osborne, Johnny Collins and the other top people in jazz on this instrument. He played only one solo item, 'Improvisation No. 1,' the other three numbers being 'Tiger Rag,' 'Honeysuckle Rose,' and some blues. The Ellington band evidently hadn't had any special arrangements made to back him, and for the most part he had only Duke, Pettiford and Greer until the last chorus of each number. On the second night at Carnegie Hall, Django had still not arrived when the time came for Duke to announce him. While Duke was apologising to the audience, Django rushed in, dishevelled, and explained that he had overslept. (This was at 10:30 P.M.!) Django is having a good time over here."

CONTRARY TO FEATHER'S quaint quip, Django was no longer having the same good time in the United States. He had been on the road away from his home in Paris for some six weeks now. He left behind his wife and 2-year-old son Babik to seek his fortune in America, but was now starting to miss the riches of his extended family.

The Gypsy was homesick.

From New York on December 5 during a brief stop on the East Coast leg of the tour, Django wrote another letter home, this time to Stéphane. In his rambling penmanship that filled four pages of hotel letterhead, he blustered to Stéphane that "*les afaires vons magnifiquement bient.*" Django proudly began listing the cities on the tour, yet his memories of the past couple weeks were clouded and he wrote that he couldn't remember all the places he'd played. Like his other letter, this one was part braggadocio, part a yearning for home. He ended with a wistful note, asking Stéphane to "*Di bien*" to a certain Georgette back in Paris, "You know, the *petite* from *Journale Music Expréss.*"

Django was believed to have also written Nin-Nin and perhaps Naguine at some point in the tour. The two letters from the United States to Lévêque and Stéphane are Django's sole surviving correspondence—and indeed the only surviving writings by Django longer than an autograph dedication.

Despite his growing loneliness, Django's tour continued on. The band traveled by train along the East Coast after the Carnegie Hall shows, playing their finale on December 7, 1946, in Detroit, where *The Detroit News* reported that Django stole the last show.

It was a fine ending to a long tour that ultimately played 21 cities in a month on the road.

AFTER THE TOUR, Django and the band made their way back to New York City, where Django was booked by the William Morris Agency into the smart Henry Hudson Hotel. Django's two-room suite became a revolving party. A gracious host, he ordered up liquor and meals from room service to feed his friends. His circle included Jean Sablon, who was then singing at New York's Versailles Club, and boxer Cerdan, who beat Georgie Abrams at Madison Square Garden in ten grueling rounds, setting off a grand round of celebration. Django met up again with Lonnie Wilfong and they ventured to Harlem's Apollo Theater one evening in January 1947 to meet Dizzy. Also among Django's admirers was an American songstress who, Django told Sablon with a wink, didn't understand a word of French.

Through his agent's arrangements, Django was scheduled to begin a four-week stand at the sophisticated Café Society Uptown at 128 East 58th. The nightclub was at the top of the social rung on New York's Upper East Side, hiring only French and Italian waiters in keeping with its Parisian cuisine and conceit. With streamlined booths, color-coordinated upholstery, and a reputation for stylish music, Café Society was the crème of the famed 52nd Street cabarets. As Delaunay remarked, it was also the "*plus froid.*"

Django opened there on December 16 and played each evening through January 11, 1947, backed by a house band led by clarinetist Edmond Hall and alternating sets with solo pianist Pete Johnson. In playing with Hall, Django was touching the roots of jazz: The venerable Hall started playing jazz in the 1920s in New Orleans bands.

For Django's premiere, the cabaret was overflowing. Sablon remembered that all of the city's show business world was there, from Paul Whiteman on down. For the evening shows, Django bought three dazzling new suits that he wore with sky-blue leather shoes and paraded about like a preening peacock: Sablon exclaimed that the effect of Django's outfits was outlandish. His guitarwork that first night was also stunning, and Sablon stated simply that "He played and created a veritable triumph."

Yet as the weeks wore on, the regimen at Café Society wearied Django, who always needed music that was new and fresh to keep his interest. Soon, he settled for playing just the four guest-solo pieces he was contracted for under strict musicians union rules. This may have been the letter of the contract but certainly not the spirit of it, and the managers complained about Django's "lack of cooperation." Sablon believed that Django was "bored to tears" by Hall's old-time ensemble. American guitarist Les Paul, who initially fashioned his own guitar playing and the music of his early ensembles on Django's, remembered going to one of the Café Society shows at Django's invitation: "Django asked me if I would come to Café Society where he was playing. I went over that same night with Lou Levy, the manager of the Andrews Sisters and a good friend of mine. He later published some of Django's works in the United States. But Django wasn't too good that night. He was uncomfortable and the rhythm section was uncomfortable." Others were impressed, however. Guitarist Johnny Smith remembered being dazzled by Django's playing at the club. Even Delaunay had to admit that Django drew large crowds that brought the house down with their applause.

Yet Django had had enough, and he refused to even play an encore despite the crowd's enthusiastic requests.

DELAUNAY KNEW about this applause firsthand because he arrived in New York at the end of December to find American distribution for his Swing label. What he found instead was a homesick and disillusioned Django. Amid the skyscrapers and theater marquees, Django regularly returned to gaze sadly at one particular gas streetlamp near Times Square as it reminded him of home.

Django also missed his French guitar. He had dreamed of the gleaming American archtops from fabled makers like Gibson, but in the end, his loyalties remained true to his Selmer. During his tour, Django telegraphed Delaunay to bring his Selmer guitar to him. When Delaunay duly arrived, he carried a new acoustic Selmer guitar sent to Django with best wishes from

Maurice Selmer, son of the firm's founder. Delaunay accidentally damaged the Selmer while in transit, although it was soon put right. Yet Delaunay came after the Ellington tour, so Django never got a chance to play his trusted guitar with the big band. Still, Django swooned when he got his hands on the Selmer. "My brother," he said to Delaunay, "all the Americans will wish they could play on this guitar! At least it's got tone, you can hear the chords like you can on the piano. Don't talk to me any more about their tinpot guitars! Listen to this, it speaks like a cathedral!" Artist endorsements were rarely so heartfelt.

Missing the gas streetlamps of Paris and his French guitar were only symptoms of a greater longing. Django wanted to go home. As Delaunay noted, "When I asked him later for his impressions of America, Django seemed to me to have lost most of his illusions. He was far from impressed by the American mentality, above all that of the women. Even the cars no longer had their old appeal for him; they were all too much alike."

Django had his share of disappointments during his American visit. The second Carnegie Hall show was a source of embarrassment, and he never got a chance to record commercially in the United States. With his sense of pride, he may have viewed this as a dismissal by the American jazz world.

There had been interest in recording him. On December 10, 1946, Stephen H. Sholes, the director of the Specialty Recording division of RCA, wrote Delaunay requesting permission to record Django. A famous scout, Sholes began in the mid-1940s supervising the recording of country western and rhythm and blues artists for RCA, producing sessions by stars such as the Sons of the Pioneers, Chet Atkins, and soon, in 1955, Elvis Presley. But in 1946, it was Django he was after.

Delaunay responded to Sholes's request on December 20, 1946: "Django's contract is over now, but I suggest you to get him a new contract for your Victor label, if you think it will be interesting for you. Django's previous contract didn't include royalties, but I guess Django would be interested to get some now." Delaunay then drafted a new contract allowing Django to record in the United States. Yet by the time Sholes received Delaunay's response, it was nearing the end of Django's time in the States, although no one knew that at the moment. Sholes contacted Django to discuss a contract, but no deal was ever made nor a session recorded.

Even if RCA wished to record Django, other hurdles stood in the way. From 1942 to 1945, American musicians were silenced from recording due to the boycott initiated by the American Federation of Musicians in a battle for radio and jukebox royalties. Now, with the ban lifted, record companies rushed to record pop stars like Bing Crosby and Frank Sinatra. Even if they had booked him, Django might not have been in the United States long enough to fit into their backed-up studio schedules.

In addition, Django lacked membership in the American musicians union, which was strict in not allowing nonmembers to play on the radio or for dances, or to record. Django mentioned in his letter to Stéphane that he talked with a union rep shortly after arriving in the United States and was told it was impossible for him to bring the full Quintette to play in America. On tour with Ellington, Django had several chances to join Ellington in the studio in Omaha and New York but never did, presumably due to union bylaws. If Django was at any of these sessions, he was only a spectator.

Now, Django was ready to say good-bye to the United States. The music had grown stale with Hall's backing band at Café Society, and while new prospects loomed, nothing was set. As of the end of January, no other venues were scheduled for Django, although agent Joe Wolfson of the William Morris Agency was laying groundwork for a tour of the West Coast as the special guest soloist with Tommy Dorsey's big band, a place in the spotlight recently vacated by Sinatra. Rumors abounded that Benny Goodman was trying to hire Django. In addition, Wolfson had music companies interested in publishing sheet music of Django's songs and solos. Yet Django had had enough. These arrangements took time, and with characteristic impatience, Django gave up on them.

"Everything had happened as though some overriding influence had made failure the only possible outcome," Delaunay wrote later, and with this, the tour would be remembered as a failure. Delaunay, the spurned agent and forgotten friend, was the historian who would have the last word. He pointed to the second Carnegie Hall concert as a Day of Judgment for Django and seemed almost to take delight in detailing Django's "appalling" behavior: "Agreed, he was applauded, he even took several bows, but the critics were not so kind as they might have been, and it is likely this incident had a great deal to do with the failure of his American tour." Yet no one but Delaunay seemed to think that this sole incident marked the whole tour as a failure. The New York critics were not as kind as they could have been, Delaunay lamented. But then critics never are. Delaunay summed up Django's American interlude with a sort of gleeful finality: "Tired of waiting and disappointed, one fine day Django decided to pack his bags and return to France."

The reason Django decided to go home was more complex and at the same time more simple—he longed for his family. Les Paul remembered a conversation he and Django had at the end of January: "He said to me one day, 'I've had it. I miss my wife and my kid. I want to go home.'" Naguine too recalled Django's return: "He could not remain separated from his child." In the end, Django's decision to return home came down to a fundamental feeling of being a stranger in a strange land. He had grown up in a communal Romany culture where he had family or "cousins" surrounding him day and night. His time in the United States had gradually become an ordeal: It was probably one of the few extended periods in his life when he was alone for more than several *hours* of time. He was cut off from his family by distance, separated from his newfound African American bandmates by language, and distanced from American society by his own Romany and French background. During the weeks of the tour with Ellington and then his stay in New York, Django became more and more alienated. It showed in his late arrival for the second Carnegie Hall concert when he was happy to while away the time reminiscing about Paris with a fellow Frenchman. It showed in his disillusionment with American cars, women, and life. And in the end, it showed in his music at Café Society.

Added to Django's homesickness was one further, more prosaic reason for his departure. In Paris on October 23, 1946, Django was issued a typical tourist nonimmigrant visa allowing him to stay in the United States just 60 days. At the start of February 1947, Django *had* to go home.

Guitarist Harry Volpe, who jammed with Django several times at Volpe's home, brought Django to the New York City harbor on February 6, where Django boarded a ship to Le Havre. Gone were the dreams of jamming with Satchmo and Dizzy. Gone were the visions of Hollywood and Dorothy Lamour. Volpe's son filmed the departure on a home cine camera: Following wishes for a bon voyage and waves from the gangplank, Django left the United States behind.

IF DJANGO'S AMERICAN TOUR truly failed, how then does one explain the music? While in the United States, Django was not presented with lucrative recording contracts or a starring role in the Hollywood film of his naïve dreams, but he did find something that money could not buy—inspiration.

New York City was the flourishing capital of jazz, and when Django arrived, American musicians welcomed him as the godfather of jazz guitar. Guitarist Johnny Smith remembered befriending Django: "I would go up [to his hotel] in the afternoon and we'd mess around together, or maybe I'd take him round the city. And at this time Les Paul was at the Paramount Theater so Django and I went down there to visit him in the afternoon." Les Paul recounted their arrival: "The doorman yelled up six floors to my dressing room, 'There's a fellow down here wants to see you. Says his name is Django Reinhardt.' I laughed at the joke and called back, 'Yeah, sure. Send him up with a case of beer and Jesus Christ, and I'll give them both an autographed picture,' because I thought someone was joshing me. So in he walks. Johnny Smith was with him, leading him around New York. I had two Epis laying on the couch. These were blonde 1939 Epi Deluxe Regent hollow-bodies, but I had added all the electronics. I had the pair in case I broke a string on stage. Johnny Smith picked up one guitar and Django picked up the other. He asked me for a pick, and I had a whole pocket full of them; the majority were Les Paul picks, round like a button. Django said that's just what he was looking for, which made me feel good. Django led off and the first number he played was 'Rose Room.' It was just the most awesome thing. Here I was in my dressing room shaving and straightening out my makeup to go on, and Django's playing guitar. It just stunned me." Johnny Smith: "We played together, but really, I was just listening because I'd heard him on record and I idolized this man from when I was younger. I'd save up my nickels and as soon as a new record came out I'd be right there. I used to play along with his solos and on the old record player they wouldn't last long and I'd wear them out, so I kept having to get new ones of the old ones too. He really made me realize that the guitar was a musical instrument and not just something to scrape on."

Jamming with Smith, Paul, and especially Ellington's band broadened Django's musical horizons more than listening to records back in Paris ever could have. Like Django, all of these musicians had grown up with swing and they were all now experimenting with modern ideas of jazz. These new influences were immediately heard in Django's music.

Django returned to France, but in the jazz he created from 1947, he never left the United States behind. His fast-paced tour and short stay in New York informed a new sensibility that he strived to put into music throughout the rest of his life.

He came to America playing swing.

He returned to Paris playing modern jazz.

12

Schism
1947–1950

HE HAD BEEN MOONSTRUCK with America. Now he was home, back in Paris in winter 1947, walking the same old streets of Pigalle, haunting the same cafés and cabarets. His old friends who ran across him found him downcast and disillusioned following his time in the United States. He told them tales of America—all about the cities and the women, all about the music and the flowered underwear. But in the end, he had to admit his dreams had failed him.

Django was bitter, but paradoxically he was also charged with a fresh energy. On his return to Paris on February 13, 1947, he immediately gathered his Nouveau Quintette around him and tuned up his Selmer guitar. Swing was now ancient history; new harmonies, new rhythms were in Django's head. Fired with inspiration from his American sojourn, he was ready to break away from the past.

Beyond his U.S. tour, 1946 had been largely a year of silence for Django, but in 1947 he would be at his prolific best. He recorded only three sessions in all of 1946, waxing just a dozen sides. Now, in the new year, Django would record 19 times in both recording and radio studios, cutting 108 sides released on four different labels. This fertile run of recordings included a variety of recent and radical compositions, but a new sensibility infused even the old classics he re-recorded—from "Minor Swing" to "Les yeux noirs." Django had not been this inspired since the late 1930s.

He began a two-month stand at Le Bœuf sur le Toit on March 6. Opening with a big band, he soon cut back to a core ensemble of just six musicians. His direction mirrored the trend in New York, where Dizzy Gillespie and Charlie Parker had in 1945 cast off the restraints of the big bands and their confining arrangements. Dizzy and Bird were performing in looser, more intimate small groups, such as the quintet they put together to play their legendary runs at

52nd Street's Three Deuces. For Django, it marked a return to old times, but also a reassessment of the basics of his music. Throughout the rest of his career, he would remain primarily focused on the tight sound of a small group.

He couldn't cast free of the past that easily, though. Even as Django was hearing a new music, Charles Delaunay was organizing yet another revival of the old Quintette. Stéphane Grappelli arrived in Paris for a short stay and Delaunay reunited them in the studio. On March 26 at the Studio Pelouze, the duo took up where they left off without missing a beat. They were backed once again by Nin-Nin and Matelo Ferret and bassist Emmanuel Soudieux. Yet despite Delaunay's attempt to revive the reliable sound of the prewar Quintette, something different was in the air. The band may have had the same instrumental lineup, but the music was fresh; Django's choice of songs showed the influence of his American trip. The session kicked off with Django's thoroughly modern composition, "R Vingt-Six." In its breathless runs of harmonizing chord changes, the song ricocheted between major voicings and dark minor-sevenths. It was part swing, part something else—in its odd intervals and syncopated rhythmic accents, it was as close to bebop as he had yet stepped. Django also reworked an American "Blues," a haunting minor-key theme that inspired him to create several recorded versions over the years. Stéphane's violin introduction was cast with shadings of Tzigane sounds before Django's guitar leaped in, exhilarating and alive.

He then led the band through an effervescent version of the bebop anthem "How High the Moon." The song was a favored launching pad for improvisation on New York's Swing Street, the beboppers playing at a fast and furious tempo, rocketing through the keys, jettisoning the old melody in search of new ones, substituting different harmonizing chords until the song was almost unrecognizable. Django and Stéphane's version did not go so far; the band was still recognizable as the Quintette. But underlying the intensity of their take was a tension and suspense, as if the band's melody was resolving in a unique direction. Stéphane's violin began by quoting the theme, swinging straight and true. Then Django's guitar ignited the song. He broke through the melody line with razor-sharp riffs, playing a raw new song, turning the theme on its head. There was no disillusionment in Django's guitar here, no bitterness, no weariness. He was searching for something, hearing a sound in his head that he was intent on capturing in his music.

DJANGO TRULY BROKE FREE of Delaunay's control during a Belgian tour in May 1947 with his Nouveau Quintette. He enlisted Soudieux, Ninine Vées, and drummer Pierre Fouad to accompany him, then turned his charms on Hubert Rostaing. The clarinetist and Django had once parted ways over financial misunderstandings during their 1942 North African trip. But history was not so easy to escape and they were now about to relive this past. "To persuade me to go to Brussels, Django promised me ten thousand francs a day," Rostaing remembered. "But when it came time to settle up, Django told me, 'But I never said that!' He was completely sincere—he'd just forgotten. Yet finally Django conceded: 'OK, since you say so.'"

In the end, none of them were paid. The concert impresario stole all the take, leaving Django and his musicians with empty pockets. The hazards of jazz were hard to elude.

There was still hope. Rostaing knew someone at the Belgian Decca label and he went to see him with the promise of bringing Django into the studio if the price was right. In their predicament, anything was better than nothing. On May 21, 1947, Django and the Nouveau Quintette were ushered into the Belgian Decca studios to circle their chairs around the mic. Delaunay was not there to dictate the playlist, and Django cut six sides that blazed a novel path.

In just three months since his return to France, he had composed a trove of new songs. These latest compositions were intriguing, taking yet another step into the future and leaving the golden days of swing behind. The session began with the pseudo-Mexican air "Porto Cabello," opening with a stately, nostalgic preamble, then exploding like fireworks, tearing the past away in a series of dazzling solo choruses of rhapsodic guitar. This song served as a warning shot: History was history, and old conventions were being thrown out the door. Archibald Joyce's "Song d'automne," while being a throwback to lyrical chanson style and a celebration of melody, provided further proof of Django's powers of harmonization, with his graceful chords and tremolos shimmering beneath the lines of Rostaing's clarinet. "Duke and Dukie" rode on a sweet theme accented by Django's sharp chordal punches; his solo phrases were long and sinuous and smooth. "Del Salle" sounded like 1940s Harlem jazz—cool and clever. Django's choruses here breathe with exotic intervals, dancing octave lines, and flurries of arpeggios, creating a minor solo master-piece. As Rostaing remembered, "What was important to him above all was the joy of music. He was always happy when he played, and the guitar was like a knife or spoon to him, something he used all the time. Every time we played together, it was a joy. It wasn't at all like playing on an assembly line."

In "Babik (Bi-Bop)" Django first tried his hand at a true bebop tune. The composition echoed his equally startling "Rythme futur," first recorded in 1940. But "Babik" was updated with jarring syncopation, discordant melo-dies, and atonal harmonies. The melody quoted Dizzy Gillespie's "Salt Pea-nuts" with its octave riffs, then modulated those octaves to create an energetic and elegant line. Django's guitar spoke the syntax of bebop but his was not the same bebop as Dizzy and Bird. Theirs was horn music, his guitar. He could play their notes, but he had to create his own language. In "Babik" he made his premiere attempt, running down razor-edged riffs. The theme, ar-rangement, and solos were exhilarating, full of a boundless joie de vivre.

Django was now in command of the electric sound and his playing was electrifying. The sound of his acoustic guitar had been rapturous, weightless notes carried away by a gossamer lightness. But now with electricity, he found new textures and new meaning to his music. This session was technically magnificent, Django adapting his acoustic techniques to the electric, from the balalaïka tremolos to stunning glissando chromatic runs. He bent blue notes, rode out the sustain, and gloried in the sonic dynamics that his newfound volume allowed. Without a doubt, the inspiration on these Belgian Decca sides came from Django's American tour and his immersion in the latest jazz. It also came from his adoption of the electric guitar, whose volume served as revenge for all the years he hammered away at his acoustic Selmer in loud, crowded nightclubs, struggling to be heard above the clatter of diners and the shuffling footsteps of dancers.

With a twist of a knob, his playing was set free.

BACK IN PARIS, a new jazz scene was blooming in the dark of cellar grottos beneath a new quarter of the city, Saint-Germain-des-Prés. Breaking away from Pigalle and Montparnasse, this was a more sophisticated and modern jazz catering to a younger crowd.

That Saint-Germain-des-Prés became the music's headquarters seemed only right. The Rive Gauche was a somnolent area of street markets, bistros, and small shops. Yet since the Occupation, it had awakened to become home to a brave new world of artists, actors, writers, and, now, musicians. Walking the warren of cobblestoned streets lined by solemn-faced buildings, one never lost sight of the spire of the gothic abbey that gave the quarter its name. The foreboding basilica, age-lined and time-darkened, seemed to cast a disapproving eye over the rising youth culture that surrounded it. In the shadow of the abbey stood two cafés that became the center of the neighborhood and of a new Parisian literary movement, the Café de Flore and Les Deux Magots. At de Flore, Jean-Paul Sartre, Simone de Beauvoir, and their family of followers gathered for their constitutional drinks and philosophical discussions and to pen their existentialist prophecies in mahogany-paneled comfort.

Below the buildings of the quarter were subterranean cellars once used to store food, wine, and the cesspools cleaned out while the city slept. Now, under the curve of the stone arches that held aloft the buildings on their staunch shoulders, bandstands were marked off and bars erected. The grottos bore the indelible scent of stone and moisture and darkness, and the fresh jazz fans who descended into their depths were laughingly labeled the Troglodytes.

The most famous of these Troglodytes was black-tressed waif Juliette Gréco, whose face and voice would come to epitomize the scene. She arrived in Saint-Germain-des-Prés in 1943 from Montpellier and soon joined the Communist youth, then tried to make it as an actress, both careers failing her. Sleeping through the daylight and coming alive at night, Gréco and her loose-knit gang made the grotto of the Café Tabou at 33 rue Dauphine their home. The cave was a true Troglodyte's tunnel. Some eight meters wide by fifteen long, it was made hospitable by an ill-tuned piano, a gaggle of tables and chairs, and a record player for spinning the latest American jazz discs. Gone was *les zazous'* sense of style: Gréco and her crowd dressed *à la américain*, the men with crewcuts, tennis shoes, and plaid shirts, the women in highnecked and tight-fitting black sweaters, ballet shoes, and, to the horror of the rest of Paris, slacks instead of dresses—couturie designed for dancing to bebop. Opening in April 1947, Le Tabou went wild in spontaneous jam sessions and shaking that would have shocked even Josephine Baker. When Le Tabou was shut down following complaints about the noise and the outrage, other grottos opened. Les Lorientais, Le Vieux-Colombier, and Le Caveau de la Huchette became the haunts of a new generation of African American and French jazzmen, from Don Byas and Lucky Thompson to Barney Wilen and Martial Solal. As Gréco said, looking back on these times, "*C'était une période nocturne mais lumineuse.*"

It was at Le Tabou that Gréco first sang. She still believed herself an actress, but when her friends heard her voice, they found something simple yet ethereal, a song they could believe in. Gréco's friend Marc Doelnitz, a failing actor and insatiable partygoer, was hired to book acts at the Rive Droite bastion, Le Bœuf sur le Toit, yet he lacked the money to hire a star like Piaf, so he decided to create one in Gréco. She took the stage and sang songs composed by novelist Raymond Queneau as well as Sartre's poems set to music by Joseph Kosma. The Troglodyte had come out of the grottos to shine over all Paris.

It was also in the Saint-Germain-des-Prés cellars that a new guitarist arrived. Henri Crolla backed Gréco at times, accompanied singer Jacques Prévert, and led his own ensembles playing a modern melodic jazz grown out of the music of his hero, Django. He was born on February 26, 1920, in Naples to a family of ambulant musicians—his mother a mandolinist, his father an accordionist, and each of his elder siblings playing an instrument in the family band, Jazz Crolla. With Mussolini's rise to power, the family fled to Paris and settled in a caravan in *la Zone* near the Porte de Choisy. By the time he was eight, Crolla was plucking a mandolin and banjo, joining the family as they played the cafés. During a midsummer's day *fête* in the Romany encampments of *la Zone*, 12-year-old Crolla overheard at a neighboring bonfire a Gypsy violin that drew him in. Standing in the shadows, he watched as a young man made music, then set down his violin and took up his guitar and played as Crolla had never heard anyone play. It was Django. As Crolla remembered, "It was something transcendent." Django—perhaps remembering his own apprenticeship with his uncle Guiligou—befriended Crolla, teaching him his first true jazz melodies. Although the Crollas were not Romanies, they lived together in *la Zone* and Henri was adopted among the Manouche. He was later adopted by another clan as well. Performing at the Club Rhumerie in Saint-Germain-des-Prés, Crolla joined the Prévert brothers, Jacques and Pierre, and artist Paul Grimault in their Groupe Octobre. He soon took over Matelo Ferret's chair in a jazz group, accompanied Gus Viseur, and was living with Django's cousin, Carmen. In 1939 as the war dawned, he was jamming at Jimmy's Bar with Django, Coleman Hawkins, Benny Carter, and Henri and André Salvador. While playing at Cannes' Palm Beach, he met singer Yves Montand and formed a duo and friendship that lasted for years. Along the way, Crolla was christened with the nickname Mille-pattes—The Centipede—for his virtuosity.

Despite his own accomplishments, Crolla remained in awe of Django's music. While performing at the Saint-Germain-des-Prés Club Schubert, Crolla looked up in horror as someone descended the steep steps into the grotto. He could tell by the hiking boots that it was Django. In a nervous flush, his fingers were paralyzed and his guitar fell silent.

Django had moved to the clubs of Saint-Germain-des-Prés. Along with Nin-Nin and Sarane and Matelo Ferret, Django was ready for a different venue, and playing his electric guitar in combos with hornmen and pianos, his sound was updated for a new generation.

ALONG WITH THE JAZZ SCENE in Saint-Germain-des-Prés came a fresh jazz record label headed by a youthful impresario. During the war years, Django jammed in clandestine clubs and *surprise-parties* with pianist Édouard Ruault. Known by his pseudo-American nom de jazz as Eddie Barclay, he and his wife, Nicole, now started a label devoted to jazz in 1945 and christened it Blue Star. Delaunay's Swing blazed the way, but it now stood for an older generation of jazz. Starting in 1947, Django and Barclay joined forces to record the first of five sessions for Blue Star. They were sessions that gave Django opportunities to explore and experiment.

Like Django, Barclay lived life on a whimsy. Born in Paris on January 21, 1921, Barclay's Auvergnat father was the manager of La Brasserie de la Poste, where Barclay grew up waiting tables, serving cold platters of oysters and steaming plates of choucroute. Yet even within these quintessentially French surroundings, Barclay fell in love with all things *américain*. He adored Hollywood movies, combing his hair straight back from his forehead and cultivating a pencil-line mustache emulating his hero, Clark Gable. He adopted the name Barclay—chosen from the title of the shop where he bought his shirts on the avenue de l'Opéra—as it sounded so American to his ear. And after making the acquaintance of Delaunay during the Occupation, he taught himself to pick out jazz tunes on the piano, playing only by ear, never learning to read.

When Eddie and Nicole Barclay started Blue Star, they had just their own savings and love of the jazz life to back them. Their apartment bathroom served as their storeroom, stacked high with towering piles of new 78s. To deliver discs to shops, Barclay loaded up his bicycle like a food porter delivering goods from the markets of Les Halles. But Blue Star never really made its name known until Barclay hooked up again with Django.

On July 6, 1947, Django recorded his first session for Blue Star at the tiny Technisonor studio. Home of the American Armed Forces Network from 1944 to 1946, it was now the base for Barclay's fledgling label. Django fronted his Nouveau Quintette with Nin-Nin, Rostaing, drummer André Jourdan, and for this session, bassist Ladislas Czabanyck. The music they cut was pure invention. "Blues for Barclay" was a rowdy jazz romp that even featured a drum solo—it didn't get any more *américain* than that. "Vette" began with strains of the classic "Shine" before breaking out into its own melody and swinging soulfully from deep within. Al Jolson's "Anniversary Song" was bittersweet and introspective, a brooding evocation of time past and passing time. And Django's own "Swing 48" was a masterpiece of *modernistique* riffing. Delaunay had been fixated on finding a certain sound with the old Quintette. Now, Barclay opened the door to a new era.

Rostaing remembered the sessions and Django's mood at the time: "Although these sessions were not prepared, we already knew the new compositions that Django wanted to record. As soon as he made them up—picking them out on the guitar—he played them to us so we could share his happiness and discover them for ourselves. We did not rehearse much at all. We practiced in each others' houses, in our dressing rooms when we played clubs; mostly we just played together in after hours jam sessions rather than in organized recording rehearsals. On the days we recorded, if Django hadn't forgotten the time or the date, he often got to the studio before us to take in its atmosphere and listen to how his guitar sounded in the room. Once in the studio, we decided on what tracks to record, and then the order of choruses and solos. Often we did not do many takes of the same title. Generally, it went off without a hitch between Django and us—the only little problems were microphone placement. In this way we put quite a few numbers in the can during these sessions, and we still had time for a drink between takes. Eddie Barclay gave us a completely free hand to choose the titles to be recorded. We were very happy with this since Django would only record music he liked. These were, of course, his own compositions, but also folk songs and current popular tunes—in fact any music he liked, which he adapted as it suited him."

With Django's freshly pressed Blue Star discs loaded on his trusty bicycle, Barclay set out across Paris to peddle their new music.

EVEN WITH THE OPENING of fresh jazz venues in Saint-Germain-des-Prés, finding ongoing work in Paris in the postwar years was a trial. Following the Belgian tour and Blue Star sessions, Django accepted a job performing for the

U.S. Army's Special Service Office to entertain troops in Germany. In mid July 1947, he assembled an ensemble with Soudieux, drummer Jacques Martinon, and pianist Eddie Bernard. Django had counted on Rostaing to join him, but at the last minute the clarinetist had another assignment. Soudieux stepped forward with a replacement named Maurice Meunier.

Soudieux recommended this clarinetist to Django—but with a word of warning. Meunier was young and green, Soudieux said. Django was used to that. He even saw it as an asset. Soudieux hesitated, then told all: Meunier knew how to play in only one key, F major. Django—who played liberally in all keys, an easy task on a guitar—couldn't believe his ears. Yet he had no other choice. Meunier was hired.

At the ensemble's first concert at the Stardust Club in Heidelberg, Meunier was all nerves—and Soudieux was even more scared. American GIs filled the hall, eager for a good time with the war over and nothing to do but drink German beer and listen to jazz. Django kicked off the first song and Soudieux looked over at the terrified Meunier: He was visibly shaking. But it only took a few notes from his clarinet for Django to spin around and look back to Soudieux. On Django's face was a huge smile.

Django and ensemble played four nights in Heidelberg before moving on to Mannheim. Django always felt that carrying anything heavy was beneath him and so had left his amplifier in Paris, believing the cabarets would have an amp to plug into. Now at the Mannheim club, he was stranded without amplification and had to try to play his acoustic guitar loud enough to be heard over a rowdy brawl of drunken soldiers who were in turn shouting to be heard above the band. Django jumped into his first songs, but the music was lost in the chaos. At the side of the stage, the American master of ceremonies was furious. Finally, after Django ended his third number, the MC told them to pack up. He called headquarters, shouting in a rage, "I asked you to send your brightest star and what do we get? Some goddamned lousy second-rate outfit!"

In the tour's final two weeks, the ensemble was sent to Frankfurt and everything again went wrong. Playing in another hall without amplification, Django's tortured guitar broke and he refused to play another note. The SSO organizers threatened to dishonorably discharge the band and ship them home without pay for any of the shows. Fortunately, Django met members of the AFN radio service who remembered his broadcasts from Orly. Under the AFN's protection, the SSO contract was smoothed over and Django happily agreed to play a broadcast concert.

When Django and band packed to catch the train back to Paris, the SSO booker dressed them down one last time. "If you weren't sacked earlier, it's only because one of the AFN executives intervened on your behalf," he shouted at them in his best drill-sergeant voice. "But I'm happy to say, your band is not likely to be back here in Germany any time soon!"

For Django, these threats brought no regrets.

BACK IN PARIS, Django again devoted himself to fatherhood. He settled his family into an apartment reigning over the place Pigalle at 32 boulevard du Clichy above the bar Clair de Lune, a musicians' rendezvous. Babik was now four years old, and Django took pride in his childish deviltries. Babik was a beautiful boy, the picture of postwar health, seeming to wear an eternal smile. Django was always ready to serenade his son on his guitar and violin, and found Babik a ukulele for him to fret with his pudgy fingers. Django spent his days lounging about in the sidewalk café below his apartment or going to the movies, always with Babik in tow. He kept his son stocked with comic books and outfitted him in an American cowboy suit with a fringed vest, a diminutive fedora in place of a true ten-gallon hat, and a pair of shiny six guns. Babik had Naguine's namesake complexion, his cheeks plump and cherry red. And he had Django's lust for life. Sharing a drink with Rostaing, Django bragged, "You know, Hubert, my son's already got an eye for girls! He's a lion! He always examines their legs. He's got the perfect character!"

Django told all that Babik was becoming a film connoisseur, just like his father. They both were enamored by cowboy and gangster films—horse operas and machine-gun concertos. "Whenever we go to the pictures," Django boasted, "Babik can tell straight away just by the music whether it's an American film!"

And Babik followed in his father's footsteps in other ways as well. Bringing Babik to Brussels with him for a series of shows in November 1948, Babik grabbed anything and everything he could lay his hands on in stores, hotels, and restaurants, spiriting them away into the depths of his pockets. Django was exceedingly proud of his four-year-old's handiwork. He boasted to Rostaing each night at the theater about his son's latest haul. "My brother, just look at what my son's pinched now!" Django beamed, ever the proud Gypsy father.

Returning to their place Pigalle apartment, Django took over the largest room as a studio and was again engrossed in painting. As Delaunay remembered, "This was not the time to talk music with him. To whatever questions you asked him, he invariably responded: 'Don't talk to me about music. At present, I'm painting.'"

Yet through autumn 1947, Django and his Nouveau Quintette were more prolific than ever. Stéphane returned to visit Paris in October, leading a 12-piece orchestra at the Sa Majesté cabaret, and Delaunay lost no time in reuniting the old Quintette yet again to record a quick session and then play a concert at Salle Pleyel on November 16.

With his Nouveau Quintette, Django recorded a long series of nine sessions at the Radio Diffusion Française studios in Montparnasse, resulting in the eventual release of 58 sides licensed to Swing and Delaunay's new label, Vogue. The RDF series were broadcast over the French national radio network on announcer Anne-Marie Duverney's "Surprise-Partie" show, airing each Saturday evening. These recordings were special, standing out from Django's commercial recordings as they were completely impromptu. While the sound quality and balance between instruments was not optimal, they are suffused with energy and daredevil improvisation. Django reinvented many of his old compositions, often elaborating and recasting the heads before diving into solos with abandon. He revived his wartime symphonic "Féerie" and launched new tunes like "Swing dynamique." Even old warhorses such as "Viper's Dream" and "Swing Guitars"—both cut at the same RDF session on August 25—were empowered with new meaning. Tunes like "Douce Ambiance," first recorded four years earlier for Delaunay, was further developed with enriched harmony, creating an ambiance even more sublime.

AT THE SAME TIME that Django was cutting himself free of his past, the Hot Club de France was breaking apart in a war of dialectics between old and new jazz. The club's patriarch, Hugues Panassié, stood staunchly for traditional jazz. Backed by his éminence grise, Mezz Mezzrow, Panassié trumpeted the music of New Orleans, Chicago, and his hero Louis Armstrong as the only real jazz. Bebop was hot jazz overheated; as Mezzrow sniped, "Them boys never play two notes where a hundred will do." Meanwhile, Delaunay—despite his eternal efforts to reunite the old Quintette—had his ears open to the latest jazz sounds. He was first inspired by Dizzy and Bird's 1945 recording of "Salt Peanuts," the symbolic anthem of the French beboppers. Now, "Salt Peanuts"—which itself signified a split from swing to bebop—was the flashpoint behind the rupture of the Hot Club.

Panassié provoked the war. Working behind the scenes in the fine tradition of medieval politics, he rallied support among traditional jazz lovers to oust Delaunay from leadership. Panassié's backing came from the Hot Clubs in the outlying French provinces, Panassié playing on their long-instilled discomfort for things Parisian. With his legions arrayed behind his cause, he called on October 2, 1947, a national assembly of the provincial Hot Clubs to denounce Delaunay. It was a coup d'état, pure and simple.

Panassié first accused Delaunay of being a dictator—a role Panassié retained for himself. Then he elaborated the counts of censure. Charge *le premier*: Delaunay hired on September 6, 1946, British jazz aficionado Leonard Feather—"an enemy of the Hot Club," or at least of Panassié—to produce recordings for the Swing label by Louis Armstrong, Panassié's "own" musician. Charge *le deuxième*: Delaunay worked behind the scenes to block Django from recording with Duke Ellington during his U.S. tour—a charge proved untrue by Delaunay's correspondence with Stephen Sholes of RCA. Charge *le troisième*: Delaunay contributed to the book *Jazz 47* under the Hot Club's name but without its permission; the revue included praise of the despised bebop as well as a contentious article by Jean-Paul Sartre. Charge *le quatrième*:

Delaunay was guilty of "pornographic propaganda exaggerating the value of be-bop." And the charges continued ad infinitum, all vaguely described as discrediting the name of the Hot Club and attacking Panassié.

Delaunay was silent in his defense. The attack was obviously personal and no appeal was going to save his face or fate. Before his inquisition, he preferred the nobility of accepting the unjust auto-da-fé.

A vote was called. Among the delegates of the 22 Hot Clubs present, just four sided with Delaunay—the clubs from Paris, Angers, Rennes, and Bordeaux, represented by its secretary, Frank Ténot. With Panassié's forces aligned against him, whether fair or foul, Delaunay resigned from the Hot Club he was instrumental in building.

Part in jest, part in cynicism, the rending of the Hot Club was labeled *le Schisme*, and Panassié and Delaunay were christened by French fans as the two Popes of Jazz. Yet Delaunay was not one to be bitter about the Schism, although he no doubt regretted it. He believed in music, not politics. Reflecting later on the Schism in his memoirs, he repented for not sending the recording of "Salt Peanuts" directly to Panassié to share this find. He believed that if Panassié had been part of the bebop revolution from the start, Panassié would have championed the new music. Yet the damage was done. The jazz association that began with such fraternity now broke apart in rancor.

In the end, the Schism was ultimately just a dialectical debacle. Panassié resumed control of the Hot Club and the Swing label partnership dissolved. But like the popes of Avignon, Panassié could not keep his power. Panassié was all spirit, but Delaunay had built the church. Panassié was a failure as an administrator and under his rule, the Hot Club de France ultimately faded away. Delaunay, meanwhile, continued on his jazz crusade, starting his own Fédération des Hot Clubs Français, ruling over the French jazz scene from his rue Chaptal offices, and recording, licensing, and issuing jazz on his Vogue label.

DJANGO WAS an unwitting pawn of Panassié's Schism and schemings. Never a paying, card-carrying member of the Hot Club, Django's allegiance was never sworn to one would-be impresario over another. Delaunay had been Django's friend, ally, and unofficial manager, but Django was quick to record for Barclay or sign on with the William Morris Agency when the opportunity arose. Now, Panassié immediately tried to enlist him.

Just days after the coup on October 4, 1947, Panassié organized with Barclay a self-serving recording session at Studio Lutetia. Ironically, given the old-versus-new battle behind the Schism, this session was shaded by bebop and in the end served Django best. He and Rostaing roared through Count Basie and Eddie Durham's "Topsy"—quaintly listed as a foxtrot on the Blue Star label. And if Django had shaken his head at the velocity of Dizzy and Bird's blowing on "Salt Peanuts," he picked with an inner fury on "Moppin' the Bride," a remake of his own "Micro."

Panassié was far from through with Django, however. In 1950, he set a guileless Django up for an interview with one of his agents, jazz writer Johnny "Scat" James. This was the sole verbatim "interview" with Django ever published—if, in fact, these were truly Django's words. First printed in the Dutch music magazine *Philarmonic* in August 1950, it was reprinted far and wide in the Belgian *Jazz Magazine* and Panassié's first issue of his new *Bulletin Hot Club de France*. This one-page interview would sour Django and Delaunay's friendship and business relationship and in the end, land Django in court defending himself against Delaunay's charges of slander.

James described visiting Django at his apartment, arriving at midday with Django still abed. While Naguine woke him, Négros served coffee. Babik—described as a little "Devil Chaser"—stormed into the room in full cowboy regalia to ambush James with an arsenal of guns and knives and war whoops that reminded James of bebop scat lines. Django finally appeared, still in his nightshirt, to watch proudly as Babik marauded his guest. The two of them then retired to Django's room and sat down amid his latest canvases.

Django was in a pessimistic mood, James noted, so he queried him as to why. "It is a long story . . ." Django began, "but the bottom line is that I don't want to work in France anymore. You know that Hugues Panassié, with the help of Grappelli and I, founded the Hot Club de France. We had an ideal, and now Delaunay is destroying everything Stéphane, Hugues, and I have been trying to build—the idealism of the French jazz musicians and jazz lovers.

"Until 1947, all was well. Hugues Panassié was the president of the Hot Club de France and Charles Delaunay had a lower place in the hierarchy. Charles felt great jealousy toward Hugues because of his big—and still growing—success, and in summer 1947, Hugues was the subject of mockery and mean intrigues with only one purpose: to make Hugues look stupid and overthrow him. There was no doubt as to who was going to win this war—Charles, of course, at least at first.

"Hugues, who always worked 100 percent for the music, is an honest man with ideals. Charles is a shrewd businessman who owes everything he has to Hugues. Everybody knows that almost all of Delaunay's discographical information [for his book *Hot discography*] was given to him by Hugues and that Charles took all the credit. And on top of that, Charles likes to give people the impression that he made the Hot Club what it is now, or at least better than what it was. It is Hugues who honestly admits that Stéphane and I have done the most work to make the Hot Club what it is.

"With all sorts of clever tricks, people managed to obstruct Hugues and even succeeded in giving him a bad image in the eyes of a public that knew nothing of the dirty games and just wanted to hear jazz music."

If this purported diatribe of Django's didn't do enough to sully Delaunay, James continued on. Django denounced the jazz festivals Delaunay organized, concerts that rivaled Panassié's own, stating that Delaunay defrauded festival backers of millions of francs—Dizzy for one was allegedly still waiting to be paid the 300,000-franc fee promised him by Delaunay. In addition, Delaunay extorted bribes from musicians such as Armstrong and Johnny Dodds for good reviews in *Jazz Hot*. Those who didn't pay up were put down.

The interview ended with a final admonition: "I have always said," Django warned, "that as soon as Charles gets power, everything we have been working so hard for will be destroyed."

This interview was clearly contrived. Django never showed any interest in French politics let alone the petty feudal wranglings behind the curtains at the Hot Club. Django worked with other impresarios and producers, such as the Jazz Club Français and Barclay, but never displayed signs of wanting to align himself with Panassié. Yet here in this purported interview, every word put in Django's mouth served Panassié's intrigues counter Delaunay. Sadly, the interview also severed Django's relationship with the man who had been fundamental in making his career.

Delaunay was a calm, patient man, but this interview cut him like an assassin's dagger. He no doubt surmised it was Panassié's handiwork, but there was no direct action he could take against Panassié's sinister machinations. And anyway, Delaunay made a poor enemy for Panassié. He was not one to fight back and seek public revenge; even years later after Panassié's death, Delaunay was forgiving in his memoirs. Instead, Delaunay wrote an indignant letter to the editor of *Philarmonic* taking the magazine to task for shoddy journalism: "With Johnny James's article, you have maliciously and without the least proof presented the personal resentments of M. Django Reinhardt and not hesitated to question my integrity."

Delaunay then responded to Django with a court summons. He sought to set the record straight.

On November 9, 1950, Django stood before magistrate René Meyer of the Tribunal Civil in the Parisian suburb of Aulnay-sous-Bois. The magistrate read the offending passages aloud and questioned Django on each statement.

Did M. Reinhardt found the Hot Club de France with M. Panassié and M. Grappelli?

"No," Django replied.

Did M. Delaunay become jealous of M. Panassié's successes during 1947?

"Not that I know of."

Was M. Delaunay the instigator of intrigues against M. Panassié?

"Not that I know of."

Did M. Reinhardt state that if M. Delaunay took control of the Hot Club "everything we have been working so hard for will be destroyed?"

"No, I never said that."

And on it went, point by point refuting the so-called interview.

The record was clarified, but the damage to Django and Delaunay's friendship was done. The evolution and revolution from swing to bebop instigated the Schism in the Hot Club. It ended with a rift between Django and his greatest fan.

THROUGHOUT 1948 and 1949, Django was torn between the new music he was hearing and calls from his audience to play the old music they knew and loved. Performing at another Quintette reunion concert with Stéphane at the Salle Pleyel near the end of 1947, Django was forced back into his old rhythms. *Jazz Hot* praised the show: "Django has certainly not played so well in public for many years. Some of his choruses recalled the splendid improviser we once knew so well. It was impossible to know which was the most impressive— the richness of his melodic invention, his technical virtuosity, or the pungency of his accompaniments. And yet somehow the old flame, the old urge to create seems to have left him." Django and Stéphane then began a several-week stand at l'ABC Théâtre on January 23, 1948, revisiting timeworn tunes in their hoary formulae. The Quintette with Stéphane's violin was simply not made for bebop.

This battle between old and new jazz raged among aficionados throughout France just as in the United States. To stand up for the old standards, Panassié announced the world's first jazz festival, to be held at the end of February 1948 in Nice. As with everything Panassié did, he had ulterior motives. His Festival de Jazz de Nice was a showcase purely for traditional jazz. Even Django's music was too modern.

Then the hostilities escalated. Just as Panassié was promoting his upcoming festival, Delaunay booked Dizzy Gillespie's bebop big band, the Hep-sations, to play a series of last-minute shows in Paris at the tail end of their European tour. Dizzy's stand in Paris came just weeks before Panassié's Nice festival, and the impassioned polemics between French jazz fans rose to full cry.

Dizzy's tour had been a nightmare. After the Swedish impresario stole off with their earnings, Dizzy and his 17-piece band made the trip to Paris without a penny in their pockets and just wine to sate their stomachs. They arrived by train from Brussels at 8:30 P.M. on February 20, 1948, and rushed across the capital straight to the bandstand for their first show. Yet during the trip, the musicians lost their book—the band's collection of arrangements.

Panassié attended one of Dizzy's Salle Pleyel shows and dismissed the music wholesale: "I love jazz—but that's not jazz!" he snarled on his way out. Dizzy's drummer, Cuban conga-master Chano Pozo, added to the uproar, driving the beat with Latin rhythms reminiscent of the tribal drumming once the heartbeat of hot jazz. It was all too much, and the last of Dizzy's Salle Pleyel concerts became a battlefield. A lone voice heckled Dizzy, "Go back to Timbuktu!"

while outside gendarmes held back hordes of fans trying to rush the doors for Dizzy's autograph.

Just as Django sought Dizzy upon his arrival in New York, Dizzy now searched out Django in Paris. He found Django playing at the ABC, a magnificent five-story cabaret on boulevard Poissonnières that served as home to the music hall stars. Django and his Nouveau Quintette were ensconced on the top floor, but the hour was late and the crowd and Django's band had left for a last bowl of onion soup in Les Halles. In walked Dizzy. Django's eyes lit up as bright as the whole City of Light. Dizzy sat in with just Django and Soudieux on bass, playing song after song, swapping solos and simply listening to each other improvise. Soudieux remembered the jam session: There, on the top floor of the ABC, Django was in heaven.

Not wanting to be outdone by the beboppers, Panassié's Festival de Jazz de Nice premiered with a lineup that included Louis Armstrong and His All-Stars featuring Earl Hines, Jack Teagarden, and Barney Bigard; Rex Stewart and band; and of course Panassié's old friend Mezzrow. Yet the program created criticism that the lineup was too American and did not include any of the prominent French jazzmen such as Alix Combelle, André Ekyan, and others—most of whom were now playing jazz with a more modern accent. France was represented only by Claude Luter and his Lorientais, provoking a protest petition signed by French musicians. To settle the controversy, Panassié's fellow organizer Michel de Bry made a last-minute call to hire Django and Stéphane. Django and company jumped on a train and performed at the grand finale on Saturday, February 28, in the Hôtel Negresco ballroom for a show broadcast live over the RDF's "Nuit de Nice" program. Still, Boris Vian, long an admirer of Django's, castigated him in *Jazz Hot* and the daily newspaper *Combat* for playing the old songs over again. "Grappelli and Reinhardt, without conviction, turned the same old crank for the thirty-sixth time," Vian wrote. It was something no one at the show complained about concerning Armstrong.

The token appearance at the Nice festival boosted Django's pride, but better yet provided an opportunity to jam with Armstrong again in clubs after hours. Pleased by the show, Django composed a melody named in honor of Panassié's event, "Festival 48." Back in Paris, Django's good mood inspired him to patch up differences with Delaunay for a recording session at which he cut the song.

In what had become a timeworn tradition, on March 10, 1948, Delaunay again led Django and Stéphane into the Studio Pelouze. Backing the duo was their now-old-fashioned lineup of two rhythm *pompeurs*—Nin-Nin and Challain Ferret—with Soudieux on bass. The ensemble recorded an odd repertoire of tunes, including their venerable composition "Bricktop" and Gershwin's "Lady Be Good," a song fittingly played on the first and now last session of the Quintette.

Django's "Festival 48" rode atop the ubiquitous changes to "I Got Rhythm" and offered a jazz history lesson in miniature. The song pasted together a scrapbook of quotes from famous melodies played with a joyous swing, all inspired by the music of Panassié's revival. And ironically, this pastiche was recorded by Delaunay. This song and session brought together the sadly severed Hot Club partnership of Panassié and Delaunay through the music of Django. But the session also marked the end of an era. It was the last time Django would record for Charles Delaunay.

WITH JOBS IMPOSSIBLE to find in Paris, Stéphane suggested reuniting the Quintette to travel to England for another tour. The old Quintette had always been more popular in England than France in the prewar era, and Stéphane had established a solid career playing jazz for Britons in the years since. With the backing of Lew Grade, a new tour of English theaters was arranged with a premiere at the Hackney Empire Theatre on March 15, 1948.

Whenever the Quintette traveled, disaster seemed in the cards. This reunion tour to England was no exception. Arriving in London on March 12, Django and ensemble were greeted not by fans but by burglars. Soudieux remembered the events: "Arriving in London, we went straight to our usual hotel. We left our luggage at the reception and went downstairs to dine in the hotel restaurant. But when we returned, all of our valises had disappeared. Django, Challain Ferret, and I found ourselves without anything left—not even a toothbrush! All we had were the clothes we were wearing. From a second-hand clothes store we rented dinner jackets, but they had enormous flaps on the pockets. We felt like ridiculous clowns and lost all enthusiasm to play. As usual, Django had all of his belongings with him in the luggage, but although he lost everything, he was calmer than any of us. He didn't even have a clean shirt left. But as soon as he'd bought a new shirt and a handkerchief, he forgot all about his loss." Soudieux, Nin-Nin, and Challain were distraught, however. Disgusted by their welcome, they turned around and departed for Paris, leaving Django and Stéphane stranded without their rhythm section.

Stéphane rushed to hire other supporting musicians. From his long sojourn in London, he was able to call together an English rhythm section for the French soloists, including rhythm guitarists Malcolm Mitchell and Alan Mindel and bassist Teddy Wadmore. Django telephoned Naguine in Paris and ordered her to London with a couple of suits and clean shirts. Then he and Stéphane led their new English Quintette in hastily opening at the Hackney Empire Theatre to rave reviews from *Melody Maker*: "Django's incredible guitaristics and Stéphane's pleasant personality and nimble violin playing" still awed the British fans. And the reporter noted with a relieved sigh, their repertoire included nothing "ultra-modern or in any way rebopish."

As with their prewar British tours, Django and Stéphane played week-long shows at the Moss Empire Theatre chain throughout London. Again the shows were variety extravaganzas, but the days of vaudeville were past, and this tour was a musical anomaly.

From the prewar glory of the music halls, Django and Stéphane next turned to the new vaudeville stage, the novel medium of the "televisor." Performing on the BBC's "Stars in Your Eyes" show from the BBC TV Studios on March 22 and 27, the English Quintette played for those lucky few who owned one of the newfangled radios with a picture screen.

From England, Django, Stéphane, and their English trio set off for Sweden to perform for several weeks in May at Stockholm's China Theatre. The Scandinavian appetite for jazz had not abated since the Quintette's 1939 tour and the reviewers and fans raved.

The English and Swedish tours may have been lucrative but the music was stale. Django and Stéphane revived their string swing from the first English tour of a decade before, yet Django's heart was now elsewhere. Following the show at London's Wood Green, where the Quintette played its "smooth cocktail of sweet and swing," the same reviewer queried Django on the dreaded subject of bop. Django's response was unequivocal: "*Je l'aime.*"

Back in Paris, Django immediately sought to play the music to which he professed his love. He joined forces with the capital's most avant-garde jazz ensemble, the Be-Bop Minstrels, toying with bebop for Sunday afternoon matinées through autumn 1948 at Le Bœuf sur le Toit, the cabaret long on the cutting edge of culture. The quaintly named Be-Bop Minstrels centered around 23-year-old Hubert and 20-year-old Raymond Fol, two Parisian brothers from a younger generation than Django, now 38. Born into a family of musicians, the Fols began piano lessons at age five, Hubert switching to violin, then clarinet before settling on alto sax while Raymond remained true to the keyboard. Raymond studied with Nadia Boulanger among others, composing classical works before being swept away by jazz during the Occupation. In forming the Be-Bop Minstrels with the backing of Delaunay, the brothers gathered American expatriate trumpeter Dick Collins, bassist Jack Smalley, and drummer Richie Frost. But with Django, the ensemble came alive. Django was inspired, playing as hard and fast as this young group of beboppers could handle.

During this time of jumping between swing and bebop, Django was also switching back and forth from acoustic to electric guitar. The science of electromagnetic pickups had progressed far from the crude pickups of just years before. French radio engineer Yves Guen and his brother Jean unveiled their first pickups in 1946, the Stimer P46 and R46. To promote their product, they naturally turned to Django, and he wholeheartedly endorsed the Stimer screwed onto the soundboard of his Selmer and amplified by the Guens' six-watt Stimer M.6 amp. The sound of the Stimer became Django's signature. It was warm and rich, at times shocking, at other times sublime. Django's electric guitar now too could speak with a human voice.

He reformed his Nouveau Quintette to perform a series of variety shows in company with chanteur Georges Ulmer in Brussels from November 22 to December 1, 1948. His ensemble included Rostaing, Vola, drummer Arthur Motta, and Django's first son, Lousson, on guitar. Mirroring Django's past with his own father, Lousson grew up in *la Zone* one step removed from Django, learning guitar from fellow Gypsies as well as mimicking Django's jazz. Just as Django had joined his father's band at the old flea-market bar La Clodoche, Lousson now was at Django's side.

For the Brussels tour, Django and Rostaing purchased a new Webster tape recorder and brought it with them, recording one of their shows at the Théâtre des Galéries. Yet while the tape recorder served to save this concert for posterity, Django also used the machine for more immediate purposes. Visiting a Belgian farm, he held the microphone to the snouts of pigs, cows, and horses, recording a menagerie of animal noises to amuse his beloved Babik.

From his Nouveau Quintette's bebop, Django was soon back to playing swing with Stéphane. Grappelli had lined up a month-long engagement for the duo at La Rupe Tarpea in Rome, arranged by a new impresario, Italian jazz connoisseur Christian Livorness.

They traveled by train first to Milan, where they played 11 nights at the Astoria Club, as magnificent a venue as postwar Milan offered. The Italian rhythm section was guitarist Franco Cerri's ensemble, which in turn was modeled after the Quintette. As well as trading riffs with Cerri, Django crossed paths with Luciano Zuccheri, a classically trained guitarist who switched to jazz under Django's inspiration and founded his own Quintetto Ritmico di Milano in 1941. Django's music had preceded him to Italy.

La Rupe Tarpea was on the via Veneto, the sweet spot of Rome's *dolce vita*. The cabaret was ominously named for the cliff over which the beautiful traitoress Tarpea was cast after showing the invading Sabines the secret path to conquer the Campidoglio. The club was a modern cliff with its own pitfalls. It attracted Rome's movie stars and nouveau riche, literati and glitterati, drawn to the all-night music and brilliant-colored cocktails *americano*. A smart venue divided in two, a restaurant occupied the ground floor and a night club filled the grotto with a dance floor. Django and Stéphane were introduced to a rhythm section of three Italians—pianist Gianni Safred, bassist Carlo Pecori, and drummer Aurelio de Carolis. Playing for dancers, then performing for diners during intermissions, they were kept working without stop. Roman doctor Mario de Crescenzo hurried to the scene when he heard word Django was in town: "I descended the stairs and there was Django with a plate of spaghetti and a bottle of chianti. I asked if I could embrace him and he said, 'I have to go and play!' So he went to the small room, where they had about 12 tables and a space for dancing. Then in came Stéphane Grappelli and an Italian rhythm group. Somebody made the point that, when you have the privilege of listening to musicians like these, you don't dance, you listen, so we started rearranging the chairs like a concert. A Dominican billionaire with two models on his arms embraced the spirit of the occasion and ordered drinks all round, and the band jammed until three in the morning." Django was billed in Italian grandiloquence as "Three Fingers Lightning," and performed a trademark virtuoso piece each night with electrifying runs to the Roman crowd's enraptured cheers.

Inspired by the music, another wealthy Italian jazz aficionado sought to record them. Count Sergio Sangiorgi funded a series of sessions organized by Livorness and captured on tape during January and February 1949 at the Radio Audizioni Italiane studios in Rome. Like the RDF "Surprise-Partie" series, the Rome RAI recordings capture Django and Stéphane in a casual mood, playing more for fun than to set down perfect renditions. There was a sense of adventure to their improvisations on a wide array of 69 jazz standards, popular songs, and Django's own compositions, from "Nagasaki," which they first recorded in 1936, to "Over the Rainbow," "Minor Swing" to "Swing 42." They even played an improvisation based on Tchaikovsky's "Starry Night."

The busy schedule was too much for Django, inspiring visions of getting away. When the recording sessions ended, he spent his earnings on a caravan and vanished for several days. As Stéphane remembered, "He preferred to live like that, for—as he said—he liked to go to sleep with the sound of rain falling on the roof."

From Rome, Django and Stéphane traveled south to Naples to perform at the Teatro Metropolitan on via Chiaia, the city's modern version of La Scala. They then caught a train back to Milan for another stand before returning home to Paris after more than two months in Italy.

The Italian trip marked Django and Stéphane's last tour and recording session together. There was no animosity between the two while in Italy; they both had matured, proven themselves together and separately, and found a contentment that allowed them to play together without the old feelings of envy on and off stage. From their first impromptu jams behind the bandstand at L'Hôtel Claridge in 1934, Django and Stéphane now each filled their own stages.

After 15 years as musical partners, they bid each other *à bientôt*.

BACK IN PARIS in springtime, Django could find no work. His fame in France had fallen from its zenith during the Occupation, when everyone adored "Nuages" and his photograph sold everywhere. France was still struggling through the postwar recession that brought a drought in bookings; according to the musicians union, 70 percent of French musicians had been out of work since 1947. Jazz not only lost its luster from the golden age during the war but even its solid fan base was fractured between New Orleans jazz and bebop. Django was disenchanted by his American tour, but he now also felt deserted by his French fans. In addition, his health was suffering. His old burn wounds never healed completely. His hand and armpit became infected during the 1949 Rome venture, and other scars were still open and needed tending with sulfa powder. Setting aside his Selmer guitar, he abandoned his apartment near place Pigalle and left Paris. He bought yet another car—this time a monstrous American Lincoln—and hitched it to a new caravan. He, Naguine, and Babik hit the road. Yet the old Lincoln was fraught with mechanical woes, and they only made it as far as Le Bourget, a dismal town just to the northeast of Paris.

The Romany encampment at Le Bourget was a no-man's land that had become a nomad's land. Alongside the right of way of the railroad tracks, caravans parked in the scrubland with no shade from the sun nor protection from the wind, rain, or snow. There was no drinking water, no sanitation except the ditches, nowhere for children to play except in the dirt.

Standing out from the encircling camp, Django's new caravan was the last word in caravans. Instead of the venerable wooden box-on-wheels of his childhood, this new caravan was fit for a Gypsy king. Made of sheetmetal bolted to a wooden frame, it was a modern trailer camper that didn't leak when the heavens rained—nor would it catch fire. Alongside Django's caravan, Négros parked her home, an old Citroën retrofitted with sleeping space in the back. Automobiles, camping vans, and metal trailers were replacing horses and the classic wooden caravans as the Manouches and Gitans evolved with the times. *La Zone* was slowly and surely being razed. Strangling the Gypsy encampments were gray apartment tenements, looking grim even when new, pushing the Romanies further out of Paris. The industrial dumps were being cleared out, the gardens and small bosques of woods leveled. Even the hedgehogs were displaced, driven further into the countryside.

Delaunay tried to enlist Django to play again. He was organizing an International Festival de Jazz de Paris at Salle Pleyel on May 8–19, 1949, and left a spot open for Django. Unlike Panassié's Nice festival, Delaunay's featured both the old and the new. Sidney Bechet—whom Delaunay was now managing in place of Django—Pete Johnson, and Oran "Hot Lips" Page shared the bill with Miles Davis's quintet featuring Tadd Dameron, James Moody, Kenny Clarke, and Barney Spieler. At the top of the bill was the festival's headliner, the Paris premiere of Charlie Parker. The show would have given Django a chance to jam with Bird, but he turned his back on the opportunity. Django had no interest in working with his old friend Delaunay. Nor even in playing his guitar.

Still Delaunay tried. With relations between himself and Django frayed, he sent his colleague Frank Ténot as emissary. "Charles sent me to ask you to participate in La Nuit de Jazz," Ténot began.

"I would go if I had the desire to play," Django replied. "How much is he paying?"

"The usual fee."

"That's not enough!" Django said, astonished by such impudence.

On another occasion, Delaunay visited Django himself with an offer to organize a concert. Delaunay dangled a tantalizing carrot before him: The pay was good, he hinted. But Django had just performed at the Salle Pleyel and been paid well. He lifted up his caravan mattress to reveal the bed of banknotes upon which he had been sleeping. He waved Delaunay off, saying, "There's money here. I don't need any more."

When Delaunay's acquaintance André Hodeir tried to move him to play, Django waved him off, saying, "I'm bored with the guitar." Hodeir pushed on, saying they were organizing a concert with the old Quintette, to which Django erupted in anger. That music was old-fashioned and the musicians were not modern enough for him any more.

Stéphane also appeared one day in Le Bourget. He came from London just to see Django, bearing an offer for another American tour, this time organized by impresario Peter Morris. Yet Stéphane found Django solemn and somber. He had no interest in the tour plans, and Stéphane left confused by his old friend's disenchantment.

Finally, saxophonist André Ekyan tracked down Django in Le Bourget. When Ekyan asked Django what he was playing these days, Django mumbled, "Nothing." Ekyan queried him further, but Django could hardly speak. It was obvious he was in pain. Finally, he opened his mouth and showed Ekyan the source of his misery—his front teeth were missing, his mouth swollen and red.

"As you can see, I obviously can't work like this," Django mumbled.

Ekyan—who studied dentistry before taking up the sax—told him he needed help immediately.

Django would have none of it. "Of course, my brother," he said, "but I'm too scared!"

The Romanies bore a deep distrust of doctors, gendarmes, and other officials, ingrained from years of abuse of power. But Django's fear came firsthand. Since his caravan fire and the prescription to amputate his leg, he had given hospitals a wide berth. Yet his current situation was serious, and Ekyan promised he would look after him. He telephoned a dentist friend and arranged an emergency appointment. Then he took hold of Django's arm and steered him straight to the dental chair. All the way there, Django argued and Ekyan persuaded. Finally Django acquiesced—as long as he could be knocked out with gas. Ekyan held his hand as he went under and the dentist pulled six of Django's teeth. Then the true emergency arrived—while Django was out, he swallowed a blood clot, blocking his throat. Immediately, his face turned blue from lack of oxygen. In a panic, the dentist reached down his throat with an instrument to clear it, then jump-started the oxygen pump to resuscitate

Django. Several days later, Django was fitted with a dental plate. It was all yet another reason to fear the medical world.

With his dazzling new white teeth in place, Django was enlisted by Ekyan to play again. Ekyan arranged a backing quintet of pianist Eddie Bernard, drummer Gaston Léonard, and bassist Jean Bouchety, and found them work at the Pavillon de l'Élysée in spring 1949. Yet the extravagant club was the wrong venue for jazz and the band fell flat. Ekyan then arranged for them to play the summer season at the Casanova in Le Touquet. From there, they toured through the French provinces, performing in Villeurbanne, Grenoble, and southward along the Côte d'Azur. On October 25, they were in Geneva, where they recorded a series of songs at the Swiss RSR radio studios to be broadcast that afternoon promoting their evening concert at the Palais d'Hiver.

At the start of 1950, Christian Livorness called from Rome with another venture. He was a founding member of the new Roman nightclub Open Gate just off the via Veneto. To inaugurate the club in style, the manager sought a class act. Livorness thought first of Django.

In spring 1950, Django and Ekyan opened at the Open Gate. Django had not been pleased with his 1949 Italian backing band, so this time they hand-picked their own ensemble of drummer Roger "Bagnolet" Paraboschi, bassist Alf "Toto" Masselier, and pianist Raphaël "Ralph" Schécroun. Yet the Roman audience were not jazz fans. Django and Ekyan were preceded by Danish swing violinist Svend Asmussen's ensemble, which was only suffered by the crowd. Ekyan remembered their reception: "The Open Gate was the famous cabaret of Roman billionaires and aristocrats, and you can imagine how we flopped with a clientele like that! There was a little Italian commercial band there with us, but they knew just what had to be done to please this audience and did it well. When we played, no one so much as looked at us—and I suspect no one even heard Django!" Trumpeter Bill Coleman and his wife Lily met up with Django at the club and reported the cabaret manager was constantly telling Django to play more softly so he wouldn't inconvenience the diners. Django simply turned his amplifier to face the wall and played on.

They made their best music in Rome off the bandstand. Italian pianist and composer Armando Trovaioli invited Django and band to his villa outside the capital. Also invited were the other name jazz musicians in town at the time—Roy Eldridge, Zoot Sims, Toots Thielemans, Ed Shaughnessy, and Benny Goodman, who Django met up with during one of the clarinetist's concerts in Rome. Only Goodman didn't show; the rest of them jammed until the sun rose. Masselier remembered that night as one of the high points of his life, Django playing one solo that lasted for half an hour—and still he had not run dry of ideas. Django was taken by composer Anton Karvas's zither soundtrack to the recent movie *The Third Man*, and Django played the theme song, using its eerie mood as a jumping off point to explorations. As Masselier said, "In my life as a musician—and I accompanied everyone, from Coleman Hawkins to Don Byas—I never heard an improviser like Django."

While in Rome during April and May, Django and band returned to RAI studios to again record under the patronage of Sangiorgi. This time, fueled by Ekyan's alto sax and clarinet, the session was infused with the spirit of bebop. As before, the songs ranged widely, from the New Orleans classic "Darktown Strutter's Ball" to improvisations on Grieg's "Norwegian Dance" and Debussy's "Rêverie." This second series of Rome sessions differed greatly from the first with Stéphane. With the violinist at his side, Django was forced to swing. Now with a sax, the mood was modern, Ekyan's horn calling on Django to best himself in his explorations.

Returning to Paris, Django was invited to join an entourage heralding Benny Goodman's arrival in France on June 6, 1950. That evening, Django attended a reception for Goodman at L'Hôtel George V off the Champs-Élysées. Goodman had been interested in hiring Django to accompany him while in the United States in 1946. Now, he was gracious in inviting Django to sit in at his band rehearsal the next day and join him onstage at his June 8 concert at the Palais de Chaillots. Goodman also asked Django to return to the United States at his side.

Out of politeness, Django agreed. Yet his dreams of fame in the promised land of jazz were jaded. Besides, Goodman remained true to his prewar sound and Django was looking to the future; he was uncertain what role he might play alongside the King of Swing. Django joined Goodman's band for rehearsals but the next night, he failed to show for the concert. In the end, Goodman returned to the United States without him.

Django meanwhile returned to his caravan at Le Bourget. Since his American tour with Ellington, his jazz world had broken apart. The Hot Club de France was history due to the schism between Panassié and Delaunay. Django and Delaunay too had gone their own ways. And whether he knew it or not at the time, Django would never work with Stéphane again. With the revolution in jazz from traditional music and swing to bebop, the fans too were divided in their allegiances; jazz in France had fallen from grace and from Django's zenith during the war, he too had lost his audience. "Nuages" was but a wistful memory, an old melody whistled by an older generation.

Back in Le Bourget, close to but yet so far from the Parisian jazz world, Django hung up his Selmer guitar in the back of his caravan.

13

A New Man
1951–1953

HIS GUITAR REMAINED hung on the wall of his caravan, silent. For some six months from July 1950 and into the New Year, dust collected on the spruce soundboard and the rosewood sides. The grease in the sealed tuning machines grew stiff from lack of use. The strings first oxidized, then began to rust.

Django likely spent his days with the other Manouche men, walking from their Le Bourget encampment to a nearby bar where they downed coffees through the morning, switching to cassis or red wine by noon. Someone would begin shuffling cards with exaggerated noise to draw players, then deal them out around the table. Bids would be made and a game of belote begun. The conversation, which might ramble from politics to gossip of Gypsy affairs, would now turn serious. Billiard balls would be racked up, then broken, another round of beer ordered. The Manouche women were the ones who typically found the money for the family to live. They were industrious, always cleaning, always cooking. In their caravans, they crafted lace or jewelry. They told fortunes, reading the mysteries in a passerby's hand. Or if times were bad, the Manouche women simply begged, their own hands held open at the mouths of the métro for spare sous.

It was Hubert Fol who lured Django back to music. The Be-Bop Minstrels alto saxman came looking for Django, keen to resurrect the ensemble. Throughout Django's life, the drive to play often came from having a musical partner in creation, someone to share inspiration, bounce lines off of, push each other to new explorations. In the beginning, it was Nin-Nin, then Stéphane, followed by a string of reedmen—Rostaing, Lévêque, Meunier, Ekyan. Now, Django found the perfect foil in Fol. With new inspiration, Django took his Selmer down from the wall, dusted it off, and tuned up the strings once again.

Fol's first hero was Johnny Hodges, the swing saxman with the dour face yet velvet tone who played Duke Ellington's melodies as though he was seducing them. Then, Fol heard Charlie Parker, and the sweetness of swing was replaced by the fury of bebop. Fol collected Bird's pioneering recordings, from "Moose the Mouche" to "Klact-oveeseds-tene"—melodies, rhythms, and ensemble performances whose ferocious energy made even the now-infamous "Salt Peanuts" of just years earlier seem suddenly tame. Just as Émile Savitry had sat Django down and played him sides by Satchmo and Ellington back in 1931, Fol now spun him the latest bebop 78s. Django's reaction was incredulous. Hearing Parker blast through "Ko Ko," Django was one of the few anywhere who instantly recognized the underlying theme as "Cherokee" and was astonished at this reworking of a standard. As bassist Pierre Michelot said, "He was in ecstasy. . . . The audacity of Bop just took his breath away. This music reached deep down inside him and little by little, his playing evolved, you could hear it, without premeditation. The phrases that belonged to the Hot Club Django were still there of course, but they were transformed." Fol remembered Django charged by a frenetic fire from the Bird and Dizzy sides. With Parker's alto sax echoing in his ears, Django was hot to jam again.

Fol soon found a venue. The *outre* novelist-singer-songwriter-trumpeter Boris Vian ran the Club Saint-Germain at 13 *bis* rue Saint-Benoît and was searching for a sensation to inaugurate its re-opening. Vian was a parttime surrealist and fulltime provocateur. Following the war, he and his trumpet backed Juliette Gréco at Le Tabou. Vian then opened Club Saint-Germain in June 1948, but had recently locked the doors while renovating the grotto. Now he was plotting a grand re-opening. As Fol and Vian were former bandmates, having played together during the Occupation in Claude Abadie's Dixieland ensemble, Fol approached him with a proposition: What better way to inaugurate the new club than with the return of Django?

Django, however, was unsure. Having not played for a time, he feared his music was out of fashion. And there was still the lingering sense of disenchantment.

In the end, something beyond jazz decided him: Vian wanted to also show Django's paintings. Now Django agreed. He was pleased to prove himself to the avant-garde with both his new music and new art.

Vian re-opened Club Saint-Germain on February 1951 surrounded by a buzz of fans anxious to see Django. On opening night, entrance was by invitation only. Meeting friends on the street, Vian scrawled out notes on paper scraps in a few illegible words that were tickets for only the crème of Paris. A *très américain* bouncer guarded the entrance from a scrum of lesser jazz fans and scenemakers not bearing invitations. Around the street grates breathing air down into the grotto, groups of Gypsies gathered like acolytes of a secret society, kneeling around the ventilators to listen to the message of Django's guitar.

Down in the depths, the cellar was packed with jazz aficionados and Tro-glodytes. Parisiennes in the latest shoulderless evening gowns, film stars, cou-ture models, government ministers, and the national theatre director-general all crowded the bar for free drinks while the best of the American expatriate musicians—beboppers Roy Eldridge, Don Byas, and Kenny Clarke as well as New Orleans stalwart Sidney Bechet—hung to the fringes. Charles Delaunay knew everyone; he began shaking hands the moment he arrived and didn't finish until the evening was over.

Fol's ensemble took the stage first, barely fitting within the curve of the ceiling. He and his pianist brother Raymond formed the foundation of Django's new sextet. The band was filled out by trumpeter Bernard Hullin with a rhythm section of bassist Michelot and drummer Pierre Lemarchand. Thus, for the first time, Django had a band with four soloists contributing melodic ideas and improvisations. Counting off, Fol led the band through the new bebop anthems, playing the rapid-fire melodies in unison with the piano and trum-pet. He was a tall, slender man dressed most nights in a suitably dark suit, and he grasped his alto sax gracefully in long fingers as if he were caressing sounds from it. As he blew, his eyes turned to the heavens. Still, *Melody Maker* re-ported that despite Fol's impressive technique, the band was ragged and rough.

Then Django joined them, and the band became an ensemble. With his Selmer guitar fitted with a Stimer S.T.48 pickup, he plugged into a tiny combo amplifier, pulled up a chair next to the piano, and without preamble, kicked off with "All God's Chillun Got Rhythm." This odd song was an ideal begin-ning. Written by Polish-born composer Bronislaw Kaper, the piece was per-formed by Duke Ellington with Harpo Marx in the Marx brothers' 1937 film *A Day at the Races* with Lindy Hoppers dancing in a make-believe Negro shantytown. Ellington made the song famous, yet Bird and Dizzy were play-ing the song on Swing Street, reinventing and empowering it in the spirit of bebop. Now, Django made the song his own. He reharmonized the chordal accompaniment and brought silence to the club with a fully electric solo. It was a simple lesson in jazz history for his young bandmates that at once fused old and new into a unique, individual statement—and the band was right be-hind him. As *Melody Maker* noted, "As soon as Django took the stand the band changed as if by magic. . . . Django gave the combination a feeling that it was now in the hands of a master."

Hubert Fol and his bandmates were all in their mid-twenties, a generation younger than the 41-year-old Django. Many of Paris's modern jazz musicians looked down on Django as the leader of the old swing era, but at the Club Saint-Germain, Django proved to all that he still sat at the top. "The chief lesson we learned from him during his stint there had to do with the total freedom with which he expressed himself," Raymond Fol remembered. "Some nights he was truly extraordinary! This came through perhaps more because of the liberties he allowed himself to take—and only he could have got away with them—than because of the ideas he hit upon. Agreed, he was no bandleader, and his amplifier was always malfunctioning, but he was a *personality*. He had his own fashion of playing his own changes—even for the American tunes he didn't know—and unconsciously fitted them up with a harmonic sequence after his own style." For his part, Django was proud to reestablish his place in Paris's jazz pantheon and listen to his electric guitar lines ricochet off the walls of the capital's premier jazz club. As he told his drummer friend Pierre Fouad, "They make me suffer sometimes, these young punks who think it's all happening *now*, that we're no good anymore, that we're finished! So one day I got angry: I began to play so fast they couldn't keep up with me! And I gave them some new morceaux to play with difficult harmonies and again they couldn't follow me! Now they have some respect for me!"

Night after night, month after month, Django built on this regard, leading the band through an array of songs that kept his accompanists guessing. He called for American pop songs such as "Smoke Gets in Your Eyes" and "Body and Soul," counted out classic jazz numbers like "I Can't Give You Anything but Love" before launching into his own beboppish "Impromptu." And of course the band performed other songs from Django's canon of compositions, including ballads and orchestral pieces such as "Nuages," "Manoir de mes rêves," and "Diminishing Blackness." Django too was happy with his sextet. He beamed with mutual admiration for Hubert Fol and his jagged-edged bebop riffs, pleased to have found yet another musical compatriot. And in Raymond Fol, Django had a truly modern pianist. Instead of pounding out the four-beat rhythm as Ralph Schécroun had done during the second Rome RAI sessions, Fol was playing rhythmic punctuation and syncopation. Together, they created music forceful and strong, making a statement for all Paris to hear.

Django's music drew other jazzmen to his bandstand. Some nights, he was joined by African American expatriates Bobby Jaspar and James Moody; on other nights, Kenny Clarke and Don Byas sat in. One evening, it was a true jam session with a trio of tenor saxes—Jaspar, Moody, and Byas all crowded onto the stage. As Michelot remembered, "Django played like a fool, his smile stretched all the way to his ears listening to the band's sound. And when it was his chorus, he turned his amplifier all the way up and played his guitar in a storm of distortion! Playing in the club, it was a space of liberation for Django. He could play completely as he wanted to play, finding all the sounds he was hearing in his head. . . . I remember him playing solos of fifteen to thirty choruses. In those days, we were still confined by the influence of 78-rpm records and their time limitations, and these long solos left us all truly astonished."

During his Club Saint-Germain stand, Django moved his family from their caravan in Le Bourget into the Hôtel Le Montana, just across the street from the cellar. This tall, narrow hotel was wedged in between more substantial neighboring buildings like an afterthought. It held just a handful of rooms on

each floor, reached by a steep stairway of switchbacks like the alps for which
the hotel was named. Django and Naguine again set up camp in a room, and
Babik made the quarter his own. Like Django before him, seven-year-old
Babik now ran at will through the winding cobbled streets. Film star Daniel
Gélin, living at Le Montana as well, remembered the days: "Jean-Paul Sartre,
who lived a large part of his life nearby at the Café de Flore where he wrote
several of his masterpieces, recalled often how little Babik swiped sugar cubes
and pastries from the terrace of the Café de Flore and then disappeared like
an arrow around the street corner. More than once, Babik returned to the
hotel with the small silver spoons that he had stolen, and Django was very
proud that his son was perpetuating this Gypsy tradition." Proud of his son,
proud of his music, it was a good time for Django and family.

   This pleasure in finding a new musical muse came alive in the Club Saint-
Germain shows broadcast on French radio from February 10 and 20, 1951.
The surviving songs were nothing novel—all part of Django's typical repertoire from years past—yet he found new meaning in the melodies and harmonies, recasting and re-inventing them. Django wasn't just playing the music,
he was playing *with* it. "While he was improvising on 'The Man I Love,' one
of his strings broke—if I remember correctly, it was the B string," Christian
Livorness said. "Quite unperturbed, he continued soloing as though nothing
had happened and it didn't seem to interrupt his melodic development in the
least." Django was taking obvious delight in reeling off runs, tossing in syncopated chords to emphasize the solos of others, spicing his fretwork with ex-
plosive riffs, and performing show tricks, from elegant glissed dashes to
lightning-fast chromatic runs that turned his two fretting fingers into a flash.
As Raymond Fol remembered, "I believe Django found at the club a pleasure
in playing that he hadn't known for a long time." Delaunay too heard the
rapture reborn in Django's music: "Every night, he was truly happy to be
working for an audience that came to listen and were appreciative. His playing was a source of good spirit and amazement to enthusiasts and musicians
alike. . . . Django was a man transformed, animated by the sacred fire of his
younger years, by this need to express himself and to renew himself, something that for a time had abandoned him." Over the past year he may have
been depressed and bitter, but the Club Saint-Germain broadcasts display a
happy man. With his guitar sounding hornlike in its electric tone, his music
was a clarion call, loud and clear, of joy.

INSPIRED BY HIS TRIUMPH at Club Saint-Germain, Django composed a series
of new tunes that he recorded during two Decca sessions with the Fol brothers and a band built on the club shows. Chief among these new compositions
was "Nuits de Saint-Germain-des-Prés," an upbeat theme charged by the
energy of nights in the grotto that fueled these recordings.

The first session took place in Paris on May 11, 1951, featuring the club band cutting four titles. For Jimmy Lunceford's classic "Dream of You," Django refitted the swing melody with his own harmonic chord sequence, making the debonair melody modern. While Fol's alto sax played the old theme, Django's guitar was a harsh counterpoint of jabbing bebop chords accenting the offbeats. This fascinating experiment married something old, something new. The other three tracks were bebop originals. Django composed "Double Whisky" in 1950 for a radio broadcast with Jacques Hélian's orchestra, Lévêque again transcribing Django's guitar notes as he composed the melody in his caravan at Le Bourget. While the main theme was cool in tone, the bridge was pure bebop with a line echoing the interludes of Bird. "Vamp" was a silky and slow after-hours melody led off with a floating improvisation by Django. His sound here was pure electric, sustained notes and resonating chords proving he was in complete command of his electric guitar. The final tune, "Impromptu," was a refinement of Dizzy's proto-bop tune "Be Bop" from the mid-1940s and one of Django's most exciting songs ever. It was both old and new, a *modernistique* bebop rendition of "Les yeux noirs." Built on the same harmonic chord structure as the Romany anthem, the melody of "Impromptu" was angular and cubist where "Les yeux noirs" was flowing and classical. Django originally recorded the song in 1950 with Ekyan in Rome, but that version went unissued. The melody now was a breathless stream of notes played in unison by Django's guitar and Fol's sax in the mode of the best Bird and Dizzy duets. The harmony jumped between minor and major chords, creating a sense of off-kilter tension and movement. It was pure bebop and it was dazzling.

As soon as the Club Saint-Germain stand ended, a rejuvenated Django was booked for the 1951 summer season at the exclusive Belgian seaside resort of Knokke het Zoute. The venue was the Knokke Casino, an ostentatious art moderne gaming temple that presided over the town's Canada Square, luring the wealthy to the green felt. Inside, the casino boasted a fantastical Venetian chandelier featuring 2,700 lamps lighting 22,000 glass crystals that glittered like diamonds above the gamblers. Django performed in the casino's New Orleans room on a bill shared with Kansas City trumpeter Oran "Hot Lips" Page. A battle-hardened veteran of Walter Page's Blue Devils and Count Basie's big band, Page was an old-school trumpetman who played the blues with a gut-bucket raunchiness. His raspy horn sound was backed by an ensemble run by French clarinetist André Reweliotty with pianist Bernard Peiffer. Page had been skeptical of playing a town with a name like Knokke het Zoute: "I figured it was going to be one sad clambake," he swore. Yet Page and Django jammed on jazz standards each night and made converts of the casino crowd. In the end, Page was so inspired by the summer's shows with Django that he named a song for the town, "Knokkin' de Zoute." For his part, Django was equally enthralled by the casino next to the bandstand and spent intermissions at the gaming tables. On his last night, luck was on his side and he won big, breaking the bank. With his pockets stuffed full of Belgian francs, he hired a taxi cab to chauffeur him the 200 miles back to Paris in regal style.

Django and Hubert Fol recast their band in January 1952 for several shows in Belgium. With trumpeter Roger Guérin, they were backed by a rhythm section of drummer Lemarchand and African American bassist Barney Spieler, then living in Paris. *Jazz Hot* was ecstatic in its report on the January 20 show at Brussels's Théâtre des Galéries: "It is above all in harmonies that the modern school has colored Django's style. Reinhardt has always been a harmonist of genius. He has the art to select the most daring note in a chord without sacrificing correctness and balance. Graced by the power of the electric guitar, this technique sends chills down the listener's spine, creating sensations that lie beyond the realm of music proper." This inspiration was kept alive back in Paris on January 30, 1952, when Django and his Belgian tour ensemble were reunited with Raymond Fol to record four more sides for Decca. The pianist's "Keep Cool" was a medium-tempo bop tune starred by a sophisticated melody theme. Django's "Flèche d'or"—Golden Arrow—was a bebop train song in honor of a famed rail line. A one-chord jam, the rhythm of the rails was echoed in Django's reverberating triplet runs. "Nuits de Saint-Germain-des-Prés" was a joyous melody with a harmony built on a series of ascending half-step minor-seventh chord modulations resolving to a major chord.

The highlight of the session was "Troublant boléro," another reworking of an old song, yet this time one of Django's own. He may have been inspired by Dizzy's explorations of Latin themes in taking up where his "Boléro" of 1937 left off. Django's new version rode on flowing rhythmic ostinatos highlighted by a complex and subtle melody, displaying the dramatic development in Django's compositional skills over the intervening years. The rhythm began again with a dancing boléro pattern before Fol and Guérin's horns made their entrance playing the mournful melody line rising now to a hopeful if jaded-sounding climax. Django's electric guitar then took over. His solo was a tour de force of audacious intervals and daring arpeggios, all accented by shimmering chords. It was bebop flamenco, sensuous guitar lines festooned with ebullient notes, rich in mood, a celebration of pure music.

IN AUTUMN 1951, Django again quit Paris. With no work or sessions scheduled, he retreated back to the peace of the countryside. This time, he hooked up his caravan and made the trek south from Le Bourget to the small village of Samois-sur-Seine.

Django first discovered Samois during a fishing venture in 1948, and always dreamed of returning. The idyllic hamlet rested along the river Seine just 40 kilometers southeast of the capital yet a world away in time and place. It was a green Garden of Eden in comparison to the city, a quiet town of small cottages built around a picturesque square, the river flowing by in a peaceful refrain beneath the overhanging branches of stately willow trees. A sole boulangerie baked the bread for the hamlet's 700 souls and two cafés served as the centers of village life. It was Django's own small corner of paradise.

He rented a house at 5 rue du Bas-Samois, a humble artisan's cottage built of plastered stone walls, the whitewash contrasting merrily with the bright-colored wooden window shutters. Django, Naguine, and Babik parked their caravan in the garden behind and moved in with their few possessions. The cottage boasted no luxuries. It had just three rooms—two small bedrooms and a large dining room with heat from an ornate porcelain-iron wood-burning stove left over from the last century. On the walls were hung Django's Selmer and his fishing rods while Naguine kept a vase full of fresh flower blooms on the dining room table. Within this small house, as one French friend, Madame Loisy, remembered, "there reigned always true chaos!"

Here, Django settled into a new routine. "Django lived in perfectly anticonformist fashion," Mme. Loisy continued. "He woke up when he wanted to, ate when it pleased him, and went to bed when he needed to. He might eat breakfast at eleven o'clock in the morning just as well as at ten o'clock at night." The family's house was just a stone's throw from the Seine, and Django often rose in the morning before the sun to go fishing. He selected a rod or two from among his collection, gathered his tackle, and quietly left the house to walk to the river where his modest wooden punt was tethered. As the morning mists cleared in the sun's rays, he spent his days on the river, his hands now working the oars, rowing upriver and drifting back downstream to troll or cast for fish.

One day, Naguine's brother-in-law came to visit. Excited to be at Django's fabled fishing spot, he asked Django, "You want to eat pike? Let's go!" They spent the day casting for fish—only for Django accidentally to hook his brother-in-law by the ear. Blood was everywhere, and Django went pale with fright, fearful he had inflicted a mortal wound. Unable to free the hook, the duo hurried home, Django leading his brother-in-law like a puppy on a leash. When another waterman halted them to ask, "Monsieur Reinhardt, did you have a good catch today?" Django cast aside his fear and pointed to his caught brother-in-law, replying, "Yes! I hooked a big fish!" After a friend in town, a Monsieur Ralph, finally freed him, they spent the rest of the day laughing over their misadventure.

On other days, Django gathered up his canvas, brushes, and oils and set up his easel along the riverbank to spend the time lost to the world amid the brilliant colors of his paints.

For his son, Django believed that Babik should follow in his own footsteps, running free in Samois to explore the world. Django insisted that Babik not attend school—against Naguine and the school administration's wishes. Only when Django was away in Paris or on tour would Naguine dress up Babik and send him off to classes at the Samois school.

In the evenings, Django strolled over to one of the town's cafés, Le Café de la Mairie, to play billiards. He joined the Billiard Club Samoisien, whose 40 members played in tournaments against teams from the neighboring village of Melun or the Samois club's arch-rivals, the Billiard Club de Fontainebleu.

At Samois's other café, L'Auberge de l'Île–Chez Fernand, Django made the acquaintance of the proprietor, Fernand Loisy. A tall, slender man always ready with coffee or a beer, he was prepared to pass the time of day chatting about the weather or fishing, arms folded atop the zinc bar. This seemingly incompatible pair—the itinerant Romany musician and the established bar owner—became fine friends. Django lacked a telephone in his Samois home and so directed calls to Chez Fernand where Loisy took messages arranging tours and concerts. Django also brought letters and contracts to Loisy, who read them aloud, then wrote responses following Django's dictation or pointed out where to scrawl his name. Beyond this assistance with the tedious details of the *gadjo* world, in Loisy, Django found a simple friend, someone to share news of the day and ask for nothing in return.

At night, Django often brought his guitar to pick out melodies at Chez Fernand or to tinker away on the bar's venerable upright piano, but he only played when among friends, never for money. He had owned some 50 automobiles in his life, but didn't care to buy another. He was loath to leave his family and his pastimes, and didn't want to worry about contracts or concerts, performing shows or tours only if he had true need of money.

In Samois, Django was content. He was entering his forties and had become more introspective than before, seeking meaning, searching for peace. Gone was his drive for all-night jam sessions and the exuberant living of *les années folles*; Django was quite simply bored by the grind of playing two and sometimes three menial gigs each day, often for diners who wished he'd simply play his background music more softly. He had lived the musician's life since he was 12. Now it was time for something more. As Gérard Lévêque stated of Django's move to Samois, "He lived the life of a pensioner—one without a pension, living just off his copyrights alone." Naguine, however, saw something deeper. She was more philosophical in describing the changes in him: "In Samois, he was no longer the Django of old. He was *un autre homme*—another man, a new man. He was now a poet. He had the time to look at the beauty of the world around him. In the evening, he might remain at the edge of the river until three in the morning. He watched the river, the movement of the trees, the concert made by the water, and he told me that there he saw the true music, he heard it all, he was crazy for it. He said to me, 'Here is the true music!'"

IN JANUARY 1953, Django left Samois with regret to play a stand at Paris's Club Ringside. Swank and swinging, the cabaret stood on the rue d'Artois, just off the Champs-Élysées. Bassist Michelot remembered this era in Django's life: "It was a time when Django wasn't much in demand anymore, so he stayed away. He wasn't one to force himself on anybody; he simply waited for someone to ask him to come and play. Why should he bother? He had a kind of fatalism that he owed to his Gypsy origins, perhaps. In Samois he led a quiet life. He was rather nonchalant by nature, and he was happy playing billiards (he was very good at it) or else fishing and painting. . . . In my opinion, Django felt that having money was the same thing as having recognition. But in 1953 he was more or less ignored. When he had a booking for two, three weeks at the Ringside (the future Blue Note) he didn't draw much of a crowd. The youngsters didn't come and listen to him and I had the feeling that he was wounded by this. But he said nothing about it. I even heard some musicians, whose names I won't mention, say that Django was past it, if not finished, just as he was going through so many changes!"

Following the Club Ringside shows, Django returned to the recording studio for the first time in a year. In a session for Decca on January 30, 1953, he reunited with Hubert Fol in a sextet featuring trumpeter Guérin, pianist Maurice Vander, Michelot, and drummer Lemarchand. The band bopped through the American tunes "Crazy Rhythm" and "Fine and Dandy," following them with the slow-tempo "D. R. Blues." But Django's new composition, "Anouman," was the highlight of the session and one of his most moving themes ever.

The derivation of the song's title was unexplained. It may have been named for the golden-faced Hindu monkey god Anouman, a legendary trickster whose exploits appeared in the Sanskrit *Mahabharata* and *Ramayana* holy books. Anouman was also a hero to some Romany, part of the Hindu pantheon that survived through time and assimilation with Catholicism. Or, "Anouman" may have been Django's phonetic spelling of the English-language phrase, "A New Man," symbolizing his own rebirth and his new music. Certainly, Naguine would have agreed.

Either way, Django's tune was at once sentimental and pastoral but also replete with world-weary acceptance and supplication, summing up a life fully lived and capturing a sense of melancholy in a melody simple yet profound. Like "Nuages," the theme was built on variations of ascending and descending arpeggios and chromatic runs, yet the melody's octave jumps were inspired by a bebop sensibility that moved far beyond the simplicity of "Nuages." The backing chords were a modulation of minor sixths, sevenths, and ninths resolving to a major key, creating a masterpiece of harmonization that just ten years earlier may have sounded wrong to ears attuned to the music of the times.

Ironically, Django played little on "Anouman." The melody was sung by Fol's alto sax, his pristine tone giving lyrical voice to the resigned longing of the theme. At the time, Fol's playing was inspired in part by the finesse of American alto saxman Gigi Gryce, then living in Paris. Still, it was a sign of Django's admiration for Fol that he arranged the piece largely for him, much as Duke Ellington wrote compositions for his favored saxman Johnny Hodges. Never before and never again would Django create a song solely for another musician—a sign of a new maturity as well as a more sophisticated sense of orchestration. Yet like Django, Fol's musical career was marked; within just a few years, Fol would quit the scene, a victim of psychological maladies. But for now, he played "Anouman" as though he believed in every note. His attack was straight and true, without any of the faked sentimentality of a quavering vibrato. Taking over the lead in the impromptu bridge, Django's guitar contribution was a short solo of just eight measures, brief but brilliant in intensity. Together, Django and Fol played with sublime purity, adding no unnecessary obbligatos nor virtuoso instrumental tricks, and the recorded song was short, well under the usual three minutes, the music fleeting but enduring. Django and Fol had said everything in the elegiac beauty of the melody.

WHILE IN THE CAPITAL for the Club Ringside shows, Django was invited to a new jazz spectacle, the likes of which had rarely been seen in Paris. Marshaled with military precision at l'Alhambra Théâtre, the May 1953 shows were headlined by saxman Lester Young and featured an epic lineup of musicians including Roy Eldridge, Oscar Peterson, Ben Webster, and Benny Carter. It was like an invading jazz army. This was Jazz at the Philharmonic, the work of American impresario Norman Granz.

Granz was the Napoléon of jazz. He was a rare combination in the jazz world—a shrewd businessman who was also a true fan. Granz began his career organizing jam sessions for Los Angeles's 331 Club and Billy Berg's Trouville. He grew attuned to civil rights issues, and during the 1943 Sleepy Lagoon murder trial and subsequent Zoot Suit Riots, he planned a jazz concert to raise legal defense funds to overturn the racist verdict. Granz was just 26, but he made the rounds enticing musicians to join the bill and then borrowed $300 to rent the Los Angeles Philharmonic Auditorium. On July 2, 1944, Granz opened the curtains on his Jazz at the Philharmonic concert with an array of stars battling on stage—Illinois Jacquet and J. J. Johnson jousting with Les Paul and Nat King Cole. The formula worked, and Granz began organizing annual concerts that turned into tours recreating down and dirty jam sessions in the safety of concert halls. Even though they were no longer held just at Los Angeles's Philharmonic Auditorium, Granz stood by the name, and Jazz at the Philharmonic soon became a household term.

Along the way, Granz built an empire. He made a fortune from the music he loved—yet he also reinvested his earnings in jazz, a novel concept in the days of well-heeled white impresarios chewing on fat cigars while their black musicians bummed cigarettes. Granz led a revolution in promoting musicians with street-smart publicity, aiding them in establishing their names to build careers; in his management stable at various times were Ella Fitzgerald and Oscar Peterson. Granz also recorded the concerts to release the first live jazz LPs, causing a sensation among jazz aficionados and creating new converts. Still, many hard-core fans and journalists decried Granz's shows and their staged cutting sessions as crass commercial grandstanding with musicians outdueling each other by striving to hit ever higher notes. Granz's musicians had few complaints, however. He was an outspoken crusader for equal rights as well as a true believer that jazz musicians were true artists. His shows featured integrated lineups of musicians performing for integrated audiences. And his musicians traveled first class all the way, receiving proper treatment whether their skin color was black or white, Granz making certain they got the best gigs in the best venues at the best pay.

Django met Granz in New York during his 1946 American tour, and they were now re-introduced backstage at the Alhambra. Granz offered him a slot in the Jazz at the Philharmonic fall 1953 tours of Europe, the United States, and Japan, outlining grand plans for his jazz spectacular and future recording sessions. Listening to Granz was for Django like hearing the prophecies of a streetcorner Gypsy fortuneteller; he must have swooned, his head full of resurrected visions of his dusty dreams finally coming true. Django happily agreed. Granz eschewed contracts as his record of serving musicians stood for itself; he believed that if a relationship was not working, a contract wouldn't make a difference anyhow. In the Alhambra's backstage wings, a handshake between Django and Granz sealed the deal.

To begin promoting Django, Granz organized a recording session through his friend Eddie Barclay. On March 10, 1953, Barclay assembled Django with backing from pianist Vander, bassist Michelot, and drummer Jean-Louis Viale to cut eight songs, including the standard "Confessin'" and Cole Porter's "Night and Day" as well as Django's own "Manoir de mes rêves," "Blues for Ike," and "Nuages." This session was released in France on a Blue Star ten-inch LP and in the United States on Granz's Clef label as *The Great Artistry of Django Reinhardt*. The Blue Star/Clef LP was just the first step in Granz's plans for Django. He would also record and release Django's Jazz at the Philharmonic concerts, and also planned that autumn to record Django in a trio with his tour rhythm section led by pianist Oscar Peterson and bassist Ray Brown. Sadly, this session was never to be.

The Blue Star/Clef session captured the quintessence of Django's many musical faces. It showed him playing chanson in Paul Misraki's "Insensiblement"; as interpreter of American standards, including "Night and Day," "Confessin'," and "September Song"; as composer with "Manoir de mes rêves" and "Nuages"; as blues player in "Blues for Ike"; and as experimenter in his exotic take on "Brazil." Underneath them all was proof of his powers of harmonization and melodic invention. As Michelot summed it up, this session was "a recapitulation of everything that he had created and everything new that he had begun creating."

The session was unique in that on all eight songs, the voice was predominantly Django's guitar—only on "Blues for Ike" and "Confessin'" does pianist Vander take choruses. On "Confessin'," one of the first jazz tunes Django ever recorded back in 1934, the length of his journey as a guitarist became clear. He plays the song here with an effortless lyrical suppleness. Michelot remembered the session with Django: "One, two, three takes at the most: he wasn't one to do the same thing twenty times over again. The first version was the best as far as he was concerned. That's when the mind is clear and the ideas are fresh. As soon as he seemed to find a tape satisfactory, we moved on to something else. He didn't belong to the category of musicians who enjoy torturing themselves. Django didn't know what the word 'problem' meant in music. His ear was extraordinary, he had an exceptional, if not unorthodox sense of swing, a limitless imagination, and faultless technique with just two fingers on his left hand. . . . He was at a crossroads in his musical expression and open to everything new. He was using an electric guitar (not the contrivance he used to tinker with in the early Forties) with complete mastery, and changing his famous sound. This doesn't change the fact that this session, which I think he liked, met with general indifference when it came out. Django intended to give his own answer to everyone who thought he was over the hill. He was bringing everyone up to date, but nobody could be bothered to look at the calendar."

In this ultimate version of "Nuages," Django made his last statement on his most famous theme. "Nuages" made him a star—stardom that proved fleeting in the fickle universe of popular music. Perhaps bitter over the vagaries of fame, Django was not one to live in the past or replay his same songs in the same way time and again. This final version of "Nuages" was alive, renewed with a sense of magic and mystery haunting his solo lines. As Gérard Lévêque remembered: "Django had found freedom again, and he went wild, exulting in it. This was a one-man fireworks display. And yet there is something intangible that I find disturbing as I listen to this ultimate recording of 'Nuages'— the most beautiful version he recorded—and the coda to 'Manoir de mes rêves,' so full of nostalgia. Something leads me to believe that Django, and many others of his people, had the gift of premonition." Michelot echoed these sentiments: "At one point he plays a phrase in such a way it makes me shiver when I listen to the record and every time I hear it I'm moved by it. Did he have a premonition he was going to leave us?"

WITH PLANS IN PLACE to tour and record with Jazz at the Philharmonic later in 1953, Django was charged by his new music. The year looked to be a busy one. He was booked to play shows in Brussels in February and a short Swiss tour in May before joining Granz for his first global tour.

With Hubert Fol back at his side, Django played a Brussels ball for Les Grands Magasins de la Bourse on Saturday, February 28. In the Belgian capital the next night, Dizzy Gillespie was performing at the Théâtre Royal des Galéries in a concert organized by the Hot Club de Belgique. Visiting Django at the Hôtel Central-Bourse just before the show, Belgian Hot Club impresario Willy de Cort invited Django to join the bill. Django politely refused, but when de Cort told him that Diz was the headliner, Django's face lit up. "I mustn't miss that!" Django eagerly replied. He got dressed, grabbed his guitar, and they rushed to the theater.

Dizzy was playing with a pared-down quintet of just a tenor sax, piano, bass, and drums. Dapper in his trademark bebop finery from his horn-rimmed glasses and goatee to his multicolored beret, his style was as shocking to fashion as his jazz was to the mainstream. Django couldn't have cared less. He sat down on a piano stool and plugged his Stimer-mounted Selmer into his small RV amp while Fol happily took the place of Bird at Diz's side. Dizzy stomped out the Ellington standard "Perdido" and the band took off. As *Jazz Hot* reported: "Django was in brilliant form and delighted everyone, including Dizzy, who seemed to have great regard for him. Almost at the start Django broke a string, but this only left us wondering what possible use it could have been, for his solo grew richer as it went on." Django's pleasure came alive through his guitar while Dizzy danced and pranced across the stage as Django played, jumping around him, gesticulating to the audience with vaudevillian antics. For "'S Wonderful," the guitar and trumpet chased each other through the song, Dizzy and Django playing like merry children. In the end, *Jazz Hot* pronounced the two "to be of the same exceptional class." But above all, the music left smiles across the faces of Django and Dizzy.

BACK IN PARIS on April 8, 1953, Django recorded his fourth contracted session for Decca. He didn't know it, but this session would be his last, and yet at the same time it represented a new beginning down a road to new directions.

Django was backed by his most modern ensemble ever—"Fats" Sadi Lallemand on vibes, bassist Michelot, and drummer Lemarchand. When pianist Vander couldn't make the date, at the last minute an unknown pianist from Algiers, Martial Solal, was called to sit in. Solal was just 25 and had arrived in Paris three years earlier to perform in the bands of Noël Chiboust and Aimé Barelli before being hired to play solo piano at the Club Saint-Germain, where Django likely first heard him. When his telephone rang inviting him to hurry down to the session, Solal thought it was a wrong number—or a practical joke. Assured that Django had indeed asked for him, he rushed to the Decca studio, thrilled and nervous at the opportunity to play with a musician of such stature. For Solal, the session passed as if in a dream. It was his first time in a recording studio and here he was to play alongside Django. He was struck by stage fright and was embarrassed by his piano work.

Django did not rehearse the ensemble and handed out no head arrangements: He simply named the key and launched into the music. As Michelot said, "For him the most important thing was freshness of spirit, spontaneity—that's why he didn't like a lot of rehearsals. He wasn't interested in going over the same thing a hundred times." Lemarchand agreed: "He was extremely spontaneous to work with. He didn't think twice—you just had to play with him! He would sometimes speed up or something and he would smile . . . but if you didn't follow him immediately, or you made a mistake, you would get the 'black look' which made you feel terrible!" The four sides cut included three covers—"I Cover the Waterfront," chansonnier Paul Misraki's "Chez Moi," and Loulou Gasté's "Le soir"—and one original, the straightforward 12-bar blues "Deccaphonie," named for the label. For "Le soir," Django asked Solal to introduce the piece with several bars of improvised solo piano. The song began with meditative choruses before kicking into a quick tempo and Django's bouncing guitar lines. In "Chez Moi," Django had a further trick to throw into the mix: he changed keys each chorus, ascending a half-step each time. Solal remembered: "It was a dangerous yet interesting exercise." The other musicians had trouble keeping up with the key changes—a facile move on a guitar—but Django relished the variety of modulating tones.

In this last session, Django was still seeking. He was always taken by the most avant garde and extreme development of a musical genre. From musette to Louis Armstrong's jazz, swing to bebop, Bach to Debussy and Ravel, the sounds that stretched the boundaries the furthest and outraged the establishment the most always held an allure. Django listened to the newest bop, including Gig Gryce's melodic orchestrations and the cool jazz of Miles Davis and his group that at times featured Gil Evans and Lee Konitz, as well as pianist John Lewis, who had been playing Paris. At 43, Django spoke through his guitar with a sound spare and understated. From the fury of his early virtuosic picking, he sought now a new virtuosity of lyricism, speaking volumes in a few phrases. He didn't toss off the same opulence of notes, but those he offered were both opalescent and iridescent. Gone were the Gypsy tricks, the showman's sleight of hand. He played instead with a confidence and wisdom as if he was sure of every note. It was a fitting last testament.

AT THE START OF MAY, Django and Naguine set off for Switzerland, where Django played dates in Geneva and Basel. Django always loved the Swiss Alps, yet during their travels, he began suffering debilitating headaches. Someone suggested that his blood pressure might be high and recommended that he consult a doctor. But after the near amputation when he was 18, the operation in London, and the visit to the dentist in 1950, Django refused to go anywhere near a doctor's office. Besides, it was just a headache.

As the tour progressed, Django then started having problems controlling his hands. Playing his guitar, his fingers were stiff, unresponsive. He complained to Naguine while they were in Basel, "I don't know what's wrong with my fingers. I'm not able to close them like before." Now even Naguine took up the chorus: He should go to a doctor. But Django again waved off the warning. "No, no, I don't want to see a doctor. I'm too afraid of their needles!"

The signs were clear, yet Django was ignorant of their meaning.

AFTER THE SWISS CONCERT dates, Django and Naguine met up with some fellow Romany and set off on the road. They borrowed a caravan to join the others in their travels, Django fishing the mountain streams for dinner. The headaches were gone and his hands seemed to be working again, and he, Naguine, and Babik spent two happy weeks in the Alps.

Returning from the Swiss dates to Samois on Friday, May 15, 1953, Django just missed Bing Crosby, who ventured from Paris in search of him, hoping to tour the United States together in a duo recreating Crosby's old dates with guitarist Eddie Lang.

Django was resigned to bad rolls of the dice; he told Naguine that luck was no longer on his side and no one understood him any more. But at the same time, Naguine sensed that he seemed content with his life. She was used to his sense of drama and fatalism. And if he missed meeting with Crosby, he could look forward to the Jazz at the Philharmonic tour.

ON THE MORNING of Saturday, May 16, 1953, Django rose early as was his fashion with plans to walk to the river Seine to fish. It was a glorious spring day and he was happy to be home. He strolled into the center of Samois to his friend Fernand Loisy's Auberge de l'Île for a cup of breakfast tea. He was sitting on the terrace and chatting happily with several regulars when he suddenly collapsed to the ground.

Alarmed, his compatriots gathered him up in their arms and carried him back to his house. Django regained consciousness just long enough to refuse a doctor one last time. Then the pains in his head grew worse, spreading throughout his right arm, and he fell into a coma. Naguine overruled Django's last wishes and sent someone to telephone for a doctor. It being Saturday, the doctor took a long time in arriving. After a hurried examination, he directed that Django be brought immediately to the Fontaineblue clinic's emergency room.

It was all too late. Doctors and hospitals could do nothing for him now. He never regained consciousness, and at four o'clock that afternoon, Django died. The cause of death was listed as cerebral hemorrhage. He was just 43.

RETURNING TO SAMOIS, Naguine and Négros hurriedly collected their belongings and moved out of their cottage at 5 rue de Bas-Samois, where the family had been so happy. They settled back into their caravan, still parked in the garden behind the house. The Manouche tradition called for vacating the abode where a beloved had died. One must always be wary of the spirit world of *moulé*.

ON THE MORNING of Tuesday, May 19, 1953, Django's coffin was carried from his house down the cobbled streets of Samois to the town's eleventh-century church. The coffin cortege was followed by Naguine, Babik, Nin-Nin, Négros, and a straggling line of Romany cousins. Inside the small chapel, some 200 Gypsies crowded into the pews along with 300 other friends and musicians—Roger Chaput, André Ekyan, Bill Coleman, Arthur Briggs, Pierre Michelot, upcoming guitarist Jean Bonal, bandleader Claude Bolling, and Charles Delaunay. The coffin was abloom with 20 wreaths of roses, lilies, and carnations, memorials from the Federation of French Hot Clubs, the Billiard Club Samoisien, and others.

After a simple service, the coffin was carted from the church, through the streets again to the Cimetière de Samois in a quiet wood on the edge of the village. He was buried on a small hillside overlooking the Seine. In a long, solemn procession, the mourners sprinkled holy water with a sprig of rosemary on the coffin and pronounced the Manouche benediction to the dead, *Akana mukav tut le Devlesa*—I now leave you to God. Then, Nin-Nin placed a symbolic guitar atop the coffin to be buried with Django.

STÉPHANE GRAPPELLI was playing a stand in Florence when Django died, and did not hear the news in time to attend the funeral. Charles Delaunay telephoned him one evening shortly after the funeral and told him of the events. "I didn't cry," Stéphane said, but hearing the news, he felt as if he had turned to stone. He couldn't breathe. He struggled as though he were suffocating. In the end he was simply silent.

FOLLOWING THE MANOUCHE mourning tradition of *zelimós*, the family moves out of the deceased's caravan, then sets it afire with all of the beloved's worldly possessions. In honor of the deceased's memory, they may keep a picture in a place of honor but they do not speak the person's name again. Their memory is honored in silence—*on n'en parle pas*.

It was thus too with Django. Following the funeral services, Naguine amassed Django's last possessions—his meager wardrobe of clothes, the collection of fishing rods and tackle of which he was so proud, his tape recorder with which he had recorded animal sounds for Babik, a batch of last home-made tapes of compositions and new music recorded in Samois, and his famous Selmer guitar. She piled Django's possessions in a pyre, struck a match, and burned them.

Django's guitar went up in flames.

Afterword
Gypsy Jazz

FOLLOWING DJANGO'S DEATH, Nin-Nin set his own guitar into its case, locked it shut, and vowed never to play again. He then disappeared. Returning into the nether regions of France that the Gypsies inhabit, he lived among his clan on the margins of French society. He collected and sold scrap metal with Ninine Vées; it was a job he and Django always loved, and now he returned to his roots. Nin-Nin's guitar remained silent in tribute to his brother.

Naguine took Babik and moved their caravan from Samois back to join their fellow Manouche. Soon after, they settled into a dreary Montmartre apartment, rootless, lost. Their sixth-floor garret had neither heat nor electricity and few of the creature comforts of even their box-on-wheels. *La Zone* was all but history. Gypsies were moving into the gray tenements strangling the city in a new noose of slums known as *la ceinture rouge*. Naguine and Babik became more of the faceless poor of Paris.

The Manouche mourn their dead following strict ritual. Homage is paid to a beloved's memory for several weeks after death. Then the family would rarely mention his name again—and would never pass his Romany name down to a succeeding generation. They might stop eating his favorite foods and visiting his favored places. His memory would never be evoked in public, and beyond a handful of memento mori, it was almost as if he never existed.

And for Django, his music would not be played again.

While non-Gypsy jazz fans continued to listen to his recordings, among Gypsies, Django's legacy was on the way to being lost.

JAZZ MARCHED ON following Django's death. Miles Davis's cool jazz. Hard bop. Free jazz. The music became more sophisticated and technical, played not for dancers but for an ever-shrinking group of enthusiasts. Few fans had interest any more in the joyous old sounds of a Gypsy guitarist. Django's *modernistique* music was left behind.

For Django's former accompanists, it was a different story. They had heard Django firsthand and the experience had left an indelible mark on their music. None of Django's Gypsy sidemen dared take a solo in Django's presence, but his death let loose a pent-up flood.

Perhaps Django's greatest admirer, Sarane Ferret continued to record and play in Montmartre and Montparnasse into the 1960s. While his brothers explored new musical directions, Sarane remained devoted to jazz in Django's mode. His band became a school for a younger generation of guitarists, including Gitan Laro Sollero and Frenchman Francis-Alfred Moerman. And keeping alive the musical progression, Sarane married Gusti Malha's daughter, Poupée. Sarane died in 1970.

Matelo Ferret created his own music. From years playing Tzigane melodies in the Russian cabarets, he forged a style of traditional Eastern European Gypsy music played on a nontraditional instrument, the guitar. He recorded several masterpieces in the coming years. In 1960 and 1966, he played alongside Jo Privat in two sessions that collectively became known as *Manouche Partie*, a nostalgic revival of the *bal musette* milieu. In 1978 Matelo recorded a two-album set for Charles Delaunay entitled *Tzigansakaïa*, an exotic medley of jazz melodies, traditional Tzigane pieces, and original compositions all played with Romany finesse.

Matelo continued to play his music in Paris's nightclubs until his death from cancer in 1989. Of all of Django's sidemen, he remained the consummate professional musician, who, like Django, lived in music. He could barely remember the name of the street he lived on, yet in his head were thousands of melodies, which he passed on to his three sons, all excellent guitarists—Michel "Sarane," Jean-Jacques "Boulou," and Elie "Elios" Ferré.

The Ferrets' cousin—the honorary "fourth brother"—René "Challain" Ferret followed Matelo's path in playing traditional Tzigane music. Throughout the 1950s, he accompanied accordionist André Verchuren and Gypsy violinist Yoska Nemeth. He married a Toulouse woman and moved to the Midi, where he continued to perform, launching a jazz group in the 1980s called Django Jazz. His son Paul "Challain" Ferret learned at his side and today plays modern jazz.

Roger Chaput, the Quintette's first rhythm guitarist, moved to Toulon to become a cartoonist after the war. He returned to music in the 1960s, touring France and recording two personal LPs, *Tonton Guitare*.

Django and Nin-Nin's cousin Ninine Vées also laid down his guitar in homage to Django, but was soon back in an ensemble with violinist Léo Slab. Vées continued to play on and off until his death in 1977. Slab moved to the Midi, where in his eighties, he recorded a stellar album *La Roulotte* with French guitarist Philippe Guignier and continued to tour as long as he could bow his fiddle.

Oscar Alémán returned to his native Buenos Aires at the outbreak of World War II. He recorded several sessions of stunning swing in Argentina that prompted a genre of South American followers of his and Django's string jazz. Following several decades of semi-retirement and obscurity, he returned with a new batch of hit LPs in Argentina in the 1970s. He died in 1980.

Marcel Bianchi remained prolific as a bandleader and recording artist in Switzerland and France. With his wife, chanteuse and guitarist Denise Varène, he performed along the Côte d'Azur for several decades starting in the 1960s.

Hubert Rostaing led a jazz ensemble in Paris through the 1950s, becoming famous for his prolific film scores.

Gus Viseur continued to play his accordion throughout, becoming a mainstay of Parisian music. After emigrating to Canada, where he had a successful career, he returned to France to live and perform into the 1970s, still with Baro, Matelo, and Matelo's son Boulou at his side. He died in 1977.

When Stéphane Grappelli died in 1997, his music was honored around the globe. To many, he was always "Django's violinist," yet Stéphane carved out his own career following their parting in 1939. He formed a fertile partnership with pianist George Shearing and recorded with numerous other jazzmen including Henri Crolla, Martial Solal, Oscar Peterson, and his disciple Jean-Luc Ponty. In 1973 when he was enticed to recreate a Quintette-style ensemble with English guitarist Diz Disley, his music found a new blossoming and he led a variety of Hot Club ensembles for years after. Throughout, he was prolific in recording, including a stellar session with violinist Yehudi Menuhin. His musical career was long and varied, but he never tired of paying tribute to Django.

Despite their falling out in their last years, Charles Delaunay remained Django's greatest fan. In 1954, Delaunay published a memoir of Django, a slim volume entitled *Django Reinhardt souvenirs*. He collected anecdotes of Django's life from the musicians he played with, writing his memoir in a nostalgic style ripe with picturesque evocations of a Paris lost. His book was hagiography pure and simple, and it became a palimpsest upon which the myth surrounding Django was built. Delaunay also continued to license and release Django's music even after their break, remaining Django's chief label into the 1950s. Following Django's death, Delaunay began a reissue program of Django's music on Vogue, uncovering recordings of concerts and collecting obscure tracks. While Django had conscientiously spent all the money he made during his lifetime, leaving his widow and son in poverty, Delaunay became a wealthy man from first his Swing label and later the Vogue recordings. He died in 1988.

Taking Django's place in the fall 1953 Jazz at the Philharmonic tour was none other than Dizzy Gillespie. Norman Granz recorded Dizzy with Oscar

Peterson and continued to promote Dizzy through the mid 1950s, taking him from a bebopper known primarily among the cognoscenti to a household name.

Naguine later moved back into a caravan. While traveling to Paris shortly after Django's death, Les Paul and Mary Ford met up with her again. Seeing her poverty, Paul pulled strings at the record companies to reinstate the royalty payments that were past due. In 1982, Babik went to court to be declared Django's sole legitimate heir and to fight to receive royalties. Learning guitar after his father's passing, he recorded and performed until his death at age 57 in 2001.

In 1959, a group of French jazz aficionados tracked down Nin-Nin and cajoled him into recording again. He needed the money and agreed to a session, which was labeled *Joseph Reinhardt joue Django*. He pulled together a band including violinist Pierre Ramonet, guitarists Jean "Cérani" Mailhes and Paul Mayer, and bassist Pierre Sim, and cut an LP of his brother's compositions as well as his own iconoclastic songs. As he explained, "I don't want to copy the familiar traits of my brother. I want to create proof of my originality and affirm my personality while conserving the famous Gypsy style. To this end, I have prepared a series of arrangements based on the themes of Django. But my repertoire also includes several of my own new compositions." His sister Sara Tsanga was more direct in describing his eccentric music: "My brother Nin-Nin? He's an arab."

Nin-Nin continued to alternate playing jazz with long stretches of silence, disappearing back onto the open road. He performed in Paul Paviot's 1957 film biography of Django and in the mid 1960s recorded several other sessions that were released on LPs and EPs. When his fellow Gypsies began to meet for a weekend each summer in the late 1960s in Samois to pay tribute to Django, Nin-Nin performed for his people in groups with his old compatriot Léo Slab, as well as Lousson and Babik.

Nin-Nin passed away in 1982, and was buried alongside Django in Samois.

Baro Ferret set aside his guitar during World War II in honor of and frustration over Django's music. He had other business to attend to anyway. Part of the Pigalle aristocracy of gangsters, he ran a series of bars, each more shady than the last one—Baro-Bar in Pigalle, La Point d'Interrogation in the suburbs, Barreaux Vert, and La Lanterne near the Porte de Champerret. They were hangouts for Gypsy gangsters, headquarters for Baro's own illicit underworld activities that ran the gamut from the black market to procuring women for the brothels. But as the Romany saying went, Neither money nor the devil remain in peace. The gendarmes kept one eye on him while rival gangsters watched as well. Police raids only interrupted his business, but he spent between 15 and 20 combined years in prison after the war.

Out of jail for a spell in 1966, Baro was enticed by Delaunay to pick up his guitar again and re-record his lost *valses bebop* that Django so admired. In several sessions starting on February 28 and ending May 2, 1966, Baro was backed by Matelo and organist Jean-Claude Pelletier, adding texture like a futuristic cymbalom. Baro was one of the pioneers exploring different time structures in jazz, including 3/4 and 6/8 time, paths later taken by musicians from Dave Brubeck to Shorty Rogers. Various versions of Baro's recordings were released on LP and EP, both entitled *Swing valses d'hier et d'aujourd'hui*. Together with his first recordings of some of these *valses bebop*, these tunes by Baro remain some of the most idiosyncratic, adventuresome, and stunning jazz masterpieces, ever bar none—including the best of Django.

After the sessions for Delaunay, Baro returned to running his enterprises, yet often hired Gypsy guitarists to play in his nightclubs. And after the bar was closed for the night, he brought out his old Selmer guitar to jam. He died in 1976, alone and uncelebrated.

IN DJANGO'S FOOTSTEPS came four *gadjé* guitarists—Jean-Pierre Sasson, Henri Crolla, Jean Bonal, and Sacha Distel. In his recordings as a leader and backing expatriate African Americans such as Lucky Thompson and Don Byas, Sasson was able to best follow Django's legacy and also play in his own voice. On a 1955 *Homage à Django Reinhardt* album including sides by Crolla, Bonal, and Stéphane, Sasson's hot rendition of Django's "Minor Swing" recast the old song in a new fashion with a modern accent and spare, stylish guitar riffs. It was an essential step away from aping the Quintette's music and toward moving ahead in French jazz.

When Crolla died in 1960 of cancer at 40, Naguine bemoaned his passing: "After him, there are no guitarists left."

In the years after Django's death, Sacha Distel was heralded as France's best jazz guitarist, winning magazine polls and recording prolifically. His style even then was pure commercialism, but once he started to sing, he realized where the money was. He put aside his guitar and became a pop vocalist. It was the trend of the times.

BY THE LATE 1950s, many Romanies had all but forgotten the jazz played by one of their own. In the Netherlands and Germany, two Sinti violinists of Django's generation were playing swing—Piotto Limburger was leading his own band while Schnuckenack Reinhardt recorded an album series, "Musik Deutscher Zigeuner." Yet few Gypsies owned a record player in their caravans, and Django's music lived on in silence in the memory of the elders. Most among the younger generations had never even heard his music. Django's legacy was mute.

Thanks to the invention of the cassette tape player, Django's jazz was restored to his own people. Starting in the 1970s, Django's music was reissued on cassette by mainstream labels such as Vogue and EMI-Pathé, and Gypsies rediscovered the music of one of their own. Cassettes were portable and inexpensive, ideal for a Romany market. This revolution of rediscovery brought a renewed interest in playing Django's music among the Manouches and Gitans, coinciding with a movement of Romany pride in Europe. Ironically, *gadjé* jazz fans had kept the heritage alive for almost two decades before it was passed back to the Gypsies. Many French Gypsies bought a copy of Delaunay's biography of Django and safeguarded it in their trailers or tenement apartments, often carefully wrapped in a plastic bag as protection against time. Even today, it's often the only book they own besides the Bible.

For a people without a documented past, here suddenly was a sense of history. Manouches and Gitans proudly played Django's music and pronounced it *mare gilia*—"our music." His legacy had been on the verge of being lost; now suddenly, it was positioned to become a mainstay of their cultural heritage. Django's guitar spoke with a new eloquence to his own people, becoming an emblem of Gypsy identity. He had become a cultural hero for a people with few heroes.

Not only was Django's music disseminated by cassette but a new generation of Gypsy guitarists emerged playing his jazz. They began by copying his song heads and solos off the tapes, faithfully picking out his choruses note for note in a near-religious devotion to his musical canon. With tape recorders, they now made their own cassettes and sold or traded them among themselves.

To the *gadjo* world, this was a lost generation of Gypsy jazz musicians. Most of them never recorded commercially as few outside their world wanted to hear this new Gypsy jazz in a dawning era of folk music and rock and roll. As some Romany musicians cursed, the world now wanted to hear only *soupe*—their slang for fluff music that tastes good but has no body. And yet with homemade cassettes, these Gypsy musicians reached their market.

Among the most famous of this lost generation was Jacques Mala, who took the nom de jazz "Jacques Montagne" in honor of Jacques "Montagne" Mailhes, a nickname meaning simply "mountain" or the summit, the best. This second Montagne accompanied Nin-Nin, Baro, and others of the elder generation, serving as a connection between the two. He even fretted his guitar with just two fingers in an attempt to replicate Django's sound. Montagne was primarily fired by Django's bebop, fashioning a hard-edged jazz. After Baro's retirement from the underworld, Montagne took over his "accounts." One day when the heat got too close, he simply disappeared for his own good. In the 1990s, he was still hiding from the gendarmes and thus, the mainstream jazz world.

Manouche Piton Reinhardt played a fierce and fast guitar, making music with a savage charm but played with the ferocious energy of early bebop. Piton was said to be so undomesticated and fiercely a Gypsy that he could not function in the *gadjo* world. Photos of him show a stately man behind a graying mustache picking out his song on a battered guitar made by luthier Jacques

Favino. Piton's sons, Coco and Sanson, learned at their father's side and were also renowned musicians. Gitans Jacquet and Cérani Mailhes and Manouche Savé Racine—who was married to Django's cousin Carmen—also never recorded commercially. A comrade of Piton's, Spatzo Adel played guitar, violin, and piano as well as backing Jo Privat on bass.

Also among this lost generation was Django's own son, Lousson, who performed regularly in Paris bars throughout the 1960s but never recorded commercially. Lousson's style was electric and modern. He died in 1992.

Others of the lost generation followed Django's bebop stylings. Laro Sollero and René Mailhes took the lead of Django's bebop and blended it with the American influences of Wes Montgomery, Joe Pass, and Jim Hall in creating a vibrant modern music. Only Mailhes recorded commercially but not until the 1990s.

During the years of the lost generation, Gitan Paul Pata from the Côte d'Azur was one of the few who got the chance to record commercially primarily because he played a melodic music that was more *soupe* than jazz. Pata claimed he was an illegitimate son of Baro Ferret, yet his musical father was Henri Crolla.

In the Midi during the 1950s and 1960s, a generation of Gitan guitarists was also playing their own brand of Django's music, blending in Corsican and flamenco influences and recording for several small labels in southern France and Lyon. Because they were able to record during this era of the lost generation, their music became influential in keeping Django's legacy alive and in passing on a southern Gitan style.

The most influential was Étienne "Patotte" Bousquet. Performing at the infamous Marseille dive Au Son des Guitares, Bousquet played with such ferocity that he at times broke all six strings with one strum of his plectrum. His music was based in Django's legacy, but also incorporated musette waltzes and Corsican melodies. He recorded a handful of EPs and LPs that kept songs such as Django's "Montagne Sainte-Geneviève" from being forgotten. In later years, Bousquet gave up on life as a musician and became a shoe vendor in the Midi's flea markets.

Paul Vidal was known mysteriously as "Tchan Tchou," a Chinese-sounding nickname bestowed on him for his slanted eyes. Born in a caravan on November 22, 1923, in Aix-en-Provence, Tchan Tchou learned guitar from his father and from watching Django, whom his father played with when Django visited the Midi. Tchan Tchou was soon performing with two other guitarists in Lyon as the Hot Club de Jazz de Lyon, playing on radio and television broadcasts, including Radio Monte Carlo concerts, and recording a first EP. In later years his recording was sporadic, including three LPs, *Guitare Party*, *Swinging Guitars*, and *Nomades*, backed by his long-time accomplice, Corsican guitarist François Codaccioni, as well as Django's one-time sidemen bassist Alf Masselier and drummer Roger Paraboschi. Tchan Tchou also accompanied Gypsy accordionist Tony "Tieno" Fallone. In later years, Tchan Tchou's chief accompanist was young Alsatian guitarist Moréno Winterstein, who would carry on the elder's guitar style and repertoire, including Tchan-Tchou's famed waltz, "La Gitane."

At the same time, Django's music was born again in a different yet related realm. Brittany cleric Clément Le Cossec founded in 1952 La Mission Évangélique Tzigane de France, an evangelical Christian church run by and devoted to Romanies. By the mid-1960s, Le Cossec's Mission won over many of Django's "followers," including Piton Reinhardt, Laro Sollero, and Louis "Vivian" Villerstein as well as Naguine. The church spread from France throughout Europe to India and the United States in the following decades. The cleric's goal was to convert Gypsies to Christianity but not convert them from being Gypsies. Thus Django's music found a home in the service of the church, transformed into devout music in the truest sense. In 1943–1944, Django tried and failed at writing a Mass for his fellow Gypsies, but now hymns were written to the scores of Django's jazz compositions and played in Gypsy church services. La Mission's musical director was violinist Pierre "Gagar" Hoffman, part of the Hoffman clan Django played with while trying to escape to Switzerland. Gypsy preacher Charles "Tarzan" Welty sang to his flock armed with his Selmer modèle Jazz guitar. And resistance hero, guitarist, and priest Armand "Archange" Stenegry recorded several hymns in 1965 backed by violinist Villerstein and Sollero's bouncing electric guitar lines in the best tradition of Django.

To his fellow Gypsies, Django's music had become sacred.

IN LA MISSION, Naguine finally found solace. Without Django, her life lacked meaning, and following the death of her life's only love, she turned to drink. Her health declined as she suffered from diabetes. Then in 1963, she was introduced to La Mission by a fellow Manouche named Hazo who invited her to a service. She was resurrected by the promise of the Gypsies' own church and its hymns set to Django's music. On February 16, 1964, she was baptized. "I was alone," she testified in La Mission's magazine, *Vie et lumière*. "Now I have found peace."

IN 1980, 13-year-old Alsatian Sinto prodigy Biréli Lagrène recorded an LP entitled *Routes to Django*. The songs were primarily originals yet the music was steeped in Django's influence. Lagrène played with a sure swing belying his age, and when Nin-Nin heard him pick his guitar, he broke into tears, stating it was Django born again.

Lagrène heralded a new generation of Gypsies playing *mare gilia*—"our music." Other child prodigies also appeared, including Matelot Ferret's two sons, Boulou and Elios. Under Matelot's tutelage, they were raised on a wide variety of musical influences and were never mere copycats of Django. Their music was some of the most daring and innovative to follow Django and the Ferrets' legacy. At the same time, Baro, Sarane, and Matelot's long-time accompanist, Francis-Alfred Moerman continued to release albums, each more beautiful than the last. On his collection, 1993 *Gitan & Tzigane magie de la guitare*, Moerman played John Lewis's homage, "Django," with a sensous grace that has never been equaled.

From Schnuckenack Reinhardt's ensemble came guitarist Häns'che Weiss, who in turn discovered prodigy violinist Titi Winterstein, who was a friend of guitarist Lulu Reinhardt. And Piotto Limburger was backed by Belgian Gypsy Fapy Lafertin, part of the Ferret clan on his mother's side. As well as playing in his group Waso with multi-instrumentalist *gadjo* Koen de Cauter, Fapy also played alongside his uncle, violinist, guitarist, and singer Eddie "Bamboula" Ferret.

Out of the Netherlands came prodigies Stochelo Rosenberg and Jimmy Rosenberg. From the Alsace were Mandino Reinhardt, Dorado Schmitt, and one of the brightest guitarists of his generation, Tchavolo Schmitt. In France, Christian Escoudé was playing modern jazz while Raphaël Fays was true to Django. Fays had learned from his father, Louis Fays, who had accompanied dance hall accordionists Verchuryen and Amiable, and also tutored Angelo Debarre. And beyond the star players were scores of others playing their guitars around the campfires.

In the 1990s, several bands began breaking away from the past to create novel takes on Django's music, sounds at once old and new. Patrick Saussois—long one of Jo Privat's accompanists—launched his Alma Sinti band with accordionist Jean-Claude Laudat while Patrick "Romane" Leguidcoq crafted novel modern compositions and arrangements based on Django's style. Dominique Cravic, together with the loose-knit ensemble Les Primitifs du Futur including musicians from Didier Roussin to cartoonist R. Crumb, celebrated the roots of musette and jazz. Thierry Robin's Gitans group created a fusion of North African, Spanish, and French Romany music strongly influenced by Matelot. And the pop group Paris Combo was infused with Django's chanson and jazz legacy, propelled by Gypsy guitarist Potzi.

At the dawn of the new millennium, two of Django's grandchildren—Babik's son David Reinhardt and Lousson's grandson Dallas Baumgartner—were beginning to perform. Today, in France, Germany, Belgium, and the Netherlands, Gypsies often teach their children Django's music note for note like a catechism, handing down *mare gilia* from generation to generation starting when children can first finger a guitar or violin. The music too had been christened with a name. Some called it Gypsy Jazz, but as the Gypsies who play it know, this was not a synthesis of two traditions—Gypsy music and jazz. Instead it was the legacy of one man who had become an emblem of a people.

FAR FROM THE RECORDING STUDIOS and the commercialism of the annual tributes in Samois-sur-Seine, New York, and elsewhere around the globe, Django's legacy best lives on in Parisian bars and bistros. Gypsy guitarists still perform in a variety of clubs for diners and jazz fans. From Russian cabarets and Saint-Germain-des-Prés jazz clubs, Pigalle nightclubs to the café Au Clarion des Chasseurs on Montmartre's place du Tertre, Django's jazz is still alive. Here, Maurice "Gros Chien" Ferret and Joseph "Babagne" Pouville performed for decades. Boulou and Elios Ferré, Moréno Winterstein, Angelo Debarre, and others also play regularly.

Yet times have changed. The music is no longer the toast of all Paris.

Untroubled by the times is a tiny bar lost amid the bustle of the Porte de Clignancourt flea market just around the corner from where Django's caravan burned during the night of October 26, 1928. La Chope des Puces is a nondescript hole in the wall on the old rue des Rosiers, lost amid antique-sellers' stalls and the bric-a-brac of the ages. Like much in the old thieves' market of Clignancourt, the bar has changed little over the decades. Within the wood-paneled walls and the tiled floor, generations of Gypsies have played their jazz, from Jacques "Montagne" Mala to Piton Reinhardt to Spatzo Adel to teenagers first flexing their fingers in public. In a corner of the bar on every weekend throughout the year, the father-and-son duo of Mondine and Ninine Garcia are La Chope des Puces's regulars. Their repertoire is eccentric—an ancient musette waltz leading into "Les feuilles mortes" played with stoptime chords echoing Miles Davis's "So What" followed with a melody by Django. While Mondine pounds out *la pompe* on a battered old Favino guitar, Ninine plays solo choruses on a gleaming new Epiphone archtop that came from a horse trade at a Pigalle music shop. The music is timeless, alive, inspiring the smattering of Gypsies and *gadjé* leaning on the bar with their coffees and beers to raise their glasses to the music.

Notes

1. Awakening, 1910–1922

1 Django was exceedingly proud: Django's later musical partner, Stéphane Grappelli, stated, "He really liked the name Django, said it sounded nice (he never liked me to call him Reinhardt, always Django)." "Stephane Grappelly Tells of Django's First Letter." Django's legal name was not "Jean-Baptiste" as often reported; his birth certificate, hospital records, and passport all list his name as "Jean."

1 Jean-Eugène Weiss: Django's father's correct name was revealed in family legal papers. Reinhardt family interview with Alain Antonietto; correspondence with author, 2002.

1 Flache ôs Coûrbôs: This is the Wallon spelling; in French it is "Flach aux Corbias." A derivative of the Latin "flaccus," "flache" is variously translated as "pond" or "depression," as in a valley. Pont-à-Celles Maire Christian Dupont correspondence with author, 2002.

2 caravan: In Django's time, the Romany term was *vurdon*. In modern days, the term is *verdine*. Caravans were also known in Gypsy slang as *vagi* and *vardò*. Doerr, *Où vas-tu manouche?* 10.

2 typical Romany caravan: Roger Spautz collected descriptions of the caravan in the 1920s in Liberchies; *Django Reinhardt*, 33–34. Just one photograph of Django's own, later caravan survives, taken in 1930–1934 by Émile Savitry. This portrait of a typical Gypsy *roulotte* comes from several sources: images by photographer Eugène Atget; Daettwyler's *Tsiganes*; and Bayol's *Rêves de roulottes*.

2 lived the family: Weiss's children—Spautz, *Django Reinhardt*, 34.

3 At 24: Négros' birthdate is uncertain: Some believed her born in 1886, other sources state 1884, thus making her about 26 at the time of Django's birth.

4 Django's sponsors and godparents: Adrien Borsin interview with Spautz, *Django Reinhardt*, 38.

4 an alias: Sara Reinhardt interview with Alain Antonietto; correspondence with author, 2003.

5 altered their own surnames: Moerman interview with author, Paris, 2001. For further descriptions of the hegira of Gypsy names, see Maximoff, *Dites-le avec des pleurs*, 28; and Yoors, *The Gypsies*, 51–52.

5 the alias Schmitt: Sara Reinhardt interview with Alain Antonietto; correspondence with author, 2003.

6 the hedgehog was feasted: Moerman interview with author, Paris, 2001. See also Poueyto, *Latcho rhaben*. The benefit of moonglow is described by Serge, *La grande histoire des bohémiens*, 94; and by Doerr, *Où vas-tu manouche?* 19–20. Hedgehog hunting and cuisine are described by Williams, *Nous, on n'en parle pas*, 37–44; and Yoors, *The Gypsies*, 15–16.

7 without a homeland: This summary comes from perhaps the sole histories of the Romanies written by a Romany, Ian Hancock's historical introduction to *The Roads of the Roma*, 9–20; and Hancock, *The Pariah Syndrome*, 55.

8 a dreaded bandit gang: Asséo, *Les Tsiganes*, 44–45; and de Foletier, *Les Tsiganes*, 210.

8 artillery shellcasings: shellcasing jewelry—Salgues, "La légende" (*Jazz Magazine*, No. 33), 20.

10 dilapidated state: Spautz, *Django Reinhardt*, 33–34.

11 "Down there": Serge (pen name of Maurice de Féaudierre), *La grande histoire des bohémiens*, 150.

12 scrap metal: Naguine Reinhardt interview with Delaunay, Delaunay Archives. Naguine said that Django and Nin-Nin "adored" to *faisait la ferraille*—literally, make metal—and even when they became musicians they remained nostalgic for their days dealing scrap. Traveling on tour in a first-class train coach, they once spotted a scrap heap out the window and began talking of the good old days. Nin-Nin would later return to dealing scrap after Django's death.

12 *père* Guillon: Salgues, "La légende" (*Jazz Magazine*, No. 33), 20; and Delaunay, *Django mon frère*, 34–35.

12 drawn to the cinema: Salgues, "La légende" (*Jazz Magazine*, No. 33), 21.

13 Sara sometimes accompanied: Sara Reinhardt interview with Alain Antonietto, "Valses pour Django" in Billard, *Django Reinhardt*, 20; and "L'histoire de Django."

14 Guiligou's tutelage: Reinhardt family interview with Alain Antonietto; correspondence with author, 2002.

14 Django played the melodies: Négros and Nin-Nin Reinhardt quoted in Salgues, "La légende" (*Jazz Magazine*, No. 33), 20–21.

14 "Once, when I returned": Négros Reinhardt quoted in Salgues, "La légende" (*Jazz Magazine*, No. 33), 21.

14 "Is that what prevents you": Salgues, "La légende" (*Jazz Magazine*, No. 33), 21.

14 Necklace of faux pearls: Salgues, "La légende" (*Jazz Magazine*, No. 33), 21.

14 by Lagardère's side: Delaunay, *Django Reinhardt souvenirs*, 26

15 Chez Clodoche: Naguine Reinhardt interview with Delaunay, Delaunay Archives; and Delaunay, *Django mon frère*, 37.

15 "Gusti" Malha: Bazin interview with Cravic, "Charley Bazin," 44; and René Mailhes interview with author, Paris, 2003.

15 Poulette Castro: Boulou and Elios Ferré interview with author, Paris, 2001; and Antonietto, "Django, la valse et le banjo . . ." in Billard, *Django Reinhardt*, 24–25.

2. *PANAM*, 1922–1928

17 Django's joy: Louis Vola stated, "One may easily imagine Django's overflowing joy. He had thus succeeded in reaching the world of the professional musician." Spautz, *Django Reinhardt*, 52.

18 Guérino bought: Naguine Reinhardt interview with Delaunay, Delaunay Archives.

20 and the night began: An account of an evening appeared in "Chez Bouscatel, un soir"; and Carco, *The Last Bohemia*, 170–71.

20 An accordionist: Noted in the newspaper *Le Courrier français*; quoted in Dubois, *La Bastoche*, 54.

20 The war was on: Quoted in "Le jargon du p'tit folkleux."

21 a pleased Bouscatel and relieved Péguri: Péguri and Mag, *Du bouge . . . au conservatoire*; quoted in "Le jargon du p'tit folkleux."

21 "people will still be dancing": Péguri and Mag, *Du bouge . . . au conservatoire*; quoted in Dubois, *La Bastoche*, 101–2.

22 his music sent women into ecstasy: Carco, *The Last Bohemia*, 172–73.

22 "a dance derived from the waltz: Péguri and Mag, *Du bouge . . . au conservatoire*, 115. Pierre Mac Orlan, the Montmartrois novelist and scholar of Parisian argot and folklore, stated in his *Images secrètes de Paris* that "the java was consecrated with its name by people calling for an encore. . . . It was an homage to a puerile argot."

23 "Here, dance is not an art": Carco, *Panam*, 48.

23 *valse manouche*: The common term *valse manouche* is a misnomer, as most of the early Gypsy banjo players in the *bals* were actually Gitans and not Manouche.

24 never-ending musical war: Malha later married Mattéo Garcia's daughter and became Garcia's son-in-law as well as musical successor. Malha's two sons, Djouan and Noye, also learned the guitar as children and followed their father into the dance halls.

24 "Reine de musette": This was not the only composition that Malha gave up or sold ownership to, although the authorship of many early musette songs is difficult to trace at best. The polka "Les triolets" was composed by Charles Péguri but later became Émile Vacher's signature song; Vacher's own version was likely arranged in concert with Malha. "La vraie valse musette" and "La Montmartroise" were both attributed to Vacher and Peyronnin but again were believed to have been composed or co-authored by Malha. And the dashing "Brise napolitaine" was a joint composition of Guérino and Malha, although it too was credited to Peyronnin. See also Alain Antonietto, liner notes to Baro Ferret, *Swing valses*; and Antonietto "Valses pour Django" in François Billard, *Django Reinhardt*, 21. In contrast to Mattéo Garcia's muted legacy, Malha got opportunities to record, both in bands and solo. Solo sessions by banjomen were rare, so the existence of these recordings were testaments to the quality of Malha's music. A session for the Javo-Disque label by "Les Frères Gusti banjoïstes" featured Malha on banjo-guitar and his brother Joseph Malha on banjo-luth performing "Souvenir de Montreuil" and "La vraie musette." Two records dating from the late 1920s or early 1930s and released on the Lutin label listed them as "Les Frères Gousti." Playing a banjo duet, Malha and his brother blazed through "Paris-Rome," "Ca c'est Paris," "La vraie valse musette," and "La Montmartroise."

24 "La valse des niglos": Sadly, there are no known recordings of Malha, or any other early musette band from the 1920s, playing "La valse des niglos."

25 back into the theme: Moerman interview with author, Paris, 2002.

26 *Panam*: The term *Panam* carried with it a nostalgia for good times and the good old days. *Panam* summoned forth an image of Paris in the period from 1900 to the 1930s, the world of the *bals musette*, and the romance of the accordion. The word *milieu* was first coined around this time to describe the world of the *bals*, the underworld of petty criminals, and *Panam*.

27 "The sounds": Brassaï, *Le Paris secret*, no folios.

28 "with a drawn knife": The bal argot was *avec couteux tirés*.

28 Frenchman Roger Chaput: Antonietto and Cravic, "Roger Chaput," 24–25.

28 "Django arrived": Chaput quoted in Gumplowicz, "Django Guitare," 90.

29 "Tête de mouton": Bazin interview with Cravic, "Charley Bazin," 44.

29 "I wonder if": Grappelli, "Django Reinhardt and the Bright Red Socks."

30 "Django made his debut": Gardoni quoted in Antonietto, "Django, la valse et le banjo . . ." in Billard, *Django Reinhardt*, 26.

30 "It must have been around 1925": Vaissade quoted in Delaunay, *Django mon frère*, 38.

31 "All of Django's family": Vaissade quoted in Delaunay, *Django mon frère*, 38.

31 "He struck his fingers to his nose": Vaissade quoted in Nevers, liner notes to *Intégrale Django Reinhardt 1*, no folios.

32 "It was several years": Vaissade quoted in Delaunay, *Django mon frère*, 38.

33 "Valse manouche": Sara Reinhardt interview with Alain Antonietto; correspondence with author, 2003. Django played the waltz at a deliberate tempo, likely slower than he played it in dance halls; this created later speculation that it may have been recorded to be transcribed for copyright, although no published version has been found.

34 Trio Ferret recordings: Baro Ferret likely learned these melodies at Mattéo Garcia and Gusti Malha's sides while accompanying them in the dance halls. Garcia's son bequeathed "Minch valse" to Baro for him to add to it; Baro likely crafted the C section but may have also revised other sections as well, so it's impossible today to know which aspects of the composition were Garcia's and which Baro's. The 1939 version of "Minch valse" was retitled in Le Trio Ferret's recording as "Ma Theo" in honor of Garcia.

34 "Montagne Sainte-Geneviève": Django never named his four waltzes. When Matelo Ferret recorded them in 1959, he visited Django's widow, Naguine, and asked her to christen them with names. "Choti" and "Gagoug" were named for Django's grandchildren, the children of his first son, Lousson. "Chez Jacquet: À la Petite Chaumière" was named for a *bal* where Django played near the Porte de Clignacourt whereas "Montagne Sainte-Geneviève" was for the *bal* in *la Mouffe* and in honor of Django's days with Guérino. Moerman interview with author, Paris, 2002.

34 "It hit me": Naguine Reinhardt quoted in Salgues, "La légende" (*Jazz Magazine*, No. 33), 23.

35 "They were from Hungary": Naguine Reinhardt interview with Delaunay, Delaunay Archives.

35 "He played": Naguine Reinhardt quoted in Salgues, "La légende" (*Jazz Magazine*, No. 33), 23.

35 Florine Mayer: Information on Florine Mayer and her family comes from Mayer-Renaud family interview with author, Paris, 2002. Florine was born April 26, 1910, in Paris, according to later Hôpital Lariboisière admittance records. Archives de l'Assistance Publique-Hôpitaux de Paris, numéro d'enregistrement 18762.

35 The Manouche had no marriage ceremony: Background on Manouche wedding practices comes from Patrick Williams, correspondence with author, 2002, as well as Williams, "Mariage Tsigane," 15.

36 "It is love": Négros Reinhardt quoted in Salgues, "La légende" (*Jazz Magazine*, No. 33), 20.

36 Porte de Clignancourt: Delaunay stated that they set up home outside the Porte de Choisy, but according to both Bella and Django's Hôpital Lariboisière records, they gave their address as 136 rue Jules Vallès in Saint-Ouen, just outside the Porte de Clignancourt in the flea market.

3. LA MUSIQUE DIABOLIQUE, 1926–1928

37 unlike anything Django had ever heard: There's question concerning the date when Django discovered jazz and Billy Arnold's band: Delaunay stated it was 1924; Chaput, who was there, claimed it was 1926. Chaput interview in Gumplowicz, "Django Guitare," 90–91. Delaunay, *Django Reinhardt*, 40–41.

37 a breadcrust to eat: Naguine Reinhardt interview with Delaunay, Delaunay Archives.

38 "Organize for me": Hayward quoted in Charters and Junstadt, *Jazz*, 65.

39 "Lieutenant Europe": Noble Sissle, *St. Louis Post-Dispatch*, June 10, 1918.

39 "A jazz musician": Coleman, *Trumpet Story*, 96.

39 "People wanted to forget": Arletty quoted in Behr, *The Good Frenchman*, 110.

42 "when the French would play": Vauchant interview in Goddard, *Jazz Away from Home*, 17.

42 "People understood": Wiener quoted in Goddard, *Jazz Away from Home*, 16.

42 "improvised" solos: Whiteman, *Jazz*, 73–74.

42 fierce superstitions: Bechet, *Treat It Gentle*, 95.

42 explore music with his hands: Delaunay, *Delaunay's dilemma*, 131.

43 Jack Hylton: There have long been doubts about the date of Jack Hylton's visit to La Java and Django's subsequent caravan fire. Delaunay stated Hylton came to La Java shortly before the fire, which he said occurred on November 2, 1928. But Hylton began a concert tour of Germany in Cologne on October 26 and during the week of November 2 was in the midst of a month-long engagement at Berlin's Scala-Theater, so it was doubtful he was in Paris during this period. The Hôpital Lariboisière's records state that Django was admitted on October 26, 1928, with burns from the fire; this date fits the known facts of Hylton's schedule as well, as Hylton was then in transit from England to Germany and could have ventured to Paris en route seeking Django. Archives de l'Assistance Publique-Hôpitaux de Paris, numéros d'enregistrement 18762 et 18763. Pete Faint correspondence with author, 2002; and Faint, internet biography of Hylton.

44 to sign contracts: Salgues, "La légende" (*Jazz Magazine*, No. 34), 30. This conversation was also remembered by Django in Corbier, "A Thonon-les-Bains."

44 chair open for Django: Salgues, "La légende" (*Jazz Magazine*, No. 34), 30–31.

4. WANDERINGS, 1928–1934

45 caravan fire: Hôpital Lariboisière records state Django and Bella were admitted on October 26, 1928, with burns from the fire. Delaunay stated the fire took place on November 2, likely based on someone's memory that the celluloid flowers were for All Soul's Day. Archives de l'Assistance Publique-Hôpitaux de Paris, numéros d'enregistrement 18762 et 18763. There are several differing descriptions of the caravan fire, the first from a magazine biography ("L'histoire de Django," *Sept jours*), that of Delaunay (*Django mon frère*, 40–41) and that of Salgues ("La légende," *Jazz Magazine*, No. 34, 31–32); this account is based on Salgues's.

46 patient number 18763: Django was logged into the Hôpital Lariboisière as "Jean Reinloardt," age 18. His profession was listed as *musicien* and he and Bella were denoted as unmarried, French law not recognizing Gypsy marriages.

47 The military had no use: Salgues, "La légende" (*Jazz Magazine*, No. 34), 33.

48 He pushed his two paralyzed fingers: Grappelli, "Stephane Grappelly Tells the Tale of Jazzdom's Magic Fingers."

48 a true miracle: Delaunay, *Django Reinhardt souvenirs*, 30.

48 nightmares of flames: Delaunay, *Django mon frère*, 41.
49 "bear cub": Salgues, "La légende" (*Jazz Magazine*, No. 35), 27.
49 Henri Baumgartner: Meyer-Renaud family interview with author, Paris, 2002.
49 "Here!": Naguine Reinhardt quoted in Salgues, "La légende" (*Jazz Magazine*, No. 34), 32.
49 "Oh, well": Django quoted in Delaunay, *Django Reinhardt*, 44.
50 Stéphane Mougin: Panassié, *Douze années*, 15.
50 "Django made up his mind": Naguine Reinhardt quoted in Delaunay, *Django mon frère*, 44.
50 nightclub Banco: There is discrepancy over where and when this stand with Eddie South took place. Delaunay stated (*Django Reinhardt souvenirs*, 31) that the Banco cabaret and the Carlton were in Monte Carlo while they were actually in Cannes. South's biographer Anthony Barnett states that the violinist was likely in Monte Carlo at the start of April 1931 and then in Cannes in August. Barnett correspondence with author, 2002; and Barnett, *Black Gypsy*, 93. See also South, "My Foreign Travels and Experiences."
51 violin play jazz: There were also other violinists playing jazz in Paris that Django may have heard, although there is no record of any encounter with them. Django could have heard Angelina Rivera, an African American female violinist who played with Josephine Baker and Spencer Williams in 1926. Louia Jones traveled to Paris in 1928 with Noble Sissle; he later became the first African American to play with the National Symphony Orchestra. Among other African American jazz violinists who also visited Paris in the 1920s at some point were Ralph "Shrimp" Jones, who had recorded in London with Louis Mitchell's Jazz Kings and directed the Plantation Orchestra; George Smith, who was originally with James Reese Europe and later with Sidney Bechet in Benny Peyton's band; Juice Wilson, who recorded with Sissle in London in 1929 and then moved on with him to Paris; and violinists Leon Abbey and William Rosemand, part of Sissle's orchestra in Paris. Anthony Barnett correspondence with author, 2002.
53 "It's not a billiards player": Savitry quoted in Delaunay, *Django Reinhardt souvenirs*, 32.
53 "Indian Cradle Song": Armstrong's recording was backed on OKeh 414123 by Jimmy McHugh and Dorothy Fields's "Exactly Like You." During the same session, Armstrong also cut versions of "Dinah" and "Tiger Rag"—songs that Django covered on his first recorded jazz sides and that remained in his repertoire for years to come.
54 "He was like a large animal": Savitry quoted in Salgues, "La légende" (*Jazz Magazine*, No. 35), 29.
54 "*Ach moune!*": Django quoted in Delaunay, *Django mon frère*, 45.
55 "Monsieur Bandit": Delaunay, *Django Reinhardt souvenirs*, 46.
55 "But why not?": Delaunay, *Django mon frère*, 47.
56 "Listen! If we play it right": Naguine Reinhardt interview with Delaunay, Delaunay Archives.
56 "I always had to go find him": Vola interview in Gaspard, "Un blues gitan," 23–24.
56 Naguine's uncle happened by: Naguine Reinhardt interview with Delaunay, Delaunay Archives.
57 "For us, houses are like prisons": Naguine Reinhardt interview with Delaunay, Delaunay Archives.
57 *moulôs*: Naguine Reinhardt interview with Delaunay, Delaunay Archives.
57 "He had fear": Mme. Ipsaïenne (daughter of Fernand Loisy) quoted in Spautz, *Django Reinhardt*, 133.

57 "He was always": Mme. Loisy quoted in Spautz, *Django Reinhardt*, 131.

57 Django's Romany cousins were suspicious: Delaunay, *Django mon frère*, 12.

57 "Some slept in the garden": Vola quoted in Delaunay, *Django mon frère*, 51.

58 "listening to Django's music": Savitry quoted in Delaunay, *Django mon frère*, 55.

59 "I need 5,000 francs": Django quoted in Salgues, "La légende" (*Jazz Magazine*, No. 36), 42.

60 "When I visited Django": Savitry quoted in Delaunay, *Django mon frère*, 51–52.

60 "This jalopy is worthless": Django quoted in Salgues, "La légende" (*Jazz Magazine*, No. 36), 42.

61 The Ferret brothers: Information in this section on the Ferret brothers is based on Moerman interview with author, Paris, 2001; Boulou and Elios Ferré interview with author, Paris, 2001, and correspondence; and Antonietto, "Matelo Ferret," 45–47.

62 The Ferrets were a clan: These names are spelled phonetically based on interviews with Elios Ferré with author, Paris, 2001. Also René Mailhes interview with author, Paris, 2003.

62 Matelo's name meant "sailor": Matelo was named Pierre at birth, but Baro was quick to use the privilege of the eldest Rom sibling: Deciding his own given name of Joseph was not strong enough, Baro appropriated his brother's name and became Pierre Joseph Ferret. Matelo then took the official name of Jean.

62 Since the revolution: Information comes from Boulou and Elios Ferré interview with author, Paris, 2001; and Kazansky, *Cabaret russe*.

63 Django and the Ferrets: Delaunay stated Django also played the Don Juan *cabaret russe* during this winter season, but the Don Juan did not open until 1937. Kazansky, *Cabaret russe*, 262.

64 Django's path had led him back: Django and Vola met film casting director Henri Diamant-Berger and became involved in the movie *Clair de Lune* shot in and around Cannes with stars Claude Dauphin and Blanche Montel. Django reportedly recorded a full soundtrack for the movie but the unfinished film never made it to screen and the soundtrack has not been found. Delaunay, *Delaunay's dilemma*, 215–16.

65 Yet by all accounts: Bazin interview with Cravic, "Charley Bazin," 44.

65 Baro's fretwork: Moerman interview with author, Charlotte, North Carolina, 2001.

66 "Jean Sablon had just bought": Ekyan quoted in Delaunay, *Django Reinhardt*, 60.

66 Django's newfound awareness: Dirats interview with author, 2002; and Schulz-Köhn, "Django—the lost years."

66 "I acted as a kind of nursemaid": Ekyan quoted in Delaunay, *Django Reinhardt*, 62–63.

67 "He was then truly a savage": Naguine Reinhardt interview with Delaunay, Delaunay Archives.

67 "Because there are spies": Django quoted in Delaunay, *Django mon frère*, 61.

68 Sablon awaited Django: Naguine Reinhardt interview with Delaunay, Delaunay Archives; and Delaunay, *Django mon frère*, 59–60.

5. LE HOT, 1934–1935

69 "One day": Grappelli quoted in Spautz, *Django Reinhardt*, 70–71. At other times over the years, Grappelli recounted the story slightly differently. The scene was always the same, yet sometimes he remembered breaking the string, other times

he and Django simply began to jam on the song "Dinah" as they were bored between sets. Sometimes it was Chaput instead of Nin-Nin who joined the duo.

71   "I look back": Grappelli, *Mon violon*, 15.

71   "This place": Grappelli quoted in Smith, *Stéphane Grappelli*, 15; and Grappelli, *Mon violon*, 18.

71   "My father saw a three-quarter violin": Anick, "Reminiscing," 10–12.

71   "Finally I was able to play": Grappelli, *Mon violon*, 22–23.

72   "I was spun upside-down": Grappelli, *Mon violon*, 46; and Smith, *Stéphane Grappelli*, 26.

72   "changed my destiny": Grappelli quoted in Smith, *Stéphane Grappelli*, 31.

72   "At the beginning when I started to play": Grappelli quoted in Smith, *Stéphane Grappelli*, 34.

72   "Grappelly" orthography: Stéphane changed his last name's orthography during this time. There are at least two versions of why he altered the spelling. Stéphane told it this way: His Italian family name was constantly mispronounced as "Grappell-eye," particularly by the British. English words such as Piccadilly, however, received the correct Italianate pronunciation, so he became "Grappelly." Others remember it differently: With Mussolini taking power in Italy and building his military might, Stéphane feared being drafted like his father had been. With the change in spelling, he sought to hide his identity from the Italian army (Lévêque interview with Fred Sharp, Paris, 1967). Either way, he reverted to the original "Grappelli" around 1969.

72   "He had a sense of spectacle": Grappelli, *Mon violon*, 58.

73   Stéphane again picked up his violin: Grappelli, *Mon violon*, 60.

73   "I started to play 'Dinah'": Grappelli quoted in Smith, *Stéphane Grappelli*, 39.

73   "It wasn't just all of Paris": Grappelli, *Mon violon*, 79.

74   But this one audience member: Django had crossed paths with Stéphane several times in the past. Stéphane remembered first spotting Django and Nin-Nin while they were busking in a Pigalle café. He also remembered seeing Django play his banjo at a *bal* on the avenue de Clichy and later, his guitar at La Boîte à Matelots in Paris with Vola. Grappelli, *Mon violon*, 80.

74   "This young man with the very hostile look": Grappelli quoted in Smith, *Stéphane Grappelli*, 43–44.

74   "We jammed all afternoon": Grappelli, *Mon violon*, 80.

74   "My life started when I met Django": Anick, "Reminiscing with Stéphane Grappelli," 10–12.

75   Panassié was the didactic leader: Information on Panassié comes from Bureau interview with author, Paris, 2002; Panassié, *Douze années*; and Patrice Panassié interview with Balmer, *Stéphane Grappelli*, 83.

75   *Jazz-Tango-Dancing*: The magazine's title inconsistently altered between *Jazz-Tango* and *Jazz-Tango-Dancing* over the years.

76   "I viewed jazz": Bureau interview with Legrand, "Jacques Bureau," 8.

77   he recommended the Hot Club: The original orthography was "Hot-Club" in *Jazz-Tango-Dancing* notices; soon, however, the hyphen was deleted. The club's first office was located at 5 rue de l'Isly, Dirats's father's hall. Information on the founding of the Hot Club comes from Bureau interview with author, Paris, 2001; and Dirats interview with author, 2002.

77   "First, organize the enthusiasts": *Jazz-Tango-Dancing*, November 1932.

77   nothing less than a crusade: If the Hot Club was akin to a church, it was also like a revolutionary political cell. While Bureau was an erstwhile Trotskyite and Panassié at Bourbonist, others who joined in the coming years had equally strong—and

disparate—political leanings. Nourry too was a royalist and Henri Bernard on the far political conservative right whereas the Alvarez brothers were communists and Gaston Brun a socialist. Bureau interview with author, Paris, 2001.

78 *Le jazz hot*: As an example of how how small the enthusiast market for jazz was in Paris at the time, *Le jazz hot* was published by Robert Corrêa's firm in Montparnasse only on the condition that Panassié guaranteed a certain number of subscriptions, which he expected to make through the Hot Club. Thus, this first book was essentially a vanity publication financed by Panassié. Panassié, *Douze années*, 121.

78 a small cadre of French jazz confreres: The Hot Club also aided the other jazz clubs forming in France: In May 1933, *Jazz-Tango-Dancing* noted there were Hot Clubs in Bordeaux, Cannes, Lille, Marseille, and Nancy; by 1947 when the movement reached its zenith, there were 71 Hot Clubs in cities across France. Tournès, *New Orleans sur Seine*, 473.

78 "I always regretted": Delaunay, "Delaunay's Delight," 2–3; and Delaunay, *Delaunay's dilemma*, 11, 17.

79 "To describe the impression": Delaunay, "Delaunay's Delight," 5.

79 "At the Claridge": Delaunay, *Delaunay's dilemma*, 101–2.

80 "One must say Django": Nin-Nin and Arthur Briggs were also supposed to perform with the band but were reported as ill that night. *Jazz-Tango-Dancing*, February 1934.

80 Bureau was particularly charmed: Bureau interview with author, Paris, 2001. The evenings spent at Le Boudon would be immortalized by Dicky Wells in his tune "Hangin' Around Boudon," recorded in 1937 with Django on guitar.

81 "He was a child": Grappelli interview with Sportis.

81 "I loved him": Crolla quoted in Tercinet, liner notes to Henri Crolla & Co., *Notre ami Django*.

81 "His lack of formal education": Rostaing interview with Goddard, *Jazz Away from Home*, 242.

81 "If anybody asked me": Panassié, "Red-Hot Strings."

81 "At that time, the guitar was only": Dirats interview with author, 2002.

82 "I was hesitant about Django's jazz": Bureau interview with author, Paris, 2001.

82 Hot Club officers: The elected officers of the Hot Club for 1933–1934 included its *comité* of Pannasié, Dirats, Auxenfans, Bureau, and Pierre Gazières with the assistance of Nourry and Léon Hoa. Membership by this time numbered just more than a hundred jazz fans. *Jazz-Tango-Dancing*, October 1933.

82 "Up until then": Dirats interview with author, Paris, 2002.

82 business: Delaunay, *Delaunay's dilemma*, 64.

82 "Panassié was never a good director": Bureau interview with author, Paris, 2001.

83 Revised Hot Club: Nourry's residence was at 126 boulevard Haussmann. Bureau interview with author, Paris, 2001; and Legrand, "Jacques Bureau," 11. Further details on the Hot Club here come from Panassié, *Douze années*, 95–97; Conte, "Les mystères d'une naissance"; and Tournès, *New Orleans sur Seine*, 40–41.

83 "Despite this setback": Nourry quoted in Delaunay, *Django Reinhardt*, 65.

84 "It was an utterly dejected": Delaunay, *Django mon frère*, 77; and Delaunay, *Delaunay's dilemma*, 84.

85 "It was a revelation": Grappelli quoted in Delaunay, *Django Reinhardt*, 73.

85 "Having Django accompany me": Grappelli quoted by Soudieux, interview with author, Paris, 2002.

86 "Nobody was quite sure": Delaunay, *Django mon frère*, 67. In later years, the band on these test sides become erroneously known as "Delaunay's Jazz." This

band name was a misnomer. On a surviving copy of the records, an unknown hand had scrawled the name and style of music as "Delaunay (jazz)" purely for identification on the label. These test takes survived thanks to Delaunay, who found them just before they were cast out in the 1930s, when they had been forgotten; he played them on his jazz radio broadcasts and later released them commercially. Delaunay, *Delaunay's dilemma*, figure 33 (no folios).

86 "Very limited": Henshaw, *Swing Guitars* column, May 1948.

86 "there was nothing to be learned": Grappelli interview with Sportis.

86 "No recording label wanted us": Grappelli, *Mon violon*, 81.

87 "We did not yet know": Delaunay, *Delaunay's dilemma*, 103.

87 "The first concert by the Quintette": Panassié, *Douze années*, 141.

87 "Our idea is to form": Fiot, "En faveur du 'jazz hot.'" Delaunay too noted this: "In 1934 the Hot Club of France, whose actions were beginning to make themselves felt, was seeking to form a French orchestra which could adequately symbolise the jazz of France and serve to represent that organization." Delaunay, "French Jazz."

87 "I was a little dubious": Nourry quoted in Delaunay, *Django Reinhardt*, 68–69.

87 jazz played on brass: Grappelli interview with Balmer, *Stéphane Grappelli*, 87.

87 Caldairou may have first heard: Abrams, *The Book of Django*, 21.

89 gasoline for the journey: Delaunay, *Delaunay's dilemma*, 102–3; and Delaunay, *Django Reinhardt*, 69.

89 "For Django it was always": Grappelli quoted in Spautz, *Django Reinhardt*, 80

89 "The recording sessions": Grappelli, *Mon violon*, 81.

90 "After several wax tests": Panassié, *Douze années*, 142–43.

91 *la pompe*: This description of *la pompe* as *leger et sec* comes from Gitan Paul "Tchan Tchou" Vidal via Alain Cola; correspondence with author, 2001. Tchan Tchou admonished Cola and his other rhythm players to keep their playing always "light and dry."

92 After the Ultraphone recording session: Chaput interview with Cravic, 1995.

6. DJANGOLOGY, 1935–1936

93 "As white as snow": Delaunay, *Django mon frère*, 68.

93 "He became aware of his importance": Delaunay, *Django mon frère*, 75–76.

94 "When Django started to have": Bureau interview with author, Paris, 2001.

94 "The strange new life Django led": Delaunay, *Django mon frère*, 76.

94 "Do you want to know": Unsigned review, *Jazz-Tango-Dancing*, February 1935.

95 "When the first four sides": Hammond, "Venuti's Rival."

95 "They are not only sensationally surprising": Hibbs, "Sensation on Strings."

95 "Here we have": Edgar Jackson, untitled review (*The Gramophone*, June 1935).

96 Cabaret de l'Enfer: Program, 1910s, author's collection; and Morrow and Cucuel, *Bohemian Paris*, 276–85.

97 "Hers is, without question, the world's most famous": Georges Sim (nom de plume of Georges Simenon), article in *Le Merle rose*, 1928; reprinted in Assouline, *Simenon*, 74–75.

98 "There was a lot of pro-black prejudice": Marshall quoted in Goddard, *Jazz Away from Home*, 26.

98 wore blackface: Delaunay, *Delaunay's dilemma*, 142.

98 As early as 1922: Tournès, *New Orleans sur Seine*, 230–31; and Shack, *Harlem in Montmartre*, 77–83.

99 "When I was asked to form a band": Briggs quoted in Delaunay, *Django mon frère*, 78.

100 Even though he could not read music: Coleman, *Trumpet Story*, 100.

100 Alemán likely first met Django: *Jazz-Tango-Dancing*, April 1935.

101 "I remember Alemán": Delaunay, "Un guitariste meconnu." Delaunay was not alone in describing Alemán as *un singe*—a monkey. Bill Coleman remembered that ex-heavyweight boxing champion Georges Carpentier used to dance at the Villa d'Este and always greeted the band members in English, calling Alemán fondly a "little monkey." Not understanding English, Alemán simply nodded politely—until one day he asked someone what the words meant. The next time Carpentier came dancing, Alemán yelled out a greeting across the dance floor in hastily learned English, "Hello Georges Carpentier, you big white monkey!" As Colemen wrote, "George laughed about it, but he never referred to Oscar as a monkey again." Coleman, *Trumpet Story*, 99.

102 This shared admiration: Boulanger and Roussin, liner notes to *Oscar Alemán*.

102 four more sides cut in Paris: Ruppli, *Discographie Swing*, 13. There is discrepancy as to when this session took place: Others list it on April 5, 1939, but Ruppli and Delaunay state that it was on May 12.

103 "For a long time": Delaunay, *Django Reinhardt*, 81.

103 "The Quintette's was an ephemeral existence": Panassié, *Douze années*, 143.

103 Yet only 20 diehard: Chaput, "Le quintet ses débuts," 14–15.

104 "One evening, Hawkins came": Grappelli quoted in Balmer, *Stéphane Grappelli*, 97.

105 "Coleman Hawkins was similar in build": Delaunay, *Delaunay's dilemma*, 91.

105 "The three pieces": N. J. Canetti, untitled review (*Melody Maker*, March 2, 1935).

106 Yet all was not well backstage: Delaunay, *Delaunay's dilemma*, 92–93.

106 Although Panassié: Panassié, *Douze années*, 197.

108 "The greater part of the record": Edgar Jackson, untitled review (*The Gramophone*, March 1936).

108 "Lack of space makes it impossible": Unsigned and untitled review (*Swing*, March 1936).

109 Italian luthier: Maccaferri worked in Paris in 1927 for his uncle Fernando Atti, who arrived in Paris in 1912 to start an accordion shop. His atelier was bought by brothers Mario and Ettore Crosio and became the foundation of the Fratelli Crosio accordion firm, beloved of musette accordionists.

110 Busato: Busato's first lutherie was located at 40 rue d'Orgemont in the Twentieth Arrondissement. Some historians believe Busato predated Selmer's use of the small oval soundhole and longer neck. Busato continued crafting guitars as well as selling proprietary accordions and other orchestral instruments until his death in 1952.

110 Di Mauro: Di Mauro immigrated to Paris in 1932 and opened his atelier in the impasse Rançon before moving to the rue de la Réunion, both in the Twentieth Arrondissement. There were in fact two Di Mauro lutheries: Antoine's brother Joseph also established his own atelier; Baro Ferret played a guitar built by Joseph, which he's shown with in a photo alongside Jo Privat from the 1950s. Antoine's son, also named Joseph, kept Antoine's workshop operating until 1993. François Charle correspondence with author; and Charle, *The Story of Selmer Maccaferri Guitars*, 230–33.

111 "Nobody had confidence": Vola interview with Fred Sharp, Paris, 1967.

111 Django's sense of humor: Chaput, "Le quintet ses débuts," 14–15.

111 "Tranchant asked for the lights": Vola quoted in Delaunay, *Django mon frère*, 81.

112 "We had a magnificent reception": Grappelli quoted in Delaunay, *Django mon frère*, 83.

112 "Django left his guitar": Savitry quoted in Delaunay, *Django mon frère*, 83–84.

113 "He left just as he arrived": Delaunay, *Django mon frère*, 84.

113 "Whenever Django had money": Soudieux interview with author, Paris, 2003.

113 "In a showroom window": Geldray interview with Ken Couper, reprinted in Cherrett, *The Genius That Was Django*, 91.

113 "After seeing a George Raft": Grappelli, "Django Reinhardt and the Bright Red Socks."

114 When his pockets turned up nothing: Lieber, "Gypsy Genuis," 9.

114 "We had no work": Grappelli quoted in Balmer, *Stéphane Grappelli*, 106.

114 "This is not to say": Lieber, "Gypsy Genuis," 8.

114 "What fortunes he threw away": Delaunay, *Django mon frère*, 15.

115 Django needed the freedom of the road: Boulanger and Roussin, liner notes to *Oscar Alemán*.

115 "He could never stand town life": Grappelli, "Stephane Grappelly Tells the Tale of Jazzdom's Magic Fingers."

116 After the last train arrived: Delaunay, *Delaunay's dilemma*, 140–41. Delaunay states this concert took place in "winter 1937," but was most likely referring to this November 28, 1936, Zürich show as it was the sole known concert the Quintette played in Switzerland in 1936–1937.

116 "Django Reinhardt was seen": *Jazz Hot*, January 1937.

7. SWING, 1937

117 Django was romance incarnate: Roger Paraboschi interview with Anne Legrand, Paris, 1999.

118 He ate his salad with his fingers: Lévêque quoted in Cruickshank, *Django's Gypsies*, 3.

118 Django adored his brother: Boyer-Davis quoted in Cruickshank, *Django's Gypsies*, 32.

118 Django began to look down on Nin-Nin: Delaunay, *Django mon frère*, 84.

119 Django couldn't be bothered to wear a watch: Beryl Davis interview with author, 2004.

119 Nin-Nin was dependable: Léo Slabiak correspondence with author, 2002.

119 in the local police station: Delaunay, *Django mon frère*, 84.

119 "If it had not been for me": Grappelli, "Django Reinhardt and the Bright Red Socks."

120 Marcel Bianchi: Charle, "Marcel Bianchi," 32–35.

120 "For a long time": Delaunay interview with Fred Sharp, Paris, 1967.

121 The motley parade of bassists: Grappelli interview with Balmer and Caine, *Stéphane Grappelli*; Balmer, *Stéphane Grappelli*, 107; and Grappelli interview with Sportis.

121 Soudieux fended off: Soudieux interview with author, Paris, 2003; and Battestini, "Emmanuel Soudieux: Django, Stéphane . . ."

121 the rivalry between the Quintette's lead duo: Soudieux interview with author, Paris, 2003.

122 "Django adored Grappelli": Naguine Reinhardt interview with Delaunay, Delaunay Archives.

122 "There was much jealousy": Vola quoted in Balmer, *Stéphane Grappelli*, 107.

122 At long last: Delaunay stated that Murrow introduced the band as "Stéphane Grappelli and His Hot Four," sparking Django's outrage. Yet on the surviving

recording of the broadcast made by a fan in England, the band is introduced by both Douglas and Murrow as the "Hot Club of France Quintet" mentioning first Stéphane and secondarily, Django—which was likely enough of a slight in itself to anger Django.

123 "Following this incident": Delaunay, *Django mon frère*, 87–88.

123 "Django was never concerned with melody": Delaunay, *Django mon frère*, 22.

123 "Often it was just the two of us": Grappelli interview with Sportis.

123 jazz record label, baptized Swing: Ruppli, *Discographie Swing*.

123 "Such an organization": The group was also known as the Fédération Internationale de Jazz. Delaunay, "As I See It"; Delaunay, *Delaunay's dilemma*, 265–67; and Stearns, "Fondation."

124 first record label in the world loyal soley to jazz: The American Commodore label is often cited as the first jazz label, but Milt Gabler did not get his label started until roughly a year after Swing. Information on Swing's founding comes from Delaunay's manuscript, "Le creation de la Marque Swing," Delaunay Archives; and Delaunay, *Delaunay's dilemma*, 230—35.

124 Delaunay and Panassié were hoping for more: Panassié, *Douze années*, 197.

125 Benny Carter: It's often stated that this session was a triumph of Carter's arranging skills yet Panassié claims Carter had failed to write the planned arrangements and everything was done impromptu in the studio by the band. Panassié, *Douze années*, 197–203.

125 "The records are really just 'jam sessions'": Hawkins quoted in Chilton, *The Song of the Hawk*, 132.

125 best-selling record ever issue: Panassié, "How We Recorded."

126 "It was an annoying habit": Panassié, *Douze années*, 189–96.

126 The label curtailed this: It was only after the session that Delaunay wrote Gramophone UK on May 28 explaining how they deviated from the list and added several other tunes in what he said "are on the whole better than any of the Quintette's previous records, for their personality as well as for the inspiration." Delaunay letters, Delaunay Archives.

127 "Django did not want to fulfill": Panassié, *Douze années*, 189–96.

127 entitled, justifiably, 'Improvisation'": This was later known as "Improvisation No. 1" to distinguish it from "Improvisation No. 2," recorded for Decca in London on September 1, 1938.

128 "It was never": Panassié, *Douze années*, 262–63.

128 Once in the studio: Adams, "I Meet Reinhardt."

129 "It was very difficult—almost impossible": Goode interview with author, London, 2003.

129 "The engineers": Panassié described this session in *Douze années*, 262–63.

129 "When he set down": Michelot quoted in Sportis, "La Galaxie Django Reinhardt," 10.

130 "With my guitar": Soudieux interview with author, Paris, 2003.

130 "Django never spoke": Soudieux interview with Anne Legrand, Paris, 1999.

130 Harpo Marx: Beryl Davis interview with author, 2004.

130 Django's lack of education: "L'histoire de Django"; and Lévêque quoted in Goddard, *Jazz Away from Home*, 241.

131 such as Soudieux to do it for him: Soudieux interview with author, Paris, 2003.

131 Describing Django's first spelling lessons: Grappelli, "Stephane Grappelly Tells of Django's First Letter."

132 African American singer Florence Embry Jones: Hughes, *The Big Sea*, 172 and 181.

133 "He was already famous": Bricktop, *Bricktop*, 199.

133 "When the last customers left": Combelle quoted in Delaunay, *Django mon frère*, 86–87.
134 "While playing, Django": MacDougald, "Is This The Best Small Swing Group?"
134 "The finest jazz concert": *Jazz Hot*, November–December 1937.
134 "Our prodigals": Delaunay, *Django mon frère*, 89.
135 drugs in general were taboos for the Manouche: Soudieux interview with author, Paris, 2003.
135 "Music was enough for us": Grappelli interview with Sportis.
136 "South had an admiration": Panassié, *Douze années*, 233–43; and Panassié, "Eddie South au Club aux Oiseaux," 10.
136 "In the presence of Django": Delaunay, *Delaunay's dilemma*, 232.
136 "He could play a fast tune": Vauchant quoted in Goddard, *Jazz Away from Home*, 274.
137 "The harmonies, that's what I love best": Django quoted in Delaunay, *Django mon frère*, 22.
137 "The violinists were very reserved": Delaunay, *Delaunay's dilemma*, 232–33.
139 "He liked great things": Grappelli, "Stephane Grappelly Continues the Story of Django: The Early Days of the Quintet."
139 "How am I to express": Panassié, untitled review (*Jazz Hot*, November–December 1937).

8. RULING BRITANNIA, 1938–1939

141 "A great roar of applause surges": Scott, "Did You See Django?"
141 Morris Levy: Unsigned and untitled review (*Melody Maker*, July 13, 1935).
141 "Rare are the records of French jazz": J. Emi, untitled review (*Jazz-Tango-Dancing*, May 1935).
142 "The Quintet is curiously static": "The French Quintet Staggers."
142 Getting into elevators: Beryl Davis interview with author, 2004.
143 "Completely out of his element": Delaunay, *Django mon frère*, 90.
143 Despite the good music and good times: Chaput interview with Dominique Cravic, 1995.
143 a towering figure: Others remember the meeting between Grade and the Quintette taking place in 1937, but Beryl Davis was certain that it was in 1936. Beryl Davis interview with author, 2004.
144 The man with the cigar: Balmer, *Stéphane Grappelli*, 110–11.
144 Beryl Davis: Davis interview with author, 2004.
145 The tour spanned almost four months: The tour included the following stands: London's Empire Theatre at Wood Green starting July 11; London's Trocadero near Elephant & Castle starting July 18; London's Empire Theatre at Shepherd's Bush starting July 25; London's Empire Theatre at Hackney starting August 1; London's Metropolitan Theatre starting August 8; north to Scotland and Glasgow's Empire Theatre starting August 15; back to London's New Empress Theatre at Brixton starting August 22; London's Palladium Theatre on Argyle Street starting September 5; London's Chiswick Empire Theatre starting September 12; and on to Manchester's Hippodrome Theatre at the start of October.
145 "playing" his penis: Balmer, *Stéphane Grappelli*, 50 and 118.
145 "If all London": Grappelli quoted in Delaunay, *Django mon frère*, 91–92.
145 Then he bought another automobile: Naguine Reinhardt interview with Delaunay, Delaunay Archives; and Grade interview with Balmer, *Stéphane Grappelli*.

146 "My dear Naguine, you must come back": Grappelli quoted in Delaunay, *Django mon frère*, 92–93.

146 As pleased as he was by the applause: Scott, "Did You See Django?"

146 "Look, they have a moon": Django quoted in Smith, *Stéphane Grappelli*, 90. Smith does not give a date for this anecdote, simply noting it took place during one of Django and Grappelli's English tours.

148 "It was all in the best traditions": Grappelli quoted in Delaunay, *Django Reinhardt*, 96.

149 The Hot Club's quarters: Delaunay, *Delaunay's dilemma*, 133–34.

150 "Every great coloured musician": Panassié's account throughout this section comes from his reminiscence "How We Recorded." It wasn't just Django who drew the American jazzmen to record for Swing. As Dicky Wells remembered, "We had champagne, wine, whiskey, and food in the studio. It was a ball." Wells, *The Night People*, 104.

150 "The air was electric": Stewart, *Boy Meets Horn*, 185.

151 "One of the most intriguing": Stewart, *Jazz Masters*, 34–35.

151 "All of the streetlamps were out": Grappelli quoted in Delaunay, *Django mon frère*, 97.

151 As with their mid-1938 English tour: The schedule included the following stands: the Empire Theatre in Hackney, London E8 starting August 1; the Metropolitan Theatre in London starting August 8; the Kilburn State Cinema in London NW6 starting August 14; Glasgow's Empire Theatre starting August 15; back to the Kilburn State Cinema starting August 22.

151 "palm-pelting": "Reinhardt, Grappelly and Co. Here Again."

152 Then, while the Quintette was playing: quoted in Delaunay, *Django mon frère*, 97–98; Grappelli, "Stephane Grappelly Tells of Django's First Letter"; and Beryl Davis interview with author, 2004.

153 Grade was forced to cancel: Further week-long shows were set for the Shakespeare Theatre in Liverpool, London's Palladium and Chiswick Empire Theatres, and the Tivoli Theatre in Aberdeen.

153 fearful of being called up: Lévêque interview with Fred Sharp, Paris, 1967.

153 "What troubles he gave me": Grappelli interview with Goddard, *Jazz Away from Home*, 245.

9. *NUAGES* 1939–1944

155 "Of course we understood": Chevalier, *The Man in the Straw Hat*, 75.

156 Bricktop had locked up her cabaret: "Cabaret Queen, Bricktop is Dead."

156 The Nazi zeal against jazz: This artwork by Ludwig Tersch was a caricature of posters for Ernst Krenek's 1925 opera *Jonny spielt auf* (*Johnny Strikes Up the Band*), a modernistic jazz fairy tale that was a hit in the Weimar Republic but despised by the Nazis for its "degenerate" vision of the future residing in America.

157 issuing lists of "unwanted" music: Four *Reichsmusikprüfstelle* lists were eventually issued, on September 1, 1938; April 15, 1940; May 15, 1941; and July 15, 1942.

157 "A nation of Germany's high cultural level": Hadamovsky quoted in Levi, *Music in the Third Reich*, 120.

158 "Never be boring": Goebbels quoted in Levi, *Music in the Third Reich*, 127.

158 "Jazz—until then the province": Delaunay, *Django mon frère*, 100.

159 Propagandastaffel had three goals: Heller, *Un allemand a Paris*, 27–28. Heller was a *sondführer* for the Propagandastaffel's literary and publishing arm.

159 "Come, my brother": Rostaing quoted in Delaunay, *Django mon frère*, 99.

160 *surprise-partie*: see descriptions in Vian, *Vercoquin et le plancton*.

161 "After the German patrol": Fouad quoted in Delaunay, *Django mon frère*, 105.

161 "None of the musicians had a pass": Boyer-Davis quoted in Delaunay, *Django mon frère*, 104–5.

161 "While one of us listened closely": Fouad quoted in Delaunay, *Django mon frère*, 103–4.

162 "I was witnessing": Delaunay, *Delaunay's dilemma*, 150.

163 *les zazous*: Panassié, *Monsieur jazz*, 185; and Loiseau, *Les Zazous*, 48.

163 Yet *les zazous* were more than just jazz fans: Loiseau, *Les Zazous*, 49.

163 At concerts, *les zazous* did not sit: Loiseau, *Les Zazous*, 35.

164 "Anything that starts with Ellington": Gestapo SS-Sturmbannführer Hans "The Fox" Reinhardt, quoted in Kater, *Different Drummers*, 194.

164 Delaunay simply translated the titles: Delaunay was not the sole one to use this subterfuge. This same "cheating" was used in Belgium and the Netherlands— and even by some bands in Germany. In 1937, the Paul Krender Orchestra recorded its version of Duke Ellington's "Karawane," released on that bastion of German music, Deutsche Grammophon. "St. Louis Blues" was retitled by Austrian jazzmen "Sauerkraut" to camouflage their favorite tune during the war.

165 Folies Belleville: Delaunay, *Django mon frère*, 105–6.

165 Clown guitar: Soudieux interview with author, Paris, 2003.

165 Invited to a soirée: Grappelli interview with Clinton, "Stephane Grappelli," 16.

166 "Django was music made man": Soudieux interview with author, Paris, 2003.

166 It was another song: Soudieux interview with author, Paris, 2003.

166 Wartime shortages of materials: Nevers, *Intégrale Django Reinhardt 10* liner notes, no folios.

167 "With a single clarinet": Combelle quoted in Delaunay, *Django Reinhardt*, 103.

168 Hitler bore a deep hatred for Gypsies: Kenrick and Puxon, *The Destiny of Europe's Gypsies*, 81.

168 "They are criminal and asocial": Behrendt quoted in Kenrick and Puxon, *The Destiny of Europe's Gypsies*, 65. The italics are Behrendt's.

168 From 1933, German Gypsies were doomed: Hancock, *The Pariah Syndrome*, 64.

169 "The officers of the Club liked": Schulz-Köhn, "Django—the lost years."

169 A longtime jazz fan: Zwerin, *La Tristesse*, 34–35.

169 "so-called Django Reinhardt": Delaunay, *Django mon frère*, 106; and Rostaing quoted in Goddard, *Jazz Away from Home*, 260.

170 "Django had a heart of gold": Paraboschi correspondence with author, 2003; and Bedin, "Django à Rome."

171 "Mélodie au crépuscule": The song has long been attributed to Django, but several of his sidemen and followers—including Matelo Ferret—were certain it was authored by Nin-Nin. Moerman interview with author, Paris, 2001.

171 Other Gypsies refrained from taking a solo: Moerman interview with author, Paris, 2001.

171 he believed himself Django's equal: Soudieux interview with author, Paris, 2003.

172 Matelo's sixtette boasted: Frenchman René Duchossoir played rhythm guitar behind Matelo. He was known as "Goudasse"—Old Shoe—a moniker bestowed on him by Matelo as Duchossoir also worked for the postal service where he had a fine pair of shoes he kept polished to a brilliant sheen. Moerman interview with author, Paris, 2001.

172 Gusti Malha: The clan included families with names translated into Spanish as Malha, Portuguese as Mala, and French as Mailhes or Maille.

173 "savage animal": Slabiak correspondence with author, 2002.

173 "There was nothing more execrable": Delaunay, *Delaunay's dilemma*, 136–37.

173 "I have no hesitation in saying": Delaunay, untitled review (*Jazz Hot*, February–March 1939).

174 Baro's earliest *valses bebop*: Published sheet music for two further *valses bebop* by Baro Ferret—"Le départ du Zorro" and "Survol de nuit"—exist in several forms (one copywritten by Éditions Léon Agel from 1951). A recording of "Le départ du Zorro" from this era has not surfaced, if indeed it was ever made. Baro may never have recorded "Survol de nuit." It's also likely that at this same time, Baro composed his other *valses bebop*—"Baro bar," "Ma zaza," "Reglement de compte," "L'inattendue," and "La jungle"—that make up his 1966 Vogue recording *Swing valses d'hier et d'aujourd'hui* for Delaunay.

174 René Mailhes: Mailhes's mother was Marie Ferret, sister of Challain Ferret. Challain's other brother, Ange, was not a guitarist but a famed horse trader. Mailhes interview with author, Paris, 2003.

175 "He would call the musicians together": Delaunay interview with Bramsen, *Django*.

175 "Every night we used to go off to the cinema": Lévêque quoted in Delaunay, *Django Reinhardt*, 113.

176 "In 'Oiseaux des îles'": Combelle quoted in Delaunay, *Django Reinhardt*, 103.

176 "I believe that he heard more music": Grappelli interview with Sportis.

176 "For the first time, Django was to conduct": Delaunay, *Django Reinhardt*, 104.

177 "Used as he was to playing": Lévêque quoted in Delaunay, *Django Reinhardt*, 114.

177 his main interest now in 1942–1943: Adams, "I Meet Reinhardt."

177 *Manoir de mes rêves*: Soudieux interview with author, Paris, 2003.

177 score was misplaced: Although Delaunay reported the full *Manoir de mes rêves* orchestral score lost, it has since been found and is in a private collection in Paris.

178 "Like Ravel or Berlioz": Grappelli interview with Sportis.

178 Mass visions: Django quoted in Corbier, "A Thonon-les-Bains."

178 "My people are savagely independent": Django quoted in Corbier, "A Thonon-les-Bains."

178 "It's true that I cannot distinguish": Django quoted in Corbier, "A Thonon-les-Bains."

178 "I don't give a damn": Delaunay, *Django mon frère*, 124–25.

179 A second recording session: Delaunay, *Django Reinhardt*, 125–26. Even though Django did not finish the Mass at this time, he remained committed to it. While traveling to Rome in 1950, he shared a train cabin with a curate who was knowledgeable about masses and Django queried him extensively on their structure. Evidently, he still wished to complete his work even then, years later. Paraboschi interview in Bedin, "Django à Rome."

179 that Django was dead: "Django Reinhardt Dead"; and "Reinhardt Death Mystery."

179 "He had no desire to work": Rostaing quoted in Delaunay, *Django Reinhardt*, 112.

180 Find guitar strings: Adams, "I Meet Reinhardt."

180 brought him hedgehog: Soudieux interview with author, Paris, 2003; and Delaunay, *Django mon frère*, 109.

180 Arthur Briggs and Charlie Lewis: Dunbar, "Trumpet Player Briggs Freed."

181 Delaunay also hid behind a code name: Loiseau, *Les Zazous*, 41.

181 hauled Delaunay: Gottlieb, "Delaunay Escapades with Gestapo," 13.

181 was tracked down by the Germans: Bureau interview with author, Paris, 2001; Bureau, "Champagne!"; and Bureau, *Un soldat menteur*.

182 some among the Romany also fought back: Kenrick and Puxon, *The Destiny of Europe's Gypsies*, 107.

182 to perform in Berlin: There were rumors Django performed in Berlin in 1942 or 1943. Several Italian jazz musicians stated they saw him play at the Femina Bar on Hohenstaufenstrasse; see Mazzoletti, *Il Jazz in Italia*. But like the other "Django" in the prison camp, this could have been one of Django's cousins. Either way, none of his French musical coterie remembered him playing in Germany during the war nor are there German accounts of him in Berlin.

182 it was compulsory to comply: Adams, "I Meet Reinhardt."

182 to marry Naguine: Delaunay stated the marriage took place on July 22, but the wedding certificate states June 21. Balen, *Django Reinhardt*, 157.

182 Thonon-les-Bains: Information on Django's time in Thonon-les-Bains and his escape attempts come from Rey correspondence with author, 2003; and Rey, "Folie à Amphion."

184 "My good Reinhardt": Quoted in Delaunay, *Django mon frère*, 114–15.

185 "So, what do you think": Delaunay, *Django mon frère*, 119–20.

185 a boy appeared as if from nowhere: Delaunay, *Django mon frère*, 119–20.

186 "Naguine had not the slightest idea": Davis-Boyer quoted in Delaunay, *Django mon frère*, 120; and Davis-Boyer quoted in Cruickshank, *Django's Gypsies*, 9.

186 "Aware of his new duties": Delaunay, *Django Reinhardt*, 119–20.

186 La Roulotte: Delaunay, *Django mon frère*, 119; and Osmont, "Autour de Django," 7.

10. *ÉCHOS DE FRANCE*, 1944–1946

188 "*C'est la guerre*": Perhaps searching for *the* secret behind Django's playing, his guitar was described in detail in three magazine articles of the time: Adams, "I Meet Reinhardt"; Henshaw, "Swing Guitars" column; and Hodgkiss, "Django's Guitar."

189 "When the Americans arrived": Naguine Reinhardt interview with Delaunay, Delaunay Archives.

189 Staff Sergeant Charlie Byrd: Byrd interview with author, 1999.

190 "On the tiny bandstand": Caen, "An Evening in Paris."

191 "We got by all right": Lévêque quoted in Delaunay, *Django Reinhardt*, 124–25.

191 Django forgot his guitar: Delaunay, *Django mon frère*, 123–24.

191 "It is clear that the majority": Galtier-Boissière, *Mon journal*, 146.

193 Army towtruck came to their rescue: Delaunay, *Django mon frère*, 126.

194 Jazz Club Mystery Hot Band: There were persistent rumors that Django recorded with Glenn Miller sometime in 1944–1945, but no recordings have been found. Delaunay, *Django mon frère*, 124.

194 musicians cryptically named: While the actual record labels show list the saxo clarinette player as "O," this was likely a misprint as the rest of the bandmembers' "names" followed alphabetical progression.

195 the Air Transport Command Band: Information on the ATC band comes from Ferreri, "Django et l'A.T.C. Band à la radio," 2; ATC tenor saxaphonist Bill Zickafoose interview with Craig L. Zavetz, www.bigbandsandbignames.com; and Platt and Wilfong interviews with Bogart, liner notes to *Django! And His American Swing Big Band*.

196 "Hello Paris": Delaunay, "Stéphane Grappelly et Django Reinhardt bavardent," 3; and Delaunay, *Django mon frère*, 127–28.

196 little news of Stéphane beyond a letter: *Jazz Hot*, No. 1, October 1945.

196 a resurrection of the Quintette: "Django Reinhardt Is Here."

196 first sounds of Django's guitar to British listeners: "Reinhardt on the Air."

197 "I opened my door": Grappelli, *Mon violon*, 126.

197 "Without premeditation": Delaunay, *Django mon frère*, 129; and Delaunay, *Delaunay's dilemma*, 234–35.

198 "From the very first note": Delaunay, *Django Reinhardt*, 132.

198 The British music press was abuzz: Naguine Reinhardt interview with Delaunay, Delaunay Archives.

198 Django was struck: "Django Reinhardt Ill." Ever the *homme d'affaires*, Delaunay sent Django condolences in an official business letter of which he kept a carbon copy on file. Delaunay letter to Django, March 7, 1946. Delaunay Archives.

198 "Échos de France": The song has often been erroneously noted as "Echoes of France," but the inventory form and label for Swing No. 229 lists the title in French.

199 "Do not order nor press again": "Échos de France" on Swing No. 229 was released in January 1947. Swing No. 229 inventory form, author's collection; Nevers, liner notes to *Intégrale Django Reinhardt 13*; and Delaunay, *Delaunay's dilemma*, 234–35.

199 "He will not play for less than 50,000 francs": Lieber, "Gypsy Genuis," 8.

199 "Django's van": Delaunay, *Django mon frère*, 132.

199 delighted in taking revenge on the gendarmes: Delaunay, *Django mon frère*, 144–46.

201 Dizzy's own compositions "Salt Peanuts": Delaunay, untitled essay in Gillespie, *To BE, or not . . . to BOP*, 330–31.

201 "inscribed the future of African American music": Hodeir, "Vers un renouveau de la musique de jazz?"

203 "How anybody can call this music jazz": Panassié, "The Unreal Jazz," 69.

204 Jimmy Reinhardt: Salgues, "La légende" (*Jazz Magazine*, No. 36), 29.

204 Among the Manouche: Information on Manouche mourning comes from Patrick Williams correspondence with author, 2002; and Williams, *Nous, on n'en parle pas*.

204 Uninspired, lacking jobs: Quoted in Delaunay, *Django mon frère*, 131.

204 It was Nin-Nin: Chaput letter to Alain Antonietto; quoted in Antonietto, "Django et la peinture" in Billard, *Django Reinhardt*, 228.

205 "Django's painting is especially interesting": Delaunay interview with Alain Antonietto; quoted in Antonietto, "Django et la peinture" in Billard, *Django Reinhardt*, 238.

205 "Your paintings": Radio broadcast from the Club St-Germain, February 1951.

206 agent for the prestigious American William Morris Agency: "'Sonny Jim' Reinhardt."

206 frustration for Delaunay: André Clergeat correspondence with author, 2001.

207 "Like the sinner who quits this ignoble world": Delaunay, *Django Reinhardt souvenirs*, 57.

207 Dorothy Lamour owned several: "Django Joining Ellington in States"; and McKean, "The Fabulous Gypsy."

11. PILGRIMAGE, 1946–1947

209 "If I was rich": Salgues, "La légende" (*Jazz Magazine*, No. 36), 29.

210 American jazz cognoscenti: *Down Beat*, November 4, 1946

210 "Swarthy Django Reinhardt": "Django Music."

210 "By legend": "Jazz by Django."

211 "We didn't communicate": Gottlieb quoted in Fisch, "Django Reinhardt."

211 we considered the "human voice": Adams, "I Meet Reinhardt."

212 And Django was not a neophyte: Along with Charlie Byrd's report of Django playing electric in Paris in 1945, others reported seeing him play electric in Marseille that year; see Cherrett, *Genius That Was Django*, 17. On Django playing electric during the 1946 Swiss tour, see "Django Joining Ellington in States"; and Gruber, "Django." Django also played electric in London days prior to coming to New York; see "Django Here."

212 "He was like a child": Grappelli interview with Clinton, "Stephane Grappelli," 16.

212 an acoustic sunburst Gibson: Les Paul interviews with author, 2000 and 2001; and John Bajo interview with author, 2001.

212 Now he was ready to play: When the tour ended on December 7 and Django returned to New York, he had plenty of time to visit the city's guitar shops. In New York, he ran into an old acquaintance, Joe Sinacore, an Italian-American studio guitarist. Sinacore had served in the U.S. Army band during World War II and met Django while stationed in Paris. Django and Sinacore could converse in a smattering of Italian, so Sinacore became Django's unofficial interpreter and tour guide. Sinacore took him to the Epiphone Company's guitar factory and showroom, where the studio guitarman was well known. Django selected an electric Epiphone hollow-body that he played through an Epiphone Electar amplifier at some later Café Society Uptown shows. Django had connections at Epiphone that were keen to have him play their guitars. In 1938, Django met the firm's top salesman and sometimes-inventor, Herb Sunshine, in Paris during a European sales tour. Epiphone was Henri Selmer's band-instruments distributor for the United States while Selmer sold Epiphone guitars in Europe. Sunshine agreed to sponsor Django's American visa application for a 1938 U.S. tour, but the war aborted further tour talk at the time. While in Paris, Sunshine also tried to convert Django to Epiphone guitars but could not lure him away from his loyalty to Selmers. Now, with Django in America, Sunshine saw the perfect opportunity to put an Epiphone in Django's hands. Sunshine, "Herb Sunshine On The Early Days," 34–38.

213 "We brought Django to America": Ellington quoted in Nicholson, *Reminiscing*, 266.

213 "Go to it, master": Django and Ellington quoted in "Django Music."

213 "What key do you want to play in": Django and Ellington quoted in "Jazz by Django."

214 "Duke Ellington came to Cleveland": *Cleveland Press*, November 5, 1949.

214 "In the hands of this virtuoso": *The Cleveland Plain Dealer*, November 5, 1946.

214 "I forget what spot I had him in": Ellington quoted in Nicholson, *Reminiscing*, 266–67.

214 After the Cleveland show: In this letter to Lévêque, Django erroneously wrote that the tour began with a show in Buffalo, New York. In a later letter to Stéphane, Django incorrectly stated the band also played shows as far west as San Francisco.

215 a growing sense of separation: Naguine Reinhardt interview with Delaunay, Delaunay Archives; and Les Paul interviews with author, 2000 and 2001.

215 flowered boxer shorts: Delaunay, *Django mon frère*, 137.

216 "*Voulez-vous coucher*": Nelson quoted in Grinnell, *Andy Nelson*, 18–20.

216 "You had to stay with him every minute": Ellington quoted in Nicholson, *Reminiscing*, 267.

216 "Django invited me to join him": Smith quoted in *Guitar Magazine*, August 1976.

217 "I remember one time we played": Greer interview with Stanley Crouch, 1979, The Smithsonian Institution Jazz Oral History Project.

217 "The concert started to a standing-room-only audience": Nelson quoted in Grinnell, *Andy Nelson*, 18–20.

217 research chemist and Chicago jazz collector Dr. John Striner: John Bajo interview with author, 2001.

218 These private recordings: Other recordings from Django's American tour may exist. The first Carnegie Hall concert of November 23, 1946, was recorded in its entirety, but the recordings of Django's set have gone missing. Portions of Ellington's performance were released at the time on the armed services's V-Discs label and Ellington's complete portion was later available on compact disc. The recordings of Django's numbers may be gathering dust in a studio vault or might have been spirited away to a collector's cache. In addition, rumors persist that at least one of Django's Café Society shows was recorded.

218 "Ah, Django": Brown interview with Patricia Willard, 1976, the Smithsonian Institution Jazz Oral History Project.

218 "Something else": Greer interview with Stanley Crouch, 1979, the Smithsonian Institution Jazz Oral History Project.

219 Ellington had not planned to hire only Django: Delaunay, *Delaunay's dilemma*, 107.

219 "By what mystery": Grappelli, *Mon violon*, 143–44.

219 "You can't write music right": Ellington quoted in Giddins, *Visions of Jazz*, 104.

220 "We stopped using the word *jazz*": Ellington interview with Michael Parkinson, *The Parkinson Show*, BBC-TV, 1973, quoted in Nicholson, *Reminiscing*, 247.

220 "The hall was packed out": Weiser, "Django aux États-Unis," 3.

221 "They presented a guitar to him": Pisano quoted in Fisch, "Django Reinhardt."

222 "Part of the trouble was Django Reinhardt": Levin, "Ellington Fails to Top Himself!"

222 *World Telegram* labeled his solos "remarkable": "Ellington Idiom at Carnegie."

222 "At his Carnegie Hall appearance": McKean, "The Fabulous Gypsy."

222 "And, though he was well received": *Metronome*, January 1947.

222 "The most talked about item": Feather, "Django's New York Debut."

223 Django stole the last show: "French Guitarist Stars."

223 in January 1947 to meet Dizzy: Delaunay, untitled essay in Gillespie, *To BE, or not . . . to BOP*, 332; and Delaunay, *Delaunay's dilemma*, 168–69.

223 "it was also the *plus froid*": Delaunay, *Django mon frère*, 139.

224 "He played and created": Sablon quoted in Delaunay, *Django mon frère*, 139.

224 "Django asked me if I would come": Les Paul interviews with author, 2000 and 2001.

225 damaged the Selmer while in transit: "Delaunay Back in Country."

225 "My brother": Django quoted in Delaunay, *Django mon frère*, 140; and Delaunay, *Delaunay's dilemma*, 108.

225 "When I asked him later for his impressions": Delaunay, *Django Reinhardt*, 139–40.

225 wrote Delaunay requesting permission: Delaunay Archives.

225 to discuss a contract: "Contrat Django Reinhardt," Delaunay Archives.

226 to join Ellington in the studio: Ellington cut five sides on November 16, 1946, at the NBC Studio while the tour was playing Omaha, Nebraska. On November 25, the day after the troubled second Carnegie Hall concert, Ellington and his band recorded for the Musicraft label in New York. And back in New York after the Detroit tour finale, the Musicraft sessions continued on December 5, 11, and 18. Yet these sessions had been arranged back in March, with no provisions or pay for anyone but Ellington's orchestra. The letter of contract between Ellington and Musicraft was signed March 16, 1946; author's collection.

226 no other venues were scheduled: "Django Out of Cafe Society"; and Delaunay, *Delaunay's dilemma*, 108.

226 "Everything had happened": Delaunay, *Django Reinhardt*, 141.

226 "He said to me one day": Les Paul interviews with author, 2000 and 2001.

226 "He could not remain separated": Naguine Reinhardt interview with Delaunay, Delaunay Archives.

227 Django was issued a typical tourist: Django's French passport #00132 was issued American visa #PV2439, good for 60 days after arrival. An extension would have had to have been applied for. United States Department of Justice Immigration and Naturalization Service Incoming Passenger Manifests and Crew Lists, New York, October 29–30, 1946, Roll Number 7210, Volume Number 15467; National Archives and Records Administration Record Group 85.

227 "I would go up": Smith interview in *Guitar Magazine*, August 1976.

227 "The doorman yelled up six floors": Les Paul began his stand at the Paramount on December 18, 1946. Paul interviews with author, 2000 and 2001.

228 Jamming with Smith, Paul: Les Paul, one of the fathers of the electric guitar, naturally had something to say on this score: "Django was very intrigued by my electric guitars [when he played them at the Paramount Theatre in 1946]. He liked their sound. He was fascinated by that electric sound. In fact, there's that film footage of him back in Paris and he's playing an acoustic blonde Epi just like mine. That guitar could have been the sister to mine. I next saw Django in Paris in 1950. We were riding in a cab going to some club and he punches me on the shoulder and says, 'Why don't they like me in the States?' I said, 'It was the background, and they weren't expecting an electric guitar. If you come back, they will surely like you.' He said, 'I don't play that bad, do I?' Well, that surprised me, I can tell you. Then he asked me, 'Do you like bebop?' I said, 'No, not in particular. I'm not too fond of it.' He said, 'That the way I want to play.' He never took my advice. That's my contribution to Django Reinhardt: He never took my advice. From 1946, he went electric and played bebop." Paul interviews with author, 2000 and 2001.

12. SCHISM, 1947–1950

231 "To persuade me": Rostaing quoted in Delaunay, *Django mon frère*, 143–44.

231 "What was important to him": Rostaing quoted in Cruickshank, *Django's Gypsies*, 12.

231 "Babik (Bi-Bop)": "Bi-Bop" was a French transliteration of "bebop," based on the long "e" sound of the French "i."

233 Henri Crolla: A young Crolla with his banjo was included in a mural painted on a pillar at La Coupole. Colette Crolla correspondence with author, 2003; and Hamon and Rotman, *Tu vois*, 224.

235 "Although these sessions were not prepared": Rostaing interview, 1973; liner notes to *Pêche à la Mouche*.

236 Maurice Meunier: Soudieux interview with author, Paris, 2003.

237 "You know, Hubert, my son's already": Django quoted in Delaunay, *Django mon frère*, 148.

237 "My brother, just look at what": Django quoted in Delaunay, *Django mon frère*, 151.

237 "Don't talk to me about music": Django quoted in Delaunay, *Django mon frère*, 147–48.

238 "Them boys never play two notes": Mezzrow quoted in Gillespie, *To BE, or not
... to BOP*, 333.

238 the rending of the Hot Club: *Bulletin Panassié*, September 25, 1947; *Bulletin du
Hot Club de France*, No. 1, January 1948; Tournès, *New Orleans sur Seine*, 106–8;
and Delaunay, *Delaunay's dilemma*, 159–63.

239 for not sending the recording of "Salt Peanuts": Delaunay, untitled essay in Gillespie,
To BE, or not ... to BOP, 330–31; and Delaunay, *Delaunay's dilemma*, 165.

239 issuing jazz on his Vogue: Delaunay, *Delaunay's dilemma*, 254–58.

240 one-page interview: James, "Interview met Django Reinhardt," 187. Translation
courtesy of Jan Brouwer. This interview was also published in the Belgian *Jazz
Magazine* (No. 7, [no date]), and Panassié's *Bulletin Hot Club de France* (No. 1,
October 1950).

241 "With Johnny James's article": Quoted in Panassié, *Monsieur jazz*, 219–23.

241 Magistrate's questioning: Transcription of Tribunal Civil, Aulnay-sous-Bois,
Delaunay Archives.

242 "Django has certainly not played so well": *Jazz Hot*, December 1947.

242 Delaunay booked Dizzy Gillespie: Vian, *Round About Close to Midnight*, 33.

243 Dizzy sat in with just Django: Soudieux interview with author, Paris, 2003.

244 With jobs impossible to find: "Reinhardt-Grappelly and French Hot Club Group
for English Tour"; and "Grappelly English Tour Fixed."

244 "Arriving in London": Soudieux interview with author, Paris, 2003; Delaunay,
Django mon frère, 150; "Burglars Greet Django on London Arrival!"; and "New
Faces in Grappelly-Reinhardt Hot Club Act." Django's guitar was likely not
stolen as Laurie Henshaw interviewed Django following the Wood Green Empire show and Django reported that he had had the guitar he was playing for ten
years. Henshaw, "Swing Guitars" column.

245 As with their prewar British tours: Django and Stéphane performed on March
15–20 at the Hackney Empire Theatre, London E8, March 29–April 4 at the
Wood Green Empire Theatre, London N22, and April 5–10 at the Chiswick
Empire Theatre, London W4.

245 trio set off for Sweden: "Grappelly and Reinhardt for Sweden." It's unclear if
Django played for the full month of May in Stockholm and then began a stand
on May 30 in Copenhagen as *Melody Maker* noted of their plans. Django and
Quintette were also advertised to play at May 24–29 at Manchester's Hippodrome Theatre and May 31–June 5 at Shepherd's Bush Empire Theatre, London W12.

245 the reviewers and fans raved: Mitchell, "Sweden Low-Down."

246 Astoria Club: Franco Cerri correspondence with author, 2003.

246 "I descended the stairs": de Crescenzo quoted in Balmer, *Stéphane Grappelli*, 158.

247 "He preferred to live like that": Grappelli, "Stephane Grappelly Tells the Tale
of Jazzdom's Magic Fingers."

247 traveled south to Naples: Delaunay reported Django played for the premiere of
the Teatro Metropolitan, but the theater had been inaugurated a year earlier, in
1948, so it was more likely just a concert.

247 70 percent of French musicians: "Grappelly-Reinhardt French Hot Club Link-Up."

248 it was a modern trailer camper: Such a modern trailer camper was known among
the Manouche as *une caravane*.

249 "Charles sent me to ask you": Frank Ténot correspondence with author, 2003;
Ténot, "Frankly Speaking" column (*Jazz Magazine*, No. 538, June 2003), 25;
and André Clergeat correspondence with author, 2002.

249 "There's money here": Michelot interview, 1988; liner notes to *Pêche à la Mouche*.

249 "I'm bored with the guitar": Hodeir quoted in Gaspard, "Un blues gitan."

249 Stepháne also appeared one day: Stéphane often confused dates: he remembered this meeting taking place in Le Bourget in 1952, by which time Django was living in Samois. Grappelli, *Mon violon*, 102.

250 "The Open Gate was the famous cabaret": Ekyan quoted in Delaunay, *Django mon frère*, 153.

250 Django simply turned his amplifier to face the wall: Lily Coleman also reported that Nin-Nin was in Rome accompanying Django. Coleman, "Rencontre à Rome avec Django," 4.

251 "In my life as a musician": Masselier interview in Bedin, "Django à Rome."

13. A NEW MAN, 1951–1953

253 "He was in ecstasy": Michelot interview, 1988; liner notes to *Pêche à la Mouche*.

253 to prove himself to the avant-garde: Delaunay interview with Alain Antonietto, quoted in Antonietto, "Django et la peinture" in Billard, *Django Reinhardt*, 238.

254 "As soon as Django took the stand": Henry Kahn, untitled review (*Melody Maker*, March 17, 1951).

254 "The chief lesson": Fol quoted in Delaunay, *Django mon frère*, 156–57.

255 "They make me suffer sometimes": Django quoted in Delaunay, *Django mon frère*, 156.

255 "Django played like a fool": Michelot quoted in Reese, "Flèche d'or," 22.

256 "Jean-Paul Sartre, who lived a large part of his life": Gélin quoted in Spautz, *Django Reinhardt*, 118.

256 "While he was improvising on": Livorness quoted in Delaunay, *Django mon frère*, 157.

256 "I believe Django found": Fol quoted in Delaunay, *Django mon frère*, 156.

256 "Every night": Delaunay, *Django mon frère*, 156.

257 "I figured it was going to be one sad clambake": "Lips, Django Just Knocked Out" in Cherrett, *Genius That Was Django*, 111; and "Hot Lips still plays pretty fierce trumpet!"

258 "It is above all in harmonies": Unsigned and untitled review (*Jazz Hot*, March 1952).

259 "Django lived in perfectly anticonformist fashion": Mme. Loisy quoted in Spautz, *Django Reinhardt*, 129.

259 One day, Naugine's brother-in-law: Naguine Reinhardt interview with Delaunay, Delaunay Archives.

259 For his son, Django believed: Mme. Ipsaïenne interview in Spautz, *Django Reinhardt*, 133.

260 only if he had true need of money: Mme. Loisy interview in Spautz, *Django Reinhardt*, 129–32.

260 "He lived the life of a pensioner": Lévêque interview, 1972; liner notes to *Pêche à la Mouche*.

260 "In Samois, he was no longer": Naguine Reinhardt interview with Delaunay, Delaunay Archives.

261 "It was a time when Django wasn't much in demand": Michelot interview, 1988; liner notes to *Pêche à la Mouche*.

261 The derivation of "Anouman": Pierre Fargeton also suggests this reading of the title in his "L'influence du *be-bop* sur la langage de Django Reinhardt."

263 To begin promoting Django: Granz interviews with Tad Hershorn; correspondence with author, 2003. Delaunay, untitled synopsis of Django's life, Delaunay Archives.

264 "a recapitulation of everything that he had created": Michelot quoted in Reese, "Flèche d'or," 23.

264 "One, two, three takes at the most": Michelot interview, 1988; liner notes to *Pêche à la Mouche.*

264 "Django had found": liner notes to *Pêche à la Mouche.*

265 "I mustn't miss that": Delaunay, *Django mon frère,* 160.

265 "to be of the same exceptional class": Unsigned and untitled review (*Jazz Hot,* April 1953); and Fol, "Dizzy Gillespie a Parigi."

265 embarrassed by his piano work: Solal interview with Anne Legrand, Paris, 1999.

266 "For him the most important thing": Michelot interview with Sportis, "Pierre Michelot."

266 "He was extremely spontaneous to work with": Lemarchand quoted in Cruickshank, *Django's Gypsies,* 13.

266 "It was a dangerous yet interesting": Solal interview with Anne Legrand, Paris, 1999.

267 "No, no, I don't want to see a doctor": Django quoted in Delaunay, *Django mon frère,* 160.

267 Django just missed Bing Crosby: Naguine Reinhardt interview with Delaunay, Delaunay Archives; and Delaunay, *Django mon frère,* 161.

267 he seemed content with his life: Naguine Reinhardt interview with Delaunay, Delaunay Archives.

267 It was all too late: "Django is dead"; and Sharpe, "Django Is Dead."

267 They settled back into their caravan: Mme. Ipsaïenne interview in Spautz, *Django Reinhardt,* 134.

268 Django's coffin was carried: Kahn, "Musicians and gypsies pay homage to Django"; and Cullaz, "Music World Mourns Reinhardt's Passing" in Cherrett, *The Genius That Was Django,* 112.

268 "I didn't cry": Grappelli interview with Clinton, "Stephane Grappelli," 16; Grappelli, *Mon violon,* 138; and Grappelli, "Stephane Grappelly Tells of Django's First Letter."

268 She piled Django's possessions in a pyre: Mme. Ipsaïenne interview in Spautz, *Django Reinhardt,* 134.

Afterword: Gypsy Jazz

269 settled into a dreary Montmartre apartment: Les Paul interview with author, 2000.

269 The Manouche mourn their dead: Williams, "Un héritage sans transmission"; and Williams, *Nous, on n'en parle pas.*

270 Matelo Ferret created his own music: Moerman interview with author, Paris, 2001.

271 Charles Delaunay remained Django's greatest fan: Delaunay published three different versions of his biography of Django over a span of 15 years. *Django Reinhardt souvenirs* was published in Paris by Éditions Jazz Hot in 1954. At the request of London publisher Cassell & Company, he edited, rewrote, and expanded his first biography to be translated into English and published as *Django Reinhardt* in 1961. In 1968, a third version was released in French as *Django mon*

frère. Each version included new stories and anecdotes and were not mere translations of each other.

272 Babik went to court to be declared Django's sole: Delaunay letter to lawyer André Schmidt stating he believed Babik Reinhardt was Django's sole legitimate heir, Delaunay Archives.

272 "I don't want to copy the familiar traits": Joseph Reinhardt interview in André, "Les Lundis du jazz."

272 "My brother Nin-Nin? He's an Arab": Sara Reinhardt quoted in Antonietto, "Joseph Reinhardt."

272 Baro Ferret set aside his guitar: Moerman interview with author, Paris, 2001; Boulou and Elios Ferré interview with author, Paris, 2001; and Pallen, "Extrait Baro Ferret."

274 Among the most famous: Jacques Montagne—Moerman interview with author, Paris, 2001; and Patrick Saussois interview with author, Paris, 2001.

274 Manouche Piton Reinhardt: Ninine Garcia interview with author, Paris, 2002.

275 Gitan Paul Pata: Moerman interview with author, Paris, 2001.

275 Étienne "Patotte" Bousquet: Alain Cola correspondence with author, 1999.

275 Paul Vidal: Moréno Winterstein interview with author, Paris, 1999.

276 "I was alone": Naguine Reinhardt, "Le témoignage," 24–25.

278 legacy of one man: Williams, "Un héritage sans transmission."

278 Maurice "Gros Chien" Ferret: Like Baro Ferret before him, Gros Chien Ferret changed his surname from "Michel" to "Maurice" as he didn't like his given name. Pouville's nickname "Babagne" was argot for "prisoner," a name he won as he loved striped shirts.

Bibliography

DISCOGRAPHIES

Antonietto, Alain. "Discographie du jazz Tsiganes." *Études tsiganes*, No. 4, 1987; No. 1, 1988; No. 2, 1988; No. 3, 1988; No. 4, 1988.
Haederli, Freddy. *Django Reinhardt: The Discography*. Geneva: self-published, August 2001 edition.
———. *Gus Viseur: The Discography*. Geneva: self-published, March 1995 edition.
Ruppli, Michel, avec le concours de Charles Delaunay. *Discographies Vol. 1: Swing*. Paris: Association Française des Détenteurs de Documents Audioviseuls et Sonores, 1989.
———. *Discographies Vol. 2: Vogue Productions*. Paris: Association Française des Détenteurs de Documents Audioviseuls et Sonores, 1992.
Vernon, Paul. *Jean "Django" Reinhardt: A Contextual Bio-Discography 1910–1953*. Aldershot, Hampshire: Ashgate Publishing, 2003.

GENERAL

Abrams, Max. "Django Reinhardt—the Jazz Gypsy." *Storyville*, No. 77, June–July 1978.
———. *The Book of Django*. Los Angeles: self-published, 1973.
Adams, Sam. "I Meet Reinhardt." *BMG*, March 1946.
André, Jacques. "Les lundis du jazz: Joseph Reinhardt." *Combat*, January 21, 1967.
Anick, Peter. "Reminiscing with Stéphane Grappelli." *Fiddler Magazine*, Vol. 9, No. 2, Summer 2002.
Antonietto, Alain. "Django: de la virtuosité tsigane . . . innée ou acquise?" *Études tsiganes*, No. 4, 1984.
———. "Histoire de la musique tsigane instrumentale d'Europe centrale." *Études tsiganes*, No. 1, 1994.
———. "Joseph Reinhardt: Le Dernier voyage . . ." *Études tsiganes*, No. 2, 1982.

————. "La musique tsigane mythe ou préjugés." *Études tsiganes*, No. 1, 1986.

————. "Matelo Ferret de la csardas au jazz . . ." *Études tsiganes*, No. 4, 1982.

————. "Nomadismes, musique et nationalisme." *Études tsiganes* No. 3, 1987.

————. Liner notes to Baro Ferret, *Swing valses d'hier et d'aujourd'hui*. © 1988 Hot Club Records HCRCD 45.

————. Liner notes to Joseph Reinhardt, *Live in Paris 1966*. © 1991 Hot Club Records HCRCD 66.

Antonietto, Alain, and François Billard. *Django Reinhardt: Rythmes Futurs*. Paris: Éditions Fayard, 2004.

Antonietto, Alain, and Dominique Cravic. "Roger Chaput: le premier compagnon . . ." *Jazz Magazine*, No. 448, May 1995.

Antonietto, Alain, and Patrick Williams. "50 Ans de jazz gitan." *Jazz Hot*, November 1985.

Asséo, Henriette. *Les Tsiganes: Une destinée européenne*. Paris: Gallimard, 1994.

Assouline, Pierre. *Simenon: A Biography*. New York: Alfred A. Knopf, 1997.

Baker, Joséphine, and Jo Bouillon. *Joséphine*. Paris: Éditions Robert Laffont, 1976.

Balen, Noël. *Django Reinhardt: Le génie vagabond*. Monaco: Éditions du Rocher, 2003.

Balmer, Paul. *Stéphane Grappelli: With and Without Django*. London: Sanctuary Publishing, 2003.

Balmer, Paul, and Judy Caine. *Stéphane Grappelli: A Life in the Jazz Century*. Music on Earth Productions, 2002.

Barnett, Anthony. *Black Gypsy: The Recordings of Eddie South: An Annotated Discography & Itinerary*. Lewes, East Sussex: Allardyce Book, 1999.

Battestini, Jean-Pierre. "Emmanuel Soudieux: Django, Stéphane . . ." *Jazz Dixie/Swing*, No. 36.

Bayol, Jeanne. *Rêves de roulottes*. Aix-en-Provence: Édisud, 2000.

Bechet, Sidney. *Treat It Gentle: An Autobiography*. London: Cassell, 1960.

Bedin, Michel. "Collette [sic] et Henri Crolla." *Jazz Hot*, No. 600, May 2003.

————. "Django à Rome: Alf 'Totol' Masselier et Roger Paraboschi." *Jazz Hot*, No. 600, May 2003.

Behr, Edward. *The Good Frenchman*. New York: Villard Books, 1993.

Bergerot, Frank. Liner notes to *Paris Musette: Swing et manouche*. © 1993 Just a Memory JAM 9122-2.

Bergreen, Laurence. *Louis Armstrong: An Extravagant Life*. New York: Broadway Books, 1997.

Billard, François, and Alain Antonietto. *Django Reinhardt: Un géant sur son nuage*. Paris: Lien Commun, 1993.

Billard, François, and Didier Roussin. *Histoires de l'accordéon*. Castelnau-le-Lez, France: Éditions Climats, 1991.

Bogart, Eric. Liner notes to *Django! And His American Swing Big Band*. © 1991 Jass Records J-CD-628.

Bonneau, Pierre. "Notes biographiques sur Django Reinhardt." *Jazz Hot*, No. 2, November 1945.

Bouchaux, Alain, Madeleine Juteau, and Didier Roussin. *L'argot des musiciens*. Paris: Éditions Climats, 1992.

Boudard, Alphonse, and Marcel Azzola. *La valse musette et l'accordéon: Bals et guinguettes*. Paris: Éditions Solar, 1998.

Boujut, Michel. "Jacques Bureau." Online. www.jazzmagazine.com/Interviews/dauj/bureau/bureau.htm.

Boulanger, Alain, and Didier Roussin. Liner notes to Oscar Alemán, *Buenos-Aires Paris 1928–1943*. © 1994 Frémeaux & Associés FA020.

Bramsen, Sten. *Django*. Denmark TV documentary, 1978.

Brassaï. *Le Paris secret des années 30*. Paris: Éditions Gallimard, 1976.

Bricktop, with James Haskins. *Bricktop*. New York: Atheneum, 1983.

Brierre, Jean-Dominique. *Le jazz français de 1900 à aujourd'hui*. Paris: Éditions Hors Collection, 2000.

Bureau, Jacques. "Champagne!" *So What*, No. 27, October 1998.

———. *Un soldat menteur*. Paris: Robert Laffont, 1992.

"Burglars Greet Django on London Arrival!" *Melody Maker*, March 20, 1948.

"Cabaret Queen, Bricktop is Dead." Huntington (WV) *Herald-Dispatch*, February 2, 1984.

Caen, Herb. "An Evening in Paris Has Some Solid Kicks." *Down Beat*, March 1, 1945.

Carco, Francis. *The Last Bohemia*. New York: Henry Holt, 1928.

———. *Nostalgie de Paris*. Geneva: Éditions du Milieu de Monde, 1941.

———. *Panam*. Paris: Librarie Stock, 1922.

Carisella, P. J., and James W. Ryan. *Black Swallow of Death*. Boston: Marlborough House, 1972.

Cassidy, Claudia. "Brilliant Solists Step Out of 'The Duke's' Orchestra to Make Concert Bow." *Chicago Daily Tribune*, November 12, 1946.

Chaput, Roger. "Le quintet ses débuts." *Jazz Hip*, No. 32, 1963.

Charle, François. "Marcel Bianchi: Premier guitariste électrique français." *Trad Magazine*, No. 44, January–February 1996.

———. *The Story of Selmer Maccaferri Guitars*. Paris: self-published, 1999.

Charle, François, with Paul Hostetter. "Selmer Guitars." *Vintage Gallery*, April 1994.

Charters, Samuel B., and Leonard Junstadt. *Jazz: A History of the New York Scene*. New Tork: Da Capo, 1981.

Cherrett, Ted, ed. *The Genius That Was Django*. Addlestone, England: self-published, 1997.

Chevalier, Maurice. *The Man in the Straw Hat: My Story*. New York: Thomas Y. Crowell, 1949.

"Chez Bouscatel, un soir." *La Haute loire*. September 17, 1906.

Chilton, John. *The Song of the Hawk: The Life and Recordings of Coleman Hawkins*. London and New York: Quartet Books, 1990.

Clinton, George. "Stephane Grappelli: 'For a few seconds I am back again with Django.'" *Guitar International*, August 1991.

Coleman, Bill. *Trumpet Story*. Boston: Northeastern University Press, 1989.

Coleman, Lily. "Rencontre à Rome avec Django." *Bulletin du Hot Club de France*, No. 523, May 2003.

Conte, Gérard. "Les mystères d'une naissance ou les premières années du Hot Club de France." *Jazz Classique Magazine*, No. 7, September 1999.

Corbier, Robert. "A Thonon-les-Bains: Django Reinhardt; premier guitariste du monde, veut composer une messe pour les 'romanis.'" Reprinted in Jean-Claude Rey, "Folie à Amphion: Django Reinhardt en Haute-Savoie au cours de l'année 1943," Société d'Histoire Locale La Salévienne/*Échos Seléviens*, No. 9, 2000, 148.

Costa, Adriana. "The Quintet of the Hot Club of France: A Historical and Analytical Study." Ph.D. dissertation, Catholic University of America, Washington, DC, January 2003.

Couvreux, Francis. "Un histoire de swing: Les pionniers." *Accordéon*, No. 5, December 1995.

Cravic, Dominique. "Charley Bazin, l'épopée de l'accordéon." *Accordéon Magazine*, No. 40, February 1999 and No. 41, March 1999.

———. Unpublished interview with Roger Chaput. 1995.

Cruickshank, Ian. *Django's Gypsies: The Mystique of Django Reinhardt and his People.* Newcastle-upon-Tyne, England: Ashley Mark, 1994.

Cullaz, Maurice, and others. "50 Ans de jazz en France." *Jazz Hot*, No. 419, March 1985.

Daettwyler, Otto, and Matéo Maximoff. *Tsiganes: Wanderndes Volk auf endloser Strasse.* Zürich: Büchergilde Gutenberg, 1959.

Daubresse, Jean-Pierre, and Daniel Nevers. "La chanson à papa." *Jazz Hot*, March 1975.

Daval, Marcel, and Pierre Hauger. "La singularité et le rôle de la musique dans l'affirmation de l'identité des Manouches d'Alsace" in Patrick Williams, *Tsiganes: Identité, évolution.* Paris: *Études tsiganes*/Syros Alternatives, 1989.

de Beauvoir, Simone. *La force des choses.* Paris: Gallimard, 1963.

de Chocqueuse, Pierre, and others. "Charles Delaunay 1911–1988: La Passion du jazz." *Jazz Hot*, No. 451, April 1988.

de Foletier, François de Vaux. *Les Tsiganes dans l'ancienne France.* Paris: Connaissance du Monde, 1961.

"Delaunay Back in Country." *Down Beat*, January 29, 1947.

Delaunay, Charles. . . . *de la vie et du jazz.* Paris: Éditions Hot Jazz, 1939.

———. "As I See It." *Jazz Record*, No. 55, May 1947.

———. "Django Reinhardt en Grand-Bretagne." *Jazz Hot*, No. 4, January–February 1946.

———. "French Jazz." *The PL Yearbook of Jazz 1946.* London: Editions Poetry London, 1946.

———. "Interview de Mme. Reinhardt." Fonds Charles Delaunay, boîte 25, Bibliothéque Nationale de France, Département de l'audiovisuel, no date but likely from 1953–1954.

———. "L'arrivée du BeBop en France." *Jazz Hot*, No. 328, June 1976.

———. "L'histoire du Hot Club de France." *Jazz Hot*, No. 19, January 1948; No. 20, February 1948; No. 21, March 1948.

———. "Le creation de la Marque Swing." Original manuscript, Fonds Charles Delaunay, Bibliothéque Nationale de France, Département de l'audiovisuel, no date [circa October 1947].

———. "Le jazz en France (1932–1944)." *Jazz Hot*, No. 250, 1969.

———. "Les debuts du jazz en France: Souvenirs par André Ekyan, Stéphane Grappelly, Alain Romans, Ray Ventura." *Jazz Hot*, No. 248, March 1969.

———. "New York 1947: Carnet de notes." *Jazz Hot*, No. 13, April 1947.

———. "Paris 1935." *Jazz Hot*, spécial No. 314, March 1975.

———. "Stéphane Grappelly et Django Reinhardt bavardent pour la première fois depuis six ans." *Jazz Hot*, No. 2, November 1945.

———. "The History of the Hot Club de France." *Coda*, November 1974, April 1976, and August 1977.

———. "Un guitariste meconnu: Oscar Aleman." *Jazz Hot*, No. 283, 1972.

———. *Delaunay's dilemma: De la peinture au jazz.* Mâcon: Éditions W, 1985.

———. *Django mon frère.* Paris: Eric Losfeld Editeur/Le Terrain Vague, 1968.

———. *Django Reinhardt souvenirs.* Paris: Éditions Jazz Hot, 1954.

———. *Django Reinhardt.* London: Cassell & Company, 1961.

———. *Hot discography.* Paris: Éditions Corrêa & Cie., 1936.

———. *Hot iconography: Lithographies.* Paris: Éditions Jazz Hot, 1939.

———. Untitled synopsis of Django's life submitted as planned film biography starring Robert De Niro to producer Louis C. Smith. Fonds Charles Delaunay, Bibliothéque Nationale de France, Département de l'audiovisuel, 1964.

Delaunay, Charles, and Philippe du Peuty. *Noirs au blanc: Portraits de jazzmen*. Paris: Éditions Porte du Sud, 1986.

Désautard, Yves. "Gus Viseur: Le mythe de l'accordéon jazz." *Accordéon*, No. 13, September 1996.

"Django a Brooklyn Bum?—Not That!" *Down Beat*, March 15, 1945.

"Django Here: Off to U.S. to Play with Ellington." *Melody Maker*, November 2, 1946.

"Django Is Dead." *Melody Maker*, May 23, 1953.

"Django Joining Ellington in States." *Melody Maker*, September 28, 1946.

"Django Music." *Time*, November 18, 1946.

"Django Out of Cafe Society." *Down Beat*, January 29, 1947.

"Django Reinhardt Dead." *Down Beat*, June 15, 1942.

"Django Reinhardt Ill: Urgent Operation." *Melody Maker*, February 16, 1946.

"Django Reinhardt Is Here." *Melody Maker*, February 2, 1946.

"Django Reinhardt: Nomade Land." *Guitar Monsters*, No. 1.

"Django's Brother Has Paree Jumping." *Down Beat*, December 1, 1945.

Doerr, Joseph "Coucou." *Où vas-tu, manouche? U Manush djiren le an u kamlepen un frai*. Bourdeaux, France: Éditions Wallada, 1982.

"Dope Cigarette Peddling among British Musicians." *Melody Maker*, February 22, 1936.

Dregni, Michael. "Boulou and Elios Ferré: In the Footsteps of Django." *Vintage Guitar*, February 1998.

———. *Django in America*. Minneapolis: Éditions Noir et Blanc, 2001.

du Peuty, Philippe, and Joëlle Ody. *Django Reinhardt*. Paris: Éditions Vade Retro, 1997.

Dubois, Claude. *Apaches, voyous et gonzes poilus: Le milieu parisien du début du siècle aux années soixante*. Paris: Éditions Parigramme, 1996.

———. *La Bastoche: Bal-musette, plaisir et crime 1750–1939*. Paris: Éditions du Félin, 1997.

———. Liner notes to *Histoires de Jo*. Djaz Records, 2000.

Dunbar, Rudolph. "Trumpet Player Briggs Freed after Four Years in Nazi Camp Near Paris." *Chicago Defender*, September 23, 1944.

"Ellington Idiom at Carnegie." *New York World Telegram*, November 25, 1946.

Faint, Pete. Biography of Jack Hylton. Online. www.jackhylton.com.

Fargeton, Pierre. "L'influence du *be-bop* sur la langage de Django Reinhardt, entre 1947 et 1953." Mémoire de maîtrise, Université Jean-Monnet, Saint-Étienne, France, September 2001.

Feather, Leonard. "Django's New York Debut." *Melody Maker*, December 7, 1946.

Ferreri, Albert. "Django et l'A.T.C. Band à la radio." *Jazz Hot*, No. 2, November 1945.

Fiot, Léon. "En faveur du 'jazz hot.'" *Jazz-Tango-Dancing*, March 1933.

Fisch, Jim. "Django Reinhardt: The Photograph, the Concert & the Guitar." *20th Century Guitar*, May 1995.

Fol, Hubert. "Dizzy Gillespie a Parigi." *Musica Jazz*, April 1948.

Franco, Maurizio. *Django Reinhardt: Dalla chitarra gitana al jazz*. Milano: Sinfonica Jazz, 2002.

"French Guitarist Stars with Ellington." *The Detroit News*, December 9, 1946.

"The French Quintet Staggers Swing Concert Audience: Ovations for Everybody." *Melody Maker*, February 5, 1938.

"Full House Hears Ellington Concert." *The New York Times*, November 11, 1946.

Gaffet, Hernán. *Oscar Alemán: Una vida con swing*. Buenos Aires: La Pintada Producciones, 2002.

Galtier-Boissière, Jean. *Mon journal depuis la Libération*. Paris: La Jeune Parque, 1945.

Gaspard, Jacques J. "Un blues gitan." *Jazz Hot*, No. 187, May 1963.

Giddins, Gary. *Visions of Jazz: The First Century*. Oxford and New York: Oxford University Press, 1998.

Gillespie, Dizzy, with Al Fraser. *To BE, or not . . . to BOP: Memoirs*. Garden City, NY: Doubleday, 1979.

Goddard, Chris. *Jazz Away from Home*. New York and London: Paddington Press, 1979.

Gottlieb, Bill. "Delaunay Escapades with Gestapo Related." *Down Beat*, September 9, 1946.

Grappelli, Stéphane. "Django Reinhardt and the Bright Red Socks." *Melody Maker*, March 13, 1954.

———. "Stephane Grappelly Continues the Story of Django: The Early Days of the Quintet." *Melody Maker*, March 6, 1954.

———. "Stephane Grappelly Tells of Django's First Letter." *Melody Maker*, March 27, 1954.

———. "Stephane Grappelly Tells the Tale of Jazzdom's Magic Fingers." *Melody Maker*, March 20, 1954.

———. "Stephane Grappelly Tells—For the First Time—the True Story of Django Reinhardt." *Melody Maker*, February 20, 1954.

Grappelli, Stéphane, as told to Dan Forte. "Stephane Grappelli on Django Reinhardt." *Guitar Player*, November 1976.

Grappelli, Stéphane, with Joseph Oldenhove and Jean-Marc Bramy. *Mon violon pour tout bagage*. Paris: Calmann-Lévy, 1992.

"Grappelly and Reinhardt for Sweden." *Melody Maker*, May 1, 1948.

"Grappelly English Tour Fixed." *Melody Maker*, March 6, 1948.

"Grappelly-Reinhardt French Hot Club Link-Up." *Melody Maker*, November 15, 1947.

Grinnell, Larry, and Andy Nelson. *Andy Nelson 1921–1995: A Fond Look at His Life in Music*. Online. www.grinnellfamily.org/webmaster/andybook.pdf.

Gruber, Ellis. "Django." *Melody Maker*, November 23, 1946.

Guitard, Jean-Louis. "La marque de Django." *Jazz Magazine*, 1976.

Gumplowicz, Philippe. "Django guitare." *Le Monde de la Musique*, No. 82, October 1985.

———. "Django guitare." *Le Monde de la Musique*, No. 82, October 1985.

"The Gypsy Evangelical Church." *The Ecumenical Review*, Vol. 31, No. 3, July 1979.

Hammond, John. "Venuti's Rival: Remarkable Hot Fiddling by Stephane Grappelly in French Record." *Melody Maker*, September 14, 1935.

Hamon, Hervé, and Patrick Rotman. *Tu vois, je n'ai pas oublié*. Paris: Éditions du Seuil/Éditions Fayard, 1990.

Hancock, Ian, Siobhan Dowd, and Rajko Djuric, eds. *The Roads of the Roma*. Hatfield, Hertfordshire: University of Hertfordshire Press, 1998.

Hancock, Ian. *The Pariah Syndrome: An Account of Gypsy Slavery and Persecution*. Ann Arbor, MI: Karoma Publishers, 1987.

Hennessey, Mike. *Klook: The Story of Kenny Clarke*. London: Quartet, 1990.

Henshaw, Laurie. "Swing Guitars" column. *Melody Maker*, May 1948.

Hibbs, Leonard. "Sensation on Strings." *Swing Music*, April 1935.

"L'histoire de Django." *Sept jours*, November 11, 1943.

Hodeir, André. "Henri Crolla." *Jazz Hot*, No. 7, May–June 1946.

———. "Hubert Fol." *Jazz Hot*, numéro special 19 bis, 1948.

———. "Vers un renouveau de la musique de jazz?" *Jazz Hot*, May–June 1946.

Hodgkiss, Allan. "Django's Guitar." *BMG*, December 1958.

———. "Rich New Wine in an Old, Old Bottle: Alan Hodgkiss recalls a brief encounter with Django Reinhardt's guitar." *Jazz Journal*, 40/4, April 1987.

Hoefer, George. "The Magnificent Gypsy." *Down Beat*, July 14, 1966.

"Hot Lips still plays pretty fierce trumpet!" *Melody Maker*, August 25, 1951.

Hughes, Langston. *The Big Sea: An Autobiography*. New York: Rinehart & Co., 1940.

Jackson, Jeffrey H. "Making Jazz French: The Reception of Jazz Music in Paris, 1927–1934." *French Historical Studies*, Vol. 25, No. 1, Winter 2002.

———. *Making Jazz French: Music and Modern Life in Interwar Paris*. Durham, NC: Duke University Press, 2003.

Jalard, Michel-Claude. "Django et l'école tsigane." *Les Cahiers du jazz*. Paris: *Jazz Magazine*, No. 1, 1959.

———. "Sous les doigts de Joseph Reinhardt." *Music-Hall*, November 1962.

James, Johnny. "Interview met Django Reinhardt." *Philarmonic*, August 1950.

"Le jargon du p'tit folkleux: Les bals musettes." Online. www.magic.fr/lvl/jargon/musique/histoire/bals.html.

"Jazz by Django." *Newsweek*, November 18, 1946.

Kahn, Henry. "Musicians and gypsies pay homage to Django." *Melody Maker*, May 23, 1953.

Kater, Michael H. "Forbidden Fruit? Jazz in the Third Reich." *American Historical Review*, No. 94, 1989.

———. *Different Drummers: Jazz in the Culture of Nazi Germany*. New York: Oxford University Press, 1992.

Kazansky, Konstantin. *Cabaret russe*. Paris: Éditions Olivier Orban, 1978.

Kenney, William H. III. "Le Hot: The Assimilation of American Jazz in France, 1917–1940." *American Studies*, No. 25, 1984.

Kenrick, Donald, and Grattan Puxon. *Les Tsiganes sous l'oppression nazie*. Toulouse: Centre de Recherches Tsiganes/CRDP Midi-Pyrénées, 1996.

———. *The Destiny of Europe's Gypsies*. New York: Basic Books, 1972.

Krümm, Philippe. "La création du musette: Un Vrai roman." *Bal Musette*, No. 1.

Le Cossec, Clément. *Mon aventure chez les Tziganes*. N.p.: self-published, 1991.

Lefort, Michel. "La musique des caravanes." *Études tsiganes*, No. 1, 1994.

———. "Le jazz des Tziganes." *Monde Gitan*, No. 4, 1991.

Legrand, Anne. "Django Reinhardt: Les débuts d'une carrière internationale." *Études*, July–August 2003.

———. "Jacques Bureau: Pionnier du jazz." *So What*, No. 22, February 1998 and No. 24, May 1998.

———. "Le fonds Charles Delaunay." *Chroniques de la Bibliothèque Nationale de France*, No. 19, July–August–September 2002.

———. "Soudieux, Michelot, Solal: c'était Django." *Jazzman*, No. 54, January 2000.

———. Unpublished interview with Emmanuel Soudieux. Paris, November 1999.

———. Unpublished interview with Martial Solal. Paris, November 1999.

———. Unpublished interview with Pierre Michelot. Paris, November 1999.

Lepidis, Clément. *Monsieur Jo: Roman d'une vie*. N.p.: Belfond/Éditions Le Pré aux Clercs, 1986.

Les génies du jazz: Django Reinhardt. Paris: Éditions Atlas, No. 5.

Levi, Erik. *Music in the Third Reich*. New York: St. Martin's Press, 1994.

Levin, Michael. "Ellington Fails to Top Himself!" *Down Beat*, December 16, 1946.

Leyh, Teddy. "Delaunay's Delight: Charles Delaunay in Conversation with Teddy Leyh." *Coda*, November 1974.

Lieber, Leslie. "Gypsy Genuis." *Rhythm Digest*, No. 1, 1947.

Loiseau, Jean-Claude. *Les Zazous*. Paris: Le Sagittaire, 1977.

Love, William C. "Mediterranean Mailbag: Django Reinhardt in a Marseille Cafe." *The Jazz Record*, July 1945.

Mac Orlan, Pierre. *Aux lumières de Paris*. Paris: Les Éditions G. Crès et Cie., 1925.

———. *Images secrètes de Paris*. Paris: René Kieffer, 1928.

MacDougald, Duncan, II. "Is This the Best Small Swing Group?" *Metronome*, 1938.

Martin, Denis-Constant, and Olivier Roueff. *La France du jazz: Musique, modernité et identité dans la première moitié du XXe siècle*. Marseille: Éditions Parenthèses, 2002.

Maximoff, Matéo. *Dites-le avec des pleurs*. Romainville, France: self-published, 1990.

Mazzoletti, Adriano. *Il Jazz in Italia: dalle origine al dopoguerra*. Rome and Bari: Laterza, 1983.

McKean, Gilbert S. "The Fabulous Gypsy." *Esquire*, June 1947.

Mezzrow, Milton "Mezz," and Bernard Wolfe. *Really the Blues*. New York: Random House, 1946.

Mingot, Françoise, François de Vaux de Foletier, and Luc Moïseef. "Joseph Doërr dit Coucou." *Études tsiganes*, No. 3, 1987.

Mitchell, Malcom. "Sweden Low-Down." *Melody Maker*, July 24, 1948.

Moerman, Francis-Alfred. "Portrait Souvenir: Sarane Ferret." *Jazz Journal*, No. 2, January–February 1987.

Monichon, Pierre. "Le genre musette." Online. www.perigord.com/asso/ar/sitedefinitif/lichon/henremu/p1.html.

Morrow, W. C., from notes by Edouard Cucuel. *Bohemian Paris of To-day*. London: Chatto & Windus, 1899.

Mougin, Stéphane. "Négromanie." *Jazz-Tango-Dancing*, October 1933.

Nabe, Marc-Edouard. *Nuage*. Paris: Le Dilettante, 1993.

Nevers, Daniel. Liner notes to *Intégrale Django Reinhardt 1–18*. © 2000–2003 Frémeaux & Associés FA301–FA318.

"New Faces In Grappelly-Reinhardt Hot Club Act." *Melody Maker*, April 3, 1948.

Nicholson, Stuart. *Reminiscing in Tempo: A Portrait of Duke Ellington*. Boston: Northeastern University Press, 1999.

Niquet, Bernard. "Eddie South: Un gentleman de la jazz bande." *Jazz Hot*, May 1969.

Osmont, Jean. "Autour de Django." *Jazz Classique*, No. 28, November 2003.

Pallen, Jean-Marie. "Extrait Baro Ferret" from *Mémoires de guitare*. Unpublished manuscript.

Panassié, Hugues. "Eddie South au Club aux Oiseaux." *Jazz Hot*, No. 19, August–September 1937.

———. "How We Recorded for the 'Swing' Label." *Jazz Express*, December 5, 1947.

———. "Red-Hot Strings." *Hot News*, May 1935.

———. "The Unreal Jazz." *Just Jazz 3*. London: Four Square Books/Landsborough Publications, 1959.

———. *Douze années de jazz (1927–1938): Souvenirs*. Paris: Corrêa, 1946.

———. *Histoire du vrai jazz*. Paris: Robert Laffont, 1959.

———. *Jazz panorama*. Paris: Éditions des Deux Rives, 1950.

———. *La bataille du jazz*. Paris: Albin Michel, 1965.

———. *La véritable musique de jazz*. Paris: Robert Laffont, 1946.

———. *Le jazz hot*. Paris: Éditions R.-A. Corrêa, 1934.

———. *Les rois du jazz*. Geneva: Ch. Grasset Editeur, 1947.

———. *Monsieur jazz: Entretiens avec Pierre Casalta*. Paris: Éditions Stock, 1975.

Paris-Musées/Pavillon des arts. *Saint-Germain-des-Prés 1945–1950*. Paris: Paris-Musées/Pavillon des arts, 1989.

Patry, Bob. "Django Reinhardt: Gypsy in His Soul." *The Mississippi Rag*, January 1994.

Paviot, Paul. *Django Reinhardt*. Production Pavox Films, 1957.

Péguri, Louis, and Jean Mag. *Du bouge . . . au conservatoire*. Paris: World Press, 1950.

Pernet, Robert. "Joseph Gustave Viseur: Le maître belge." *Accordéon*, No. 57, September–October 2000.

Perrault, Gilles. *Paris under the Occupation*. New York: Vendome Press, 1989.

"Pierre 'Matelo' Ferré (1918–1989): La fin d'une epoque." *Jazz Swing-Journal*, No. 12, March–April 1989.

Poueyto, Jean-Luc, ed. *Latcho rhaben: Cuisine Tsigane*. Pau, France: L'Instep Formation, 1994.

Privat, Jo. *Jo Privat partitions*. Paul Beuscher, 1985.

Randlemon, Marba. "Reinhardt as a 'Subversive': The Battle of Form DSP-33." *Guitar Player*, November 1976.

Reese, Jérôme. "Flèche d'or: Django, le be-bop et la guitare électrique." *Jazz Hot*, No. 401, June 1983.

"Reinhardt Death Mystery: New York Report Unconfirmed." *Melody Maker*, August 22, 1942.

"Reinhardt, Grappelly and Co. Here Again." *Melody Maker*, August 26, 1939.

"Reinhardt-Grappelly and French Hot Club Group for English Tour." *Melody Maker*, December 27, 1947.

Reinhardt, Naguine. "Le témoignage de la Guigne Reinhardt—veuve du célèbre guitariste Django Reinhardt." *Vie et lumière*, No. 18, 1964.

"Reinhardt on the Air." *Melody Maker*, January 12, 1946.

"René Mailhes: Souvenirs." Online. www.lechodescuilleres.com.

Rey, Jean-Claude. "Folie à Amphion: Django Reinhardt en Haute-Savoie au cours de l'année 1943." Société d'Histoire Locale La Salévienne/*Échos Seléviens*, No. 9, 2000.

Rimia, Pierre. "La séance privée d'août 1933." Online. www.silicone.fr/algo/séance.htm.

"Roger Paraboschi: Le batteur de Django à Rome en 1950." Online. www.lechodes cuilleres.com.

Roussin, Didier. "Les Tsiganes, le musette, la guitare et le banjo." *Études tisganes*, No. 1, 1994.

"Rumors That Django Lives." *Down Beat*, October 1, 1942.

Salgues, Yves. "La légende de Django Reinhardt." *Jazz Magazine* No. 33, January 1958; No. 34, February 1958; No. 35, March 1958; No. 36, April 1958; No. 37, May 1958; No. 38, June 1958; No. 39, July 1958; No. 40, August 1958; No. 41, September 1958.

Sartre, Jean-Paul. "New York City." *Jazz* 47, May 1947.

Schaap, Walter E. "Jazzmen Abroad." *Jazz Information*, Vol. 1, No. 9, November 7, 1939; Vol. 1, No. 11, November 24, 1939; Vol. 1, No. 13, December 8, 1939.

Schmitz, Alexander, and Peter Maier. *Django Reinhardt: Sein Leben, Seine Musik, Seine Schallplatten*. Gauting-Buchendorf, Germany: Oreos Verlag, 1985.

Schulz-Köhn, Dietrich. "Django—the lost years." *Melody Maker*, February 14, 1970.

———. *Django Reinhardt: Ein portat*. Wetzlar, Germany: Pegasus Verlag, 1960.

Scott, Charlie. "Did You See Django?" *BMG*, August 1963.

Serge. *La grande histoire des bohémiens*. Paris: Éditions Karolus, 1963.

Shack, William A. *Harlem in Montmartre: A Paris Jazz Story between the Great Wars*. Berkeley: University of California Press, 2001.

Sharp, Fred. "Django Reinhardt." *Jazz Hot*, No. 283, 1972.

———. Unpublished interview with Charles Delaunay, Louis Vola, and Gérard Lévêque. 1967.

Sharpe, A. P. "Django Is Dead." *BMG*, July 1953.

Shipton, Alyn. *Groovin' High: The Life of Dizzy Gillespie*. Oxford and New York: Oxford University Press, 1999.

———. *A New History of Jazz*. London and New York: Continuum, 2001.

Smith, Geoffrey. *Stéphane Grappelli*. London: Pavillion Books, 1987.

Snowball, David. "Controlling Degenerate Music: Jazz in the Third Reich" in *Jazz & the Germans: Essays on the Influence of "Hot" American Idioms on 20th-Century German Music*. Hillsdale, NY: Pendragon Press, 2002.

"'Sonny Jim' Reinhardt Was Born in Brooklyn!" *Melody Maker*, February 4, 1945.

South, Eddie, with F. Avendorph. "My Foreign Travels and Experiences." *Chicago Defender*, December 12, 1931; December 19, 1931; December 26, 1931; January 2, 1932; and January 16, 1932.

Spautz, Roger. *Django Reinhardt: Mythe et réalité*. Luxembourg: RTL Édition, 1983.

Sportis, Félix W. "Jean Sablon." *Jazz Hot*, No. 499, April 1993.

———. "La galaxie Django Reinhardt." *Jazz Hot*, No. 499, 1993.

———. "Pierre Michelot." *Jazz Hot*, No. 499, April 1993.

———. "Stéphane Grappelli." *Jazz Hot*, No. 499, April 1993.

Stearns, Marshall. "Fondation de la fédération internationale des hot clubs." *Jazz Hot*, September–October 1935.

Stewart, Rex. *Boy Meets Horn*. Ann Arbor: University of Michigan Press, 1991.

———. *Jazz Masters of the Thirties*. New York: Macmillan, 1972.

Sunshine, Herb, as told to Tom Wheeler. "Herb Sunshine on the Early Days of Epiphone and Guild." *Guitar Player*, August 1980.

Ténot, Frank. "Frankly Speaking" column. *Jazz Magazine*, No. 538 (June 2003).

———. "Le jazz en France pendant l'Occupation." *Jazz Magazine*, No. 263, March–April 1978.

———. "Le proces Delaunay." *Jazz Magazine*, No. 349.

Tercinet, Alain. "Django Reinhardt, la tête dans les nuages." *Jazzman*, No. 54, January 2000.

———. Liner notes to Henri Crolla, *Notre ami Django*. © 2001 Gitanes Jazz Productions 014 062-2.

Tournès, Ludovic. *New Orleans sur Seine: Histoire du jazz en France*. Paris: Librairie Arthème Fayard, 1999.

Transcription of Tribunal Civil, Aulnay-sous-Bois, Fonds Charles Delaunay, Bibliothéque Nationale de France, Département de l'Audiovisuel, boîte 69.

Usher, Terry. "The *Melody Maker*, Django Reinhardt and Hot Club de France CC." *Melody Maker*, 1938.

Vian, Boris. "Hommage à Django Reinhardt." *Arts*, No. 467, June 9, 1954.

———. "Hubert Rostaing." *Jazz Hot*, No. 7, May–June 1946.

———. "Le français Charles Delaunay est célèbre dans le monde entier pour avoir fait l'inventaire de tous les disques de jazz enregistrés à ce jour." *Combat*, September 26, 1946.

———. *J'irai cracher sur vos tombes*. Paris: Éditions du Scorpion, 1946.

———. *Round About Close to Midnight: The Jazz Writings of Boris Vian*. London: Quartet, 1988.

———. *Vercoquin et le plancton*. Paris: C. Bourgois, 1947.

Vigneron, Éric. "Jo Privat ou 'l'argodéon.'" *Accordéon*, No. 5, December 1995.

"V-J Day Brought Cheering to Nations and a Famed Guitarist to Ellington." *Chicago Defender*, November 16, 1946.

Warnod, André. *Les bals de Paris*. Paris: Les Éditions G. Crès, 1922.

Weiser, Jimmy. "Django aux États-Unis: Lettre d'Amérique." *Jazz Hot*, No. 11, December 1946.

Wells, Dicky, as told to Stanley Dance. *The Night People: The Jazz Life of Dicky Wells.* Washington, DC, and London: Smithsonian Institution Press, 1991.

Whiteman, Paul, and Mary Margaret McBride. *Jazz.* New York: J. H. Sears, 1926.

Wiggins, Edgar. "Montmartre: The World's 'Hot Spot': Where 'Smart Boys' Go to Learn How Dumb They Are." *Chicago Defender*, October 14, 1933.

Williams, Patrick. "Django: vous et moi." Online. www.jazzmagazine.com.

———. "Mariage Tsigane." *Études tsiganes*, No. 4, 1985.

———. "Maro bravlepen i maro vàgo maro graj: un répertoire de chansons manouches." *Études tsiganes*, No. 1, 1994.

———. "Un héritage sans transmission: le jazz manouche." *Ethnologie française*, No. 3, 2000.

———. *Django Reinhardt.* Marseille: Éditions Parenthèses, 1998.

———. *Mariage Tsigane une cérémonie de fiançailles chez les Rom de Paris.* Paris: L'Harmattan, 2000.

———. *Nous, on n'en parle pas: Les vivants et les morts chez les Manouches.* Paris: Éditions de la Maison des sciences de l'homme, 1993.

Yoors, Jan. *The Gypsies.* Prospect Heights, IL: Waveland Press, 1967.

Zwerin, Mike. *La Tristesse de Saint Louis: Swing under the Nazis.* London: Quartet Books, 1985.

Acknowledgments

IT MAY BE A CONTRADICTION in terms to try to schedule an interview with a Gypsy. Even today, Romanies live on the edges of Parisian society. The horrors and glories of *la Zone* are long gone, the color and squalor of the encampments of caravans near-forgotten history. Yet old habits—and the residue of generations of racism—die hard. The Gypsies of Paris live within French society but safely hidden from sight. If you want to track down the address or telephone number of a certain Gypsy guitarist who followed in Django's footsteps, good luck. He's likely unlisted in phone directories, may have an alias, simply not have an address or phone, or be on the road. Some things haven't changed after all.

I faced all these dilemmas when I wished to contact René Mailhes. At 78 René was the last of his generation of Gitan guitarists. On his father's side, he is a direct link back to Gusti Malha. On his mother's side, he is of the Ferret clan, his mother the sister of Challain Ferret and cousin of Baro, Sarane, and Matelo. René was of the Gypsy bebop generation, and he played alongside Baro, Lousson Reinhardt, Laro Sollero, and nearly everyone else.

I asked several of my Romany acquaintances if they knew René's whereabouts. Elios Ferré responded: René hung out at Café les Boulistes somewhere near the Porte de Vanves flea market. Tracking down the café's address on the internet from across the Atlantic, I wrote to René in care of the café: I would be in Paris on Saturday, March 15, stopping by the bar for a coffee at 10 A.M.

Then I had to find the café. Wandering north from the flea market up a back street named for Gaullist chieftain Vercingétorix, I walked for blocks through a *quartier* wisely passed over by tourist guidebooks. At long last I came across the café, a true hole in the wall. Asking after René Mailhes, I was greeted with a shrug of the shoulders. The bartender had never heard of him, nor seen sign of any letter. Tired and disappointed after my search, I ordered *un café* to regain my strength for the hike home.

And then in walked René Mailhes. He had indeed miraculously received my letter—somehow—and he was happy to talk history with *un américain*. In fact, he brought some friends with him—other Ferret clan guitarists, the son of Jacquet Mailhes, cousins of Christian Escoudé, and more. Coffee was ordered for all, belote cards shuffled, and we talked for some three hours until lunch was served.

Serendipity aided me throughout the research and writing of this book. I met Boulou and Elios Ferré far from Paris in a Minnesota blizzard before they played a concert. They couldn't get their rented amps to function nor get anyone to understand their French; I was able to do both, and a friendship formed, resulting in many meetings in Paris.

Perhaps most miraculously of all, I found the family of Django's first wife in Paris. Beyond her Romany name Bella, no *gadjé* knew anything of her story. Mentioning my project to French friends living in Minneapolis, Valérie Ferment and Pierre-François van de Moortele, they by chance told a doctor friend, Jean-Christophe Germain, back home. He and his father happened to have been the family's physicians for several generations. And thus, a meeting was arranged, photo albums brought out, music played, and a whole side of Django's shadowy history unveiled.

Django's story is indeed mysterious. He left behind just two or three letters from the later years of his life when he learned to write. There are only several recorded interviews with him, most of which were meant for radio airplay and discuss only his latest recordings or his painting exhibits. Even then, he responded to questions like the card sharp he was, answering only *oui* or *non*, never giving anything away. There are also few printed interviews: The journalistic style of the time called for feature articles with the subject's own words paraphrased instead of quoted and lost amid the purple prose. The sole purported verbatim interview with Django led to a lawsuit for slander. And there are but a bare handful of known professional and amateur film clips of him. Except for his music, Django is all but a ghost haunting history.

The enigma surrounding Django was part of the thrill in writing this book. Others have tried to decipher his story before me, including novelist James Jones. After the success of *From Here to Eternity*—which praised Django's playing in several passages—Jones moved in 1958 to Paris's Île Saint-Louis with plans to write his second novel based on Django's life. He interviewed Naguine, Nin-Nin, and others, and began sketching out a storyline to be entitled *No Peace I Find*. But the disparate accounts and vagaries of the anecdotes overwhelmed him and his novel was never finished. To many Gypsies, a good tale is often more intriguing than the truth—especially when told to *gadjé*.

For me, this book is about Paris as much as it is about Django. I first stayed in the city for a time when I was ten and was inspired as much by the Champs-Élysées and Notre-Dame as by the métro, cemeteries, and sewers. Yet this is only part of the beginning of the mystery of Paris for me: No one in my family remembers any details about where we stayed for all that time—neither the *faubourg* nor even vague geographical coordinates. Thus, Paris exists for me as a fantastical city, each streetcorner, bistro, and café creating a strange, yet true sense of déja vù. My fascination for Paris old and new continues in these pages.

Anyone who writes history naturally owes a debt to the researchers and historians who came before, and I offer my thanks and compliments above all to Alain Antonietto, the master historian of *jazz tsigane*. His tireless assistance and sharing of information, recordings, and photographs has been generous and kind.

I thank as well Patrick Williams, and the writings of Claude Dubois, Daniel Nevers, Didier Roussin, François Billard, Charles Delaunay, Roger Spautz, Geoffrey Smith, and Chris Goddard.

And yet this book is based above all on interviews and correspondence that brought Django's life alive again. Among the Manouches and Gitans of France, my thanks to *la famille* Reinhardt; the family of Florine "Bella" Mayer and Lousson Baumgartner—Augustine "Poupée" Renaud, Marie-Thérèse "Minou" Garcia, Jeannot Garcia, and Michel Heil; Boulou and Elios Ferré and Paul "Challain" Ferret; the daughter of Django's cousin, Carmen Ziegler, Jeanne "La Poule" Ziegler; Pierre "Copain" Vées, Tony Weiss, and Mano Weiss/Dray. For their music and their memories, I also thank René Mailhes, Ninine Garcia, Moréno Winterstein, and Patrick Saussois.

Among the Hot Club de France founders, I was fortunate to spend thoroughly enjoyable and uproarious times with Jacques Bureau in Meudon-sur-Seine reminiscing and hearing in his own words the history of jazz, surrealism, and politics in France. I'm only sorry I never got to meet Monsieur Bureau's great friend and partner in crime, Hugues Panassié. I also thank Elwyn Dirats for evoking Paris in the 1920s and Django. I am unfortunate never to have met Charles Delaunay, as everyone I talked with spoke of him in glowing terms, both as a person and for his contributions to jazz. For sharing memories of Delaunay and Django, my thanks to Frank Ténot of *Jazz Magazine* and André Clergeat, Disques Vogue artistic director. I also thank Fred Sharp for sharing his correspondence with Delaunay, and Anne Legrand for all of her time, assistance, and friendship during several visits to the Fonds Charles Delaunay at the Bibliothèque Nationale de France.

Of the Quintette members, Django's sidemen, and other musicians, I cannot thank Emmanuel Soudieux enough. At a mere 85 years of age, Monsieur Soudieux not only regaled me with phenomenal stories of Django and the olden days but also acted most of them out in his Montparnasse apartment.

I owe a great debt to Francis-Alfred Moerman for his long reminiscences, tours of his old haunts in Paris, and musette guitar lessons. Without Francis, this book would never have even gotten started.

I thank Léo Slabiak for his spirited correspondence, *souvenirs*, and great music. I also thank Franco Cerri, Roger Paraboschi, Beryl Davis, and Coleridge Goode.

In France and the rest of Europe, I thank Colette Crolla; Ludovic Tournès; François Charle; Jean-Pierre Favino; Luc Degeorges; Romane; Koen de Cauter; Sophie Riché and Agnès Masson at Archives de l'Assistance Publique–Hôpitaux de Paris; Christian Gauffre at *Jazz Magazine*; Guy Chauvier at *Jazz Classique*; Pierre Fargeton; Jean-Claude Rey; Gérard Lepere at *Échos Saléviens*; Alexis Blanchart at Iris Music; Evelyne Pommeret at *Études tsiganes*; Christian Dupont, Mayor of Pont-à-Celles; Mike Zwerin; Fere Scheidegger; Jan Brouwer; Freddy Haederli; and Wolfram Knauer at the Jazz-Institut Darmstadt. In Italy, I thank Maurizio Franco; Daria Masullo at RAI; and Marc Masselin. In Great Britain, my thanks to Judy Caine and Paul Balmer.

In North America, I thank Charlie Byrd; Les Paul; Oscar Peterson and Joanne Bain; Gary Giddins; Mark Pritcher; Alain Cola; John Jorgenson; John Reeves; François Rousseau; Jacques Mazzoleni; Tad Hershorn; Paul Vernon; Peter Anick; Duncan Schiedt; Gino Francesconi and Rob Hudson at Carnegie Hall; Ted Gottsegen; Patrick Caissy; and Charles Fuller at *Down Beat*.

I owe special thanks to a handful of fellow collectors and historians—Scot Wise, John Bajo, John Roth, and Dominique Cravic. It's been fun, and I could not have written this book without you.

My thanks to Valérie Ferment, Pierre-François van de Moortele, and Jean-Christophe Germain for their assistance, good food, and good times.

On the editorial front, I offer my appreciation to my agent, Paul Bresnick, and everyone at Oxford University Press—especially Kim Robinson, Eve Bachrach, Sara Leopold, and Joellyn Ausanka. Thanks to others who have read and advised on my manuscript at earlier stages, including Eric Dregni, Margret Aldrich, and for her knowledge of all sorts of esoterica, Sigrid Arnott. A thank-you as well to Paul Elie for insightful advice.

Finally, a thanks to my family—Sigrid, Nico, and Marco—for the time they've allowed me and the obsession they've shared.

The research and writing of this book was tinged by sadness. During the time I was at work, too many of the protagonists passed on—Stéphane Grappelli, Babik Reinhardt, Jo Privat, René "Challain" Ferret, René "Didi" Duprat, Paul "Tchan Tchou" Vidal, Maurice Ferret, and Didier Roussin.

Index